Kantian Conceptual Geography

Kantian Conceptual Geography

Nathaniel Jason Goldberg

OXFORD
UNIVERSITY PRESS

OXFORD
UNIVERSITY PRESS

Oxford University Press is a department of the University of
Oxford. It furthers the University's objective of excellence in research,
scholarship, and education by publishing worldwide.

Oxford   New York
Auckland   Cape Town   Dar es Salaam   Hong Kong   Karachi
Kuala Lumpur   Madrid   Melbourne   Mexico City   Nairobi
New Delhi   Shanghai   Taipei   Toronto

With offices in
Argentina   Austria   Brazil   Chile   Czech Republic   France   Greece
Guatemala   Hungary   Italy   Japan   Poland   Portugal   Singapore
South Korea   Switzerland   Thailand   Turkey   Ukraine   Vietnam

Oxford is a registered trademark of Oxford University Press
in the UK and certain other countries.

Published in the United States of America by
Oxford University Press
198 Madison Avenue, New York, NY 10016

© Oxford University Press 2015

All rights reserved. No part of this publication may be reproduced, stored in
a retrieval system, or transmitted, in any form or by any means, without the prior
permission in writing of Oxford University Press, or as expressly permitted by law,
by license, or under terms agreed with the appropriate reproduction rights organization.
Inquiries concerning reproduction outside the scope of the above should be sent to the
Rights Department, Oxford University Press, at the address above.

You must not circulate this work in any other form
and you must impose this same condition on any acquirer.

Library of Congress Cataloging-in-Publication Data
Goldberg, Nathaniel Jason.
Kantian conceptual geography / Nathaniel Jason Goldberg.
pages cm
Includes index.
ISBN 978-0-19-021538-5 (hardcover : alk. paper)   1. Kant, Immanuel, 1724-1804.
2. Kant, Immanuel, 1724-1804. Kritik der reinen Vernunft.   3. Space.   I. Title.
B2798.G596 2015
193—dc23
2014019313

For Maria
for sacrificing so much

CONTENTS

PREFACE & ACKNOWLEDGMENTS "Dostoevsky is Immortal!" xi

PART ONE Establishing Kantianism's Borders

ONE Dualism, Principlism, Kantianism 3
  1. Kantianism 6
  2. Kantianism and Kant's *Critique of Pure Reason* 12
  3. Contrasting Views 18
  4. The Plan of This Work 25
  5. Naturalism 29

PART TWO Exploring Kantian Territory

TWO Philip Pettit 33
  1. Response-Dependence 34
  2. Pettit's Response-Dependence and Kantianism 40
  3. From Kantianism to Noumenalism 46
  4. Complicating the Debate 49
  5. Pettit's Trilemma 54
  6. Lessons for Kantian Conceptual Geography 55

THREE Thomas Kuhn 58
  1. Pettit and Kuhn on Language Learning 59
  2. Kuhn's Kantianism 66
  3. Residual Issues Concerning Kuhn's Kantianism 72
  4. From Kantianism to Incommensurability 74
  5. Lessons for Kantian Conceptual Geography 79

FOUR Donald Davidson 80
  1. Radical Interpretation and Kantianism 82
  2. Language Learning and Kantianism 91
  3. Reconcilable and Irreconcilable Differences 100
  4. The Curious Case of Swampman 101
  5. Lessons for Kantian Conceptual Geography 104

PART THREE Defending Kantianism's Borders

FIVE Defending Dualism 109
1. Scheme/Content Dualism and (My) Dualism 111
2. First Half of Davidson's Argument Against the Scheme Side 115
3. Second Half of Davidson's Argument Against the Scheme Side 119
4. Evaluating That Second Half 125
5. Davidson's Argument Against the Content Side 127
6. Dualism Defended 132
7. Lessons for Kantian Conceptual Geography 133

SIX Defending Principlism 136
1. Kant's Principlism 138
2. Classic Arguments Against Kant's Principlism 144
3. Carnap's Principlism 146
4. Quine's Arguments Against Carnap's Principlism 150
5. Friedman's Principlism 154
6. Defending Friedman's Principlism 159
7. Principlism Defended 162
8. Lessons for Kantian Conceptual Geography 162

PART FOUR Looking for New Land within Kantianism's Borders

SEVEN From Dualism to a Kantian Account of Meaning 167
1. Kantian Account of Meaning 168
2. Kantian Account Explored 173
3. Platonic Realist Account of Meaning 175
4. Aristotelian Realist Account of Meaning 177
5. Berkeleian Idealist Account of Meaning 181
6. Lockean Hybridist Account of Meaning 182
7. Hegelian Pragmatist Account of Meaning 184
8. Lessons for Kantian Conceptual Geography 186

EIGHT Problems That a Kantian Account of Meaning Faces 188
1. First Three Putative Problems: Indeterminacy, Relativism, and Incommensurability 188
2. Fourth and Fifth Putative Problem: Infinite Regression and Truth-Value Relativism 192
3. Sixth Putative Problem: Empirical-Property Relativism 194
4. Seventh Putative Problem: A Plurality of Empirical Worlds 199
5. Eighth Putative Problem: Movability Between Empirical Worlds 202

6. The Unity of Reason 208
   7. Lessons for Kantian Conceptual Geography 212

NINE From Principlism to Kantian Thoughts on Truth 214
   1. Anthropocentric Kantian Thoughts from Kant 215
   2. Ethnocentric Kantian Thoughts from Kuhn, Carnap, and Friedman 219
   3. Un-Principled Kantian Thoughts from Pettit and Quine 224
   4. Logocentric Kantian Thoughts from Davidson 228
   5. The Historical Story in Full 232
   6. Lessons for Kantian Conceptual Geography 233

PART FIVE Lessons for Us

TEN "Some Idea Had Seized the Sovereignty of His Mind" 237
   1. Subjectivity, Objectivity, Principles, and the Empirical 238
   2. Response-Dependence, Noumenalism, and Incommensurability 240
   3. Subjective Scope and Relevant Timing 242
   4. Dualism and Principlism Defended 244
   5. Meaning, Subjectively Empirical Worlds, and Empirical Truth 246
   6. Dostoevsky Is (Still) Immortal! 250

WORKS CITED 253

INDEX 265

PREFACE & ACKNOWLEDGMENTS

"Dostoevsky Is Immortal!"

In Mikhail Bulgakov's fantasy-satire *The Master and Margarita* (1995/1967) Satan and his minions visit Soviet Moscow. One day Satan's minions try entering a restaurant affiliated with the Moscow Association of Writers. Lacking a membership card they are turned away. Incredulous one of them asks whether Dostoevsky himself would face such treatment. The receptionist replies: "Dostoevsky is dead" (p. 300). Indignant one of them declares: "Dostoevsky is immortal!"

Admittedly Satan's minions are up to mischief. We might however sympathize with them a bit. Not only are they having as much trouble with Soviet bureaucracy as Soviet citizens themselves had. But (and to my point) the receptionist could have chosen her words more carefully. Though Dostoevsky the man is dead, Dostoevsky the novelist lives on in the sense that his work continues to inspire others, implicitly or explicitly, in their own discussions of humanity, humility, and the divine.

This book is not about Fyodor Dostoevsky of course. Nor is it about Immanuel Kant—though Bulgakov's first chapter does involve him.[1] It is instead about how, though Kant the man is dead, Kant the philosopher likewise lives on in the sense that his work continues to inspire others, implicitly or explicitly, in their own discussions of knowledge, meaning, and reality. Dostoevsky and Kant are both preeminent in their fields because each redefined the conceptual

---

1. The chapter centers around Satan's arguing with two Muscovites about Immanuel Kant's take on proofs of God's existence. Ellendea Proffer in her critical commentary explains: "This entire argument [about Kant's proofs] ... is the nucleus of the philosophical and thematic structure of the novel" (1995, p. 339). Moreover Mikhail Bulgakov presents his third chapter as a new proof of God's existence to be added to Kant's count.

space in which subsequent generations exercise their minds. Kant even promised an "altered method of our way of thinking" (1998/1787, Bxviii). Both he and Dostoevsky delivered.

The debt of those generations, myself included, to Dostoevsky and Kant is therefore great. So is my individual debt to others. Thanks go to Paul Bourdon, Matthew Burstein, Gregory Cooper, Wayne Davis, Hilary Gaskin, Paul Gregory, Steven Kuhn, Mark Lance, Margaret Little, Charles Lowney, Kirk Ludwig, James Mattingly, Wendy Parker, Brandon Patterson, James Petrik, Howard Pickett, John Reuscher, Duncan Richter, W. Lad Sessions, Nancy Sherman, Ásta Sveinsdóttir, Linda Wetzel, and Tadeusz Zawidzki for feedback on various ideas. Thanks also go to Matthew Gill, Andrew Howat, Chauncey Maher, Wojciech Malecki, Thane Naberhaus, Mark Piper, Matthew Rellihan, and Angela Smith for comments on various chapters. And special thanks go to Mark LeBar for comments on the entire text as well as advice throughout. Without them *Kantian Conceptual Geography* would have been incalculably worse.

Likewise thanks go to Robert Hanna and Jeff Malpas for their invaluable reviews; Peter Ohlin, Emily Sacharin, and everyone else at Oxford University Press for their expertise; and Peter Mavrikis for coordinating production. Thanks also go to the following journals and presses for permission to draw from previously published work. Parts of Chapter Two draw from "Response-Dependence, Noumenalism, and Ontological Mystery," *European Journal of Philosophy* 17 (2008): 469–88. Parts of Chapter Three draw from "Interpreting Thomas Kuhn as a Response-Dependence Theorist," *International Journal of Philosophical Studies* 19 (2011): 729–52. Parts of Chapter Four draw from "Swampman, Response-Dependence, and Meaning," in *Donald Davidson on Truth, Meaning, and the Mental*, ed. Gerhard Preyer (Oxford University Press, 2012): 148–66. Parts of Chapter Five draw from "Davidson, Dualism, and Truth," *Journal for the History of Analytic Philosophy* 1 (2012): 0–19. And parts of Chapter Six draw from "Historicism, Entrenchment, and Conventionalism," *Journal for General Philosophy of Science* 40 (2009): 259–76. Without them *Kantian Conceptual Geography* would have been calculably worse.

Finally thanks go to James Mahon for managing a philosophically engaged philosophy department; and Melina Bell, Christian Jennings, Carey McCallum, Violet McCallum, Jason Miles, Lyndon Sayers, Florentien Verhage, Nicole Walker, and Michelle Yoon for moral and esthetic support. General thanks go to Washington and Lee University and its leadership, including President Kenneth Ruscio, past and present Provosts June Aprille and Daniel Wubah, and past and present Deans Hank Dobin and Suzanne Keen, for a wonderful academic home, excellent students, and generous Lenfest summer fellowships and an even more generous Lenfest sabbatical fellowship that facilitated the writing of this work. Thanks as well go to Daniel Kaplan, Anya Rozonoer, and Natalie Spector for introducing me to Bulgakov. Most importantly thanks go to my in-laws, Aida, Larry, and Nelson; my brother, Frank; my parents, Doris and Stephen; and my dearest, Maria, for being in my life. Without them *Kantian Conceptual Geography* would not have been.

PART ONE

Establishing Kantianism's Borders

ONE

Dualism, Principlism, Kantianism

Philosophers are pretty bad at plenty of things. Our conclusions, even if resulting from valid reasoning, are often difficult to believe. Our forays into empirical matters have historically ranged from merely false to outright laughable. And our incessant attempts to lay philosophical issues, if not philosophy itself, to rest have all come up short. (Perhaps on this last point at least we professionals should be grateful.)

Philosophers are not however quite so bad at two things in particular. The first is drawing on our own history to make contemporary philosophical views more comprehensible. As Wilfrid Sellars remarks:

> The history of philosophy is the *lingua franca* which makes communication between philosophers, at least of different points of view, possible. Philosophy without the history of philosophy, if not empty or blind, is at least dumb (1968, p. 1).

In this book I draw on the history of philosophy, and especially Immanuel Kant's *Critique of Pure Reason* (1998/1787), to illuminate issues in analytic epistemology, philosophy of language, and metaphysics. Kant is a pivotal, perhaps *the* pivotal, figure of the past several centuries in the Western tradition. In the *Critique of Pure Reason* in particular Kant synthesized views of his early-modern predecessors (rationalist and empiricist) and established much of the agenda for his nineteenth-, twentieth-, and twenty-first-century successors (idealist, pragmatist, neo-Kantian, analytic, and Continental). To this day epistemologists, philosophers of language, and metaphysicians engage in issues that Kant indelibly shaped. Moreover, even when Kant did not himself shape them, his conceptual resources remain rich enough to illuminate them just the same. As Otto Liebmann is attributed as saying: "One can philosophize with Kant or against Kant; but one cannot philosophize without Kant."[1] In fact Sellars himself continues:

> Thus, if I build my discussion of contemporary issues on a foundation of Kant exegesis and commentary it is because, as I see it, there are enough close parallels between the problems confronting him and the steps he took to solve them, on the one hand, and the current situation and its demands, on the other, for it to be helpful to use him as a means of communication, though not, of course, as a means only.

Now my project is not Sellars's. My discussion of contemporary issues is not built on as robust a foundation of Kant exegesis and commentary as is his. Nor are the problems, situation, and demands of which Sellars speaks mine. Regardless, like Sellars, I do use Kant as a means of communication—though not, of course, as Sellars surely does not, as a means only.

The second thing at which philosophers are not quite so bad is engaging in what I call 'conceptual geography'. By this I mean roughly what Gilbert Ryle means by "logical geography" (2000/1949, p. 7). Ryle explains: "Many people," and I might specify even many philosophers, " ... know by practice how to operate with concepts, anyhow inside familiar fields. ... They are like people who know their way about their own parish, but," Ryle continues, they "cannot construct or read a map of it, much less a map of the region or continent in which their parish lies" (pp. 7–8). Ryle would have us philosophers be conceptual geographers—exploring, surveying, and mapping how concepts relate to one another and the broader conceptual world.[2]

My aim in *Kantian Conceptual Geography* is to mate Sellars's and Ryle's methods to increase our understanding of myriad concepts, or issues, in epistemology, philosophy of language, and metaphysics. Following Ryle, engaging in *conceptual geography* illuminates the way around not merely our parish but also our region and continent. Following Sellars, engaging in conceptual geography that is *Kantian* permits exploring, surveying, and mapping these

---

1. Indeed see J. Alberto Coffa (2008/1991), who argues that the "semantic" tradition—analytic philosophy concerning meaning, from Bernard Bolzano's to Willard van Orman Quine's—developed in reaction to Immanuel Kant's notion of pure intuition. (See Chapter Six, §2.) See Robert Hanna (2001), who argues that Coffa's lesson extends to analytic philosophy generally. And see Richard Rorty (1981), who argues that analytic philosophy is Kantian in his (not my) sense. Kant's influence has been at least as great, not to mention more explicit, in ethics, political philosophy, and allied fields. (See below.)

2. Wilfrid Sellars (1991/1963, essay 5, §§39–41) himself has something like my notion of conceptual geography in mind.

conceptual connections by drawing on ideas from Kant. We thereby learn the way around our conceptual continent by speaking philosophy's *lingua franca* with a Kantian accent.

Now let me be clear. I am not contributing to Kant scholarship, though I do consider some of what Kant says.[3] Nor am I arguing that there always have been explicit historical connections between Kant's claims and what I identify as various "Kantian" ones, though I do note connections where they exist. Nor am I attempting to establish the truth of particular claims, though I do defend theses drawn from Kant, and when there is reason to prefer a Kantian view to a non-Kantian one I do say so.[4] Instead in *Kantian Conceptual Geography* I am engaging *in* Kantian conceptual geography: exploring conceptual connections among myriad issues by appealing to Kantian tools.

There are six reasons that engaging in Kantian conceptual geography is of the utmost importance to analytic philosophy. First, and foremost, doing so maps out issues that are themselves of the utmost importance to analytic philosophers in ways that are informative and often unexpected. These issues include the nature of the subjective, objective, and empirical; potential scopes of the subjective; what can (and cannot) be said about a subject-independent reality; empirical concepts and their content, empirical terms and their meaning, and empirical properties and their nature; analyticity, syntheticity, apriority, and aposteriority; constitutive principles, acquisitive principles, and empirical claims; meaning, meaning indeterminacy, meaning relativism, meaning incommensurability, and truth-value relativism; logically possible *versus* subjectively empirical worlds; and the nature of empirical truth.

Second, engaging in Kantian conceptual geography surveys Kantian territory itself, the totality of philosophical positions in conceptual space that are "Kantian" in the sense explained below. Because (as also explained below) such territory is prominent and expansive, we analytic philosophers ignore it at our own peril.

Third, engaging in Kantian conceptual geography reduces disciplinary disparity. Though the applicability of Kant's views to analytic versions of what Kant himself would count as "practical" philosophy (ethics, political philosophy, and allied fields) might come as no surprise, their applicability to correlative versions of "theoretical" philosophy" (epistemology, metaphysics, and allied fields) might. Theoretical philosophy is the domain of the *Critique of*

---

3. See §2 and Robert Howell (2013) for recent analytic Kant scholarship.

4. See Leslie Stevenson (2011) for recent analytic philosophy that does attempt to establish the truth of particular Kantian claims.

Pure Reason, and my concern is with analytic epistemology, philosophy of language, and metaphysics (as well as overlapping areas in philosophy of mind and science) in particular. Kantian ethics is a recognized field in analytic philosophy, while Kantian epistemology, Kantian philosophy of language, and Kantian metaphysics are not. In *Kantian Conceptual Geography* I consider what these other fields would look like.[5]

Fourth, engaging in Kantian conceptual geography makes apparent that there are *implicit* instances of Kantian epistemology, philosophy of language, and metaphysics already in analytic philosophy. Moreover these instances illustrate how prominent and expansive Kantian territory is. In particular, while I look at many different views, I examine at length those of Philip Pettit, Thomas Kuhn, Donald Davidson, Rudolf Carnap, Willard van Orman Quine, and Michael Friedman. Though important in their own right, I consider their views because doing so is the best way that I know to explore Kantian territory itself.

Fifth, engaging in Kantian conceptual geography discloses new land within Kantianism's borders that has until now remained uncharted. In particular I come upon a Kantian account of meaning and Kantian thoughts on truth. This is especially valuable because meaning and truth are issues especially central to analytic philosophy as well as philosophy *tout court*.

And sixth, engaging in Kantian conceptual geography engages in philosophical conceptual geography generally. Surveying Kantian territory surveys the territory of other views that touch it at its borders. As I explain here and in the chapters that follow, engaging in Kantian conceptual geography illuminates various forms of realism, idealism, pragmatism, and hybrid views. By allowing us to see Kantianism as a distinct sort of approach, it thereby puts other approaches into greater relief. Engaging in Kantian conceptual geography therefore reveals a better understanding of philosophy writ large.

The remainder of the chapter proceeds as follows. In §1 I define what I mean by 'Kantianism'. In §2 I show that I call the view 'Kantianism' because theses definitive of it can be drawn from Kant's *Critique of Pure Reason*. In §3 I consider views that contrast with Kantianism. In §4 I provide the plan of this work. Finally in §5 I address a worry concerning naturalism.

1. KANTIANISM

'Kantianism' means different things to different people. Though I elaborate on my definition below, let me state here that by 'Kantianism' I mean any view

---

5. See Hanna (2011) for more on such disparity and his diagnosis.

that *does* satisfy Empirical Dualism (hereafter 'Dualism') and *may* satisfy Subjective Principlism (hereafter 'Principlism'):

DUALISM: All empirical concepts, terms, or properties are linked essentially to subjective and objective sources.[6]

PRINCIPLISM: The subjective source of all empirical concepts, terms, or properties takes the form of subjective principles.[7]

Kantianism combines these:

KANTIANISM: All empirical concepts, terms, or properties are linked essentially to subjective and objective sources. The subjective source may take the form of subjective principles.

Dualism concerns how certain epistemological, linguistic, and metaphysical items are ineluctably bound to both minded subjects and mind-independent objects. Principlism concerns the form that such subjective binding might take. And Kantianism incorporates both. In §2 I show that Dualism and Principlism can both be drawn from the *Critique of Pure Reason*. That is why I call their resulting view 'Kantianism'. Here I make three preliminary points and then explain the theses in detail.

First, while satisfying Dualism is necessary and sufficient for a view to be Kantian in my sense, satisfying Principlism is neither. A view can maintain that empirical concepts, terms, or properties are linked essentially to a subjective source generally rather than any principle specifically. On such a view there would be no subjective principles. As I understand it, there would be no claims, distinct from any empirical ones, that are the form or basic epistemological or linguistic unit that the subjective source of empirical concepts, terms, or properties takes. All empirical concepts, terms, or properties would be linked essentially to subjective and objective sources holistically.

Second, while not all kinds of Kantianism satisfy Principlism, many of the most influential ones do. Moreover views that satisfy Dualism and Principlism treat them both as indispensable. Hence, though satisfying Dualism is necessary and sufficient for a view to be Kantian while satisfying Principlism is neither, Principlism's prominent role in kinds of Kantianism earns it its place

---

6. Michael Friedman describes this and related dualisms as "Kantian dualism" (2010c, p. 621). Kurt Gödel describes Kant's transcendental idealism as a "fruitful viewpoint [that draws] a distinction between subjective and objective elements in our knowledge" (1995/1946, p. 240). I limit myself to analyses of *empirical* concepts, terms, and properties throughout.

7. In the *Critique of Pure Reason* Kant himself writes: "Synthetic *a priori* judgments are contained as principles in all theoretical sciences of reason" (1998/1787, A10/B14). See §2. As I explain in Chapter Six, §1, I am using 'principle' in my sense, which is not quite Kant's.

in its definition. Let me therefore talk about Kantianism—or Kantians, who are committed to it—as coming in "Principled" and "un-Principled" kinds. Recurring to my geographic image, let us understand Dualism as establishing Kantianism's *external* border, separating it from other conceptual territories. Let us likewise understand Principlism as establishing an *internal* border, separating Principled and un-Principled kinds of Kantianism from themselves.

And third, I have formulated Dualism, Principlism, and therefore Kantianism as concerning empirical concepts, terms, *or* properties. That is because many who are usefully counted as Kantian tend to focus on only one or two of these at times or overall. As I explain in §2, however, Kant can himself be understood as focusing on all three. The disjunctions are therefore meant to be inclusive.[8]

Now that we have noted these preliminaries, let me explain Dualism and Principlism in detail. What are the "subjective" and "objective" sources of which Dualism speaks? By 'subjective source' I mean the specific conceptual, linguistic, or perceptual capacities in an individual subject's mind, shared across a group of subjects' minds, or encoded in a subject's or subjects' language or (other) conventions. Different philosophers have chosen different elements of this set. As I explain in §2, as I understand Kant himself, **substance** is an *a priori* concept (1998/1787, B6, A181–89/B224–32) because it derives purely from the conceptual capacities inherent in a human subject's mind (her transcendental unity of apperception). Assuming that Kant is right, **substance** would count as subjective in my sense.

Conversely by 'objective source' I mean a source that is not subjective. Such a source might include objects in the world. Though not usually so conceived, sensations deriving from those objects would count as objective in this sense also. So would the world itself, in itself, or considered in itself, if construed in a subject-independent way.[9] Now, given Dualism, empirical concepts are linked essentially to both subjective and objective sources. As I explain in §2, as I understand Kant, **gold** is an empirical concept (A721–22/B749–50) because it derives from the human subject's mind as it conceptualizes and intuits sensations from a subject-independent, and so an objective, world.[10] With certain

---

8. As we see in Chapter Eight, §6, anyone committed to Kantianism concerning concepts, terms, *or* properties is ultimately committed to Kantianism concerning concepts, terms, *and* properties—at least construed ontologically (more below).

9. Understanding an objective source as not subjective is understanding it in a negative sense. Understanding that such a source might include these things is understanding it in a positive sense. These correlate with Kant's own understanding of a noumenon in negative and positive senses, respectively. See Chapter Eight, §5.

10. For Kant, because concepts of the understanding and forms of intuition are both *a priori*, they are both subjective in my sense. They also correlate roughly with conceptual and perceptual capacities, respectively.

caveats, such a world would, for Kant, be "noumenal." I consider this below and in the chapters that follow.

What does it mean for empirical concepts, terms, or properties to be "linked essentially" to subjective and objective sources, as Dualism dictates, and for that subjective source to "take the form of subjective principles," as Principlism proposes? Each can mean one of two things. As I explain in more detail in the chapters that follow, first, concepts, terms, or properties that are linked essentially to subjective and objective sources would be *constituted essentially out them*. Such sources go into the concepts', terms', or properties' *very being*. In that sense subjective and objective sources go into the *content* of the concepts, *meaning* of the terms, or *nature* of the properties. Expanding Kant's example, as I understand him, the content of **gold**, meaning of 'gold' in English, and nature of gold would all be constituted, or constructed, essentially out of something subjective (a subject's specific conceptual, linguistic, or perceptual capacities) and something objective (something independent of these). What **gold** and 'gold' express, and what gold is, derive from both. All empirical concepts, terms, and properties would be so constituted. And, because a subject's constituting concepts, terms, and properties brings her into not only ontological but also epistemological contact with them, the subject could in principle come to learn all those concepts, terms, and properties also. We see examples of this in Chapters Three and Four.[11]

Correspondingly one way for a subjective source to "take the form of subjective principles" is for those principles themselves to be *constitutive of* these concepts, terms, or properties. The principles would partly be constitutive of the concepts', terms', or properties' *very being*. In that sense these principles would partly be constitutive of the *content* of the concepts, *meaning* of the terms, or *nature* of the properties. Kant's own principles are synthetic *a priori* judgments, one example of which is his First Analogy: "In all changes of appearances substance persists, and its quantum is neither increased nor diminished in nature" (B224). As I explain in §2, I understand Kant's idea—at least if construed constitutively (more below)—as twofold. On the one hand, this principle is a claim, distinct from any empirical one, that is the form or basic epistemological or linguistic unit that the subjective source of empirical concepts, terms, or properties takes. On the other hand, by applying this and other (subjective) principles to (objective) sensation, the subject can constitute the content of **gold**, meaning of 'gold' in English, and nature of gold. All empirical concepts, terms, and properties would be so constituted. Again the subject could in principle come to learn all those concepts, terms, and properties too.

---

11. See Nathaniel Goldberg (2004a) for Kant's own account in the *Critique of Pure Reason* of empirical-concept constitution and in turn acquisition.

Hence the first way of understanding "linked essentially" and to "take the form" is *ontological*. All empirical concepts, terms, or properties are constituted, or constructed, essentially out of subjective and objective sources—where the subjective source may take the form of principles constitutive of those concepts, terms, or properties. By 'Ontological Kantianism' let me therefore mean any kind of Kantianism that *does* satisfy an ontological version of Dualism and *may* satisfy an ontological version of Principlism, respectively:

> ONTOLOGICAL DUALISM: All empirical concepts, terms, or properties are constituted essentially out of subjective and objective sources.
>
> ONTOLOGICAL PRINCIPLISM: The subjective source of all empirical concepts, terms, or properties takes the form of subjective principles constitutive of those concepts, terms, or properties.

Ontological Kantianism itself is this:

> ONTOLOGICAL KANTIANISM: All empirical concepts, terms, or properties are constituted essentially out of subjective and objective sources. The subjective source may take the form of subjective constitutive principles.

According to Ontological Kantianism, all empirical concepts, terms, or properties owe their *very being* to subjective and objective sources. What it is to *be* a particular concept, term, or property—and so to *have* a particular content, meaning, or nature, respectively—depends on both kinds of sources. Something deriving from the subject and something deriving from objects jointly constitute the concept, term, or property. Moreover that something deriving from the subject may take the form of constitutive principles.

The second thing that empirical concepts', terms', or properties' being "linked essentially" to subjective and objective sources, and for a subjective source's to "take the form of subjective principles," can mean is this. Starting with the former locution, concepts, terms, or properties that are linked essentially to subjective and objective sources would be *acquired by a subject's appealing essentially to* them. Such sources go into the subject's *very knowledge* of the concepts, terms, or properties. In that sense subjective and objective sources go into the subject's *learning* the concepts, terms, or properties—without impacting their content, meaning, or nature, respectively, themselves. Now it might sound infelicitous to say that properties are acquired, or learned, in the sense in which concepts and terms are acquired, or learned, so let me bracket talk of "acquiring" properties.[12] Regardless **gold** or 'gold' would itself be acquired, or learned, by a subject's appealing essentially to something subjective (her specific

---

12. Nonetheless in Chapter Eight, §3, I use the notion of learning empirical properties to explain my notion of a subjectively empirical world.

conceptual, linguistic, or perceptual capacities) and something objective (something independent of these). Its mastery would depend on both. The world (or sensations therefrom) has within it delineations from which a subject in virtue of her specific conceptual, linguistic, or perceptual capacities can acquire concepts or terms. Objective reality would have these delineations on offer but only by appealing to her specific capacities could the subject learn these concepts or terms as opposed to others. Reciprocally that she learns these *specific* ones is no accident. She learns them by appealing essentially to *her* specific capacities. Moreover, though she would not constitute them, there would be no reason that the subject could not learn all such concepts or terms. Her specific capacities are necessary and sufficient in principle for her to master every one.

Correspondingly the other way for a subjective source to "take the form of subjective principles" is for those principles to be *acquisitive* of these concepts, terms, or properties. The principles would be partly acquisitive of, by which I mean that they would allow a subject to come to *know*, the concepts, terms, or properties. In that sense these principles would partly allow the subject to acquire the concepts, terms, or properties—without impacting their content, meaning, or nature, respectively, themselves. Because it might still sound infelicitous to say that properties are acquired, or learned, in the sense in which concepts and terms are acquired, or learned, let me continue to bracket talk of "acquiring" properties. Regardless recall Kant's principle: "In all changes of appearances substance persists, and its quantum is neither increased nor diminished in nature" (B224). This time I understand Kant's idea—now construed acquisitively (again more below)—also as twofold though not in quite the same way. On the one hand, this principle is again a claim, distinct from any empirical one, that is the form or basic epistemological or linguistic unit that the subjective source of empirical concepts, terms, or properties takes. On the other hand, by applying this and other (subjective) principles the subject can this time acquire **gold** or 'gold'. Now, on the current acquisitive understanding, only by appealing essentially to her own specific conceptual, linguistic, or perceptual capacities in the form of principles can the subject acquire these specific concepts or terms. Regardless that the subject learns these *specific* ones as opposed to others is again no accident. That she does so is due essentially to *her* specific capacities. Her specific capacities are still necessary and sufficient in principle for her to master every empirical concept or term.

Hence the second way of understanding "linked essentially" and to "take the form" is *epistemological*. All empirical concepts, terms, or properties are acquired, or learned, by a subject's appealing essentially to subjective and objective sources—where the subjective source may take the form of principles acquisitive of those concepts, terms, or properties. By 'Epistemological Kantianism' let me therefore mean any kind of Kantianism that *does* satisfy an epistemological version of Dualism and *may* satisfy an epistemological version of Principlism, respectively:

> EPISTEMOLOGICAL DUALISM: All empirical concepts, terms, or properties are acquired by a subject's appealing essentially to subjective and objective sources.
> EPISTEMOLOGICAL PRINCIPLISM: The subjective source of all empirical concepts, terms, or properties takes the form of subjective principles acquisitive of those concepts, terms, or properties.

Epistemological Kantianism itself is this:

> EPISTEMOLOGICAL KANTIANISM: All empirical concepts, terms, or properties are acquired by a subject's appealing essentially to subjective and objective sources. The subjective source may take the form of subjective acquisitive principles.[13]

According to Epistemological Kantianism, all empirical concepts, terms, or properties owe a subject's *very knowledge* of them to subjective and objective sources. What it is to *master* a particular concept, term, or property depends on both kinds of sources. Something deriving from the subject and something deriving from objects jointly allow the subject to acquire the concept, term, or property. Moreover that something deriving from the subject may take the form of acquisitive principles.

Hence, with Dualism at its core, Kantianism can be Ontological or Epistemological, and each of these can be Principled or un-Principled. That results in four kinds of Kantianism. In Chapter Two I examine an un-Principled Epistemological Kantianism that exists in the analytic literature, and in Chapters Three and Four each I examine a Principled Kantianism that is both Ontological and Epistemological. So there is time to try out my Kantian classifications on various views. Nonetheless, though this is not a work in Kant scholarship, it is instructive to see here how all these theses can be drawn from Kant's *Critique of Pure Reason* and specifically his discussion of transcendental idealism. Doing so also explains why I am calling the view that results from Dualism and Principlism 'Kantianism' in the first place.

2. KANTIANISM AND KANT'S *CRITIQUE OF PURE REASON*

Discussing any aspect of the *Critique of Pure Reason* is risky. As Kant's biographer Manfred Kuehn reports, in Kant's day

---

13. Though I bracketed "acquisition" talk above, in Epistemological Dualism, Principlism, and Kantianism the brackets come off.

in Jena two students fought a duel because one had accused the other of not understanding the *Critique*, claiming that he needed to study it for thirty years before he could hope to understand it and then for another thirty years before being allowed to comment on it (2002, pp. 318–19).

Coming to grips with transcendental idealism, the *Critique's* unifying thread, can itself be perilous. As Robert Hanna relates: "Kant's eighteenth-century near-contemporary, the dramatic poet Henrich Kleist, fully grasped this point"—the point being transcendental idealism and its consequences for free will—"and it nearly drove the poor man mad. Taking the *Critique of Pure Reason* utterly seriously ..., Kleist suffered a nervous breakdown generally known as his 'Kant crisis'" (2006, p. 226). Nor are the perils necessarily any less in our own century. As the *Guardian* headlined on September 16, 2013: "Unreasonable critique of Kant leads to man being shot in Russian shop" (Alexi Anishchuk 2013).[14] Kant exegesis is not for the timid.

Further, even bracketing the possibility of duels, breakdowns, and bullets, such exegesis remains highly contested. I myself therefore aim to achieve not so much exegetical fidelity as thematic acquaintance with Kant's transcendental idealism. I would be content to provide an understanding of a view recognizably like Kant's even if not quite Kant's own, but which is useful to consider in understanding Kant's broad themes. I proceed by assuming generic ontological and epistemological construals of Kant's transcendental idealism to draw Ontological and Epistemological Dualism, Principlism, and Kantianism from them. I close by relating influential construals of transcendental idealism in the analytic literature to Ontological and Epistemological Kantianism themselves.

According to both generic construals of transcendental idealism, the basic unit of knowledge is the judgment. Judgments are something like complete thoughts. They result from the combination of intuitions and concepts. Intuitions are themselves singular representations in space and time, while concepts are general representations under which intuitions are subsumed. Intuitions are then either pure, deriving entirely from the transcendental subject's *a priori* forms of space and time (due to the subject's mind or transcendental unity of apperception), or empirical, deriving from both these *a priori* forms and sensation somehow arising from things in themselves (on an ontological construal) or things considered in themselves (on an epistemological construal). Concepts are also either pure, being nothing but the transcendental subject's *a priori* categories, or empirical, being constituted (on an

---

14. Likewise RT.com, the website for the Russia-based RT news network, headlined: "Impure reason: Russian man shot in heated Kant philosophy debate" (TV-Novosti 2013).

ontological construal) or acquired (on an epistemological construal) by the transcendental subject from empirical intuitions *via* the categories.[15]

Consider concepts. *A priori* concepts are candidates only for constitution. As I understand Kant, *a priori* concepts like **substance** are the categories. They are constituted essentially out of only a subjective source, the transcendental subject's mind in the form of her transcendental unity of apperception. By contrast empirical concepts are candidates for either constitution or acquisition, depending on which construal of transcendental idealism is operative. On an ontological construal, empirical concepts like **gold** are constituted essentially out of the transcendental subject's mind and sensation somehow arising from things in themselves. Sensation and the subject jointly create the concept. Conversely, on an epistemological construal, empirical concepts like **gold** are acquired by the subject by her appealing essentially to her own mental resources and sensation somehow arising from things considered in themselves. The subject does not constitute **gold**; she contributes nothing to its content. Rather she acquires the concept from sensation insofar as sensation affects her conceptual and intuitive capacities. The subject reads the concept off sensation, though it is not luck that it can be so read. The subject reads just those concepts that her specific subjective manner of conception and intuition allows.

Further, throughout the *Critique* Kant speaks of concepts as "predicates." And predicates are terms. This suggests that on both construals we might take transcendental idealism to entail correlative claims about *a priori* terms like 'substance' and empirical terms like 'gold' in English. Nor does Kant always distinguish predicates from the properties that they name. This suggests that we might also take transcendental idealism to make correlative claims about *a priori* properties like being substantial and empirical properties like being gold. In fact Kant identifies empirical cognition with experience itself: "[The categories] serve only for the possibility of **empirical cognition**. Such cognition, however, is called **experience**" (1998/1787, B147). Kant is therefore concerned with empirical concepts, terms, *and* properties, on the one hand, and well as their *a priori* correlates, on the other.

Hence I can draw Ontological Dualism concerning empirical concepts, terms, and properties from Kant's view as I understand it. All empirical concepts, terms, and properties would be constituted essentially out of subjective

---

15. For Kant, both *a priori* forms and concepts are subjective in my sense. As I explain in Chapter Six, §1, pure intuition itself is something like the mental canvass on which subjects perceive experience but which is structured prior to experience by the pure forms of space and time. Kant's *a priori* (or pure) forms and concepts therefore correlate roughly with perceptual and conceptual capacities, respectively.

and objective sources. What content **gold** has, meaning 'gold' in English has, and nature gold has derive jointly from something subjective and something objective. Kant can therefore be seen as an Ontological Kantian concerning all three. Moreover, on this construal, Kant would be committed to Ontological Principlism too. While I discuss this in more detail in Chapter Six, let me note here that the subjective source of these concepts, terms, and properties takes the form of principles, Kant's synthetic *a priori* judgments. Kant himself explains: "Synthetic *a priori* judgments are contained as principles in all theoretical sciences of reason" (A10/B14).[16] As we saw in §1, such principles include Kant's claim about substantial persistence. **Gold**, 'gold', and gold are constituted essentially out of this and other such synthetic *a priori* judgments applied to sensation. On this view Kant's synthetic *a priori* judgments are constitutive principles. They are distinct from the empirical concepts, terms, and properties—and ultimately empirical claims, Kant's synthetic *a posteriori* judgments—whose constitution they make possible. Ontological Dualism, Principlism, and Kantianism can therefore all be drawn from Kant's transcendental idealism as I understand it.

Likewise I can draw Epistemological Dualism concerning at least empirical concepts and terms from that view too. All empirical concepts and terms would be acquired by a subject's appealing essentially to subjective and objective sources. Kant can therefore be seen as an Epistemological Kantian concerning them as well. What use **gold** and 'gold' in English have derives jointly from something subjective and something objective. Moreover, on this construal, Kant would be committed to Epistemological Principlism also. The subjective source of these concepts and terms again takes the form of principles, again Kant's synthetic *a priori* judgments. **Gold** and 'gold' (but not necessarily gold; see §1) are acquired by a subject's appealing essentially to Kant's principle of substantial persistence and other such synthetic *a priori* judgments applied to sensation. On this view Kant's synthetic *a priori* judgments are acquisitive principles. They are distinct from the empirical concepts and terms—and ultimately empirical claims, synthetic *a posteriori* judgments—whose acquisition they make possible.

Though 'Kantianism' does mean different things to different people, I am therefore justified in calling both ontological and epistemological versions of the main view under consideration in this book 'Kantianism'. Moreover it is noteworthy how influential analytic construals of transcendental idealism relate to Ontological and Epistemological Kantianism themselves. Because

---

16. Nonetheless, as I explain in Chapter Six, §1, I am using 'principle' in my sense, which is not quite Kant's.

their projects differ from mine, proponents of these construals emphasize different things from what I have been emphasizing. I adjust for that by understanding their construals in terms of mine.

Peter F. Strawson (1975) and Paul Guyer (1987) construe transcendental idealism as an *ontological* thesis according to which things in themselves are distinct from things as they appear to us. We might think of things in themselves and things as they appear to us as comprising two different worlds. Consonant with Strawson's and Guyer's views, we can understand things as they appear to us in particular (and presumably concepts and terms for them, and their properties) as being constituted essentially out of subjective and objective sources. The subjective source would be the transcendental subject's mind, while the objective source would be sensation somehow arising from things in themselves. Strawson's and Guyer's construals therefore approximate a kind of Ontological Kantianism.[17]

Conversely Henry Allison (2004) construes transcendental idealism as an *epistemological* thesis according to which things considered in themselves are distinct from things considered as they appear to us. We might think of things considered in themselves and things considered as they appear to us as comprising two different aspects of the same world. Consonant with Allison's view, we can understand concepts and terms for (but not necessarily properties of; see §1) things considered as they appear to us in particular as acquired by a subject's appealing essentially to subjective and objective sources. The subjective source would be the transcendental subject's mind, while the objective source would be sensation somehow arising from things considered in themselves. Allison's construal therefore approximates a kind of Epistemological Kantianism.[18]

Less known though no less interesting, Rae Langton (2004/1998) construes transcendental idealism as an *ontological* thesis with an *epistemological* consequence. It is an *ontological* thesis because it distinguishes two kinds of properties: intrinsic properties, which are properties of things in themselves, and relational properties, which just are things as they appear to us. We might think of intrinsic properties and relational properties as comprising two different sets of properties in the same world. Langton's construal has an *epistemological* consequence because it counsels "epistemic humility": we

---

17. Peter F. Strawson speaks of the "metaphysics of transcendental idealism" (1975, part 4). See Charles Parsons (1992, pp. 83–88) for how Strawson's and Paul Guyer's construals compare. Richard E. Aquila's (1983) and James Van Cleve's (2003/1999) construals are similar to Strawson's and Guyer's.

18. Graham Bird's (1962) construal is similar to Henry Allison's.

should acknowledge that can know only relational properties.[19] Consonant with Langton's view, we can understand relational properties (and presumably concepts and terms for them) in particular as constituted essentially out of subjective and objective sources. The subjective source would be the transcendental subject's mind, while the objective source would be those intrinsic properties. Langton's construal therefore nevertheless approximates a kind of Ontological Kantianism.

Finally, less known, no less interesting, but more complicated, Hanna (2006) offers two construals of transcendental idealism. He calls the first 'strong transcendental idealism'. Based on a strict understanding of Kant, strong transcendental idealism is roughly the same as Strawson's and Guyer's construals. Strong transcendental idealism is therefore as an *ontological* thesis, or two-world view, approximating a kind of Ontological Kantianism. Hanna calls the second construal 'weak transcendental idealism'. A related but allegedly more defensible view, weak transcendental idealism is a *semantic* (or as Hanna prefers "cognitive-semantic") thesis. As I understand it, weak transcendental idealism relies on two claims. One is the *epistemologico-ontological* claim that our forms of intuition (which are epistemological) are isomorphic with space and time in themselves (which are ontological). The other is the *semantic* claim that our forms of intuition are satisfied (in Alfred Tarski's [2008/1944] technical sense) by space and time in themselves. Apparently a subject's empirical concepts and terms, presupposing (at least) her forms of intuition, are themselves satisfied by things in space and time in themselves—and so by things in themselves. We might think of space and time, and things, in themselves as comprising the world in itself that our forms of intuition, and empirical concepts and terms, necessarily possibly represent.[20] Consonant with weak transcendental idealism, we can understand those concepts and terms in particular as acquired by a subject's appealing essentially to subjective and objective sources. The subjective source would be the transcendental subject's mind and in particular her forms of intuition (and presumably other capacities).

---

19. Confusingly Nenad Miščević calls Rae Langton's epistemic humility "metaphysical modesty" (2011, p. 80).

20. As I understand Hanna (2006, ch. 6.1), because our intuitive forms are isomorphic with space and time in themselves, it is necessarily *possible* for us to represent in intuition things in space and time in themselves. It is not however necessarily *necessary* because space and time in themselves do not require our representations to exist. Nonetheless Hanna wrongly concludes from this that the "best modal logic for discussing metaphysical issues in a Kantian context is either C. I. Lewis's system S4 alone, or else some conservative extension of S4" (p. 304). Our *necessarily possibly* representing something that *actually* exists—which, Hanna thinks, space and time in themselves do—requires S5.

The objective source would be space and time, and things, in themselves.[21] Because on Hanna's view our empirical concepts and terms necessarily possibly represent things in themselves, we acquire rather than constitute them. Weak transcendental idealism therefore ultimately approximates a kind of Epistemological Kantianism.

3. CONTRASTING VIEWS

So far I have explained what Kantianism is and why I call the view 'Kantianism' in the first place. Here I put Kantianism into better focus by considering what it is not. As we saw in §1, Principlism establishes an internal border, separating kinds of Kantianism from one another. Dualism establishes an external border, separating Kantianism from views contrasting with it altogether. Thus any view that denies Dualism contrasts with Kantianism. In fact many views deny Dualism, thereby existing in conceptual space external to Kantian territory. To demonstrate this, I again draw on the history of philosophy in the service of conceptual geography.

As I understand them, both *Platonic* and *Aristotelian realism* maintain that all empirical concepts, terms, or properties are linked essentially only to an objective source, reality or the world itself. While the corresponding realists may not always concur with all of Plato's or Aristotle's claims, they do concur with Plato when he proclaims, and Aristotle agrees, that "species [have] ... natural joints" (*Phaedrus* 265e). The world (Plato's "nature") already comes carved. It has "real classes" (*Statesman* 262b). Thus

> [s]uppose, for example, that we undertake to cut something. If we make the cut in whatever way *we* choose and with whatever tool *we* choose, we will not succeed in cutting. ... If we try to cut contrary to nature, ... we'll be in error (*Cratylus* 387a).[22]

---

21. Hanna does maintain that, according to Kant, because "[w]e cannot *empirically* meaningfully assert either that things-in-themselves exist or that they do not exist[,] ... we must be *systematically agnostic* about them" (p. 15, first emphasis mine). We should therefore methodologically eliminate them (pp. 15, 197–98). Nonetheless there are two reasons that, even for Hanna, there would still be an objective source. First, discussions of subjective and objective sources are not empirical discussions. Nor are Hanna's weak or strong transcendental idealisms empirical theses. Any inability *empirically* meaningfully to assert that things in themselves do or do not exist is irrelevant. Second, methodological eliminativism is not eliminativism.

22. The *Phaedrus* translation is Alexander Nehamas and Paul Woodruff's; *Statesman*, C. J. Rowe's; *Cratylus*, C. D. C. Reeve's—all in John M. Cooper (1997).

These "species," or "real classes," do not depend on how *we* choose to cut. They are not constituted essentially out of, nor do we acquire them by appealing essentially to, our own specific conceptual, linguistic, or perceptual capacities. These species or real classes instead have "natural joints." They derive not at all from subjects but entirely from objects themselves. Platonic and Aristotelian realists however differ concerning how they understand those natural joints. The Platonic realist understands them as existing "*ante res*," or prior to the objects in the world whose speciation they make possible. The Aristotelian realist understands them as existing only "*in rebus*," or in the objects in the world whose speciation they make possible. The difference between Platonic and Aristotelian realism is the difference between those joints being Platonic forms (existing in a supermundane realm) or Aristotelian essences (existing in the mundane realm), respectively.[23]

Regardless, for both kinds of realism, all empirical concepts, terms, or properties just are the concepts, terms, or properties that they are purely in virtue of the objective world alone.[24] No empirical concept, term, or property would be constituted essentially out of a subjective source at all. For the Platonic and Aristotelian realist, all empirical concepts, terms, or properties are constituted essentially out of the world itself. They all pre-exist the subject. Neither would any be acquired by a subject's appealing essentially to a subjective source. All such concepts, terms, or properties are acquired by the subject in virtue of reality revealing itself to her independent of anything about her specific conceptual, linguistic, or perceptual capacities. Subjects sometimes simply can—with practice and luck—conceive of, name, and perceive its species. Nonetheless subjects can in principle always come up short. There is nothing specific about any subjects (or essential to their modes of acquisition) that guarantees that they could in principle acquire these concepts or terms. Neither is there anything specific about any subjects (or essential to their modes of acquisition) that guarantees that only they would acquire them. A subject's specific conceptual, linguistic, or perceptual capacities are irrelevant.

It is useful to contrast these kinds of realism with Epistemological Kantianism. According to an Epistemological Kantian, subjects can in

---

23. Platonic and Aristotelian realism are species of the "metaphysical" realism that Hilary Putnam (1978, part 4; 1981, ch. 3) contrasts with internal realism, and the "cosmocentric" realism that Philip Pettit (2002, ch. 2) contrasts with global response-dependence. As I understand them, both internal realism and global response-dependence are kinds of Kantianism. See Chapter Seven, §4, on internal realism, and Chapters Two, Three, and Four on global response-dependence, respectively.

24. I formulate Kantianism's contrasting views as concerning concepts, terms, *or* properties, for the same general reason that I formulated Kantianism as such. See §1.

principle learn all empirical concepts, terms, or properties. That is because, according to the Epistemological Kantian, the acquisition process is linked essentially to the subject. It is no accident that the subject acquires the specific concepts and terms that she does (that is how she is built), and no certainty that other creatures could in principle acquire the same (that need not be how they are built). Platonic and Aristotelian realists disagree with both. Hence, when the Platonic or Aristotelian realist theorizes about empirical concepts, terms, or properties, she need not take specific subjective manners of conception, language, or perception, into account. When the Epistemological (or for that matter Ontological) Kantian theorizes about empirical concepts, terms, or properties, she does. I elaborate on all this in Chapter Two.

The opposite extreme of Platonic or Aristotelian realism is *Berkeleian idealism*. As I understand it, Berkeleian idealism maintains that all empirical concepts, terms, or properties are linked essentially only to a subjective source. In fact, for such an idealist, there is no world, or anything else, beyond the subjective. For George Berkeley (2000/1713) himself, there are only ideas and minds having them. Empirical concepts, terms, or properties are purely subjective creations, even though once some mind constitutes them others can acquire them.[25] Hence, when the Berkeleian idealist theorizes about empirical concepts, terms, or properties, she can take only specific subjective manners of conception, language, or perception into account.

The Platonic and Aristotelian realist and Berkeleian idealist therefore differ from the Kantian by maintaining that *all* empirical concepts, terms, or properties are linked essentially only to one source. They simply disagree about what that source is. Then there are those who maintain that *only some* empirical concepts, terms, or properties are linked essentially to two sources. As I explain in Chapter Two, John Locke (1979/1689, II.8) and two analytic "response-dependence" theorists, Mark Johnston (1989, 1993) and Crispin Wright (1988, 1989, 1999/1992, 1993), maintain that only some empirical concepts, terms, or properties are so linked. Locke distinguishes primary from secondary qualities and their concepts, while Johnston and Wright distinguish response-dependent concepts, terms, and properties from response-independent ones. As I explain there, secondary qualities and their response-dependent relatives are linked essentially to responses of normal human beings under normal conditions of observation to objects in the world. Those responses, relying on specifically human conceptual, linguistic, or perceptual capacities, are the subjective source; objects in the world, the objective

---

25. According to George Berkeley (2000/1713, §48), God is the mind ("spirit") doing the constituting. Berkele*ian* idealism is consistent with subjects constituting their own concepts, terms, or properties.

source. Conversely primary qualities and their response-independent relatives are linked essentially only to an objective source. Nothing about the subject's specific nature is required for their constitution or the subject's acquisition thereof. Specific subjective capacities are irrelevant.

Hence Locke's secondary qualities and secondary-quality concepts, and Johnston and Wright's response-dependent concepts, terms, and properties, resemble the Kantian's empirical concepts, terms, and properties. They are all linked essentially to subjective and objective sources. In fact, as I explain in Chapter Two, in the *Prolegomena to Any Future Metaphysics* (2010/1783, 4: 288–98) Kant himself regards all empirical properties as secondary qualities. Conversely primary qualities and their concepts, and their response-independent relatives, resemble the Platonic and Aristotelian realist's empirical concepts, terms, and properties. They are all linked essentially only to an objective source. Thus Locke, Johnston, and Wright have a hybrid account. Because it traces explicitly to Locke, I identify any proponent of such an account as a *Lockean hybridist*. Hence, when the Lockean hybridist theorizes about empirical concepts, terms, or properties, she needs to take specific subjective manners of conception, language, or perception into account only for some of them.

Finally some think that *no* empirical concept, term, or property is linked essentially to a subjective or objective source in the first place. Such thinkers deny that it is philosophically useful to talk of distinctly "subjective" or "objective" sources at all. On certain readings such thinkers include Georg Wilhelm Friedrich Hegel (1977/1807); the American Pragmatists Charles Sanders Peirce, William James, and John Dewey (in their various writings); and more recently Sellars (1991/1963, 1968), Richard Rorty (1981), John McDowell (1996), and Robert Brandom (1998). The group also includes Donald Davidson (2001d/1984, essay 13; 2002, essays 3, 9–14), who at one point (2002, p. 154), at Rorty's (1990b) urging, saw himself as belonging to the American Pragmatist tradition, though, as I explain in Chapters Four and Five, is in fact a Kantian.[26]

On certain readings these thinkers agree that all empirical concepts, terms, or properties are inextricably tied to human practices embedded within

---

26. See also Rorty (1990a). Donald Davidson later (2005a, ch. 3) ceases identifying as an American Pragmatist. Nonetheless his pairing (which I examine in Chapter Four) of interpreter and speaker, and teacher and language learner, are philosophical descendants of Georg Wilhelm Friedrich Hegel's pairing of master and slave. Each member of each pair is engaged in a social practice constitutive of each one's status in the pair. And, because these statuses are co-constituted and arise from a common source, the practice itself, the statuses are themselves not ultimately distinct. In fact Hegel and Davidson each use their pairs to argue against Dualism. As I explain in Chapter Four, however, Davidson is committed to Dualism, and, in Chapter Five, his arguments against Dualism fail.

a naturally evolving world. Such practices allegedly afford us no legitimate notions of subjectivity or objectivity of the sort that I have tried to provide. Though "subjective" and "objective" might appear in these thinkers' vocabulary, they would not mean by them anything substantive or consequential. For, as they might maintain, the "spectator theory of knowledge" (Dewey), according to which we can distinguish "subject and object" (Dewey), "scheme and content" (Davidson), and "mind and world" (McDowell), is bankrupt. It is implicated in the "Myth of the Given" (Sellars, Rorty, McDowell, Brandom) or "myth of the subjective" (Davidson), and therefore its opposing "Myth of the Taken" (McDowell) or "myth of the objective" (I might add). The so-called "subjective" and "objective" are themselves in a way identical, manifesting as the unfolding of "spirit" dialectically through history (Hegel). Truth itself is a matter not of corresponding to some objective reality (Rorty, Davidson, McDowell, Brandom) but of what works (James, Rorty) or would work were our practices ideal (Peirce). Or perhaps 'truth', though formally indefinable, gets its content from our practice of interpreting persons (Davidson). Because all these accounts trace, implicitly or explicitly, to Hegel, and many make practices central, I identify any proponent of such an account as a *Hegelian pragmatist*.[27] Hence, when the Hegelian pragmatist theorizes about empirical concepts, terms, or properties, she would not regard as philosophically significant specific subjective manners of conception, language, or perception. That is because she would deny any philosophical usefulness of the alleged subjective/objective distinction itself.

Kantianism, Platonic and Aristotelian realism, Berkeleian idealism, Lockean hybridism, and Hegelian pragmatism are therefore all territories in the broader conceptual world.[28] Admittedly not all philosophical views are uncontroversially located in exactly one territory each. Philosophers, including those considered in this book, propose views that sometimes shift and employ language

---

27. See Louis Menand (2002) for Hegel's influence on Charles Sanders Peirce, William James, and John Dewey. Sellars, Rorty, John McDowell, and Robert Brandom are all explicit about their debt to Hegel and American Pragmatism. See below for Sellars and McDowell.

28. Where would the neo-Kantians of the late nineteenth and early twentieth century fit? Because members of the Marburg School—most famously Hermann Cohen, Paul Natorp, and Ernst Cassirer—reject Kant's distinction between the understanding (responsible for a subjective source of empirical concepts, terms, and properties) and sensibility (responsible for an objective source), they would be Hegelian pragmatists. Insofar as members of the Baden or Southwest School—most famously Wilhelm Windelband, Heinrich Rickert, Jonas Cohn, Emil Lask, and Bruno Bauch—retain some role for sensibility distinct from the understanding, they would be Kantian. See Rudolf A. Makkreel and Sebastian Luft (2010) for more on neo-Kantianism, and Konstantin Pollok (2010) for its influence on analytic philosophy.

that is sometimes ambiguous. This however is neither surprising nor problematic. It is not *surprising* because shifting views and ambiguous language might accompany all great thinkers. When their ends are extensive, their means and meanings might sometimes meander. It is not *problematic* because in what follows I note shifts and ambiguity where necessary while being charitable where possible. And this has in fact allowed me to locate views in one territory each much of the time.

Of course other expositors might locate the same views elsewhere. Hence my conceptual geography might occasionally be revisionary. Nor is that *problematic*. Geographers do occasionally correct each other's maps. My conceptual geography might however be *surprising*. Specifically it may or may not be controversial for Plato, Aristotle, Berkeley, Locke and certain contemporary response-dependence theorists, and Hegel and the American Pragmatists (and perhaps Rorty and Brandom) to be Platonic realists, Aristotelian realists, Berkeleian idealists, Lockean hybridists, and Hegelian pragmatists, respectively. It likely is controversial for Davidson to be a Kantian while Sellars and McDowell are not. As I explained, Davidson denies dualisms underlying Kantianism. Conversely Sellars and McDowell are themselves sometimes regarded as those Kantians with the greatest contemporary relevance for analytic epistemology and allied fields.[29] How then could I understand Davidson, and Sellars and McDowell, as I do? Because I discuss Davidson in subsequent chapters, let me say something about Sellars and McDowell here.

One reason that Sellars and McDowell are often regarded as Kantians is that Kant's transcendental idealism is their explicit starting point. Yet in this Sellars and McDowell are no different from Hegel. Nor is this enough to make Sellars or McDowell, let alone Hegel, Kantian in my sense. To appreciate this, consider one issue in particular that Sellars and McDowell discuss. It is the issue of non-conceptual content, the allegedly purely sensory, and so in my sense objective, subject matter of certain mental states.[30] The analytic debate concerning non-conceptual content traces explicitly to Strawson's student Gareth Evans (1982), who argues that there is such content.[31] Fred Dretske (1969, 1991/1981), Christopher Peacocke (1995), Michael Tye (1997), and Susan Hurley (2002/1998) argue similarly.

---

29. Previously Clarence Irving Lewis (2004/1929) and Strawson (1975) were so regarded. See Kenneth R. Westphal (2010) for more on Lewis's, Strawson's, and Sellars's debt to Kant.

30. Non-conceptual content would be Davidson's (2002, essays 3, 10, 11; 2005b, essay 4) "empirical content" as it figures in mental states. See Chapter Five, §5.

31. Hanna (2006, ch. 2.1) traces *both* sides in the non-conceptual content debate ultimately to Kant.

Conversely Sellars (1991/1963, essay 5) argues that there is no non-conceptual content. That is one conclusion of his argument against the Myth of the Given. As I would put it, Sellars contends that no non-conceptual content, which would be objective, can be merely "given" to the mind, which would be subjective. In fact, for Sellars, noticing objects in the world presupposes already having concepts for them:

> [I]nstead of coming to have a concept of something because we have noticed that sort of thing, to have the ability to notice a sort of thing is already to have the concept of that sort of thing, and cannot account for it (p. 176).

According to Sellars, the world itself can ground our mental states only if our epistemological access to it is already conceptual. The very idea of non-conceptual content is inconsistent. Non-conceptual content, the "Given," therefore does not exist. In fact, as Rorty observes, Sellars "attack[s] the distinction *between* what is 'given to the mind' *and* what is 'added by the mind'" (Rorty 1997, p. 5, emphases mine)[32]—between, in my terms, the objective and the subjective as traditionally understood by philosophers.

McDowell in turn extends Sellars's argument against non-conceptual content by maintaining that "conceptual capacities are not exercised *on* non-conceptual deliverances of sensibility. Conceptual capacities are already operative *in* the deliverances of sensibility themselves" (1996, p. 39, emphases mine). Conceptual capacities would be subjective in my sense; non-conceptual deliverances of sensibility, which would be sensation, objective. Rather than the subjective being exercised *on* the objective, McDowell is therefore saying, the subjective is already operative *in* the objective. So *non*-conceptual content in particular is impossible. McDowell continues: "We must not suppose that receptivity," the capacity to take in the objective, "makes an even *notionally* separable contribution to its co-operation with spontaneity," the capacity to generate the subjective (p. 41, emphasis mine). But then we cannot maintain even the *notion* that objective and subjective sources separably contribute to anything, the content of mental states or otherwise. If however (and now I am perhaps extending McDowell's argument myself) we cannot maintain even the *notion* of separable contributions, then neither can we maintain that they "co-operate." Without being notionally *separable*, they cannot be said to *co*-operate, or work *together*. Instead, as I understand McDowell, the world *itself* is already conceptual. That is the sense in which the subjective is already

---

32. Rorty also explains that Sellars's work "links up with that of the American pragmatists" (1997, p. 5, n. 5).

operative in the objective. Hence nothing is merely Given (from the objective) *or* Taken (by the subjective). We reject both Myths, and with it dissolve the philosophical distinction between mind (and subjectivity) and world (and objectivity).[33]

Hence, while neither Sellars nor McDowell denies the ordinary distinction between subjective and objective, or mind and world, they do challenge the usefulness of the traditional philosophical distinction. That is why they deny the existence of non-conceptual content. And that is enough for me to count both as Hegelian pragmatists. Nor might my counting them as such be surprising. Sellars calls his most influential work (1991/1963, essay 5) "incipient *Meditations Hegeliennes*" (p. 148), while McDowell claims that he "would like to conceive [his own] work ... as a prolegomenon to a reading of the *Phenomenology* [Hegel 1977/1807]" (1996, p. ix).

4. THE PLAN OF THIS WORK

Now that we know what Kantianism is, what the relation between Kantianism and Kant's transcendental idealism is, and what Kantianism is not, we should consider what lies ahead in this book. *Kantian Conceptual Geography* divides into five parts.

We are nearly done with Part One, "Establishing Kantianism's Borders." Here in its sole chapter, Chapter One, "Dualism, Principlism, Kantianism," I have defined each of these terms. I have thereby established Kantianism's external border, Dualism, separating it from other views, some of which we have considered. I have also established Kantianism's internal border, Principlism, separating Principled and un-Principled kinds of Kantianism from themselves.

In Part Two, "Exploring Kantian Territory," we see that there are views within Kantianism's borders that are alive and well in analytic epistemology, philosophy of language, and metaphysics. I explore these views to illustrate the breadth of those borders and with it its rich and diverse interior. I have

---

33. See Sally Sedgwick (1997) for more on "McDowell's Hegelianism." As she explains, McDowell sees two tendencies in Kant. From the standpoint of experience, Kant takes conceptual capacities to be "inextricably implicated" (McDowell 1996, p. 10) or "drawn on" (p. 87) *in* receptivity. While this makes Kant sound like a Hegelian pragmatist, from the standpoint of transcendental idealism, Kant takes spontaneity to impose its forms and categories *on* "prior deliverances of receptivity" (p. 10). According to Sedgwick, both McDowell and Hegel retain the former idea while rejecting the latter. Thus Rorty could be talking about McDowell too when he explains that Sellars himself "emphasiz[es] the passages in Kant which anticipate Hegel" (1997, p. 9).

therefore chosen to focus on three analytic philosophers who provide an especially expansive view.

In Chapter Two, "Philip Pettit," I focus on Pettit. As I explain there, Pettit stands out among nearly all his analytic peers for range of research, including not merely epistemology, philosophy of language, and metaphysics, but also ethics and philosophy of mind. He has contributed to political science too. More importantly for my purposes, Pettit's notion of *global response-dependence* further liberates Kantianism from Kant's transcendental idealism. As Johnston's and Wright's response-dependence is related to Locke's view, so Pettit's global response-dependence is related to Kant's. Though Pettit is not as well-known as the other two analytic philosophers on whom I focus in Part Two, appealing to him helps me explain their views also. Moreover from Pettit we learn that Kantianism can take the subjective source of all empirical concepts, terms, or properties to be *anthropocentric* in scope. Conceptual, linguistic, and perceptual capacities can be had by subjects *qua* human. I also consider a debate concerning *noumenalism*, the thesis that reality has an intrinsic nature or aspect that remains unknowable.

In Chapter Three, "Thomas Kuhn," I focus on Kuhn. As I explain there, Kuhn was arguably the most famous philosopher of science of the last century, having contributed to epistemology, philosophy of language, and metaphysics as well. Kuhn's views have been taken up by philosophers of all persuasions, besides historians, literary theorists, political scientists, and sociologists also. More importantly for my purposes, by establishing that Kuhn too can be understood as a global response-dependence theorist, I expand my exploration of Kantianism itself. From Kuhn we learn that Kantianism can take the subjective source of all empirical concepts, terms, or properties to be *ethnocentric* in scope. Conceptual, linguistic, and perceptual capacities can be had by subjects *qua* community member. I also consider the connection between Kantianism and *incommensurability*, which on my construal obtains between linguistic units (terms, sentences, theories, languages) that are not completely intertranslatable.

In Chapter Four, "Donald Davidson," I focus on Davidson. As I explain there, Davidson enriched our understanding of thought, language, and reality more deeply and systematically than perhaps any other analytic philosopher. Davidson's views are far-reaching, regarded by some as continuous with American Pragmatism, seen by others as consonant with many in the Continental tradition, and connected in his final years by Davidson himself to views in Chinese philosophy; Davidson also inspired linguists and literary theorists alike. More importantly for my purposes, by establishing that Davidson himself offers different global response-dependence theories, I expand my exploration of Kantianism too. From Davidson we learn that Kantianism can take the subjective source of all empirical concepts, terms, or properties to be *idiocentric* in scope. Conceptual, linguistic, and perceptual capacities can be had by subjects *qua* individual. We also learn that Kantianism can take the subjective source to be *logocentric* in scope. Capacities can be had subjects *qua* language user. Finally, by considering an irreconcilable difference among Davidson's response-dependence theories, we learn as well that Kantianism can be *ahistoricist* or *historicist*. Capacities can be those that a subject would or did exercise, respectively.

Then I turn to Part Three, "Defending Kantianism's Borders." Regardless of whether Kant's views in the *Critique of Pure Reason* are defensible, I establish that Dualism and Principlism are. This reassures us that my definition of 'Kantianism' in Part One and exploration of Kantian territory in Part Two are not for naught. It also furthers my aim of increasing our understanding of myriad issues in epistemology, philosophy of language, and metaphysics. Much about a view and issues related to it can be learned from its defense.

In Chapter Five, "Defending Dualism," I defend Dualism against its most serious challenge. That challenge is ironically from Davidson himself. For Davidson presents a series of arguments meant to show the unintelligibility of the very idea of subjective and objective sources of concepts, terms, or properties. I conclude that the most determined case against Dualism can be disqualified. Moreover I thereby reaffirm Davidson's Kantian credentials recognized in Chapter Four.

In Chapter Six, "Defending Principlism," I defend Principlism against its most important challenges, culminating in those of Davidson's mentor, Quine. I do so by demonstrating that there is a version of Principlism, Friedman's, that remains unimpugned by any of these challenges. Though this does not prove Principlism true, it does shift the burden to those who think it false.

Next I turn to Part Four, "Looking for New Land within Kantianism's Borders." There we learn that there is land within Kantianism's borders that no one has yet charted. *Qua* Kantian conceptual geographer, I survey rather than settle on that land. Nonetheless I do indicate whether we have reason to prefer that Kantian land to any other.

In Chapter Seven, "From Dualism to a Kantian Account of Meaning," I rely on Dualism to disclose a Kantian account of meaning. We thereby learn what a Kantian account of meaning is, different ways in which it can be formulated, and different examples of such an account itself. We also learn how a Kantian account differs from other kinds of accounts of meaning. In fact we learn that each account that contrasts with Kantianism—Platonic and Aristotelian realism, Berkeleian idealism, Lockean hybridism, and Hegelian pragmatism—has a correspondingly contrasting account of meaning. And we learn that there exist prominent accounts of meaning in the analytic literature approximating nearly all these. Along the way we see that a Kantian account does not face problems that these other accounts of meaning face. I conclude that we have reason to prefer a Kantian account of meaning to them.

In Chapter Eight, "Problems That a Kantian Account of Meaning Faces," I consider putative problems that such an account does face. Most striking are the relativism of the empirical world, possible plurality of empirical worlds, and possible movability between empirical worlds. For each I consider whether the putative problems are genuine and if so offer multiple replies. I thereby show that we have even more reason to prefer a Kantian account of meaning to other such accounts. Besides all that I show as well that anyone committed to Ontological Kantianism concerning concepts, terms, *or* properties is committed to Ontological Kantianism concerning concepts, terms, *and* properties. In Kant's own spirit I conclude that Kantianism entails a "unity of reason"—a unity among concepts, terms, and properties, as well as epistemology, philosophy of language, and metaphysics themselves.

In Chapter Nine, "From Principlism to Kantian Thoughts on Truth," I rely on Principlism to disclose not a Kantian account of but instead Kantian thoughts on empirical truth in particular. We thereby learn how, for the Principled Kantian, all empirical claims depend on, and are therefore necessarily consistent with, subjective principles. We also learn about attempts to join Kantian thoughts on truth with analyses of instrumental or pragmatic value. Then we see what the un-Principled Kantian can say. Though I do not consider putative problems that Kantian thoughts on truth face, I do show that appreciating such thoughts nevertheless illuminates the nature of empirical truth itself.

While at the end of each chapter in Parts Two, Three, and Four I draw lessons for Kantian conceptual geography, finally I turn to Part Five, "Lessons for Us," where I draw lessons for us. There in its sole chapter, Chapter Ten, "Some Idea Had Seized the Sovereignty of His Mind," besides drawing those lessons, I also look back at the full expanse of Kantian territory relative to the broader conceptual world.

Hence in this book I am not determining the truth of any particular claim, not even Kantianism itself. I am instead doing something more important. I am appealing to Kantianism to engage in conceptual geography by exploring issues of the utmost importance to analytic epistemology, philosophy of language, and metaphysics. This involves working out implications, noting compatibilities and incompatibilities, comparing and contrasting views, and ultimately surveying the lay of the conceptual land. Admittedly my exploration does provide a defense of some views and reason to prefer others. Regardless *Kantian Conceptual Geography* remains a work in Kantian conceptual geography: exploring conceptual connections among myriad issues by appealing to Kantian tools. Moreover, since some sort of conceptual geography is necessary for a fair and complete determination of the truth of any particular claim, conceptual geography is logically prior to any such determination. Since appealing to Kantianism in particular is an especially useful tool, one might think of Kantian conceptual geography as a *prolegomenon* to any future epistemology, philosophy of language, or metaphysics—Kantian or otherwise.

5. NATURALISM

I close by addressing a potential worry. Many philosophers take consistency with naturalism to be a *desideratum* on any philosophical project. Likewise many regard anything Kantian as committed to transcendental philosophy—a kind of "first" philosophy, an attempt to appeal to something logically prior to natural science. Since naturalism is (perhaps) the view that no such appeal is legitimate, many philosophers might therefore see my project as misguided.

Let me offer three replies. First, for all the importance assigned to it, 'naturalism' has no clear or univocal meaning. This is so across philosophy as well as within its fields. Jerry Fodor (2005/1975) and McDowell (1996) are both self-identifying naturalists and philosophers of mind, yet one would be hard pressed to identify more than a handful of substantive theses on which they agree.[34] Even the construal that I just suggested, that naturalism is the view that no appeal to anything logically prior to science is legitimate, is vague. What counts as science? Is it just physics or any knowledge (if any) that reduces without remainder to it? Is it just the sciences of the so-called "physical" world, perhaps the world independent of human beings, and not also the "social," or human, world, that presumably overlaps with the physical? And are we to understand this (or these) science (or sciences), whatever it (or they) turn out to be, as the science (or sciences) of today or some idealized end of inquiry? Further, is naturalism a thesis in epistemology, admonishing an appeal to anything that scientists think we cannot *know*; philosophy of language, admonishing an appeal to anything to which scientists think we cannot *refer*; metaphysics, admonishing an appeal to anything that scientists think does not *exist*; or something else? Until naturalism is clarified, making consistency with it a *desideratum* is hardly illuminating.

Second, my project is to explore the conceptual geography of myriad issues in epistemology, philosophy of language, and metaphysics by appealing to theses that can be drawn from the *Critique of Pure Reason*. It is not to establish the truth of any particular claim, "naturalistic" or otherwise. So, if naturalism concerns the truth of particular claims, then Kantian conceptual geography is consistent

---

34. See Jerry Fodor (1995) on this point.

with it after all. In fact worries concerning naturalism would be posterior to my project.

And third, scientists themselves consider how their concepts relate. They themselves thereby explore, survey, and map the conceptual lay of their own particular land. To the extent that scientists occasionally are conceptual geographers, if naturalism concerns particular methodologies, then Kantian conceptual geography is itself naturalistic.[35]

---

35. See Joel Smith and Peter Sullivan (2011b) for discussion of naturalism and transcendental philosophy. See Barry Stroud (2009/1996) for discussion of "the charm of naturalism" in analytic philosophy.

PART TWO

Exploring Kantian Territory

TWO

Philip Pettit

Philip Pettit has contributed to nearly every area of analytic philosophy: from ethics and political philosophy, to epistemology, metaphysics, philosophy of language, and philosophy of mind. He has also contributed to related areas in political science. Concurrent with parts of this, Pettit has proposed his theory of global response-dependence.[1] In this chapter we see that Pettit's global response-dependence is a kind of un-Principled Epistemological Kantianism. Moreover we see that Pettit's theory, like Immanuel Kant's own transcendental idealism, takes the subjective source of empirical concepts, terms, or properties to be anthropocentric, *i.e.*, centered on paradigmatic human (*anthropos*) responses—and ultimately specifically human conceptual, linguistic, and perceptual capacities. Finally we see that Pettit's Kantianism, and in fact all kinds of Kantianism, entail noumenalism, the thesis that reality possesses an intrinsic nature or aspect that remains unknowable.

The chapter proceeds as follows. In §1 I explain response-dependence by appealing to the historical view of John Locke and contemporary views of Mark Johnston and Crispin Wright. In §2 I show that Pettit's global response-dependence theory is a form of un-Principled Epistemological Kantianism. In §3 I present Michael Smith and Daniel Stoljar's argument that Pettit's theory entails noumenalism and then present Pettit's reply. In §4 I engage Pettit, and Smith and Stoljar's, debate. In §5 I show that Pettit is committed to a trilemma and then resolve it. Finally in §6 I draw lessons for Kantian conceptual geography generally.

---

1. Philip Pettit's major works include Pettit (1996, 1997, 1998, 2001, 2002, 2005, 2010); John Braithwaite and Pettit (1992); Frank Jackson, Pettit, and Michael Smith (2004); Geoffrey Brennan and Pettit (2006); Christian List and Pettit (2011); and José Luis Martí and Pettit (2012). Pettit (1998; 2002, part I; 2005; Jackson and Pettit 2002) discusses global response-dependence.

1. RESPONSE-DEPENDENCE

As we saw in Chapter One, 'response-dependence' names various views in analytic philosophy inspired by Locke (1979/1689, II.8). Here I can be more precise. According to Locke, certain concepts (his "ideas of secondary qualities") and properties ("secondary qualities") are linked essentially to responses of normal human beings under normal conditions of observation to objects in the world. As I understand Locke, an object falls under the concept **red** and is red if and only if normal human beings under normal conditions of observation would conceive of and perceive the object as such. Moreover what it is for something to fall under the concept and have the property just is for it to be so conceived and perceived. The connection is essential to the conception and perception.

Hence Locke's account of secondary-quality concepts and properties links them essentially to subjective and objective sources. The subjective sources are responses of normal human beings under normal conditions of observation, involving the subject's conceiving of and perceiving certain objects in certain ways. These responses themselves rely on specifically human conceptual, linguistic (insofar as language is itself linked to conception and perception), and perceptual capacities. The objective source are objects in the world—objects to which these paradigmatically human subjects would respond.

Conversely Locke's account of primary-quality concepts and properties links them essentially only to an objective source. For Locke, an object in the world falls under **solid** and is solid without any essential connection to subjective responses, human or otherwise. While an object cannot fall under **red** or be red unless normal human beings under normal conditions of observation would conceive of and perceive it as such, an object can fall under **solid** and be solid without any such conception or perception. While secondary-quality concepts and properties are anthropocentric, or centered on paradigmatic human responses, primary-quality concepts and properties are not.[2] Finally, because **red** and red, and **solid** and solid, are all empirical, Locke thinks that only some empirical concepts and properties are linked essentially to subjective and objective sources. He is therefore a Lockean hybridist in the sense offered in Chapter One.

Johnston (1989, 1993), who coined the term 'response-dependence', has proposed the following as a generalization of Locke's view:

> If C, the concept associated with the predicate 'is C', is a concept interdependent with or dependent upon concepts of certain subjects' responses

---

2. The notion of a secondary quality traces to Galileo (1957/1623). See Jonathan Bennett (1971), Colin McGinn (1983), and Peter M. S. Hacker (1991) for more on the primary-/secondary-quality distinction.

under certain conditions, then something of the following form will hold *a priori*:

  x is *C* iff In *K*, *S*s are disposed to produce *x*-directed response *R*
  (or
  x is such as to produce *R* in *S*s under conditions *K*) (1989, p. 145).[3]

Johnston limits the application of this to evaluative concepts like **good** and sensory concepts like **red**. As I explain below, Johnston aims ultimately to demonstrate the "interdependence" of concepts with subjective responses to objects in the world (1989, pp. 145, 147; 1993, pp. 105–06). For Johnston, it holds (or is) *a priori* that something is an instance of **good** if and only if in suitable conditions, suitable subjects are disposed to produce a something-directed response that it is good. I take Johnston's point in more natural wording to be that *a priori* something is good if and only if a suitable subject under suitable conditions would conceive of it as falling under **good**. Johnston is therefore committed to the view that, for the appropriate concepts, this holds *a priori*:

  CONCEPT: Something is *x* if and only if a suitable subject under suitable conditions would conceive of it as falling under *x*.

Moreover Johnston's analysis also references the predicate (or term) ⌜is *C*⌝ (or ⌜*C*⌝). Since other response-dependence theories are explicit about it, and it does no injustice to Johnston's, I can also say that on his view it likewise holds *a priori* that something is good if and only if a suitable subject under suitable conditions would in English call it 'good'. Hence Johnston is committed to the view that, for the appropriate terms, this too holds *a priori*:

  TERM: Something is *x* if and only if a suitable subject under suitable conditions would in English call it ⌜*x*⌝.

Finally, though Johnston is not explicit about it, his analysis pertains to properties also.[4] It holds *a priori* as well that something is good if and only if a suitable subject under suitable conditions would perceive it as good. Generalizing we see that Johnston is committed to the view that, for the appropriate properties, this holds *a priori* also:

  PROPERTY: Something is *x* if and only if a suitable subject under suitable conditions would perceive it as *x*.

---

3. *Cf.*: "The concept *F* = the concept of the disposition to produce *R* in *S* under *C*, where *R* is the manifestation of the disposition, *S* is the locus of the manifestation and *C* is the condition of manifestation" (Mark Johnston 1993, p. 103).

4. See David Yates (2008).

Three things about Concept, Term, and Property are noteworthy. First, for Johnston, Concept, Term, and Property do all hold *a priori*. What does this mean? There are ontological and epistemological senses of apriority. As I understand it, the ontological sense concerns sources, faculties, or places from which things that are *a priori* derive. This is the sense of *a priori* employed in Chapter One when I explained that Kant's synthetic *a priori* judgments are meant to derive from a subjective source, the transcendental subject's mind. Conversely the epistemological sense of *a priori* concerns how *a priori* claims (or judgments, propositions, or statements) can be justified or verified. *A priori* claims can be justified or verified independently of experience or anything about objects in the world. They can be justified or verified subjectively, perhaps by appealing to a subject's mind or language and so in the latter case the meaning of her terms. At least concerning claims these two senses of *a priori* are mutually entailing. If some claim is *a priori* because it derives entirely from a subjective source, then it is *a priori* because it can be justified or verified independently of an objective source. Conversely, if some claim is *a priori* because it can be justified or verified independently of an objective source, then it is *a priori* because it derives entirely from a subjective source.[5]

Johnston and subsequent response-dependence theorists want their biconditionals to hold *a priori* in (at least) the epistemological sense. For Johnston, Concept, Term, and Property hold *a priori* insofar as they can be justified or verified independently of experience in particular. For him, it makes no sense to say that there is an empirical test to determine whether something falls under **good**, is in English called 'good', or is good, if and only if a suitable subject under suitable conditions would conceive of or perceive it as such. Neither, for Locke, does it make sense to say that there is an empirical test to determine whether something falls under **red** or is red if and only if a suitable subject under suitable conditions would conceive of or perceive it as such. In each case those claims are taken to follow from what we *conceive* of when we think, or *mean* when we say, that something is good or red. That would make Johnston's biconditionals in particular hold *a priori* in an ontological sense of deriving subjectively—including (to focus on this) from the meaning of our terms and ultimately our language.

Now I said that there are three noteworthy things about Concept, Term, and Property. While the first is that, for Johnston, they hold *a priori*, the second is that, for him, Concept, Term, and Property elucidate rather than reduce

---

5. As I explain in Chapter Six, §1, both senses of apriority are in Immanuel Kant (1998/1787). Robert Hanna (2001, ch. 5.2) calls Kant's ontological sense 'semantic' because it concerns the source of the (semantic) content of cognition. As R. Lanier Anderson (2010, p. 78) explains, the epistemological sense is normally taken to be basic in Kant.

or eliminate the sense in which concepts, terms, and properties, respectively, are response-dependent. For Johnston, the appearance of ⌜x⌝ and its cognates on both sides of each biconditional is not only unproblematic. It is in fact required. I return to this below.

And third, for Johnston, the relevant subjects and conditions are (ultimately) to be specified non-trivially. By a 'suitable subject' Johnston would follow every explicit response-dependence theorist in meaning a normal human being—roughly one with unfettered conceptual, linguistic, and perceptual capacities. By 'suitable conditions' he would follow them in meaning normal conditions of observation, *i.e.*, conditions under which normal human beings can exercise such capacities. Thus Johnston follows every explicit response-dependence theorist in proposing a view that is anthropocentric in the same way in which Locke's view of secondary-quality concepts and properties is anthropocentric. Admittedly, for Johnston, what is normal (and unfettered) is unclear. Self-identified response-dependence theorists tend to leave specification to others.[6] Ironically, as I explain in Chapters Three and Four, non-self-identified response-dependence theorists tend to take up the task of specification themselves.

Johnston's work is pioneering, and in the chapters that follow I return to it often. Here I compare it with Wright's. Wright offers the following "modest generalization" (1999/1992, p. 109) of Johnston's own view:

For all S, P: P if and only if (if CS then RS),

where ["]S["] is any agent, "P" ranges over all of some wide class of judgments (judgments of color or shape, or moral judgments, or mathematical judgments, for instance), "RS" expresses S's having of some germane experience (judging that P, for instance, or having a visual impression of color, or of shape, or being smitten with moral sentiments of a certain kind, or amused) and "CS" expresses the satisfaction of certain conditions of optimality on that particular response (pp. 108–09).[7]

Wright's analysis is of properties. According to him, for any suitable subject (or agent) and judgment, the judgment is true if and only if, if the subject is in normal (or optimal) conditions then the subject responds by making that judgment. Thus, for any suitable subject and judgment that something is red,

6. As I mention in §2, Pettit (2002, essay 5) is an exception.

7. See also Crispin Wright (1988; 1989, pp. 246–58; 1999/1992, pp. 108–10; 1993, p. 77). Wright later suggests formulating response-dependence biconditionals thus: "If CS, then (it would be the case that P if and only if S would judge that p)" (1999/1992, pp. 117–20; see also 2002, pp. 388–97).

the judgment is true if and only if, if the subject is in normal conditions then she responds by making that judgment. And, for Wright, the subjects and conditions are centered on human beings, making his view, like Johnston's (and Locke's), anthropocentric.

Wright can endorse some version of Property if not also Concept and Term. Moreover I can extract from Wright's view four requirements for *any* biconditional to express a response-dependence relation. The first three requirements coincide with the noteworthy features of Johnston's biconditionals. First, response-dependence biconditionals hold *a priori*. Second, such biconditionals are non-reductive and non-eliminative. And third, such biconditionals are (ultimately) to be specified non-trivially.[8]

Now following Johnston I take satisfying these three requirements to be necessary and sufficient for a biconditional to express a response-dependence relation. Wright however adds a fourth requirement, which on my view is optional. It is that response-dependence biconditionals are read in a constitutively asymmetric manner. They are in Wright's terms 'extension-determining' rather than 'extension-reflecting'. According to Wright, that something is red if and only if normal human beings under normal conditions of observation judge that it is red must *determine*, or constitute, what it is for the thing to be red. It must not merely *reflect*, or describe, any ontologically antecedent redness. For Wright, something is red *because* normal human beings under normal conditions of observation judge that it is red rather than (and certainly not also) *vice versa*.[9]

There are two reasons that one might think that response-dependence biconditionals need not satisfy Wright's fourth requirement. Either reason is on my view appropriate. First, one might agree with Johnston that response-dependence biconditionals express constitutive *interdependence* between concepts, terms, or properties, on the one hand, and subjective responses to objects in the world, on the other. Though he does not put it this way, Johnston could maintain that something is good because normal human beings under normal conditions of observation judge it to be good *and also vice versa*. *Contra* Wright, there would be no constitutive asymmetry. In fact, as I understand him, Johnston discounts the extension-determining/reflecting distinction not because he thinks that there is no determining but because he thinks that the determining is symmetric.

---

8. See Wright (1988, pp. 19–22; 1989, p. 247; 1999/1992, pp. 114–17; 1993, pp. 77–82) regarding the first requirement and Wright (1989, pp. 247–48; 1999/1992, pp. 112, 120–23; 1993, p. 78) regarding the third. The second requirement is implicit in these and proximal passages.

9. See Wright (1999/1992, ch. 3. append.; 1993, pp. 77–82; 2001, pp. 191–99). See Johnston (1993) for criticism and Wright (1999/1992, ch. 3. append.) for his reply.

Second, one might think that response-dependence biconditionals express *no* constitutive relations in the first place. Instead they merely describe (Wright's "reflect") ontologically antecedent facts. There would be no constitutive asymmetry (*à la* Wright) or symmetry (*à la* Johnston), respectively, at all. Nonetheless, as I understand things, one holding such a view would still be a response-dependence theorist if she accepted Wright's first three requirements.

Perhaps it is not difficult to understand why I count Johnston as a response-dependence theorist. Though he discounts the extension-determining/reflecting distinction, he does think that responses determine (or constitute) his target concepts, terms, and properties. He merely thinks that the determination is symmetric. This second case, concerning extension-reflecting, involves no determining (or constituting) at all. To appreciate why I nevertheless count someone supporting this second case as a response-dependence theorist as well, let me contrast her with a Platonic or Aristotelian realist, considered in Chapter One.

Both Platonic and Aristotelian realists think that the world reveals its joints directly to a subject, independent of her specific conceptual, linguistic, or perceptual capacities. Hence, if either a Platonic or Aristotelian realist happened to accept some biconditional like Concept, Term, or Property (which is doubtful), then she would read it as reference-reflecting herself. Nonetheless she would *also* maintain that any such biconditional would at best be true accidentally. Nothing from a subject's specific conceptual, linguistic, or perceptual capacities would be necessary or sufficient when combined with an objective source to determine or reflect properties of objects in the world. The world reveals itself to subjects, but only with practice and luck can they sometimes conceive of, name, and perceive its objects as they really are. As we saw in Chapter One, such realists allow that the subject can in principle always come up short in her conceptual, linguistic, and perceptual results. Hence, according to such realists, the truth of biconditionals like Concept, Term, or Property—*were* any true—would itself be due to practice and luck on the part of the subject rather than her specific conceptual, linguistic, and perceptual capacities responding to objects in the world.

Conversely, according to someone who is a response-dependence theorist but reads her biconditionals in a response-reflecting way, those biconditionals would be true not merely due to practice and luck on the part of the subject. They would be true due to the subject's specific capacities responding to objects in the world as such. For those capacities would be in principle necessary and sufficient for her to learn the requisite concepts, terms, and properties. There would be nothing accidental about that at all. While both Platonic and Aristotelian realists allow the subject to come up short even in principle, a proponent of the case that I am imagining would not. Put differently, though both Platonic and Aristotelian realists would be sympathetic with an extension-reflecting reading (if any) of Wright's biconditionals, they would reject that such biconditionals hold *a priori*. They would reject Wright's first requirement on response-dependence biconditionals. Conversely a proponent of the view that I am imagining would accept that they so hold. She would accept Wright's first requirement.

Besides Johnston and Wright, other influential response-dependence theorists include Michael Smith (1989), John McDowell (2001/1998, essays 6, 7, 10), David Wiggins (1998, essays 3, 5), and Pettit (1998; 2002, part I; 2005; Frank Jackson and Pettit 2002). I consider Pettit next.[10]

2. PETTIT'S RESPONSE-DEPENDENCE AND KANTIANISM

Pettit's response-dependence theory follows from his account of language learning. I consider that account in Chapter Three. Let me here focus on the theory itself.

Pettit's theory is jointly of terms and concepts. According to him, response-dependent terms and concepts are

> those terms and concepts that are biconditionally connected, as an a priori matter, with certain more or less primitive responses: in particular, with responses of a perceptual or affective character (1998, p. 55).

For convenience let me focus on terms. Pettit asks us to suppose that ⌜P⌝ in English names a semantically basic term. By 'semantically basic' he means a term learned *via* exposure to ostensible objects. For Pettit, learning ⌜P⌝ would

---

10. Many response-dependence theorists regard various parts of their biconditionals as rigid designators. Consider:

> Something is red if and only if normal human beings under normal conditions of observation would conceive of it as falling under **red** and in English call it 'red'.

They might treat 'red', 'normal human beings', 'normal conditions of observation', '**red**', 'English', or "red" as referring to the same objects—the objects to which they refer in the actual world—in all possible worlds in which the objects exists. There are two reasons that I do not discuss rigidity. First, the Kantians on whom in Part Two I focus are Pettit, Thomas Kuhn, and Donald Davidson. And Pettit makes rigidity peripheral to his concerns, Kuhn (1990) argues that it is irrelevant, and Davidson (2002, p. 29) rejects it. Second, and relatedly, differences among Pettit, Kuhn, and Davidson do not concern rigidity. As I engage in Kantian conceptual geography *via* Pettit's, Kuhn's, and Davidson's views, therefore, discussing rigidity illuminates little territory.

involve a primitive response. Semantically basic terms are themselves then response-dependent because their mastery depends on "contingencies of subjective response" (2005, p. 181) that paradigmatic human beings have to their referents. They are acquired by a subject's relying on specifically anthropocentric conceptual, linguistic, and perceptual capacities. Pettit explains:

> something is *P* if and only if it is such that it would seem *P*—people would be disposed to use '*P*' to ascribe the corresponding property to it—under normal conditions of observation (2002, p. 136).

Pettit's examples are color terms. He maintains that something is red, and in English called 'red', if and only if a suitable subject under suitable conditions would respond to it as red. Generalizing to any semantically basic term, we see that Pettit is committed to the view that this holds *a priori*:

CONCEPT-AND-TERM: Something is *x* if and only if normal human beings under normal conditions of observation would conceive of it as falling under *x* and in English call it ⌜*x*⌝.

As we just saw, Pettit does maintain that "something is *P* if and only it is such that it would seem *P* ... under normal conditions of observation," where ⌜*P*⌝ names a property rather than a term. Nonetheless Pettit does not offer a response-dependence theory of properties. According to him, while 'red' (and **red**) are response-dependent, red is not: "[L]ike a spectral reflectance, [red] may be the sort of thing that can exist in the absence of the community and in the absence of any thinking thing" (Jackson and Pettit 2002, p. 99). Likewise Pettit explains: "Under the story developed here, a response-dependent predicate—a response-dependently mastered predicate—like 'is red' ascribes an objective property to things, perhaps a particular spectral reflectance" (Pettit 2002, p. 14), where an objective property would be a property that is what it is without any essential connection to subjects. It would be a property of objects in the world in themselves or considered in themselves—a distinction to which I return in §3. Still Pettit maintains that what allows us to identify the objective property of red *as* red are its effects on us. That a suitable subject under suitable conditions perceives something as red if and only if it is red is not, on Pettit's view, an ontological fact about red. It is instead an epistemological fact about how we identify red and a linguistic fact about what in English we call 'red'. Regardless of what red really is, we know red when we see it because under normal conditions of observation red looks red to us. We then call it 'red'. Thus, Pettit maintains, response-dependent terms (and concepts) refer to "pre-existing things" (2002, p. 75)—things that pre-exist our responses. Red is itself "a mind-independent"—and therefore itself a pre-existing—"property" (1998, p. 62). It is a property of objects in the world independent of any subjects, even if the property is recognized only (and in fact essentially) by subjective responses to it. So, while Concept-and-Term is meant on Pettit's view to apply to all semantically basic concepts and terms, he has no correlate for properties.[11]

Does Pettit endorse the four requirements on response-dependence biconditionals that I extracted from Wright's view? He endorses the first. Like Wright and Johnston, Pettit takes his response-dependence biconditionals to hold *a priori*. That something is red if and only if normal human beings under normal conditions of observation would conceive of it as falling under **red** and in English call it 'red' is, for him, insusceptible to empirical justification or verification. That makes it *a priori* in the epistemological sense. In fact, presumably for Pettit, it is *a priori* in this epistemological sense because claiming that something is red under just those circumstances is itself a statement of what we *mean* when we say that it is red. That makes it *a priori* in the ontological sense of deriving from the meaning of our terms and ultimately our language.

Pettit also endorses Wright's second requirement. Like Wright and Johnston, he thinks that response-dependence biconditionals are non-reductive and non-eliminative. Pettit's biconditionals can and must contain versions of ⌜P⌝ on both sides.

Likewise, like Wright and Johnston, Pettit endorses the third requirement, that response-dependence biconditionals are to be specified non-trivially. Though I cannot discuss it here, Pettit (2002, essay 5) himself specifies normality conditions on subjects and conditions of observation.

Finally Wright's fourth requirement is that response-dependence biconditionals are read as extension-determining rather than extension-reflecting. As we saw in §1, Johnston disagrees with the requirement, and on my view satisfying it is not necessary for a biconditional to express a response-dependence relation. Now Pettit himself says nothing about Wright's extension-determining/reflecting distinction. Regardless he would reject Wright's fourth requirement. Because Pettit thinks that his response-dependence biconditionals express ontologically antecedent facts, he would read them as merely reflecting those facts. Focusing on red, Pettit

---

11. Pettit (Pettit 2002, pp. 14, 98; Jackson and Pettit 2002, pp. 105–09) allows that *some* properties are response-dependent. He maintains that something is nauseating if and only if a suitable subject under suitable conditions would perceive it as nauseating, where the property itself is ontologically interdependent with those responses. Nonetheless Pettit also offers "another account" (Jackson and Pettit, p. 107). Nauseating is whatever property *realizes* the property that Johnston identifies as response-dependent. As I explain in §3, for Pettit, such a realizer-property would be an objective, or response-independent, property in the world that we nevertheless identify *via* its effects on us.

explains: "The story told here assumes that the property materializes without any influence from how we see things" (2002, p. 12). The biconditional is not to be read as extension-determining. He adds: " ... things will look red under favourable conditions and deserve to be described as red only because—causally, because—they have the property, and not the other way around" (p. 15). Pettit would read his biconditionals as extension-reflecting.[12] He therefore differs from Johnston, who (implicitly) reads such biconditionals as symmetrically extension-determining, and Wright, who (explicitly) reads them as asymmetrically extension-determining.

Pettit differs from Johnston and Wright in another way also. Like Locke, Johnston and Wright maintain that *only some* empirical concepts (to focus on these) are linked essentially to subjective and objective sources. Locke is committed to the view that only some empirical concepts are secondary-quality in nature, and Johnston and Wright, though preferring 'response-dependent', agree. Like Locke, Johnston and Wright are therefore Lockean hybridists.

Conversely Pettit maintains that *all* empirical concepts (and terms) are so linked. For, according to Pettit, all such concepts and terms are either semantically basic, and so response-dependent, or defined *via* semantically basic ones. They are all therefore connected in an *a priori* manner to anthropocentric responses and ultimately capacities. Pettit even calls all concepts and terms "anthropocentric" (2002, pp. 13–17, 53–58). In fact Pettit plays Kant to Johnston and Wright's Locke. In the *Prolegomena to Any Future Metaphysics* (2010/1783, 4: 288–98) Kant himself maintains that all empirical properties are secondary qualities, and I might apply his reasoning to all empirical concepts and terms.[13] While Locke is a local secondary-quality theorist, Kant is a global secondary-quality theorist. Likewise, while Johnston and Wright are local response-dependence theorists, Pettit is a global response-dependence theorist. Moreover both Johnston (1989, p. 148) and Pettit (2002, p. 90) themselves understand Kant as a global response-dependence theorist.[14] And Pettit (2002, pp. 18–20, 50, 90, 96–115) likens his own view to Kant's.

---

12. Pettit maintains that this is consistent with "the objectivist thesis" (p. 52) and "epistemic servility" (2002, p. 78), which amount to the same.

13. See Hilary Putnam (1981, essay 3), James Van Cleve (1995), and Rae Langton (2004/1998, ch. 7).

14. If Pettit (2002, p. 50) is right, then Putnam (1981, p. 63) construes Kant the same. Moreover Henry Allison (2004, p. 34) contends that Kant is the first to give a global "anthropocentric" theory of knowledge, while Hanna claims that Kant provides an "anthropocentric scientific realism" (2006, p. 33). Kant himself explains in the *Critique of Pure Reason*: "We can accordingly speak of space, extended beings, and so on only from the *human* standpoint" (1998/1787, A26/B42, emphasis mine).

We can now finally see how my discussion of Pettit helps us explore Kantian territory. Pettit is committed to the view that all empirical concepts and terms are connected in an *a priori* manner to subjective and objective sources—where the subjective source are paradigmatically human responses (and ultimately capacities); the objective source, objects in the world to which those responses (and ultimately capacities) are directed. And this *a priori* connection amounts to the essential link of the sort that Kantianism requires. According to Pettit, though anthropocentric responses are not constitutive of those concepts and terms, they are nevertheless essential to our acquiring them. That is enough to establish Pettit's commitment to Dualism:

> DUALISM: All empirical concepts, terms, or properties are linked essentially to subjective and objective sources.

Pettit's commitment is in particular to empirical concepts and terms, and not properties.

Now, as we saw in Chapter One, Dualism can come in one of two kinds. It can be *ontological*, and so those concepts and terms would be constituted essentially out of subjective and objective sources. Or it can be *epistemological*, and so those concepts and terms would be acquired by a subject's appealing essentially to these sources. Pettit's Dualism is epistemological:

> EPISTEMOLOGICAL DUALISM: All empirical concepts, terms, or properties are acquired by a subject's appealing essentially to subjective and objective sources.

He merely restricts it to concepts and terms. Though empirical concepts and terms would not be the concepts and terms that they are were they not linked essentially to normal human beings under normal conditions of observation, that link is acquisitive not constitutive. Anthropocentric responses do not determine the content of **red** or meaning in English of 'red'. Instead they allow subjects to master semantically basic concepts and terms and *via* being defined in terms of them semantically complex ones too. For Pettit, therefore, all empirical concepts and terms are acquired by a subject's appealing essentially to a subjective source, anthropocentric responses (and ultimately anthropocentric conceptual, linguistic, and perceptual capacities), and an objective source, objects in the world to which those responses are directed.

As we also saw in Chapter One, some Kantians, Epistemological or otherwise, are committed to Principlism as well:

> PRINCIPLISM: The subjective source of all empirical concepts, terms, or properties takes the form of subjective principles.

Pettit however is not. Epistemological Principlism in particular is not part of his view:

EPISTEMOLOGICAL PRINCIPLISM: The subjective source of all empirical concepts, terms, or properties takes the form of subjective principles acquisitive of those concepts, terms, or properties.

For Pettit, there are no claims, distinct from any empirical ones, that are the form or basic epistemological or linguistic unit that the subjective source of empirical concepts, terms, or properties takes. Subjective capacities operate holistically in response to objects in the world in general. That subjective source, which is ultimately those capacities, does not take the form of subjective principles in particular. For Pettit, there are no acquisitive principles as opposed to empirical claims. He has no correlate of Kant's synthetic *a priori* judgments.[15]

I explore un-Principled Kantianism further when in Chapters Five and Six I consider Willard van Orman Quine's view. Regardless we can see here that Pettit's commitment to Epistemological Dualism entails his commitment to Epistemological Kantianism:

EPISTEMOLOGICAL KANTIANISM: All empirical concepts, terms, or properties are acquired by a subject's appealing essentially to subjective and objective sources. The subjective source may take the form of subjective acquisitive principles.

Pettit's view simply concerns only concepts and terms, and rejects the existence of acquisitive principles.

So Pettit is an analytic philosopher who is a Kantian. Exploring his view has therefore helped us appreciate Kantianism's conceptual expansiveness by making us aware of global response-dependence as one way of understanding it. It has also illustrated a kind of Kantianism that is both epistemological and un-Principled. Pettit helps us appreciate Kantianism's conceptual expansiveness in another way too. If Smith and Stoljar (1998) are right, then Pettit, like Kant himself, is committed to noumenalism. And noumenalism occupies a central space in all Kantian lands.

---

15. Nor is Concept-and-Term itself a subjective principle. It is instead a statement of Pettit's global response-dependence. Likewise, for Kant, a statement of transcendental idealism is not a synthetic *a priori* judgment—in my terms a subjective principle—either. This is Allison's point when he calls transcendental idealism "*meta*epistemological" (2004, p. 35, emphasis mine). Concept-and-Term and statements of transcendental idealism are statements *about* rather than *within* each theorist's Kantianism.

3. FROM KANTIANISM TO NOUMENALISM

Seeing why Smith and Stoljar think that Pettit is committed to noumenalism requires seeing how they understand his global response-dependence. Smith and Stoljar take Pettit to maintain that our responses to objects in the world are to dispositional properties affecting us in certain ways. We would respond to an object as red, and in English call it 'red', not necessarily because the object appears red at the moment (perhaps the lighting is off), but because the object has the disposition to appear red to normal observers under normal conditions. Now Smith and Stoljar assume that every disposition has a non-dispositional base. Moreover, because our responses are always to dispositions and never to their bases, the nature of the bases themselves remains unknowable. We can know only that they support the disposition to which a response-dependent term refers.

Smith and Stoljar conclude that Pettit is committed to noumenal realism, or "noumenalism," their version of which is this:

> [T]here is an independent reality, but the intrinsic nature of that reality is unknowable. The world is a certain way in and of itself but, given the nature of our concepts [and terms], we cannot think or say what that way is, but can only ever think or say what relations the world stands in to us (1998, p. 87).

And Smith and Stoljar take noumenalism to be a *reductio ad absurdum* of Pettit's global response-dependence.

Pettit agrees that noumenalism follows from his view. Nonetheless he thinks that noumenalism is more benign than Smith and Stoljar realize. For Pettit (2002, overview to part I, essay 3) urges that noumenalism itself has ontological and epistemological construals. According to the ontological construal, which Pettit rejects, response-dependent terms refer to worldly dispositions that cause normal observers under normal conditions to respond in certain ways. This is Pettit's gloss of the view that Smith and Stoljar attribute to him. On this first construal of noumenalism the referent of 'red' is whatever dispositional property plays the *role* of looking red to those observers under those conditions.[16] Pettit calls this kind of property a 'role-property'. Role-properties are response-dependent: properties whose nature depends on subjective responses to their non-dispositional bases. Regarding red, the role-property is whatever property plays the role of looking red to us subjects.

---

16. This amounts to Johnston's (1989, 1993) view. Johnston therefore eventually (1993) talks about "response-dispositional" rather than "response-dependent" concepts.

Pettit acknowledges that, if response-dependent terms refer to role-properties, then we can know nothing about the nature of the bases that underlie them. Pettit calls the properties comprising those bases 'realizer-properties'. Realizer-properties *realize* the dispositional, or role, properties to which Smith and Stoljar think Pettit is committed. And realizer-properties would be response-*in*dependent: objective features of the world itself. Realizer-properties would inhere in Pettit's "pre-existing things" (2002, p. 75). Keeping with the letter of Smith and Stoljar's phrasing, let me say that noumenalism construed ontologically is the thesis that reality possesses an intrinsic "nature," comprised of realizer-properties, that remains unknowable.

We can understand all this in terms of construals of Kant's own transcendental idealism considered in Chapter One. Noumenalism construed ontologically can be either "two-property" or "two-world." As Smith and Stoljar understand it, Pettit's construal is *two-property*. One set of properties, role-properties, supervenes on a second set of properties, realizer-properties, their non-dispositional bases; and we can know nothing about the bases themselves. This resembles Rae Langton's (2004/1998) construal of transcendental idealism. Langton's distinction between relational and intrinsic properties correlates with the distinction between role- and realizer-properties, respectively. Conversely we can also understand noumenalism construed ontologically as *two-world*. The world of role-properties can be taken to supervene on a distinct world of realizer-properties; we again can know nothing about the latter. That resembles Peter F. Strawson's (1975) and Paul Guyer's (1987) construal of transcendental idealism. Strawson's and Guyer's distinction between things as they appear to us and things in themselves correlates with the distinction between a world comprised of role-properties and one comprised of realizer-properties. On either a two-property or two-world understanding, however, noumenalism construed ontologically maintains that reality possesses an intrinsic "nature" that remains unknowable.

The second construal of noumenalism, which Pettit accepts, is epistemological. According to it, 'red' refers not to the dispositional property that plays the role of looking red but to the non-dispositional property that realizes the disposition to look red. This, Pettit notes, is to understand the referents of response-dependent terms *themselves* as realizer-properties. According to Pettit, the realizer-property to which 'red' refers might be something "like a spectral reflectance" (Jackson and Pettit 2002, p. 99). Nonetheless Pettit concedes: "[W]e use [response-dependent] terms to ascribe certain objective properties," realizer-properties, "*in virtue of* the fact that those properties have certain disposing effects on us" (2002, p. 19, emphasis mine). Red, understood as a realizer-property, has the disposing effect of causing us to *perceive* red, even if this effect is not itself constitutive of the *nature* of red.

Though red is response-independent, and so is the property that it is in virtue of its objective features, we nevertheless identify and name red *via* its effects on us. Moreover, by understanding response-dependent terms as referring to realizer-properties, Pettit maintains that we can take noumenalism to be the epistemological thesis that there exists a single set of properties (or world comprised thereof), realizer-properties, that we can nevertheless *know* only in their effects not in themselves. Noumenalism now does not concern limitations on the properties to which we can refer. We do refer to objective properties, realizer-properties, in the world. Instead it concerns limitations on what we can know about those properties. Keeping with the spirit of Smith and Stoljar's phrasing, let me say that noumenalism construed epistemologically is the thesis that reality possesses an intrinsic "aspect" that remains unknowable.

We can understand this too in terms of construals of Kant's transcendental idealism. Noumenalism construed epistemologically is "two-aspect." We respond only to one aspect of realizer-properties, their effects on us, and so we can know them only in their effects. This resembles Henry Allison's (2004) construal of transcendental idealism. According to Allison, there is only one world, the world in itself, with two aspects: considered in itself and considered as it appears to us. Realizer-properties considered in themselves cannot be known. Realizer-properties considered as they appear to us can be. Pettit adds that our terms refer to realizer-properties in themselves nevertheless.

Reminding Smith and Stoljar that he takes properties to be response-independent, Pettit (2002, pp. 112–14) contends that noumenalism should be construed epistemologically. For Pettit, the lesson of noumenalism is not that there is some ontologically mysterious second set of properties or world underlying our experience but that we should be epistemologically humble. Though there is only one set and world, and our terms refer to it, we can nevertheless know realizer-properties only in their effects. We can never know them in themselves. While we have linguistic access to the world as it really is, we must not be arrogant in our epistemological pronouncements. For we can *know* the world only insofar as it affects us. And, Pettit claims, even if ontological mystery is problematic, "epistemic humility" (as he calls it) is not. He sees no problem with noumenalism construed epistemologically.

Here as well we can understand this in terms of construals of transcendental idealism, though this time we must correct Pettit. While what Pettit says does not otherwise affect his view, he nevertheless chooses the wrong pedigree for this epistemic humility. He appeals to Langton's (2004/1998) ontological construal of transcendental idealism to support it. Yet Langton's distinction between relational and intrinsic properties correlates with the distinction between role- and realizer-properties. This is the distinction that Pettit rejects. Though, as we saw in Chapter One, Langton's construal does counsel epistemic humility, Pettit should appeal to Allison's epistemological construal of transcendental idealism instead. Allison's distinction between things considered in themselves and things considered as they appear to us correlates with the distinction between realizer-properties in themselves and realizer-properties insofar as they affect us. That is the distinction that Pettit accepts. Moreover, for Allison, we should still be epistemologically humble. We can never know things considered in themselves. In fact, according to Guyer, Allison's construal of transcendental idealism amounts to nothing *but* a "recommendation of epistemological modesty" (1987, p. 336.) While Guyer means this as a vice, Pettit would take it as a virtue.

Regardless of Pettit's misunderstanding of Kant scholarship, I agree with him that noumenalism can be construed ontologically or epistemologically. And I grant Pettit that the former entails a second set of properties or world, while the latter entails a second aspect of this set or world—and so consequently counsels epistemic humility about the set or world, comprised of his "realizer-properties," themselves. I do not however agree with Pettit, or Smith and Stoljar, that either construal of noumenalism is problematic. Noumenalism construed ontologically limits the properties to which we can refer, while noumenalism construed epistemologically limits the aspect of properties that we can know. They are simply limitations of different sorts. For my part, Pettit can construe noumenalism either way. In fact, as I explain next, these different construals are not so easily segregated. To demonstrate this, I complicate Pettit, and Smith and Stoljar's, debate by comparing Pettit's view to that of another analytic Kantian, Thomas Kuhn.

4. COMPLICATING THE DEBATE

In Chapter Three I argue that Kuhn's view can be construed as a variant of Pettit's. I do so by comparing Kuhn and Pettit on how we learn terms. Here I make a more modest point. While Pettit follows Johnston, Wright, and all other self-identifying response-dependence theorists in focusing on *anthropocentric* responses, Kuhn focuses on *ethnocentric* responses. As Kuhn explains, the concepts and terms that human beings employ depend on the community (*ethnos*) of which they are members. Community membership specifically rather than species membership generally is relevant.[17]

Kuhn offers several examples of his ethnocentric theory of concepts and terms. I consider several in Chapter Three but only one here. It concerns

---

17. Pettit raises the possibility of ethnocentric response-dependence only to drop it, noting that the "a priori connection ... introduce[s] a relativity to our species, *perhaps even our culture*" (2002, p. 44, emphasis mine).

astronomical objects. The example also introduces Kuhn's (2002) notion of a lexical taxonomy (or "lexicon").[18] According to Kuhn, a lexicon is a set of kind terms figuring as nodes in a network structured according to species–genus relations of objects in the world to which scientists in particular historical communities respond. Kuhn explains that the (Anglophonic) Ptolemaic teaches neophytes in his community to respond to the sun, the moon, Venus, Mercury, Mars, Jupiter, and Saturn by constructing a lexicon in which 'the sun', 'the moon', 'Venus', 'Mercury', 'Mars', 'Jupiter', and 'Saturn' figure under 'planet'. The Ptolemaic therefore categorizes planet as the genus of which the sun, the moon, Venus, *etc.*, are species. The Copernican conversely teaches neophytes in her community to respond to the same objects with 'the sun', 'the moon' 'Venus', 'Mercury', 'Mars', 'Jupiter', and 'Saturn', respectively, too. Nonetheless the Copernican structures the last four under 'planet', the first under 'star', and the second under 'satellite'. The Copernican therefore categorizes planet as the genus whose species include Venus, Mercury, Mars, Jupiter, and Saturn; while star and satellite are themselves genera whose species include the sun and the moon, respectively.

Kuhn is right that the Ptolemaic responds to the sun as a planet while the Copernican responds to it as a star. He is also right that part of those responses include countenancing the taxonomic relations between each one's terms for these objects. Nor is this ethnocentrism an expression of Kuhn's controversial earlier claim, which I consider in Chapter Three, that members of different communities "are responding to a different world" (2012/1962, p. 111). Kuhn's mature (2002) view is that members of different communities respond to the same world though they categorize objects in that world differently.[19] The Ptolemaic and Copernican agree that the sun exists. They simply disagree on whether to categorize it as a planet or a star.

Though his theory does not countenance such ethnocentric differences, Pettit would have to endorse some degree of ethnocentrism. Otherwise he would be ignoring the real, and in Kuhn's astronomical example really obvious, taxonomic differences between communities. Yet endorsing even this tame ethnocentrism commits Pettit to the possibility of a different kind of ontological mystery. Consider the question of why the Ptolemaic and Copernican categorize the sun differently. Pettit can give either one of two answers. Because the first answer entails a variety of ontological mystery while

---

18. As I explain in Chapter Three, §2, this replaces Kuhn's earlier notions of a paradigm (2012/1962) and disciplinary matrix (2012/1970, 1979).

19. Nonetheless, as I explain in Chapter Eight, §6, Kuhn cannot maintain this mature view. Regardless Pettit can.

the second does not, and Pettit's epistemological construal of noumenalism prevents adjudicating between the two answers, Pettit cannot know whether he is committed to this different variety of mystery itself.

Let me take things slowly. The first answer that Pettit can give to the question of why the Ptolemaic and Copernican categorize the sun differently relies on a distinction that, as I explain in Chapter Three, Pettit employs in his account of language learning. The distinction is between instantiation and exemplification. According to Pettit (2002, pp. 4, 36), exemplification is relative to the interests and abilities, and ultimately responses, of human beings. For him, while an object *instantiates* all the realizer-properties inherent in it, human beings take the object to *exemplify* far fewer. Pettit's first answer to the question would be that different communities habituate their members to have different interests and abilities. They would then have been habituated into being interested in and able to respond to different things. Consequently members of different communities can take the same object to exemplify different realizer-properties.

Perhaps the Ptolemaic's and Copernican's interests and abilities cause them both to perceive the sun's motion as geocentric, while only the Copernican's cause her to recognize such motion as merely apparent. Because the Ptolemaic regards the sun's (apparent) geocentric motion as indicating its being a planet, while the Copernican regards the sun's (real) stationary motion relative to the earth as indicating its being the earth's star, the former regards the sun *as* a planet while the latter regards it *as* a star. The Ptolemaic, responding to one set of exemplified properties (disposing him to perceive apparent motion), takes the sun to be a planet. The Copernican, responding to a different set (disposing her to perceive apparent *and* real motion), takes it to be a star. According to this first answer, the Ptolemaic and Copernican categorize the sun differently because they are responding to different realizer-properties. The Ptolemaic's and Copernican's term 'motion' when applied to the sun would itself then refer to different realizer-properties.

The second answer that Pettit can give relies on degrees of ethnocentrism. Pettit could maintain that, though the Ptolemaic and Copernican both take the sun to exemplify the same set of realizer-properties, they each respond to those properties *sometimes in less* and *sometimes in more* ethnocentric ways. Consider how this might work with red. For Pettit, Chinese and Americans alike respond to the same property as red, insofar as normal observers of each community under normal conditions perceive objects that exemplify that property as red. Nonetheless Chinese might *also* respond to the property by perceiving it as the color worn by brides, while Americans might perceive it as a color not worn by brides. The same property, red, can therefore elicit multiple responses. Some responses, like perceiving the color red, might be shared between communities. Others, like perceiving the color worn by brides, might not be.

Similarly, for Pettit, the Ptolemaic and Copernican could both respond to the same set of realizer-properties that the sun exemplifies, insofar as under normal conditions both regard the object that exemplifies that set as the sun. Nonetheless the Ptolemaic might *also* respond to those properties by categorizing the sun as a planet. The Copernican might herself do so by categorizing the sun as a star. Perhaps the Ptolemaic is disposed to respond to the set of properties causing the sun's motion by perceiving that motion as geocentric, while the Copernican, differently habituated, is disposed to respond to the same set by perceiving the sun's motion as relatively stationary *vis-à-vis* the earth. As with red so with the sun, each community habituated its neophytes to respond in ways that are shared between communities *and* in ways that are not. According to this second answer, the Ptolemaic and Copernican categorize the sun differently because they are responding to the same set of realizer-properties differently. This time the Ptolemaic's and Copernican's 'motion' when applied to the sun would refer to the same realizer-properties, even though the Ptolemaic and Copernican would be affected by those realizer-properties differently.

Thus Pettit can give two answers to the target question. The Ptolemaic and Copernican respond to *either* different realizer-properties *or* the same realizer-properties differently. Now these two answers cannot both be right. They make conflicting claims. Which is right? Pettit's epistemological construal of noumenalism makes it impossible to know. Since, if Pettit is right, we can know realizer-properties never in themselves but only in their effects, we can never know whether members of different communities respond to either different realizer-properties or the same realizer-properties differently. We can then never know whether members of different communities refer to different or the same properties either. Moreover, as Kuhn claims (and I explain in Chapter Three), adopting a different set of responses to the world by adopting a different lexicon, and so changing communities, is definitive of a scientific revolution. But then the *same person* before and after a revolution responds (and so refers) to either different or the same realizer-properties also. For the same person could switch from being a Ptolemaic to being a Copernican.

How does this concern Pettit's debate with Smith and Stoljar? Pettit rejects the idea that we respond to a set of role-properties underlain by a different set of realizer-properties. Construing noumenalism epistemologically permits him to maintain instead that there is only one set of properties, realizer-properties, though we can know these properties only in their effects. I have now shown that Pettit must say that members of different communities—and so even potentially the same person at different times—respond to either different or the same realizer-properties, and Pettit cannot know which. On his view, therefore, members of different communities *refer* to either different or the same realizer-properties. Hence they may or may not have linguistic access to the same parts of the world. Let me call the total set of realizer-properties a 'realm' of properties and part of that set a 'province'. For Pettit, therefore, though there is no separate inaccessible realm of properties, there may be separate inaccessible provinces. If members of different communities respond to different realizer-properties, then they respond to different provinces. If they respond to the same realizer-properties differently, then they respond to the same realm differently. And Pettit's epistemological construal of noumenalism prevents him from knowing which it is.

Now consider these two possibilities more closely. The first is a form of ontological mystery. Because members of different communities are limited in referring not to an entire realm but only to particular provinces of properties, let me call it 'provincial ontological mystery'. According to provincial ontological mystery, members of different communities can refer only to some properties. There are provinces of properties of the world as it really is that they cannot access. Calling this form of ontological mystery 'provincial' distinguishes it from what I may now call 'realm ontological mystery', the variety that Smith and Stoljar proposed and of which Pettit disposed. Regardless, according to both forms of ontological mystery, human beings are disconnected from the world as it really is. On the realm variety the disconnect is total. On the provincial variety the disconnect is partial. Regardless the Ptolemaic still cannot refer to the same set of properties to which the Copernican can. The Ptolemaic has no linguistic access to that *part* of the world as it really is.

The second possibility, that members of different communities can have linguistic access to the same properties but are nevertheless *affected* by those properties differently, is a form of epistemic humility. It entails that members of different communities, though able to refer to the same properties in themselves, can know those properties only in effects that differ *between* communities. Let me say that this second possibility encourages 'provincial epistemic humility'. Here the provincialism concerns not the properties but their responders. Though members of different communities can refer to realizer-properties in themselves, they can know those properties only in the effects that they have on them as members of one particular community (or province of responders) as opposed to another. Conversely the form of epistemic humility that Pettit adopts might be called 'realm epistemic humility'. According to it, human beings can know realizer-properties in their effects on them as members of the human realm at large. Now on this second possibility provincial epistemic humility does obtain. The way in which the Ptolemaic knows the motion of the sun differs from the way in which the Copernican knows it, even though Ptolemaic and Copernican alike, when they refer to the sun's 'motion', refer to the same set of realizer-properties in themselves. Regardless the lesson of epistemic humility in its provincial and realm form is that the Ptolemaic and Copernican—as well as the rest of us—should be humble when making epistemological pronouncements. In the provincial form in particular human beings can know the properties of worldly objects only in their own provincial ways.

5. PETTIT'S TRILEMMA

What does this mean for Pettit's commitment to noumenalism and Kantianism? Smith and Stoljar argued that Pettit's theory came at the cost of noumenalism. While I remain unsure how costly noumenalism ultimately is, Pettit himself tried to discount that cost by construing noumenalism epistemologically. I have now shown that the cost of this epistemological construal might itself be more expensive than Pettit realizes. For Pettit cannot know whether he is committed to provincial ontological mystery. And, because Pettit agrees with Smith and Stoljar that ontological mystery should be avoided, he should want to avoid the provincial variety also. Pettit therefore faces a trilemma:

(a) He can construe noumenalism ontologically, as Smith and Stoljar think that he does. But then he is committed to realm ontological mystery.
(b) He can construe noumenalism epistemologically to avoid realm ontological mystery. But then he cannot know whether he is committed to provincial ontological mystery. And provincial ontological mystery remains a form of ontological mystery.
(c) He can reject his theory altogether. So goes Pettit's global response-dependence and with it his Kantianism.

Which horn should Pettit choose? For starters, Pettit should choose (b) over (a). For (b) is an epistemological limitation. Pettit cannot *know* whether he is committed to a form of ontological mystery. Conversely (a) is an ontological limitation. Pettit *is* committed to a form of ontological mystery. And Pettit himself prefers epistemological limitations. Moreover, following out Pettit's reasoning, possibly inaccessible parts of an otherwise accessible world, as *per* (b), is probably less mysterious than an inaccessible world, as *per* (a).

Should Pettit then accept not knowing whether he is committed to provincial ontological mystery, (b), or reject his theory altogether, (c)? Here again Pettit should choose (b). As I have said, neither construal of noumenalism strikes me as problematic. And, if Pettit himself has reason to choose (b) over (a), then he has no reason not to choose (b) over (c). In fact not knowing whether separate inaccessible provinces of properties exist is arguably even intuitive. Perhaps scientific habituation puts human beings in linguistic touch with different realizer-properties in the world, sometimes different properties in objects with which members of different communities are already familiar. When Copernicus challenged geocentrism, he might be understood as having challenged astronomers to respond to more properties inherent in the sun than only those to which they were already responding. While the Copernican could agree with the Ptolemaic that the sun appears to revolve around the earth, the Copernican could insist that only she herself is in touch with enough properties in the world to recognize that the revolution is merely apparent. The world is large and complex. It is not so strange to think that the parts of it are accessible to us in virtue of the community that we keep. Nor is it so strange as to make Pettit reject his global response-dependence, and so his Kantianism, altogether. Pettit should choose (b) over (c) as well as (a). Regardless we have seen that ontological and epistemological construals of noumenalism are not so easily segregated.

6. LESSONS FOR KANTIAN CONCEPTUAL GEOGRAPHY

In this chapter we have seen how Pettit's global response-dependence theory of concepts and terms is a kind of Kantianism. We have then seen how I complicated Smith and Stoljar's debate with Pettit concerning noumenalism and concluded that Pettit should choose the middle horn of the resulting trilemma. In this conclusion I draw five lessons for Kantian conceptual geography generally.

First, global response-dependence *is* a form of Kantianism. By connecting all empirical concepts, terms, or properties in an *a priori* manner to subjective responses to objects in the world, global response-dependence links all empirical concepts, terms, or properties essentially to subjective and objective sources. Global response-dependence is therefore a way of liberating Kantianism from Kant's own transcendental idealism.

Second, while I focused on Pettit's response-dependence theory, which is global, I did introduce Johnston's and Wright's response-dependence theories, which are local. We can now appreciate what would happen to Johnston's and Wright's theories were they themselves globalized. While Pettit's is a kind of Epistemological Kantianism concerning no constitution at all, globalized versions of Johnston's and Wright's would be kinds of Ontological Kantianism concerning constitution in different directions. Johnston (implicitly) claims that subjective responses are *symmetrically* constitutive of certain concepts, terms, and properties. These concepts, terms, and properties are constitutively interdependent with those responses. Wright (explicitly) claims that subjective responses are *asymmetrically* constitutive of certain concepts, terms, and properties. These concepts, terms, and properties constitutively depend on those responses. Hence, were they globalized, then Johnston's response-dependence would be a kind of symmetric Ontological Kantianism, while Wright's would be a kind of asymmetric Ontological Kantianism. But then, while Epistemological Kantianism, because it involves no constitution, comes in only one kind, Ontological Kantianism, because constitution can be symmetric or asymmetric, comes in two.

Third, though we focused on Pettit's global response-dependence, we can now appreciate that *every* kind of Kantianism entails noumenalism. For every kind of Kantianism satisfies some version of Dualism:

DUALISM: All empirical concepts, terms, or properties are linked essentially to subjective and objective sources.

And Dualism itself entails noumenalism. By requiring that there be subjective and objective sources, Dualism requires that there be an objective one—a source independent of the subject. That source might be the world in itself, if noumenalism is construed ontologically, or the world considered in itself, if noumenalism is construed epistemologically. Regardless of how noumenalism is construed, however, all empirical concepts, terms, or properties would have subjective and objective sources mixed. But then possessing such concepts or terms, or perceiving such properties, would not allow us to know any objective source in itself or considered in itself. Conversely, any non-empirical concepts, terms, or properties (were there any) would be purely subjective. So possessing such concepts or terms, or perceiving (if this is even the right word) such properties, would not allow us to know any objective source in itself or considered in itself either. And those are the only options for the Kantian. We can then never know any objective source in itself or considered in itself. Keeping with Smith and Stoljar's spirit, we can understand noumenalism as the thesis that reality possesses an intrinsic nature *or* aspect that remains unknowable. No matter how we understand noumenalism, however, every kind of Kantianism entails it.[20]

---

20. Hence all construals of transcendental idealism considered here and in Chapter One, §2, entail noumenalism. Because Peter F. Strawson's (1975) and Paul Guyer's (1987) construals are two-world, they entail noumenalism construed ontologically. Because Allison's (2004) is two-aspect, it entails noumenalism construed epistemologically. Because Langton's (2004/1998) is two-property, it entails noumenalism construed ontologically—even though it also counsels epistemic humility. Because Hanna's (2006) strong transcendental idealism is roughly the same as Strawson's and Guyer's construals, it entails noumenalism construed

Fourth, Pettit's case in particular reveals that noumenalism construed ontologically is correlated with Ontological Kantianism, while noumenalism construed epistemologically is correlated with Epistemological Kantianism. If all empirical concepts, terms, or properties are constituted essentially out of subjective and objective sources, then there is an objective source ontologically independent of the subject, perhaps the world in itself, its intrinsic nature remaining unknowable. If all empirical concepts, terms, or properties are acquired by a subject's appealing essentially to subjective and objective sources, then there is an objective source epistemologically independent of the subject, perhaps the world considered in itself, its intrinsic aspect remaining unknowable.

And fifth, as my complicating Pettit, and Smith and Stoljar's, debate reveals, ontological and epistemological construals of noumenalism are not so easily segregated.[21] If Pettit himself construes noumenalism epistemologically, then he cannot know whether he is committed to a kind of provincial noumenalism construed ontologically. As I have suggested, however, none of this need be problematic.

---

ontologically. Hanna's weak transcendental idealism is more complicated. As I understand it, weak transcendental idealism maintains that our empirical concepts and terms necessarily possibly represent things in space and time in themselves, because our forms of intuition are isomorphic with space and time in themselves. But then things in themselves can be known only insofar as a subject can intuit them. They can never be known in themselves. Hanna's weak transcendental idealism therefore entails noumenalism construed epistemologically. Admittedly Hanna *also* argues for methodological eliminativism about things in themselves. He maintains that, according to Kant, because "[w]e cannot empirically meaningfully assert either that things-in-themselves exist or that they do not exist[,] ... we must be *systematically agnostic* about them" (p. 15). We should therefore methodologically eliminate them (pp. 15, 197–98). Nonetheless there are two reasons that noumenalism still follows. First, discussions of noumenalism are not empirical discussions. Nor are Hanna's weak and strong transcendental idealisms empirical theses. Any inability empirically meaningfully to assert that things in themselves do or do not exist is irrelevant. Second, methodological eliminativism is not eliminativism.

21. I reached this conclusion partly by arguing that Pettit has reason to allow a kind of Kantianism more subjective in scope than his, *viz.*, Kuhn's ethnocentrism (on which I focus in Chapter Three). Instead of Kuhn's ethnocentrism, I could have appealed to Davidson's idiocentrism (on which I focus in Chapter Four). That makes ontological and epistemological construals of noumenalism even less easily segregated.

THREE

Thomas Kuhn

Thomas Kuhn was arguably the most famous philosopher of science of the last century. His contributions extended as well to epistemology, philosophy of language, and metaphysics—not to mention the history and sociology of science too. Kuhn was also however among the most controversial philosophers of recent times. His *magnum opus*, *The Structure of Scientific Revolutions* (2012/1962), reflects this tension. Having sold more than one million copies, *Structure* is potentially the most popular book of academic philosophy of the twentieth and twenty-first centuries. Yet the same work, though influential among academic philosophers also, has more often been criticized than complimented by them.[1]

Since his death Kuhn's *corpus* has received renewed attention.[2] Here I explain how Kuhn's contributions to epistemology, philosophy of language, and metaphysics in particular allow me to understand him as a global response-dependence theorist. Doing so thereby allows me to understand him as a Kantian and so to continue my exploration of Kantian territory. Moreover focusing on Kuhn reveals two things relevant to my aim. First, as was suggested in Chapter Two, Kantianism can be, like Philip Pettit's (and Immanuel Kant's), *anthropocentric*, or centered on generally human conceptual, linguistic, and perceptual capacities. But it can also be, like Kuhn's, *ethnocentric*, or centered on specifically community conceptual, linguistic, and perceptual capacities. Second, Kuhn's Kantianism, like all kinds of Ontological Kantianism concerning terms that allow there to be relevantly distinct subjects—subjects with relevantly distinct subjective capacities—entails the possibility of non-intertranslatable terms, theories, or languages. Kuhn calls such terms, theories, and languages 'incommensurable'.

1. See K. Brad Wray (2012).

2. See Nathaniel Goldberg (2011, p. 1).

The chapter proceeds as follows. In §1 I show that, while Pettit offers an account of language learning that is anthropocentric, Kuhn offers one that is ethnocentric. In §2 I show that Kuhn is in fact an ethnocentric Kantian. In §3 I explore residual issues concerning Kuhn's Kantianism. In §4 I show why Kuhn's ethnocentric Kantianism, as well as all other kinds of Ontological Kantianism concerning terms that allow there to be relevantly distinct subjects, entail the possibility of incommensurability. Finally in §5 I draw lessons for Kantian conceptual geography generally.

1. PETTIT AND KUHN ON LANGUAGE LEARNING

Because as I understand him Kuhn implicitly subscribes to a kind of global response-dependence, and Pettit provides the only explicit example of such a theory, let me start by considering Kuhn in the context of Pettit. As we saw in Chapter Two, Pettit takes his global response-dependence theory to follow from his account of language learning. Here I explain that account.

Pettit begins his account of language learning by acknowledging that any finite set of examples instantiates an infinite number of properties.[3] For Pettit, a ripe tomato, cardinal, and fire truck all instantiate the properties of being red, being material, being observable from my window, *etc*. Pettit next postulates that all human beings have a "ground-level disposition or habit ... to extrapolate spontaneously in a given direction, taking the examples to be instances of a kind" (2002, p. 142). As we saw in Chapter Two, Pettit (2002, p. 36; Frank Jackson and Pettit 2002, p. 103) distinguishes instantiation from exemplification. Though any such set of examples *instantiates* an infinite number of properties, human beings take it to *exemplify* a finite set of properties based on what we find salient. Unlike instantiation, exemplification is relative to human interests and abilities and in turn responses. Presented with the tomato, cardinal, and truck, human beings tend to extrapolate spontaneously in the direction of taking them to exemplify being red. If Anglophonic we would call them 'red'. Pettit next postulates that human beings have a higher-order disposition or habit to refuse to endorse extrapolations if discrepant across persons or times, and a practice to explain such discrepancies. Suppose that someone takes those objects to exemplify being green. We would be disposed to reject that extrapolation, trying to discern what went wrong. Because of the

---

3. See Philip Pettit (2002, pp. 3–10, 35–48, 65–67, 97, 142–49). As we saw in Chapter Two, §3, Pettit is discussing realizer-properties. I understand Thomas Kuhn (especially 2002) as discussing realizer-properties, or properties of Pettit's "pre-existing things" (2002, p. 75), because I take him not to be an Ontological Kantian concerning properties—though I revise this view in Chapter Eight, §6.

centrality of dispositions and habits to it, Pettit calls his account of language learning 'ethocentric':

> The sort of story I have told about how we might get the concept of redness [and term 'red'] can be described as 'ethocentric'. It gives centre stage to habits of response and practices of self-correction, and both notions are captured in the Greek word *ethos* (2002, p. 66).

Now such ethocentrism differs from the eth*n*ocentrism some degree of which, I argued in Chapter Two, Pettit should endorse. Pettit's ethocentrism makes dispositions and habits central to language learning. Because of this ethocentrism, Pettit thinks that semantically basic terms are response-dependent. Their mastery depends on "contingencies of subjective response" (2005, p. 181) to their referents, which are Pettit's "pre-existing things" (2002, p. 75). Conversely eth*n*ocentrism concerns *whose* subjective responses are relevant. For the ethnocentrist, the relevant responses are those of normal members of a community under normal conditions of observation. Pettit, though endorsing ethocentrism in language learning, (at least officially) endorses anthropocentrism in subjective scope.

Kuhn conversely endorses ethocentrism in language learning and ethnocentrism in subjective scope. Like Pettit, Kuhn makes dispositions and habits central. Unlike Pettit, Kuhn thinks that they are shared across not human beings generally but members of a community specifically. Consider Kuhn's own account of how normal members of a community under normal conditions of observation learn terms in English like 'swan', 'goose', and 'duck' (1979, pp. 308–19; 2002, p. 51); 'pendulum' (2012/1962, pp. 118–20, 150); and 'planet', 'moon', 'star', and their relatives (2002, pp. 15, 94). Kuhn begins his discussion of the first set by observing that "a given stimulus can evoke a variety of sensations" (1979, p. 308). This resembles Pettit's point that objects instantiate multitudes of properties, some not salient to our categorizations. Nonetheless, unlike Pettit, Kuhn claims that whatever spontaneous extrapolation there is must be shaped and guided by a teacher from a particular community. Only then can the learner learn which properties (or stimulations due to them) are salient for her community. Teaching is central to the process of taking objects to exemplify one property rather than another:

> I ask that you imagine a small child on a walk with his father in a zoological garden.... During the afternoon now at hand, he will learn for the first time to identify swans, geese, and ducks. Anyone who has taught a child under such circumstances knows that the primary pedagogic tool is ostension.... Father points to a bird, saying, "Look, Johnny, there's a swan." A short time

later Johnny himself points to a bird, saying, "Daddy, another swan." He has not yet, however, learned what swans are and must be corrected: "No, Johnny, that's a goose." Johnny's next identification of a swan proves to be correct, but his next "goose" is, in fact, a duck, and he is again set straight. After a few more such encounters, however, each with its appropriate correction or reinforcement, Johnny's ability to identify these waterfowl is as a great as his father's (2002, p. 309).

Kuhn concludes that Johnny

has learned all this without acquiring, or at least without needing to acquire, even one criterion for identifying swans, geese, or ducks. ... Johnny, in short, has learned to apply symbolic labels to nature without anything like definitions or correspondence rules. In their absence he employs a learned but nonetheless primitive perception of similarity and difference (p. 313).

Kuhn surmises that such considerations apply to amateur ornithologists and professional physicists alike.[4]

Hence Kuhn, like Pettit, thinks that learning his privileged class of terms occurs through dispositions to extrapolate in response to ostended examples. Johnny is disposed to extrapolate in response to birds in the garden. Kuhn, like Pettit, thinks that there are higher-order dispositions that enforce conformity in these extrapolations. If Johnny exhibits inconsistent identifications of waterfowl, then his father corrects him. Kuhn, like Pettit, therefore offers an ethocentric account of language learning. Moreover Kuhn, like Pettit, thinks that individual learning is done in a social environment. The example is simplistic, but Johnny and his father comprise such an environment. Further, Kuhn, like Pettit, thinks that learning ostensibly *via* extrapolation is psychologically and logically prior to following explicitly articulated rules. This in fact is Kuhn's conclusion. Finally, though not explicit about it, Kuhn, like Pettit, thinks that concepts are learned along with terms. Johnny can think to himself as well as say aloud what is and is not a swan.[5]

---

4. That Kuhn intends his analysis to extend to non-scientific terms is further evidenced by his non-scientific examples (1999, p. 34; 2002, pp. 36, 48, 56, 93). See below and §2.

5. While Pettit's terms, like 'red', are adjectives referring to properties, Kuhn's terms, like 'pendulum', are nouns referring to objects instantiating properties. Nonetheless Pettit (1998, p. 63) suggests that we learn the noun 'water' response-dependently. We can thus learn 'pendulum' also. Further, nouns and adjectives are interconvertible: 'red' and 'red object', and 'pendulum' and 'being a pendulum'. Kuhn (2002, pp. 67–69) even thinks that we learn nouns like 'force', 'mass', and 'weight' response-dependently.

Nonetheless Kuhn's ethocentric account of language learning, unlike Pettit's, is ethnocentric in subjective scope. While Pettit urges that anthropocentric conformity becomes important when deciding whether an individual's extrapolation is adequate, Kuhn maintains that ethnocentric teaching goes into an individual's extrapolation *ab initio*. Kuhn talks about the teacher as a member of a community ostending to objects *for* the learner rather than the learner extrapolating without initial guidance *ab initio*. Pettit's "primitive" responses, which Pettit maintains are anthropocentric and corrected only *ex post facto*, require on Kuhn's view social guidance. As Kuhn puts it, Johnny "employs a *learned* but nonetheless *primitive* perception" (2002, p. 313, emphases mine). His father's role as community indoctrinator is indispensable initially, which Pettit would deny.

Likewise, for Kuhn, unlike for Pettit, different communities can teach their learners to extrapolate differently and so to categorize the same objects as different kinds. We can appreciate this by considering Kuhn's other examples. Early on Kuhn (2012/1962, pp. 118–20, 150) urges that after Galileo human beings would respond to a tethered weight by conceiving of it as falling under **pendulum** and (if Anglophonic) calling it a 'pendulum'. Before Galileo human beings would respond to the same object by taking it instead to be a constrained body with a slow descent. As we saw in Chapter Two, Kuhn later (2002, pp. 15, 94) explains that the (Anglophonic) Ptolemaic teaches learners in his community to respond to the sun, the moon, Venus, Mercury, Mars, Jupiter, and Saturn by constructing a lexical taxonomy (or "lexicon") in which 'the sun', 'the moon', 'Venus', 'Mercury', 'Mars', 'Jupiter', and 'Saturn' figure under 'planet'. The Ptolemaic thereby taxonomizes these objects by treating planet as the genus whose species include the sun, the moon, Venus, *etc*. He conceptualizes them likewise. Conversely the (Anglophonic) Copernican teaches learners in her community to respond to the same objects with 'the sun', 'the moon', 'Venus', 'Mercury', 'Mars', 'Jupiter', and 'Saturn' also. Yet the Copernican structures the last under 'planet', the first under 'star', and the second under 'satellite'. The Copernican thereby taxonomizes these objects by treating planet as the genus whose species include Venus, Mercury, Mars, Jupiter, and Saturn; while star and satellite are the genera whose species include the sun and moon, respectively. She conceptualizes them likewise too.[6]

Hence, on Kuhn's view, for members of a community to learn a concept or term, they must learn how that concept or term is connected to responses of normal members of that community under normal conditions of observation

---

6. As we saw in Chapter Two, §§4–5, the Ptolemaic and Copernican respond to either different realizer-properties or the same realizer-properties differently. This distinction is unimportant here.

for that community to objects in the world. Moreover, for Kuhn, these objects are tantamount to Pettit's "pre-existing things" (Pettit 2002, p. 75). Whatever object the pre-Galilean and post-Galilean conceptualize differently must "pre-exist" their conceptualizations lest there be no object *to* conceptualize differently. For Kuhn, before Copernicus human beings taxonomized the sun as a planet by conceiving of it as falling under **planet** and calling it a 'planet'. After Copernicus human beings taxonomized the sun as a star by conceiving of it as falling under **star** and calling it a 'star'. Hence the sun itself must pre-exist.[7]

For Kuhn, what size is a community? Sometimes it is as small as a specific scientific community "of perhaps one hundred members" (2012/1962, pp. 177–78) at a particular historical time. Other times it is as large as more or less all humans at a particular historical time (*e.g.*, those after Galileo). In fact, though Kuhn writes mostly about historically situated scientific communities, his ethnocentrism applies to all empirical concepts and terms rather than just scientific ones. Nor by 'community' does Kuhn mean all and only those who seem to use the same language. Some communities are smaller. As we saw above, even Johnny and his father could comprise a community. Though they are not its only members, they could be. Other communities are larger. Catalan and Cantonese speakers could both be Copernicans.[8]

Let me connect all this to response-dependence. Kuhn maintains that a pendulum for a community just is an object that normal members of that community under normal conditions of observation for that community would conceive of as falling under **pendulum** and in English call a 'pendulum'. Because a community is not necessarily identical with all those who seem to speak the same language, let me specify that the English in question is English as it would be used by that community were anyone in fact to use it.[9] It would be their community's (potential) *dialect*. Likewise a planet for a community just is an object that normal members of that community under normal conditions of observation for that community would conceive of as falling under **planet** and in English as used by that community call a 'planet'.[10] Generalizing

---

7. I explain this in §3 and qualify it in Chapter Eight, §6.

8. Nor need Kuhn deny that there are responses or capacities shared by all human beings. He could simply explain them ethnocentrically. Perhaps 'pendulum' would be linked essentially to responses of our post-Galilean community to objects in the world, while 'red' would be linked essentially to responses of all human communities to objects in the world.

9. See Chapter Seven, §§2, 4.

10. Because English as used by that community need not be English as used by our community, this formulation respects what, as I explain in §3, Kuhn says about incommensurability.

we see that Kuhn is committed to the view that this holds for any taxonomic concept or term:

ETHNOCENTRIC CONCEPT-AND-TERM: Something is x for a community if and only if normal members of that community under normal conditions of observation for that community would conceive of it as falling under x and call it ⌜y⌝ to mean x in their language.

I have said that they would call it ⌜y⌝ to mean x, and so kept the variables distinct, because the community's language (or dialect) is not necessarily the same as mine, the meta-language in which I phrased the biconditional.

Regardless Kuhn's Ethnocentric Concept-and-Term resembles those response-dependence biconditionals to which, as we saw in Chapter Two, Mark Johnston, Crispin Wright, and Pettit are committed. Is Kuhn himself committed to the four requirements on response-dependence biconditionals that I extracted from Wright's view?[11] The first requirement is that response-dependence biconditionals hold *a priori*. Indeed, for Kuhn, it is unintelligible for a normal Copernican under normal conditions of observation to be unable to identify which objects according to her community are conceived of as falling under **planet** and called 'planet'. Responses of requisite community members to objects are definitive for their community of what objects fall under a particular concept or are called a particular term. Hence Ethnocentric Concept-and-Term is *a priori* in the epistemological sense of being insusceptible to empirical justification or verification within the requisite community.[12] But that is because it is *a priori* in the ontological sense of deriving purely from a subjective source, the community's lexicon. The biconditional is insusceptible to empirical justification or verification *because* it is meant to express linguistic relations encoded in a community's lexicon. And such a lexicon, as part of that language, is itself a subjective source.

Wright's second requirement is that response-dependence biconditionals be non-reductive and non-eliminative. In fact, to say that something is a planet for a community if and only if normal members of that community under normal conditions of observation for that community would conceive of it as falling under **planet** and in English as used by that community call it 'planet'

---

11. See Crispin Wright (1988, pp. 19–22; 1989, p. 247; 1999/1992, pp. 114–17; 1993, pp. 77–82) regarding the first; Wright (1989, p. 247–48; 1999/1992, pp. 112, 120–23; 1993, p. 78), the third; and Wright (1999/1992, ch. 3. append.; 1993, pp. 77–82; 2001, pp. 191–99), the fourth. The second requirement is implicit in these and proximal passages.

12. Of course it would be susceptible to such justification and verification within a *different* community. See §2.

just is to treat it as non-reductive and non-eliminative. Variants of 'planet' can and must occur on both sides of the biconditional.

Wright's third requirement is that such biconditionals are to be specified non-trivially. Kuhn himself explains who normal members of a community under normal conditions of observation would be. Such members would have been indoctrinated into their particular community sometimes through years of implicit and explicit instruction, a process that Kuhn describes. There is no triviality here.

Finally Wright's fourth requirement is that response-dependence biconditionals be read as extension-determining rather than extension-reflecting. As we saw in Chapter Two, neither Johnston nor Pettit accepts this requirement nor need any response-dependence theorist do so. Nonetheless it is worth detailing Pettit's, Wright's, and Johnston's positions to see whom Kuhn follows. Focusing on concepts and terms:

(a) *Pettit* implicitly reads response-dependence biconditionals as extension-reflecting. He thinks that such biconditionals describe (or "reflect") ontologically antecedent facts. He is concerned with the mastery of concepts and terms, where their mastery acquisitively depends on subjective responses to objects in the world.
(b) *Wright* explicitly reads response-dependence biconditionals as extension-determining. He thinks that such biconditionals constitute (or "determine") ontological facts in an asymmetric way. He is concerned with the content of concepts and meaning of terms, where their content and meaning constitutively depend on subjective responses to objects in the world.
(c) *Johnston* explicitly rejects Wright's distinction because he thinks that response-dependence biconditionals express ontological interdependence. He thinks that such biconditionals constitute ontological facts in a symmetric way. He is concerned with the content of concepts and meaning of terms, though now their content and meaning and the correlative subjective responses to objects in the world are constitutively interdependent.[13]

Whom does Kuhn follow? Kuhn's account of language learning *concerns* learning or mastery. It has to do with acquisition. The neophyte Copernican acquires 'planet' from her community. So, for the neophyte, the relevant biconditional is extension-reflecting. It describes an ontologically antecedent

---

13. See Pettit (2002, especially pp. 12, 13, 15, 52, 78), Mark Johnston (1993), and Wright (1999/1992, ch. 3. append.; 1993, pp. 77–82; 2001, pp. 191–99), respectively.

fact. Hence Kuhn follows Pettit. Nonetheless the community also *establishes* that ontologically antecedent fact. What the Copernican community says 'planet' means for them just is what it means for them. From the perspective of the community itself (and so experts in it), therefore, the relevant biconditional concerns a constitutive relationship. Hence Kuhn also follows Wright or Johnston.

That Kuhn's account of language learning concerns constitution and so meaning becomes clearer next. So is its relation to how that same account also concerns acquisition and so mastery. Only in the section that follows do I try to answer whom Kuhn follows besides Pettit—Wright or Johnston.

2. KUHN'S KANTIANISM

So far we have seen that Kuhn is committed to Ethnocentric Concept-and-Term concerning taxonomic concepts and terms, and that his commitment satisfies (at least) Wright's first three requirements on response-dependence biconditionals. If Kuhn is committed to Ethnocentric Concept-and-Term concerning *all* empirical concepts or terms, then he is committed to Dualism:

DUALISM: All empirical concepts, terms, or properties are linked essentially to subjective and objective sources.

In fact Kuhn is committed to Ethnocentric Concept-and-Term concerning all empirical concepts and terms. Though he is never explicit that concepts and terms not learned ostensibly are conceptually and linguistically connected to those that are, the historicist turn that Kuhn helps inaugurate brings with it the broader lesson that *whatever* we scientists and laity alike can think or say about the world depends on how our historically situated community's practices, theories, and values teach us to respond to that world. It depends on our historically informed conceptual, linguistic, and perceptual capacities. In the concluding chapter of Kuhn (2012/1962, ch. 13) and its postscript (2012/1970) Kuhn argues against the intelligibility of seeing ourselves coming closer to describing the world independently of our community's historical perspective. "[T]he Archimedean platform outside of history," he explains, " ... is gone beyond recall" (2002, p. 115; *cf.* p. 95). We cannot recover an ahistorical platform—where such a platform, independent of our community's historical purview, would be anthropocentric if not even more general. In fact, according to Kuhn, we never had access to such a platform, or perspective, in the first place.

Kuhn must therefore be committed to something like Pettit's view, in ethnocentric form, that all empirical concepts and terms for a community are learned in response to ostended examples or are connected with those that are. Given this globalism and Kuhn's account of language learning we have grounds to maintain that his Dualism is epistemological:

EPISTEMOLOGICAL DUALISM: All empirical concepts, terms, or properties are acquired by a subject's appealing essentially to subjective and objective sources.

While Kuhn is an Epistemological Dualist concerning concepts and terms, he is not one concerning properties. Kuhn does not think that we acquire properties by appealing essentially to subjective and objective sources—or anything else. Properties are there for us to conceive of and name rather than acquire. Regardless the subjective source of concepts and terms, which we do acquire, are ethnocentric responses. Those responses would themselves be grounded on ethnocentric conceptual, linguistic, and perceptual capacities. The objective source is objects in the world. As we saw in §1 and Chapter Two, the Ptolemaic and Copernican conceive of and name the same object in the world, the sun, differently. The Ptolemaic conceives of it as a **planet** and in English as used by that community names it a 'planet'; the Copernican, **star** and 'star'.

Nonetheless, Kuhn, unlike Pettit, is not merely an Epistemological Dualist. He is also an Ontological one. Kuhn, unlike Pettit, is concerned not only with the mastery of terms and concepts but also with their meaning and content, respectively. To appreciate this, consider what Kuhn says about paradigms, disciplinary matrices, and (as I have discussed) lexical taxonomies or lexica.

Kuhn (2012/1962) is responsible for introducing 'paradigm' into ordinary English. His uses for it however are hardly univocal. Margaret Masterman (1970) identifies twenty-one, and Kuhn (2012/1970; 2002, p. 127) basically agrees. Kuhn's general idea however is that a paradigm is a set of shared examples embodying problems, solutions, methods, and values around which a scientific community coalesces. Paradigms are essential to what Kuhn calls 'normal science'. Physicists appealing to examples from (*e.g.*) classical mechanics to explain physical phenomena engage in normal science when such appeals dominate the discipline. Normal science contrasts with revolutionary science, where there is no dominant set of examples; the community instead seeks one. Some physicists might continue appealing to examples from classical mechanics, while others could appeal to examples from relativity theory, where no set dominates. The eventual dominance, in this case of relativity theory, signals the completion of a scientific revolution. Orthogonal to the distinction between normal and revolutionary science is Kuhn's distinction between immature and mature sciences. Immature sciences have never had a dominant set of examples—a "paradigm" in short. Consequently they have never had periods of normal science or scientific revolutions. Perhaps before Aristotle there were competing accounts of motion, none having significantly more adherents than any other. Mature sciences have had at least one paradigm and so at least one period of normal science.

Moreover Kuhn's general model of immature science likely describes his thoughts on the nature of disciplines outside science. Since there is no "Archimedean platform outside history" (2002, p. 115) for scientists or laity, we all understand the world relative to sets of examples embodying ethnocentric commitments. It is just that outside science, like during periods of immature science, no such set dominates. Because Kuhn's most developed accounts involve mature sciences, however, I focus on these.

Kuhn eventually (2012/1970; 1979, essay 12) disambiguates his notion of a paradigm into symbolic generalizations, ontological views, values, and exemplars associated with a "disciplinary matrix." A disciplinary matrix is itself the set of beliefs required for someone to have to be a member of a scientific community. Ultimately Kuhn (2002, essays 1–4, 11) speaks instead of a "lexical taxonomy" or "lexicon." As we saw in §1 and Chapter Two, a lexicon is a set of kind terms figuring as nodes in a network structured according to the species–genus relations of objects in the world to which scientists in particular historical communities respond. We have seen two such lexica, the competing astronomical ones. By focusing on lexica Kuhn distills the conceptual and linguistic components of his original notion of a paradigm from its evaluative and exemplary ones. Though shared values and examples remain important, Kuhn attends less to them.[14]

I can focus on lexica to show that Kuhn's Kantianism is not only Ontological but also Principled. Kuhn's lexica are themselves meant implicitly to contain subjective principles, or claims, distinct from any empirical ones, that are the form or basic epistemological or linguistic unit that the subjective source of empirical concepts, terms, or properties take. In fact, Kuhn explains, lexica are a variant on Kant's synthetic *a priori* judgments, Kant's own version of subjective principles. In explaining this Kuhn appeals to Michael Friedman's discussion of Hans Reichenbach, who gives an ontological construal of transcendental idealism. Kuhn approvingly writes of

> Friedman's [2010b/1993] description of Reichenbach's [1965/1920] distinction between two meanings of the Kantian a priori, one which "involves unrevisability and ... absolute fixity for all times" while the other means "'constitutive of the concept of the object of knowledge'." Both meanings make the world in some sense mind-dependent, but the first disarms the

---

14. See Paul Hoyningen-Huene (1993, ch. 4), Alexander Bird (2002, ch. 3), and James Marcum (2012) for more on paradigms, matrices, and lexica.

apparent threat to objectivity by insisting on the absolute fixity of the categories, while the second relativizes the categories (and the experienced world with them) to time, place, and culture.

"Though it is a more articulated source of constitutive categories," Kuhn continues, "my structured lexicon resembles Kant's a priori when the latter is taken in its second, relativized sense" (2002, p. 245, Friedman's ellipsis).[15] Because Kuhn's—as well as Friedman's and Reichenbach's—concern is with Kant's *a priori* that is "constitutive of the concept of the object of knowledge," all three have in mind Kant's synthetic *a priori*. While Kant's analytic *a priori* judgments are meant merely to analyze or clarify knowledge, Kuhn's lexica and Kant's synthetic *a priori* judgments (ontologically construed) are instead meant to be constitutive of empirical knowledge. Kant's synthetic *a priori* judgments and Kuhn's lexica are each meant to provide the conceptual resources within which empirical claims—Kant's synthetic *a posteriori* judgments and Kuhn's empirical claims proper—can be articulated and empirically verified. They are therefore also necessary relative to the empirical claims that they make possible.

Nonetheless Kuhn sees his lexica as not sharing the first meaning of Kant's synthetic *a priori*. While Kant's synthetic *a priori* judgments are meant to have "absolute fixity for all time" (at least for human beings), Kuhn's lexica are meant to depend on "time, place, and culture." Kant's principles are anthropocentric. Kuhn's, which are relative to a historically situated community, are ethnocentric. Kuhn summarizes his acceptance of the first and rejection of the second meaning of Kant's synthetic *a priori* when he calls himself "a Kantian with movable categories" (2002, p. 264; *cf.* pp. 29–30, 36, 52, 104). Lexica, though constitutive of empirical knowledge, move along with community membership. In Peter

---

15. Kuhn is quoting Michael Friedman (2010b/1993, p. 50), who is translating Reichenbach. See J. Alberto Coffa (2008/1991, ch. 10) for discussion of Reichenbach's distinction and an alternate translation closer to Reichenbach's original (1920, p. 46) German. Reichenbach himself translates the passage: "Kant's concept of a priori has two different meanings. First, it means 'necessarily true' or 'true for all times', and secondly, 'constituting the concept of the object'" (1965/1920, p. 48). In Chapter Six, §3, I consider Hans Reichenbach's, and in Chapter Six, §5, Friedman's, views directly. Moreover Albert Einstein apparently agrees with Reichenbach:

> The theoretical attitude here advocated [in the general theory of relativity] is distinct from that of Kant only by the fact that we do not conceive of the "categories" as unalterable (conditioned by the nature of the understanding) but as (in the logical sense) free conventions. They appear to be *a priori* only insofar as thinking without the positing of categories and of concepts in general would be as impossible as is breathing in a vacuum (1970/1949, p. 674).

Lipton's (2003) phrase Kuhn is "Kant on wheels." Kuhn's Ontological Kantianism has community mobility.[16]

Hence, for Kuhn, empirical concepts and terms for a community depend in a constitutive manner on responses of its members, encapsulated in their lexicon. Kuhn's account of language learning therefore concerns mastery *and* meaning. Moreover, by constituting the meaning of terms and the content of concepts, normal members of a community under normal conditions of observation would themselves learn them. 'Planet' means what it does for the Copernican insofar as she (and her fellows) give it that meaning and thereby also master it. This is enough to make Kuhn's Dualism not only Epistemological but also Ontological:

> ONTOLOGICAL DUALISM: All empirical concepts, terms, or properties are constituted essentially out of subjective and objective sources.

Kuhn's Ontological Dualism, like his Epistemological one, concerns concepts and terms, and not properties. The content of empirical concepts and meaning of empirical terms for a community depend on responses of normal members of that community under normal conditions of observation for that community to objects in the world. The subjective source of empirical concepts and terms are subjective responses as grounded on lexica used in those concepts' and terms' constitution and subsequent acquisition. These lexica are subjective in the sense of being imposed by community members, in virtue of community-wide agreement upon concepts and terms, on objects in the world that the community investigates. Moreover that agreement would itself result from conceptual, linguistic, and perceptual capacities shared across the community. The objective source of empirical concepts and terms are those objects, independent from the subject. As we saw in §1, Kuhn's objects are tantamount to Pettit's "pre-existing things" (2002, p. 75).

---

16. Kuhn's debt to Kant traces to his first year of college when he took a course in the history of philosophy:

> Spinoza didn't hit me very hard, Descartes and Hume were both in the current, I could understand them easily; *Kant was a revelation*.... Oh it's important to the story because I go round explaining my own position saying I am a Kantian with movable categories. It's got what is no longer quite a Kantian a priori, but that experience [of taking the class] surely prepared me for the Kantian synthetic a priori. And I do talk about the synthetic a priori (2002, p. 264, emphasis mine).

Kuhn (2012/1962, p. xi, n. 1) also acknowledges the influence of Alexandre Koyré and other neo-Kantian historians of science, who argue for the role of constitutive principles and conceptual breaks in the history of science.

Further, subjective principles implicit within these lexica are themselves meant to be distinct from the empirical claims that the lexica make possible. For Kuhn, the claim that the sun is a species of star is taxonomic. In fact it is *a priori* in both epistemological and ontological senses. It is *a priori* in the former sense because it is insusceptible to empirical justification or verification within the Copernican community. It is *a priori* in the latter sense because it derives from a subjective source, that community's lexicon. Conversely, for Kuhn, the claim that the sun is 1.496×10^8 km from the earth, though drawing on taxonomic concepts, is empirical. It is susceptible to empirical justification and verification within the Copernican community, because it derives from subjective and objective sources—the subject's lexicon and objects in the world that that lexicon taxonomizes, respectively. According to Kuhn, the distance between the sun and earth can be measured, while the sun's being a star is instead part of what members of the Copernican community mean by 'sun' and 'star'. Finally, because the subjective principles implicit within lexica are themselves constitutive of these empirical claims and so their component concepts and terms—they provide the terms within which the empirical claims can be articulated and empirically verified—they are constitutive principles. Hence Kuhn is committed to Ontological Principlism:

> ONTOLOGICAL PRINCIPLISM: The subjective source of all empirical concepts, terms, or properties takes the form of subjective principles constitutive of those concepts, terms, or properties.

Kuhn however is committed not only to Ontological but also to Epistemological Dualism. His commitment to lexica commits him to principles not only constitutive of the content of empirical concepts and meaning of empirical terms but also acquisitive of their mastery. By appealing to these lexica community members can learn the requisite concepts and terms themselves. Implicit within the lexica are acquisitive principles. Hence Kuhn is committed to Epistemological Principlism too:

> EPISTEMOLOGICAL PRINCIPLISM: The subjective source of all empirical concepts, terms, or properties takes the form of subjective principles acquisitive of those concepts, terms, or properties.

He is therefore committed to Ontological and Epistemological Kantianism *in toto*:

> ONTOLOGICAL KANTIANISM: All empirical concepts, terms, or properties are constituted essentially out of subjective and objective sources. The subjective source may take the form of subjective constitutive principles.
>
> EPISTEMOLOGICAL KANTIANISM: All empirical concepts, terms, or properties are acquired by a subject's appealing essentially to subjective and objective sources. The subjective source may take the form of subjective acquisitive principles.

In each case Kuhn's focus is on concepts and terms. And, because Kuhn is committed to Principlism, in each case his Kantianism is Principled.

3. RESIDUAL ISSUES CONCERNING KUHN'S KANTIANISM

Three residual issues concerning Kuhn's Ontological Kantianism in particular remain. The first traces to an unanswered question from §1. Recall Ethnocentric Concepts-and-Term:

> ETHNOCENTRIC CONCEPT-AND-TERM: Something is x for a community if and only if normal members of that community under normal conditions of observation for that community would conceive of it as falling under x and call it ⌜y⌝ to mean x in their language.

As we saw in §1, Kuhn would follow *Pettit* and read this biconditional as extension-reflecting in describing ontologically antecedent facts. But we saw as well that he would also follow either *Wright* and read the biconditional as asymmetrically extension-determining or *Johnston* and read the biconditional as symmetrically extension-determining. Whom else besides Pettit does Kuhn follow? Now that we know that Kuhn is an Ontological Kantian, this amounts to asking whether Kuhn is committed to what in Chapter Two I counted as a kind of asymmetric or symmetric Ontological Kantianism. Alas Kuhn himself never says anything allowing me to answer this. We should then treat his Kantianism as simply Ontological. Empirical terms in some manner constitutively depend on ethnocentric responses to objects in the world. We can then say that, for Kuhn, all empirical terms mean what they do *in virtue of* such responses and objects.

The second residual issue concerns an apparent tension in Kuhn's Ontological Kantianism concerning properties. In §2 I argued that the way to understand Kuhn's (2002) claim that the Ptolemaic and Copernican respond to the same objects by conceiving of and naming them differently is to understand him as an Ontological Kantian concerning concepts and terms, and not properties. Properties would be "pre-existing," instantiated by something like Pettit's "pre-existing things" (2002, p. 75). Nonetheless Kuhn earlier (2012/1962) writes in ways suggesting that he is an Ontological Kantian concerning properties too. According to him, members of different communities "are responding to a different world" (p. 111), those before a scientific revolution "lived in a different world" (pp. 116–17), and "though the world does not change with a change of paradigm, the scientist afterwards works in a different world" (p. 121). Such a "different world" would be a world instantiating different properties. Here Kuhn seems to be an Ontological Kantian concerning concepts, terms, *and* properties.

There are two strategies to handle this apparent tension. The former is to attempt to understand Kuhn's earlier (2012/1962) remarks as not committing him to Ontological Kantianism concerning properties. The latter is to acknowledge that Kuhn initially (2012/1962) is an Ontological Kantian concerning properties but eventually (2002) changes his mind. Though his project differs from mine, Ian Hacking (1983, pp. 108–11; 2010) construes Kuhn consistently with the former. According to Hacking, Kuhn is a *transcendental nominalist* because Kuhn thinks that (as I would put it) subjective responses to the world are structured, not by Kant's constitutive principles, which are epistemological (involving judgments), but by constitutive principles implicit within lexica, which are linguistic (involving names). The world is one of individual objects with properties, though how these objects are taxonomized depends on responses that subjects would have to them.[17] According to Hacking, Kuhn's transcendental nominalism is *revolutionary* because Kuhn thinks that taxonomies change radically over time. Hacking explicates Kuhn's statement about "different worlds":

The world does not change, but we work in a new world. The world that does not change is a world of individuals. The world in and with which we change is a world of kinds. The latter changes; the former does not. After a scientific revolution, the scientist works in a world of new kinds (Hacking 2010, p. 306)

rather than a new world *simpliciter*. The world and its properties therefore "pre-exist" in Pettit's sense. Members of different communities are responding to the same world ("the world does not change") but do so by conceiving of and naming objects in it differently (and so "work in a new world," *i.e.*, "a world of new kinds").

I am unsure whether Hacking can absolve Kuhn from all apparent commitments to Ontological Kantianism concerning properties. I am therefore tempted to adopt the latter strategy of seeing Kuhn as simply having changed his mind. Now in Chapter Eight I show that one cannot be an Ontological Kantian concerning concepts and terms without also being one concerning properties. Nonetheless what matters here is that by presenting Kuhn as having changed his mind I can explain why Kuhn ceased

---

17. Jeffrey K. McDonough explains: "Scientific revolutions alter the existence of mind-dependent kinds, but leave untouched the existence of ontologically independent individuals" (2003, p. 346). "Mind-dependence" amounts to response-dependence, while "ontologically independent individuals" would be Pettit's "pre-existing things" (2002, p. 75).

talking about "worlds"—even if in Chapter Eight I explain that he should not have done so.

The third and final residual issue concerning Kuhn's Ontological Kantianism concerns noumenalism, which, as we saw in Chapter Two, is the thesis that reality possesses an intrinsic nature or aspect that remains unknowable. We also saw that all kinds of Kantianism entails noumenalism. If empirical concepts, terms, or properties are linked essentially to subjective and objective sources, then we cannot conceive of, name, or perceive anything about the world independent of the subjective. The world therefore possesses an intrinsic nature (if construed ontologically) or aspect (if construed epistemologically) that remains unknowable. Kuhn's Kantianism would then entail noumenalism too.

In fact Kuhn himself acknowledges that it does:

> Underlying all these processes of differentiation and change, there must, of course, be something permanent, fixed, and stable. But, like Kant's *Ding an sich*, it is ineffable, undescribable, undiscussible. Located outside of space and time, this Kantian source of stability is the whole from which have been fabricated both creatures and their niches, both the "internal" and the "external" worlds (2002, p. 104).

This construal of noumenalism is ontological. Kuhn's description is similar to Michael Smith and Daniel Stoljar's own, itself ontological: "The world is a certain way in and of itself but, given the nature of our concepts, we cannot think or say what that way is" (1998, p. 87). Kuhn's and Smith and Stoljar's descriptions are dissimilar only insofar as Kuhn's concerns an independent world that stays fixed across ethnocentric changes, while Smith and Stoljar's concerns an independent world *simpliciter*. Regardless Kuhn's commitment to noumenalism is clear.[18]

4. FROM KANTIANISM TO INCOMMENSURABILITY

In Chapter Two we learned from Pettit not only that Kantianism can be anthropocentric in subjective scope but also that it entails noumenalism. Here

---

18. Kuhn does not realize that noumenalism could be construed epistemologically—as positing "something permanent, fixed, and stable ... ineffable, undescribable, undiscussible" *only in itself and not in its effects*. That might explain why Kuhn "later repudiated (in conversation with us) that notion of a *Ding an sich*" (James Conant and John Haugeland 2002, p. 7). Nonetheless Kuhn never repudiated it in print, and his reasoning that his view entails noumenalism remains valid. Moreover, as we saw in Chapter Two, §5, ontological and epistemological construals of noumenalism are not so easily segregated. More fundamentally, because

we learn from Kuhn not only that Kantianism can be ethnocentric in scope but also that all kinds of Ontological Kantianism concerning terms that allow there to be relevantly distinct subjects—subjects with relevantly distinct subjective capacities—entail the possibility of incommensurability.

'Incommensurability', like 'paradigm', is one of Kuhn's catchphrases. Kuhn initially (2012/1962, chs. 9–11) presents his incommensurability "thesis" as a series of theses denying any common measure (perspective, method, language) against which members of different communities can fully and impartially compare their observations, values, and terms. Kuhn eventually (2012/1970 and after) distinguishes incommensurability concerning observations, values, and meaning.[19] He then ceases talking about the observational variety, and, though writing occasionally (1979, essay 13) about value incommensurability, focuses on meaning incommensurability, which he identifies with intranslatability:

> The phrase 'no common measure' becomes 'no common language'. The claim that two theories are incommensurable is then the claim that there is no language, neutral or otherwise, into which both theories, conceived as sets of sentences, can be translated without residue or loss (2002, p. 36).

Now, if there is no language into which two theories can be translated without residue or loss, then the two theories are themselves non-*inter*translatable without residue or loss.[20] I take this to be Kuhn's general notion of (meaning) incommensurability.

Moreover, though Kuhn talks about theories and sentences, in the same article (2002, essay 2) he also talks about lexica and individual terms (2002, pp. 52–53). Later still (especially 2002, essays 5, 11) he refines meaning incommensurability into a lexical-taxonomic form, using his astronomical example to illustrate. According to him (2002, p. 53), because the Ptolemaic and Copernican lexica taxonomize objects in ways that are non-isomorphic with

---

he is an Ontological Kantian, Kuhn is committed to noumenalism construed ontologically; see Chapter Two, §6.

19. Howard Sankey and Hoyningen-Huene call these "perceptual," "methodological," and "semantic...components" (2001, p. ix), respectively, of Kuhn's account of incommensurability.

20. That can happen if and only if only one language is intranslatable into *the* other, or both languages are non-intertranslatable into *each* other. See Goldberg and Matthew Rellihan (2008) for more on (asymmetric) intranslatability. As I explain in Chapter Five, Donald Davidson himself worries about non-intertranslatability. See Hoyningen-Huene (1993, ch. 6) and Sankey (1993) for more on Kuhn on incommensurability. See Sankey (1994) and Sankey and Hoyningen-Huene (2001) for more on incommensurability generally.

one another, 'planet' in the Ptolemaic and Copernican lexica cannot be systematically correlated while respecting the taxonomic structures in which these terms are embedded. Since Kuhn regards the possibility of such correlation as a necessary condition on translatability, he maintains that the Ptolemaic's and Copernican's 'planet' are non-intertranslatable and therefore incommensurable in his specific taxonomic sense.[21]

While Kuhn's general notion of incommensurability has received sustained attention, his specific taxonomic variety has not.[22] There are three reasons for this. First, compared to Kuhn's notion of a paradigm, his notion of a lexical taxonomy has itself received little attention. Second, Kuhn provides little exposition of lexical incommensurability beyond what I myself have discussed. And third, besides examples like his from astronomy, it is unclear that what is important about incommensurability, on Kuhn's or anyone else's view, does concern taxonomy. Concerning the third, theories that are most uncontroversially incommensurable, for Kuhn or anyone else, are not necessarily incommensurable merely because of non-isomorphic species–genus relations. When Mendelian geneticists talk about "dominant and recessive traits," and molecular geneticists talk about "ribonucleic and deoxyribonucleic acids," these differences are not merely taxonomic. They concern entirely different models of heredity, with entirely different parts and processes, and so with terms for all these that are non-intertranslatable without residue or loss generally. Likewise, even in Kuhn's original case of Newton's and Einstein's 'mass' (2012/1962, pp. 98–103), incommensurability arises because the meaning of their shared term is non-intertranslatable without residue generally, not because of any taxonomic mismatch specifically. In both cases non-isomorphic taxonomy is if anything secondary.

Let me therefore adopt Kuhn's general notion of (meaning) incommensurability when discussing his view. Two theories, and so their component sentences and terms, are incommensurable if and only if they are non-intertranslatable without residue or loss. Further, there might be entire languages that are non-intertranslatable without residue or loss also. We can say that terms or languages that are so incommensurable are at least partially non-intertranslatable also. Moreover this general notion of incommensurability subsumes Kuhn's specific notion of taxonomic

---

21. Kuhn (2002, p. 36; 1999, p. 34) explains that incommensurability arising between lexica does so only for a small number of terms. He also offers the non-intertranslatability of the French 'esprit' and 'doux' into English (2002, p. 48), English 'sweet' into French (p. 56), and English 'mat' into French (p. 93) as examples of incommensurability outside science.

22. See however Sankey (1998), McDonough (2003), and Ian Hacking (2010).

incommensurability. *Because* the Ptolemaic and Copernican take 'planet' to figure in a non-isomorphic species–genus hierarchy, the Ptolemaic and Copernican mean by it non-intertranslatable things.

I agree with Kuhn that his specific ethnocentric view does entail incommensurability (and therefore *at least* its possibility). As I would put it, ethnocentric Ontological Kantianism says that the meaning of terms is community-specific and denies that there is a common measure (or language) against (or into) which members of *different* communities can compare (or intertranslate) them.[23] There is no Archimedean platform. Members of different communities are therefore

> unable to communicate all of their experiences across the lexical divide. Though individuals may belong to several interrelated communities (thus, be multilinguals), they experience aspects of the world differently as they move from one to the next (Kuhn 2002, p. 101).

The Ptolemaic is unable fully to communicate to the Copernican his experiences of seeing planets move across the sky, because the Copernican, unlike the Ptolemaic, does not experience the sun and moon as planets. Though Kuhn treats the sun as tantamount to one of Pettit's "pre-existing things," neither the Ptolemaic nor Copernican can categorize the sun in non-community specific terms. Even I can categorize the sun as a planet *as according to the Ptolemaic* or a star *as according to the Copernican* but not both simultaneously.[24]

Nonetheless, going beyond Kuhn, I can ask the following. Would anthropocentric Ontological Kantianism concerning terms entail incommensurability also? It would entail at least its possibility. While Kuhn denies that anthropocentrism is true, Pettit provides a model for it. According to Pettit, terms like 'red' in English are connected in an *a priori* manner to paradigmatic human responses. Though Pettit's Kantianism is epistemological, and so does not concern meaning and would not entail incommensurability, we can imagine an ontological kind that would. On that view 'red' in English would have a human-specific meaning. Were there a language specifically non-human, then 'red' in English might be non-intertranslatable into it. In phrasing closer to Kuhn an object might be "taxonomized" as red *according to human beings* and as something else *according to non-human beings* but not both simultaneously. Admittedly we so far have no uncontroversial example of another species with

---

23. Were there a common measure (or language), then they would not be different communities.

24. See Goldberg and Rellihan (2008) for another reason that, for Kuhn, incommensurability obtains.

conceptual, linguistic, or perceptual capacities necessary to "taxonomize" objects one way, and so mean by their terms one thing, rather than another. Nonetheless such a species is possible. Incommensurability itself is then possible given anthropocentric Kantianism too.

Let me make this more precise. As I explain in Chapter Seven, Kuhn's view amounts to an example of what I there call a 'Kantian account of meaning'. According to Kuhn's ethnocentric Ontological Kantianism concerning terms, 'planet' in English as used by a particular community would mean planet for that community in virtue of normal members of that community under normal conditions taking it to mean planet. Though not all (or even any) members of that community might speak English, 'planet' in English as used by that community would mean planet for any member of that community who did. Conversely, according to the correlative anthropocentric account, 'red' in English as used by human beings generally would mean red for them in virtue of normal human beings under normal conditions taking it to mean red. Though not all human beings speak English, 'red' in English would mean red for any human being who did. Since both ethnocentrism and anthropocentrism deny that there is a neutral language—between communities and species, respectively—both entail that incommensurability is at least possible.

This generalizes. The possibility of incommensurability follows from any kind of Ontological Kantianism concerning terms if and only if it allows there to be relevantly distinct subjects, and so more than one relevantly distinct set of specific conceptual, linguistic, and perceptual capacities. Ethnocentric Ontological Kantianism concerning terms allows that. Kuhn spent a career discussing consequences of different (for him, historically situated) communities conceiving of, naming, and perceiving objects in the world differently. Members of different communities would be relevantly distinct from one another. Anthropocentric Ontological Kantianism concerning terms allows it also. Though we have no uncontroversial example of a species other than ours possessing conceptual, linguistic, and perceptual capacities necessary for empirical thought or language in any uncontroversial sense, this kind of Kantianism allows there to be other such species. They would simply not be ours. Hence, while in Chapter Two I expanded Pettit's debate with Smith and Stoljar from a species-specific case to a community-specific one, here I expanded Kuhn's notion of incommensurability from his community-specific case to a species-specific one.[25]

---

25. Perhaps anthropocentrism should therefore be named 'species-centrism'. Nonetheless, as ethnocentrism accommodates our community and others, so I take anthropocentrism to accommodate our species and others.

5. LESSONS FOR KANTIAN CONCEPTUAL GEOGRAPHY

In this chapter we have seen how understanding Kuhn as a global response-dependence theorist allows me to understand him as a Kantian of an ethnocentric, Ontological and Epistemological, Principled kind. We have also seen the connection between Ontological Kantianism concerning terms and incommensurability. In this conclusion I draw three lessons for Kantian conceptual geography generally.

First, as we began to see in Chapter Two, language learning is integrally connected to Kantianism. Moreover language learning can have both ontological and epistemological, or only epistemological, consequences. In Kuhn's case language learning involves both acquiring terms and constituting their meaning. For him, because all terms are either acquired or constituted response-dependently, or semantically grounded on those that are, both Epistemological and Ontological Kantianism follow. In Pettit's case language learning involves only acquiring terms. For him, because all terms are either acquired response-dependently, or semantically grounded on those that are, only Epistemological Kantianism follows.

Second, instead of following Johnston, Wright, Pettit, and all other explicit response-dependence theorists (and John Locke and Kant) in identifying a suitable subject under suitable conditions with a normal human being under normal conditions of observation, Kantians can follow Kuhn in identifying them with normal members of a community under normal conditions of observation for their community. Kantians can therefore be anthropocentric or ethnocentric.

And third, both ethnocentric and anthropocentric Ontological Kantianism concerning terms entails the possibility of incommensurability. In fact that possibility follows from any kind of Ontological Kantianism concerning terms that allows there to be relevantly distinct subjects. Terms could then mean what they do partly in virtue of relevantly distinct subjective sources, without there being sufficient subjective sources that are shared.

FOUR

Donald Davidson

Donald Davidson was influential outside philosophy generally, outside analytic philosophy specifically, and inside analytic philosophy itself. Outside philosophy generally, Davidson's work on truth-conditional semantics inspired a research program in linguistics, while his take on the interpretation of literary texts has itself been taken up by literary theorists. Outside analytic philosophy specifically, Davidson's views have been seen as consonant with those of the Continental tradition and especially Hans-Georg Gadamer; Davidson has inspired those trying to reinvigorate the American Pragmatist tradition of which Davidson is sometimes seen as part; and in his final years Davidson connected his view to Chinese philosophy himself.[1]

Davidson was however first and foremost an analytic philosopher. In fact he contributed more deeply and systematically to our understanding of thought, language, and reality than perhaps any other analytic philosopher. The *deepness* of Davidson's contributions is partly evidenced by their continued prominence. Davidson's is a live position in many areas.[2] Their *systematicity* is partly evidenced by their connection to his notion of radical interpretation, offered to answer the question: "What is it for words to mean what they do?" (2001d/1984, p. xiii). Much of Davidson's philosophy of language, epistemology, and action theory in particular depends on his answer. Though it is too early to tell,

---

1. See §2 for more on Donald Davidson's truth-conditional semantics, and Davidson (2005b, essays 10–12) for his thoughts on literary interpretation. See Jeff Malpas (2011a, essays 9–14) for comparisons between Davidson and Hans-Georg Gadamer; Chapter One, §2, for Davidson's connection to American Pragmatism; and Bo Mou (2006) for his connection to Chinese philosophy.

2. See Mark de Bretton Platts (1997), Ernest Lepore and Kirk Ludwig (2007, 2009), and Lepore and Barry Lower (2011).

Richard Rorty might be right when he writes: "Histories of twentieth-century philosophy will have to include a sizable chapter on Davidson" (2011, p. 6).

Radical interpretation was not however Davidson's only language-related account. Like both Philip Pettit and Thomas Kuhn, Davidson also provided an account of language learning. Further, like them, Davidson drew ontological and epistemological consequences from it. In this chapter I explore Davidson's accounts of radical interpretation and language learning. I thereby further explore Kantian territory. Staying with my general strategy, I show that Davidson's accounts can be understood as different global response-dependence theories of terms and ultimately different kinds of Kantianism.[3] This allows me to demonstrate that Kantianism need not be *anthropocentric*, according to which all empirical concepts, terms, or properties are linked essentially to specifically human (*anthropos*) capacities, as Immanuel Kant and Pettit maintain. Nor need it be *ethnocentric*, according to which all such concepts, terms, or properties are linked essentially to specifically community (*ethnos*) capacities, as Kuhn maintains. Kantianism can also be *idiocentric* or *logocentric*. According to the former, all empirical concepts, terms, or properties are linked essentially to specifically individual (*idios*) capacities—capacities had by subjects *qua* individual. According to the latter, all empirical concepts, terms, or properties are linked essentially to specifically language user (*logos*) capacities—capacities had by subjects *qua* language user generally.

Admittedly appealing to Davidson when exploring Kantianism might seem strange. Davidson does admit that of all historical philosophers "Kant's influence has been the most pervasive" (1999a, p. 64) on him. Nonetheless, as I explain in Chapter Five, Davidson argues against what I mean by 'Kantianism' by arguing against Dualism in particular. Yet, as I also explain, Davidson's arguments fail. Given that failure, and that his accounts of radical interpretation and language learning otherwise would commit him to different kinds of Kantianism, I am entitled in this chapter to take them to be kinds of Kantianism.[4]

The chapter proceeds as follows. In §1 I show that Davidson's account of radical interpretation can be understood as *one* response-dependence theory of terms and so one kind of Kantianism. In §2 I show that Davidson's account

---

3. Mark Johnston (1991, pp. 171–73) and Alex Byrne (1998) argue that Davidson's account of radical interpretation is a response-dependence theory of belief. Regardless Johnston's argument is sketchy, and Byrne's establishes only one direction of the requisite biconditional and so is insufficient. None makes the connection to either terms or Kantianism.

4. See Richard N. Manning (2011, §1) for different aspects of this tension.

of language learning can be understood as *two different* response-dependence theories of terms and so two different kinds of Kantianism. In §3 I highlight differences among these three kinds. In §4 I show that one difference makes Davidson's accounts inconsistent and then suggest a resolution. Finally in §5 I draw lessons for Kantian conceptual geography generally.

1. RADICAL INTERPRETATION AND KANTIANISM

Davidson officially introduces radical interpretation in an eponymous article (2001d/1984, essay 9) and elaborates on it throughout his career (*e.g.*, 2002, essay 10; 2005a, ch. 3). Nonetheless Davidson first invokes the notion in his landmark essay (2001d/1984, essay 2) on truth and meaning. There he uses Alfred Tarski's (2008/1944) semantic conception of truth to devise an account of meaning. According to Tarski, specifying conditions under which each sentence in a language is true defines what truth in that language is. Consider sentences of this form, embodying Tarski's "Convention T":

(T) ⌜s⌝ is true in the object language if and only if p.

(T)'s grammatical subject, ⌜s⌝, is a sentence in the object language. Its predicate, ⌜is true in the object language if and only if p⌝, is a predicate in the meta-language. Tarski's intended object languages are formal languages free of ambiguity and paradox. They are also already interpreted or assigned meanings. In (T) ⌜p⌝ is the meta-linguistic translation of ⌜s⌝, derived by recursively matching ⌜s⌝'s subsentential parts with objects or properties that they satisfy. Tarski maintains that any adequate theory of truth for a language must *via* this recursive method imply for every ⌜s⌝ a corresponding ⌜p⌝.

Davidson modifies Tarski's account in three ways. First, he (2001d/1984, essay 2) applies it to natural languages. Unlike Tarski, Davidson therefore cannot forbid ambiguity, must accommodate paradox, and must also maintain that all natural-language locutions can be logically regimented.[5] Second, Davidson eventually (essay 9) speaks officially not of "sentences" but of sentence "utterances," indexed to a speaker, time, and place. The *object* language is the *speaker's* language. Regardless Davidson continues to speak unofficially of

---

5. On ambiguity Davidson (2001d/1984, p. 30) argues that, if ambiguity in the object language is preserved in the meta-language, then no problems arise. On paradox Davidson (pp. 28–29) counsels that we accept the intertranslatability between object and meta-language except concerning the object language's truth-predicate. (See Chapter Five, §2.) On regimentation Davidson (essays 2, 4, 5) notes that many natural-language locutions have been regimented and hopes that eventually all are.

"sentences," and so do I. And third, while Tarski contends that one can define truth in a language by presupposing a notion of translation (and so meaning), Davidson (essay 2) wishes to determine sentences' interpretation (and so meaning) by presupposing the concept of truth. I return to this last point in Chapter Nine.

Though the details of Tarski's and Davidson's formal apparatus are interesting, we can already appreciate Davidson's conclusion.[6] It is that constructing a resulting "Tarski-style" truth theory for a natural language amounts to constructing a meaning theory for that language. For Davidson, a Tarski-style truth theory for a language *interprets* the language if and only if it correlates all the sentences of the language with their truth conditions.[7] Moreover the systematic correlation, generated *via* Tarski's recursive method, ensures that individual terms make similar semantic contributions regardless of the sentence in which they occur. Terms then mean what they do in virtue of their compositional role in sentences, making good on Davidson's earlier (2001d/1984, essay 1) claim that sentential meaning must be compositional.

Davidson soon realized however that systematically correlating truth conditions is insufficient to limit the possible number of truth-condition assignments to plausible interpretations. Davidson eventually (2001d/1984, essay 9) explains how a radical interpreter—an idealized interpreter with no prior insight into a speaker's language—would construct truth theories based on a speaker's observable behavior and environment. According to Davidson, the radical interpreter constrains her substitution instances of ⌜p⌝ by the principle of charity. Though Davidson offers different versions of the principle, he ultimately understands it as requiring that in basic cases the radical interpreter correlate a speaker's sentences with truth conditions that describe what from the interpreter's perspective would be perceptually salient features of the environment were the interpreter in the speaker's spot.[8] Basic cases concern ostensible

---

6. See Bjørn T. Ramberg (1991, p. 50) for similar bracketing of Davidson's apparatus.

7. See Davidson (2001d/1984, essay 8) and Lepore and Ludwig (2009, ch. 12) for sentences that are not statements.

8. The principle of charity traces to Neil Wilson: "We select as designatum [of proper names] that individual which will make the largest possible number of ... statements true" (1959, p. 532). Willard van Orman Quine (1964, §13) expands Wilson's use by arguing that we should attribute to others our own logical constants. As we saw above, Davidson expands Quine's own use. See Nathaniel Goldberg (2004c) for Davidson's earlier formulations of the principle and Lepore and Ludwig (2007, pp. 185–92) for this later one. Davidson also bifurcates the principle:

> The Principle of Coherence prompts the interpreter to discover a degree of logical consistency in the thought of the speaker; the Principle of Correspondence prompts the

objects. As Davidson suggests (2001a, p. 294; 2002, p. 121), in basic cases the radical interpreter makes these correlations by triangulating ostensible objects with the speaker.[9] The interpreter thereby attributes to the speaker beliefs that she herself would have, themselves serving as substitution instances of ⌜p⌝. Further, applying the principle of charity in tandem with Tarski's recursive method entails that in non-basic cases the interpreter attributes to the speaker beliefs based on those attributed in basic cases.[10]

How does this concern response-dependence and Kantianism? By a 'normal radical interpreter under normal conditions of radical interpretation' I mean an interpreter whose evidence is limited to the sort just described (a speaker's observable behavior and environment), whose conditions of interpretation allow her to perceive that evidence (her senses are unobstructed, the speaker's behavior is overt, *etc.*), and who can construct a Tarski-style truth theory given that evidence (she has the requisite memory, combinatorial abilities, *etc.*) *via* the principle of charity. Now suppose that some speaker utters "La rosa es roja," and that by responding to this and other utterances given the speaker's environment a normal radical interpreter under normal conditions of radical interpretation would construct a charitable, Tarski-style truth theory according to which the radical interpreter *interprets* "La rosa es roja" to mean that the rose is red. On Davidson's view "La rosa es roja" then *means* that the rose is red. For "La rosa es roja" means that the rose is red if and only if a normal radical interpreter under normal conditions of radical interpretation would interpret it to *have* that meaning. And by determining what a sentence means the radical interpreter determines what its component terms mean.[11]

---

interpreter to take the speaker to be responding to the same features of the world that he (the interpreter) would be responding to under similar circumstances. Both principles can be (and have been) called principles of charity: one principle endows the speaker with a modicum of logical truth, the other endows him with a degree of true belief about the world (2002, p. 211).

My formulation is roughly Davidson's Principle of Correspondence. I do not have a correlative Principle of Coherence because I maintain that Davidson gets coherence from the recursive nature of T-sentence construction.

9. Davidson explores triangulation over a series of articles (2001a; 2001c; 2002, essays 3, 7, 8, 12–14; 2005b, essay 9). See Goldberg (2009b).

10."The interdependence of belief and meaning springs from the interdependence of two aspects of the interpretation of speech behavior: the attribution of beliefs and the interpretation of sentences" (Davidson 2001d/1984, p. 195). See Simon Evnine (1991, chs. 6, 7), Jerry Fodor and Lepore (1992, ch. 3), Hans-Johann Glock (2003, ch. 6), and Lepore and Ludwig (2007, part II) for more on radical interpretation.

11. As I explain in §3, Davidson thinks that interpretation is nevertheless indeterminate.

We can appreciate that Davidson is committed to this biconditional as follows. According to him, *if* a radical interpreter would interpret a speaker to mean something, then that is what the speaker does mean: "What a fully informed interpreter could learn about what a speaker means is all there is to learn" (2002, p. 148).[12] And, if a fully informed interpreter could do this, then Davidson's idealized interpreter, the radical interpreter, would do so. Elsewhere Davidson explains: "[T]here can be no more to meaning than an adequately equipped person can learn and observe; the interpreter's point of view is therefore the revealing one to bring to the subject" (2005a, p. 62). Again, if a radical interpreter would interpret a speaker to mean something, then that is what the speaker does mean. Conversely, "[a]s a matter of principle, then, meaning, and by its connection with meaning, belief also, are open to public determination" (2002, pp. 147–48), and "[m]eaning is entirely determined by observable behavior" (2005b, p. 56). Meaning therefore must be open to public determination by the radical interpreter, who interprets based on publicly observable behavior and environment, and determinable by the radical interpreter, for whom such behavior and environment are sufficient for interpretation. Hence *only if* a radical interpreter would determine that a speaker means something by her terms does she mean it.

Though, as I explain below, doing so is not especially intuitive, I can formulate Davidson's biconditional similarly to how I formulated the biconditionals to which, as we saw in Chapters Two and Three, respectively, Pettit and Kuhn are committed. Davidson would be committed to this:

RI TERM: Something is x for a speaker if and only if a normal radical interpreter under normal conditions of radical interpretation would interpret the speaker's term ⌜y⌝ for it to mean x in the speaker's language.

Similar to what I said in Chapter Three concerning Kuhn's Ethnocentric Concept-and-Term, I have said here that the radical interpreter would interpret the speaker's ⌜y⌝ to mean x, and so kept the variables distinct, because the speaker's language is not necessarily the same as mine, the meta-language in which I phrased the biconditional. Now Davidson is explicit that any interpreter's responses are constrained by "the way we are constructed (evolution had something to do with this)" (2002, p. 202) and that, "[i]f some such discriminative mechanisms were not in our genes, none could be learned" (p. 118). This would apply to the radical interpreter's construction (or evolution) and discriminative mechanisms (in her genes) also. Thus the radical

---

12. Byrne (1998, p. 203) takes the continuation of this quotation—"the same goes for what the speaker believes"—to show that Davidson holds a response-dependence theory of belief. Nonetheless the quotation corroborates only one direction of the requisite biconditional.

interpreter's responses are subjective insofar as they are grounded on how she is constructed (or evolved) and therefore mechanically (and genetically) discriminates. Hence those responses rely on her specific conceptual, linguistic, or perceptual capacities.[13] Conversely the radical interpreter's responses are responses *to* the speaker and the objects that the interpreter triangulates with her. And the speaker's behavior, those objects, and the environment generally are all independent of the subject. They are from the perspective of the interpreter objective. They are therefore from that perspective part of the interpreter-, and so subject-, independent world.

Hence RI Term connects terms to subjective and objective sources. Moreover, for Davidson, because there *can* be no more to meaning than what a radical interpreter *can* learn, and meaning is *in principle* radically interpretable, RI Term expresses an essential connection between radical interpretation and meaning. It is no accident that 'la rosa es roja' means that the rose is red if and only if a normal radical interpreter under normal conditions of radical interpretation would interpret it to have that meaning. It is essential. It follows from the nature of radical interpretation and meaning itself.

Now, like Pettit's and Kuhn's biconditionals, RI Term does not tell us whether Davidson is after a response-dependence theory of terms or properties. We know however that Davidson is after (at least) an account of interpretation and so is concerned (at least) with terms. Something is red for a speaker if and only if a radical interpreter would interpret her term for it to mean red, because *what it is for some term to mean red* depends on the interpreter's subjective responses to objects in the world. Regardless, as I suggested, formulating Davidson's view as a canonical response-dependence biconditional is not especially intuitive. I can reformulate it as follows. As *per* RI Term, Davidson is committed to the claim that 'roja' in a speaker's language means red if and only if a normal radical interpreter under normal conditions of radical interpretation would interpret it in that language to have that meaning. Generalizing we see that Davidson is committed to the following, which I call 'RI' (*simpliciter*):

> RI: For any empirical term in L, the term means what it does if and only if a normal radical interpreter under normal conditions of radical interpretation would interpret it in L to have that meaning.[14]

RI involves the same subjective and objective sources as does RI Term. The radical interpreter's responses (and ultimately specific conceptual, linguistic, and

---

13. See also Davidson (1999b, p. 732; 2002, pp. 120, 212; 2005b, p. 136).

14. In Chapter Five, §3, we see that Davidson is committed to this for all terms, empirical or otherwise. Here I limit myself to the empirical ones.

perceptual capacities) are subjective. The speaker's behavior and environment, including objects in the world that interpreter and speaker triangulate—all falling under 'normal conditions of radical interpretation'—are objective.

Let me focus on RI. If Davidson thinks that RI satisfies the first three of the four requirements that in Chapter Two I extracted from Crispin Wright's view, then he is committed to its being a response-dependence biconditional.[15] Does he? Wright's first requirement is that response-dependence biconditionals hold *a priori*. Indeed, for Davidson, RI is *a priori* in both the epistemological and ontological senses that I discussed in Chapters Two and Three. It is epistemologically *a priori* insofar as it is insusceptible to empirical justification or verification. Davidson takes the connection between meaning and radical interpretation to be "a matter of principle" (2002, p. 147). He never constrains his theorizing by empirical findings or presents it as vulnerable to empirical results. RI is ontologically *a priori* insofar as it is meant to derive from a subjective source. Davidson (1994, p. 121; 2004, p. 128) maintains that his account of radical interpretation limns conceptual connections among meaning, belief, desire, truth, speaker, and interpreter. For Davidson, RI derives from those conceptual connections and so presumably what he means by 'radical interpretation' and 'meaning'. As I explained above, Davidson treats the connection between radical interpretation and meaning as essential.[16]

Wright's second requirement is that response-dependence biconditionals be non-reductive and non-eliminative. Davidson never claims to reduce meaning to or eliminate it in favor of anything else. As Ernest Lepore and Kirk Ludwig observe, for Davidson, the position of the radical interpreter is "the fundamental standpoint from which to consider questions of thought and meaning" (2007, p. 338). The radical interpreter can determine all the semantic details of a situation. And radical interpretation itself leaves the analysis in terms of meaning. As we saw above, Davidson's canonical work on meaning opens: "What is it for words to mean what they do?" (2001d/1984, p. xiii). Davidson's aim is elucidation rather than reduction or elimination. 'Meaning' and its cognates can and must appear on both sides of RI.

---

15. See Crispin Wright (1988, pp. 19–22; 1989, p. 247; 1993, pp. 77–82; 1999, pp. 114–17) regarding the first; Wright (1989, p. 247–48; 1993, p. 78; 1999, pp. 112, 120–23), the third; and Wright (1999/1992, ch. 3. append.; 1993, pp. 77–82; 2001, pp. 191–99), the fourth. The second requirement is implicit in these and proximal passages.

16. I say more in Chapter Nine, §4, about what Davidson takes to be the conceptual connection between radical interpretation and meaning. Davidson makes other claims intended to be *a priori*, e.g., "What makes interpretation possible is that we can dismiss a priori the chance of massive error" (2001d/1984, p. 169). See Glock (2003, pp. 251–52), Manning (2006), and Lepore and Ludwig (2007, pp. 168–69, n. 138–39, p. 331, n. 250). In Chapter Five I consider what amount to Davidson's arguments against Dualism, themselves intended to be *a priori*.

Wright's third requirement is that response-dependence biconditionals are to be specified non-trivially. As we saw above, Davidson analyzes what is involved in being a normal radical interpreter under normal conditions of radical interpretation. He spent much of his career doing so. There is no triviality here.

Finally, as we saw in Chapters Two and Three, satisfying Wright's fourth requirement is on my view optional for a biconditional to be response-dependent. Nonetheless it is worth considering whether RI does satisfy it. That requirement is that the biconditional be read as extension-determining rather than extension-reflecting. Let me focus on terms to recall all possible options, from Pettit, Crispin Wright, and Mark Johnston:

(a) *Pettit* implicitly reads response-dependence biconditionals as extension-reflecting. He thinks that such biconditionals describe (or "reflect") ontologically antecedent facts. He is concerned with the mastery of terms, where their mastery acquisitively depends on subjective responses to objects in the world.

(b) *Wright* explicitly reads response-dependence biconditionals as extension-determining. He thinks that such biconditionals constitute (or "determine") ontological facts in an asymmetric way. He is concerned with the meaning of terms, where their meaning constitutively depends on subjective responses to objects in the world.

(c) *Johnston* explicitly rejects Wright's distinction because he thinks that response-dependence biconditionals express ontological interdependence. He thinks that such biconditionals constitute ontological facts in a symmetric way. He is concerned with the meaning of terms, though now their meaning and the correlative subjective responses to objects in the world are constitutively interdependent.[17]

Whom does Davidson follow? He cannot follow Pettit. His account of radical interpretation is meant to answer: "What is it for words to mean what they do?" It is not meant to answer: "What allows us to master words?" Radical interpretation is not an account of language learning. It concerns meaning rather than mastery, and so constitution rather than acquisition. Does Davidson follow Wright in thinking that RI expresses a constitutive *dependence* of meaning *on* responses or Johnston in thinking that it expresses a constitutive *interdependence between* meaning and responses? Davidson never says anything allowing me to answer this. Let me therefore acknowledge that he is offering some

---

17. See Philip Pettit (2002, especially pp. 12, 13, 15, 52, 78), Johnston (1993), and Wright (1999/1992, ch. 3. append.; 1993, pp. 77–82; 2001, pp. 191–99), respectively.

kind of account of meaning and so some kind of ontological theory of terms. RI entails that empirical terms in some manner constitutively depend on what a normal radical interpreter under normal conditions of radical interpretation interprets them to mean. We can then say that, for Davidson, all empirical terms mean what they do *in virtue of* the subjective and objective sources associated with radical interpretation.

Now, for Davidson, the radical interpreter can interpret all of a speaker's empirical terms. The meaning of each would be linked essentially to the radical interpreter's responses to the speaker's behavior and environment. And, as we saw above, those responses are subjective, while the speaker's behavior and environment are objective. All of a speaker's empirical terms are therefore linked essentially to subjective and objective sources. Hence RI is a form of Dualism:

DUALISM: All empirical concepts, terms, or properties are linked essentially to subjective and objective sources.

Davidson's focus is on terms. Moreover, because Davidson's Dualism concerns meaning rather than mastery, it is ontological. Hence RI is an instance of this:

ONTOLOGICAL DUALISM: All empirical concepts, terms, or properties are constituted essentially out of subjective and objective sources.

Davidson also is committed to Ontological Princiblism:

ONTOLOGICAL PRINCIPLISM: The subjective source of all empirical concepts, terms, or properties takes the form of subjective principles constitutive of those concepts, terms, or properties.

For him, not just any responses but only charitable ones—ones guided by the principle of charity—are relevant. In basic cases the radical interpreter correlates a speaker's sentences with truth conditions that describe what from the interpreter's perspective would be perceptually salient features of the environment were the interpreter in the speaker's spot. The principle of charity offers the subject the source, her own subjective capacities, to interpret her speaker's utterances. The subjective source of the meaning of a speaker's terms takes the form of the principle of charity itself. In fact the principle of charity is doubly subjective. On the one hand, as I explain in more detail in Chapter Five, for Davidson, the principle derives from the subject's "underlying methodology of interpretation" (2001d/1984, p. 197). And that methodology, though, according to Davidson, the only one that interpreters have, is nevertheless a convention that they follow. On the other hand, as we just saw, the principle of charity requires that the radical interpreter rely on her own responses and ultimately capacities. And, as we saw above, Davidson is explicit that any interpreter's responses (and so capacities) are constrained by "the way we are constructed (evolution had something to do with this)" (2002, p. 202) and that, "[i]f some such discriminative mechanisms were not in our genes, none could be learned" (p. 118).

Further, for Davidson, the principle of charity is distinct from any claims about what particular terms mean. The principle—that in basic cases the radical interpreter correlate a speaker's sentences with truth conditions that describe what from the interpreter's perspective would be perceptually salient features of the environment were the interpreter in the speaker's spot—is distinct from the interpretive claim that 'roja' in Spanish means red. Such interpretive claims are susceptible to empirical justification and verification. Davidson explains:

> A theory of meaning (in my mildly perverse sense) is an empirical theory, and its ambition is to account for the workings of a natural language. Like any theory, it may be tested by comparing some of its consequences with the facts (2001d/1984, p. 24).

Interpretive claims are therefore empirical, deriving from the radical interpreter's applying the principle of charity (a subjective source) to a speaker's observable behavior and environment (which, from the interpreter's perspective, is an objective source). According to Davidson, however, the principle of charity is not itself empirical. It "cannot be a factual question" (Davidson quoted in Hans-Johann Glock 2003, p. 252) whether the principle of charity applies to speakers. If it cannot be factual, then it must be *a priori*. The principle of charity is itself therefore insusceptible to empirical justification or verification. That makes it epistemologically *a priori*. Davidson even calls the principle "synthetic *a priori*" (2001b/1980, p. 221). In fact, as Kant himself maintains that "[w]e cannot **think** any object except through categories" (1998/1787, B165), embedded in his synthetic *a priori* judgments, so Davidson maintains that we cannot *interpret* any utterances except through the principle of charity. Unlike Kant's synthetic *priori* principles, however, which are meant to derive from the subject's transcendental unity of apperception, Davidson's synthetic *a priori* principle is meant to derive from conventions of interpretation. That makes it metaphysically *a priori*.[18] Hence Davidson is a Principled Ontological Kantian concerning terms:

> ONTOLOGICAL KANTIANISM: All empirical concepts, terms, or properties are constituted essentially out of subjective and objective sources. The subjective source may take the form of subjective constitutive principles.

---

18. See Goldberg (2012a, §4). See Kathrin Glüer (2006, pp. 347–48) on the connection between the principle of charity's constitutivity and its synthetic apriority. Stephen Turner (2011) argues that Davidson's appeal to normativity itself requires synthetic apriority.

Indeed Davidson explicitly regards the principle of charity as a constitutive principle in the philosophy of mind (2001b/1980, essays 12, 13), and given RI he implicitly treats it as one in the philosophy of language.

Two more things about radical interpretation need saying. First, as we saw in Chapter Two, all Kantians are committed to noumenalism. And, as we saw in Chapter Three, Ontological Kantians concerning terms can be committed to the possibility of incommensurability. Yet Davidson (2001d/1984, essay 13) argues from radical interpretation against both the intelligibility of noumenalism and the possibility of incommensurability. Because these arguments both allegedly follow from his arguments *against* Dualism, I postpone discussion of them until Chapter Five, where I consider Davidson's arguments themselves.

And second, Davidson does not think that we ourselves are radical interpreters. We do not explicitly construct charitable truth theories, even if we might do so implicitly. Nor do we rely solely on a speaker's observable behavior and environment. We always have some prior insight into a speaker's language, based on previous encounters, hunches, *etc*. Davidson introduces radical interpretation to show the minimal evidence required to interpret a speaker's terms: "The point of the 'epistemic position' of the radical interpreter is not that it exhausts the evidence available to an actual interpreter, but that it arguably provides sufficient evidence for interpretation" (1994, p. 121). For Davidson, though we ordinary interpreters bring background knowledge to interpretation, radical interpretation is all that an interpreter *would* need to interpret a language.[19] Regardless, insofar as we bring more than is necessary, our results (if acquired carefully, *etc*.) would be consistent with those of the radical interpreter. Moreover, as I explain in §5 and Chapter Five, Davidson would maintain that the principle of charity is itself necessary for *any* language user—radical interpreter or otherwise—to interpret a speaker's sentences.

2. LANGUAGE LEARNING AND KANTIANISM

Davidson discusses language learning in several different articles (2002, essays 2, 3, 6, 8, 9, 13; 2004, essay 9; 2005b, essays 1, 4, 7, 8, 9). He imagines language learning in basic cases—which, as we saw in §1 in the context of radical interpretation, concern ostensible objects—like this. When a teacher thinks that a learner is looking at a chair, the teacher utters, "Chair," and ostends to the

---

19. Fodor and Lepore (1992, ch. 3) and Fodor (1994) are therefore wrong that, for Davidson, all interpretation is radical.

chair. The learner correlates utterances of "chair" with her teacher's ostensions. Davidson explains:

> The teacher is responding to two things: the external situation and the responses of the learner. The learner is responding to two things: the external situation and the responses of the teacher. All these relations are causal. Thus the essential triangle is formed which makes communication about shared objects and events possible. But it is also this triangle that determines the *contents* of the learner's terms and thoughts when these become complex enough to deserve the term (2002, p. 203, emphasis mine).

Hence triangulation is crucial not only to radical interpretation but also to language learning. Here we see some of the connection that Davidson draws between language learning, responses, and meaning (or "content").[20] In fact Davidson's account of language learning

> is not just a story about how we learn to *use* words: it must also be an essential part of an account of what words refer to, and what they *mean*. ... [I]n the simplest and most basic cases, words and sentences derive their meaning from the objects and circumstances in whose presence they were learned (2002, pp. 43–44, emphasis mine).

Now Davidson does not maintain that every term in one's language was learned directly *via* triangulation. He describes only the "simplest and most basic" cases. Regardless, Davidson explains, "for someone to think or say that the cat is on the mat"—or anything else—"there must be a causal history of that person that traces back, directly or indirectly, to the triangular experiences" (2001a, p. 293). The causal history would be *direct* insofar as the learner learned any of her terms *via* triangulation. That is how above the language learner learned 'chair'. The causal history would be *indirect* insofar as the learner learned any of her terms by appealing to terms that she learned *via* triangulation—and so by appealing to terms *like* 'chair'.[21]

---

20. By 'terms' and 'thoughts' 'contents' Davidson means what I mean by terms' 'meaning' and concepts' 'content' (or subject matter), respectively.

21. See Catherine J. L. Talmage (1997), Claudine Verheggen (1997, 2007), Peter M. S. Hacker (1998), Steven Yalowitz (1999), John Fennell (2000), William Child (2001), Peter Pagin (2001), Glock (2003, p. 260), Martin Montminy (2003), Ingar Brink (2004), Maria Lasonen and Tomáš Marvan (2004), Jason Bridges (2006), and Goldberg (2009b, pp. 265–67) for more on Davidson on language learning.

This suggests that Davidson's account of language learning can itself be understood as a response-dependence theory of terms. A term's use and meaning both depend on how a language learner learned to use that term in response to objects in the world. It also suggests that Davidson's account is a form of Epistemological *and* Ontological Kantianism. It is a form of *Epistemological Kantianism* insofar as the "triangle" determines "how we learn to *use* words." That makes language learning an account of learning or mastery. It is a form of *Ontological Kantianism* insofar as employing triangulation to learn how to use words "must also be an essential part of an account of what words ... mean." That makes it an account of meaning.[22]

Something else about Davidson's account of language learning is noteworthy. The learner's own 'chair' is used to mean, and does mean, chair if and only if she *herself* learned it to mean chair. Learners learn the mastery and meaning of their own terms, though their teachers help. For Davidson, therefore, while there is overlap between the use and meaning of different individuals' terms, what I have been calling a language learner's "language" amounts to an evolving *idiolect*. Every speaker speaks a language that is strictly speaking unique and changing. That is why Davidson maintains that "there is no such thing as a language, not if a language is anything like what many philosophers and linguists have supposed" (2005b, p. 107).[23] Hence, as we saw in Chapter Two, Pettit's account of language learning is *anthropocentric*. The mastery of terms is centered on paradigmatic responses of human beings generally. As we saw in Chapter Three, Kuhn's account of language learning is *ethnocentric*. The mastery and meaning of terms are centered on paradigmatic responses of members of communities specifically. As I explain here, Davidson's account of language learning is *idiocentric*. The mastery and meaning of terms are centered on paradigmatic responses of an individual particularly.

We can now see the connection between this and response-dependence. By a 'normal language learner under normal conditions of language learning' I mean a language learner who has adequate perceptual and other cognitive abilities to learn a term's use and meaning by being in a triangular situation with her teacher or by appealing to terms learned in such a situation. For Davidson, *if* such a learner learned that her terms have a certain use

---

22. "The Davidsonian claim regarding the role of triangulation is, in this respect, not merely an *epistemological*, but an *ontological* thesis—it concerns the grounds for the possibility of content, or, to put the matter more directly, it concerns the very *being* of content" (Malpas 2011b, p. 263) or meaning.

23. See Davidson (2001d/1984, pp. 276-77; 1993, p. 117; 2002, pp. 88-89, 114-15; 2005a, p. 52; 2005b, essay 7, 8) for his understanding of languages as idiolects. See Davidson (2001d/1984, essay 11; 2002, p. 89; 2005b, essays 7, 8) for his understanding of idiolects as evolving.

and meaning, then they have that use and meaning in her language. Think of our example learner and 'chair'. Conversely, for Davidson, *only if* such a learner learned that her terms have a certain use and meaning do they have that use and meaning in her language. The biconditional in this direction is implicit in Davidson's talk of how learning is an "*essential* part of an account of what words ... mean" (2002, p. 43, emphasis mine) and so are also used. Further, as I explain in §4, Davidson (2002, essay 2) presupposes this direction of the biconditional with his thought-experimental Swampman. Swampman never learned what any terms mean, from which Davidson concludes that Swampman's terms cannot mean anything. Contrapositively Swampman's terms would have meaning (and could be used as such) only if Swampman had learned what they mean.

So Davidson is again committed to a biconditional. Moreover this biconditional can also be formulated, even if not especially intuitively, similarly to how I formulated the biconditionals to which Pettit and Kuhn are committed:

LL TERM: Something is x for a speaker if and only if as a normal language learner under normal conditions of language learning she learned to call it ⌜y⌝ to mean x in her language.

As in §1, I have said here that the language learner learned to call something ⌜y⌝ to mean x, and kept the variables distinct, because the learner's language is not necessarily the same as mine, the meta-language in which I phrased the biconditional. Regardless the language learner's responses as she and her teacher triangulated objects in the world are subjective—grounded on her specific conceptual, linguistic, or perceptual capacities. Moreover, for Davidson, as (as we saw in §1) the radical interpreter's responses are constrained by "the way we are constructed (evolution had something to do with this)" (2002, p. 202) and, "[i]f some such discriminative mechanisms were not in our genes, none could be learned" (p. 118), so the language learner's own responses are likewise constrained. Conversely those objects that the teacher and learner triangulate, and from the learner's perspective her teacher's responses themselves, are objective. They are from that perspective part of the learner-, and so subject-, independent world.

Hence LL Term connects terms to subjective and objective sources. Moreover, for Davidson, because learning is an *essential* part of what words mean, and a creature like Swampman who did not learn what words mean *cannot* mean anything by them, LL Term expresses an essential connection between language learning and meaning. For Davidson, it is no accident that 'chair' means chair if and only if a normal language user under normal conditions of language learning learned that it means chair. It is essential. It follows from the nature of language learning and meaning themselves.

Now, as with RI Term, LL Term does not itself tell us whether Davidson is after a response-dependence theory of terms or properties. We again however know independently that Davidson is after (at least) an account of language learning and so (at least) one of terms. Something is red for a learner if and only if as a normal language learner under normal conditions of language learning she learned to call it some term to mean red, because *what it is for some learner to master the term* and *for that term to mean red* depends on her having learned to call it that. Regardless, as with radical interpretation, formulating Davidson's view on language learning as a canonical response-dependence biconditional is not especially intuitive. My reformulation of LL Term is however more complicated. As *per* LL Term, Davidson is committed to the claim that 'roja' in (an individual's) Spanish (idiolect) *both* is used to mean *and* does mean red if and only if a normal language learner of (that) Spanish under normal conditions of language learning learned that the term has that meaning and use.[24] Generalizing we see that Davidson is committed to the following, which I call 'LL' (*simpliciter*) to parallel RI as an account of meaning:

> LL: For any empirical term in *L*, the term means what it does if and only if a normal language learner of *L* under normal conditions of language learning learned that the term has that meaning.[25]

'Roja' in Spanish means red if and only if a normal learner of the language under normal conditions of language learning learned that the term has that meaning. But we can also see that Davidson is committed to the following, which I call 'LL-A', an account of language learning concerning *acquisition* in particular:

> LL-A: For any empirical term in *L*, the term has the use that it does if and only if a normal language learner of *L* under normal conditions of language learning learned that the term has that use.[26]

'Roja' in Spanish is used to mean red if and only if a normal language learner of the language under normal conditions of language learning learned that the term has that use. Both LL and LL-A involve the same subjective and objective sources as LL Term does. The language learner's responses as she and her teacher triangulated objects in the world (and ultimately the learner's specific

---

24. I follow Davidson in talking about English, Spanish, *etc.*, languages. Nonetheless Davidson and I both mean the speaker's particular English, Spanish, *etc.*, idiolect. See Davidson (2005b, essay 8) as well as Ian Hacking (1986) and Lepore and Ludwig (2007, ch. 1).

25. As we saw in §1 with RI, Davidson is committed to this for all terms, empirical or otherwise. Again I limit myself to the empirical ones.

26. As with RI and LL, Davidson is committed to this for all terms.

conceptual, linguistic, or perceptual capacities) are subjective. Those objects and her teacher's responses to them—all falling under 'normal conditions of language learning'—are objective.

Let me focus on LL and LL-A. If Davidson thinks that LL and LL-A satisfy the first three of the four requirements extracted from Wright's view, then he is committed to their being response-dependence biconditionals. Wright's first requirement is again that such biconditionals hold *a priori*. Indeed, for Davidson, both LL and LL-A are *a priori* in both epistemological and ontological senses. They are epistemologically *a priori* insofar as they are meant to be insusceptible to empirical justification or verification. As Davidson takes the connection between meaning and radical interpretation to be "a matter of principle" (2002, p. 147), so he takes the connection between meaning and language learning to be one also. Nor does Davidson ever constrain his theorizing, concerning radical interpretation or language learning, by empirical findings or present either as vulnerable to empirical results. Conversely LL and LL-A are ontologically *a priori* insofar as they are meant to derive from a subjective source, here Davidson's conception of language learning and its connection to meaning. As Davidson maintains that his account of radical interpretation limns conceptual connections among meaning, belief, desire, truth, speaker, and interpreter, so he would likely maintain that his account of language learning limns those connections among meaning, language learning, and many of these others also. For Davidson, LL and LL-A therefore both derive from those connections and so presumably what he means by 'language learning' and 'meaning'.[27]

Wright's second requirement is that response-dependence biconditionals be non-reductive and non-eliminative. Nowhere does Davidson try to reduce meaning or use to or eliminate either in favor of anything else. LL and LL-A aim to elucidate rather than reduce or eliminate meaning or use. 'Meaning' and its cognates can and must appear on both sides of LL, and 'use' can and must appear on both sides of LL-A.

Wright's third requirement is that response-dependence biconditionals are to be specified non-trivially. In fact Davidson analyzes what is involved in being a normal language learner under normal conditions of language learning. Features of language learners engaged in language learning are described throughout his later work.

---

27. Davidson makes other claims intended to be *a priori*. See Davidson (2001d/1984, p. 169). See also Glock (2003, pp. 251–52), Manning (2006), and Lepore and Ludwig (2007, pp. 168–69, n. 138–39, p. 331, n. 250). See Chapter Five, where I consider Davidson's *a priori* arguments against Dualism.

Finally Wright's fourth requirement, which Davidson need not accept to be a response-dependence theorist, is that response-dependence biconditionals express a constitutive asymmetry. Here again are all three options:

(a) *Pettit* is concerned with the mastery of terms, where their mastery acquisitively depends on subjective responses to objects in the world.
(b) *Wright* is concerned with the meaning of terms, where their meaning constitutively depends on subjective responses to objects in the world.
(c) *Johnston* is concerned with the meaning of terms, though now their meaning and the correlative subjective responses to objects in the world are constitutively interdependent.

Whom does Davidson follow here? For starters, Davidson follows Pettit. Davidson's account of language learning, like Pettit's, is "a story about how we learn to *use* words." Mastery is the aim, which is what LL-A encapsulates. Nevertheless, Davidson continues, his account " ... must also be an essential part of an account of what words ... *mean*" (2002, pp. 43–44, emphases mine). Meaning is also the aim, which is what LL encapsulates. By constituting a term, and so creating its meaning, a learner herself acquires the term, and so learns its use. Hence, besides following Pettit for LL-A, Davidson must follow Wright or Johnston for LL. Whom does he follow there? Davidson never says anything allowing me to answer this either. Let me therefore acknowledge that Davidson is offering besides his account of mastery some kind of account of meaning. LL entails that empirical terms in some manner constitutively depend on what a normal language learner under normal conditions of language learning learned them to mean. We can then say that, for Davidson, all empirical terms mean what they do *in virtue of* the subjective and objective sources associated with language learning.

Now, as we have seen, Davidson thinks that every term in a learner's idiolect "traces back, directly or indirectly, to the triangular experiences" (2001a, p. 293) involved in language learning. So LL and LL-A would themselves apply to every empirical term. The meaning and mastery of each would be linked essentially to the language learner's responses to objects as triangulated with her teacher as well as her teacher's behavior given them. LL and LL-A would themselves therefore be forms of Dualism:

DUALISM: All empirical concepts, terms, or properties are linked essentially to subjective and objective sources.

They both concern terms. Because LL concerns meaning rather than mastery, it is also an instance of this:

ONTOLOGICAL DUALISM: All empirical concepts, terms, or properties are constituted essentially out of subjective and objective sources.

Conversely, because LL-A concerns mastery rather than meaning, it is instead an instance of this:

EPISTEMOLOGICAL DUALISM: All empirical concepts, terms, or properties are acquired by a subject's appealing essentially to subjective and objective sources.

So, regarding language learning, Davidson is both an Ontological and an Epistemological Kantian. He is a Principled one in each case too. The principle of charity functions in language learning much as it does in radical interpretation. Teacher and learner are guided in their triangulations by assuming that each would agree on perceptually salient features of the environment. As we saw in §1, this would amount to each attributing to the other beliefs that she would herself have in the other's spot. In basic cases only by taking her teacher to be responding to the object to which she herself would respond in her spot can the learner triangulate objects with the teacher in any systematic fashion. Only by assuming that the teacher would find the same objects perceptually salient can the learner have some idea at what the teacher's responses are directed.[28] Reciprocal considerations apply to the learner. Again, as I explain in §5, Davidson would maintain that the principle of charity is necessary for *any* language user to learn any terms from *any other* language user at all.

The principle of charity is therefore the form that the subjective source of the interpreter's as well as the learner's and teacher's empirical terms takes. It offers the subject the source, the language user's own subjective capacities, to make sense of objects that she and her interlocutor are triangulating. This time we might understand the principle as deriving not from the subject's "underlying methodology of interpretation" (2001d/1984, p. 197) but from her underlying methodology of language learning. The principle still directs all language users to rely on their own responses, which are constrained by things like "the way we are constructed (evolution had something to do with this)" (2002, p. 202) and "some such discriminative mechanisms ... in our genes" (p. 118). So the principle remains subjective in the sense of being methodological or conventional, and relying on genetic mechanisms. Now methodology, convention, and genetic mechanisms are subjective sources. That makes the principle of charity ontologically *a priori*. Moreover, for Davidson,

---

28. See Davidson (2002, p. 121).

the principle is again distinct from any empirical claim, here about what terms mean or how they are used. It is presupposed by language learning without itself being susceptible to empirical justification or verification. As Davidson takes the connection between meaning and radical interpretation to be "a matter of principle" (2002, p. 147), so he would take the connection between meaning and language learning to be such a matter too. That makes the principle of charity epistemologically *a priori* also.

Hence Davidson is committed to Ontological Principlism concerning language learning:

ONTOLOGICAL PRINCIPLISM: The subjective source of all empirical concepts, terms, or properties takes the form of subjective principles constitutive of those concepts, terms, or properties.

Focusing on LL, we see that a learner's terms mean what they do in virtue of the learner's applying the principle of charity, essential to triangulation, to her teacher and environment. Likewise, focusing on LL-A, we see that a learner's terms are mastered in virtue of the learner's applying the principle of charity, essential to triangulation, to her teacher and environment too. Davidson is then committed to Epistemological Principlism as well:

EPISTEMOLOGICAL PRINCIPLISM: The subjective source of all empirical concepts, terms, or properties takes the form of subjective principles acquisitive of those concepts, terms, or properties.

And in virtue of being committed to two kinds of Dualism Davidson is committed to two kinds of Kantianism:

ONTOLOGICAL KANTIANISM: All empirical concepts, terms, or properties are constituted essentially out of subjective and objective sources. The subjective source may take the form of subjective constitutive principles.

EPISTEMOLOGICAL KANTIANISM: All empirical concepts, terms, or properties are acquired by a subject's appealing essentially to subjective and objective sources. The subjective source may take the form of subjective acquisitive principles.

In each case his focus is on terms. And each of these kinds of Kantianism is Principled. Moreover LL, as a kind of Ontological Kantianism, treats the principle of charity as a constitutive principle, while LL-A, as a kind of Epistemological Kantianism, treats it as an acquisitive principle.

Finally we know that all Kantians are committed to noumenalism and that Ontological Kantians concerning terms can be committed to the possibility of incommensurability. As I explained in §1, I sort all this out for Davidson in Chapter Five.

3. RECONCILABLE AND IRRECONCILABLE DIFFERENCES

Hence encapsulated in RI Davidson's account of radical interpretation commits him to Ontological Kantianism. Encapsulated in LL Davidson's account of language learning also commits him to Ontological Kantianism, while encapsulated in LL-A it commits him instead to Epistemological Kantianism:

> RI: For any empirical term in L, the term means what it does if and only if a normal radical interpreter under normal conditions of radical interpretation would interpret it in L to have that meaning.
> LL: For any empirical term in L, the term means what it does if and only if a normal language learner of L under normal conditions of language learning learned that the term has that meaning.
> LL-A: For any empirical term in L, the term has the use that it does if and only if a normal language learner of L under normal conditions of language learning learned that the term has that use.

RI, LL, and LL-A differ in three noteworthy ways. The first two are reconcilable. The third is not.

First, RI involves interpreting a *language*, presumably something having multiple speakers, while LL and LL-A entail that languages are really evolving idiolects and so have only one speaker. Nonetheless, though when discussing radical interpretation Davidson does speak about truth and meaning "in a language," he could also speak about truth and meaning "in an idiolect." A radical interpreter's interpretation of one speaker's Spanish (*e.g.*) would at least in small details differ from her interpretation of another speaker's. No two speakers mean exactly the same thing by all their terms.[29] Davidson's accounts of radical interpretation and language learning can both support the view that meaning is speaker-specific. In fact Davidson later maintains that the charitable, Tarski-style truth theories that the radical interpreter would construct are themselves more specific than even idiocentric: "I shall therefore treat theories of truth as applicable in the first place to individual speakers *at various periods or even moments of their lives*" (2005a, p. 52, emphasis mine). In radical interpretation the "speaker" is an individual on a particular occasion. Davidson can likewise in language learning treat the "learner" as an individual on a particular occasion. This makes sense of his own claim in language learning that languages are *evolving* idiolects. For Davidson, therefore, the subjective scope of RI, LL, *and* LL-A is not idiocentric generally but "occasionalist" specifically. Nonetheless, because an occasionalist account would still be idiocentric, I continue to count Davidson as an idiocentrist.

---

29. See Davidson (2005b, essay 7).

Second, according to Davidson (2001d/1984, p. 154), any radical interpreter could interpret a term to mean $x_1, x_2, x_3, \ldots,$ or x_n, with compensatory adjustments elsewhere; and there would be no fact of the matter about which is *the* right interpretation. Because radical interpretation requires constructing truth theories based on a speaker's observable behavior and environment, possible interpretations are not unrestricted. Nonetheless a radical interpreter could in principle interpret 'roja' in Spanish to mean green if she interpreted 'rosa' to mean grass and made similar systematic interpretations elsewhere. This is Davidson's thesis of the indeterminacy of interpretation (or "indeterminacy of meaning" [2001d/1984, p. 154]).[30] It follows from RI. Nonetheless Davidson claims no correlative thesis concerning language learning, following from LL or LL-A. Regardless interpretive indeterminacy would itself apply to language learning. The radical interpreter could use different interpretations to track what the language learner learns—concerning meaning, LL, or mastery, LL-A. From the interpreter's perspective the language learner could learn that 'roja' in Spanish means, or is merely used to mean, red *or* green, provided that either is consistent with an overall interpretation of the learner's language. Though indeterminacy applies only to interpretation, that interpretive indeterminacy itself applies to language learning.

And third, RI connects terms to responses that a subject *would* have, while LL and LL-A both connect terms to responses that a subject *did* have. RI is therefore *ahistoricist* insofar as it requires no history of actual responses. It shares this ahistoricism with the response-dependence biconditionals that I extracted from Johnston, Wright, Pettit, and Kuhn. Nonetheless LL and LL-A are both *historicist* insofar as they do require a history of actual responses. They share this historicism with no biconditional that I have considered. Unlike the first two, this third noteworthy difference among RI, LL, and LL-A is irreconcilable. We see this by considering the curious case of Swampman.

4. THE CURIOUS CASE OF SWAMPMAN

In §1 we made the casual acquaintance of Davidson's (2002, essay 2) thought-experimental Swampman. Here is a proper introduction:

Suppose lightning strikes a dead tree in a swamp; I am standing nearby. My body is reduced to its elements, while entirely by coincidence (and out of different molecules) the tree is turned into my physical replica. My replica,

---

30. Davidson (2001d/1984, pp. 24–26) introduces the notion of the indeterminacy of interpretation in his essay on truth and meaning (essay 2) and mentions it throughout his *corpus*. He thinks that it is innocuous. See Chapter Eight, §1.

Swampman, moves exactly as I did; according to its nature it departs the swamp, encounters and seems to recognize my friends, and appears to return their greetings in English. It moves into my house and seems to write articles on radical interpretation. No one can tell the difference.

But there *is* a difference. ... [Swampman] can't mean what I do by the word 'house', for example, since the sound 'house' Swampman makes was not learned in a context that would give it the right meaning—or any meaning at all. Indeed, I don't see how my replica can be said to mean anything by the sounds it makes, nor to have any thoughts (2002, p. 19).

Because Swampman's sex and gender would both be male, and because it is unclear why Swampman's lacking a causal history would negate either, let me regard Swampman and Davidson both as men. We can then ask how each and *his doppelgänger* compare.

For starters, because Swampman would exhibit the same behavior in the same environment as Davidson would, each would utter, "House," when asked what each calls a house. "No one can tell the difference. But," Davidson explains, "there *is* a difference. ... [Swampman] can't mean what I do by the term 'house' ... since the sound 'house' Swampman makes was not learned in a context that would give it the right meaning." In fact, Davidson is saying, since Swampman never learned what his terms mean, Swampman's 'house' cannot have any meaning. That verdict appeals to LL. 'House' in Swampman's language means house if and only if Swampman learned that 'house' means house. Since Swampman never learned that 'house' means house (or anything else), Swampman's 'house' cannot mean house (or anything else). Davidson's account of language learning is an Ontological Kantianism that is both *idiocentric* and *historicist*. It is *idiocentric* because Swampman's language is his own. The homophony between his and Davidson's 'house' does not endow the former with meaning from the latter. It is *historicist* because a term's meaning is dependent on a history of subjective responses. Having no history, Swampman's 'house' can have no meaning.

Though not realizing it, Davidson's other Ontological Kantianism, RI, contradicts this. If no one can tell the difference between Swampman and Davidson, then no radical interpreter can tell the difference either. Now on Davidson's view a radical interpreter would interpret Davidson's own terms to have meaning. But then, because Davidson and Swampman would exhibit the same behavior in the same environment, a radical interpreter would interpret Swampman's terms to have meaning also. Though RI can be idiocentric—the radical interpreter is interpreting Swampman's terms and not necessarily anyone else's—it is ahistoricist. The meaning of Swampman's terms is independent of any history of subjective responses.

Hence, according to RI, Swampman's terms have meaning, while, according to LL, they do not. The ahistoricist Ontological Kantianism of RI and historicist Ontological Kantianism of LL are inconsistent. How should Davidson resolve this? Three resolutions in particular come to mind. Davidson could (i) reject both RI and LL, (ii) retain RI and reject LL, or (iii) reject RI and retain LL.[31]

We have seen no reason that Davidson should reject both RI and LL. So drastic a move would be unmotivated. So I need not consider (i).

There are two reasons for Davidson to choose (ii) over (iii). First, the cost of rejecting RI is relatively high. As I explained at the outset, Davidson stands apart from perhaps all other analytic philosophers in the deepness and systematicity of his view. Its systematicity is itself partly evidenced by the connection of so much of what he says to radical interpretation, which RI encapsulates. In *philosophy of language* Davidson (2001d/1984, essay 2) anticipates RI when he proposes that a charitable, Tarski-style truth theory amounts to a meaning truth. RI then becomes his account of interpretation (2001d/1984, essay 9), which he elaborates throughout his career (*e.g.*, 2002, essay 10; 2005a, ch. 3). In *epistemology*, because Davidson (2001d/1984; 2002; 2005a, ch. 3) maintains that terms and concepts are interpreted together, the connection between RI and concepts is central to his results. As I explain in Chapter Five, whether or not Davidson succeeds, he relies on RI to argue against the very idea of a conceptual scheme and with it conceptual relativism and empiricism (2001d/1984, essay 13), as well as against skepticism about other minds and the external world (2002, essay 10, 14).[32] Finally, as I explain in Chapter Nine, in *action theory* Davidson (2004, essays 8, 10; 2005a, ch. 3) maintains that the radical interpreter determines what a speaker means, believes, and desires, and can in turn discern a speaker's behavior as actions. RI binds Davidson's work in theoretical and practical philosophy itself.[33] Conversely LL is not significantly integrated into Davidson's other positions. It has little to do with the rest of Davidson's philosophy of language. It has almost nothing to do with his epistemology. And it has nothing to do with his action theory.

That is the first reason to choose (ii) over (iii). The second is this. Meaning is by nature connected to interpersonal communication. And the purpose of meaningful utterances is in their primary instance to allow language users to

---

31. As I show elsewhere (2012b, §6), conjoining RI and LL into a single account amounts to (ii), while disjoining them amounts to (iii). See Goldberg (2008b, 2012b) for Lepore and Ludwig's (2007, pp. 337–39) discussion of Swampman.

32. See Goldberg (2003) for Davidson's argument against skepticism about the external world.

33. See Goldberg and Mark LeBar (2012) for this binding.

coordinate behavior. Meaningful utterances are the means *by which* language users collectively respond to their environment. In fact language itself developed to allow individuals to act together toward common aims. And interpersonal communication proceeds by concerned parties interpreting one another and responding in turn. The connection between meaning and communication, and therefore interpretation, is conceptually basic. Admittedly communication ordinarily *presupposes* language learning. Teachers teach students what expressions mean so that they can interpret and be interpreted by others. But this presupposition is not necessary. By introducing Swampman Davidson makes us choose whether meaning is more closely connected to interpretation or learning. We should choose the former. Swampman means by his words what Davidson himself would because Swampman and we could coordinate our behavior *via* those words as easily as Davidson and we could. This is the essential role of meaning, and as the Swampman thought experiment illustrates learning need not be part of it. Davidson should retain RI and reject LL. He should choose (ii) overall.[34]

So far we have been considering RI and LL, Davidson's two kinds of Ontological Kantianism. Where does this leave LL-A, his Epistemological Kantianism? LL-A needs to be rejected too. From RI it follows that Swampman's terms have the same meaning as Davidson's would. It also follows that they have the same use. LL-A however entails that Swampman's terms have no use at all, because Swampman was never a normal language user under normal conditions of language learning. So Davidson should retain RI and reject both LL and LL-A. Hence, while in Chapter Two I engaged in Pettit's debate concerning noumenalism, and in Chapter Three I myself debated whether Kuhn's notion of incommensurability applies beyond his ethnocentric cases, here I resolved Davidson's debate between ahistoricism and historicism themselves.

5. LESSONS FOR KANTIAN CONCEPTUAL GEOGRAPHY

In this chapter we have seen how Davidson's accounts of radical interpretation and language learning amount to different response-dependence theories of terms and ultimately different, and inconsistent, kinds of Kantianism. We have also seen how Davidson should resolve the inconsistency. In this conclusion I draw six lessons for Kantian conceptual geography generally.

First, language learning can entail Epistemological Kantianism, as it does for Pettit, or Epistemological and Ontological Kantianism, as it does for Kuhn

---

34. Nor does everyone share Davidson's (2002, essay 2) view that Swampman's utterances are meaningless. See Goldberg (2008b, p. 382, n. 24).

and Davidson. This is so even though in Davidson's case it should be taken to entail only Ontological Kantianism as encapsulated in RI.

Second, while Pettit, Kuhn, and Davidson on radical interpretation are ahistoricist Kantians, Davidson on language learning is a historicist Kantian. Hence all Kantians can come in those two kinds based on whether a term's meaning or mastery is independent of or dependent on a history of subjective responses. They can concern the relevant timing of the subjective.

Third, while Pettit is an anthropocentric Kantian, and Kuhn is an ethnocentric Kantian, Davidson is an idiocentric Kantian. Hence all Kantians can come in these three kinds based on which subjects' responses are relevant: human beings generally, members of a community specifically, or individuals particularly, respectively.

The fourth lesson requires deeper extraction. So far I have understood anthropocentrism, ethnocentrism, and idiocentrism as concerning subjective responses. But I can also understand them as concerning subjective principles— where those principles *guide* those responses in virtue of being the form that the responses take. Though Pettit has no such principles, Kant does; for him, those principles, his synthetic *a priori* judgments, are anthropocentric. They are meant to guide normal human beings under normal conditions of observation. That is one role of the categories and forms of intuition embedded in synthetic *a priori* judgments. Likewise subjective principles implicit within Kuhn's paradigms (and ultimately lexica) are themselves ethnocentric. They are meant to guide normal members of communities under normal conditions of observation. That is one role of paradigms. Hence all Kantians can be anthropocentric, ethnocentric, or idiocentric concerning responses *and* principles guiding them.

Fifth, these responses and principles can come in yet another variety. For Davidson's subjective principle, the principle of charity, is *logocentric*. The principle of charity is intended to be a principle guiding anyone possessing or capable of possessing language (*logos*) when interpreting or language learning generally. It is centered on paradigmatic language user responses (and ultimately capacities) generally. Davidson's aim is to answer "What is it for words to mean what they do?" (2001d/1984, p. xiii) not "What is it for *human* words to mean what they do?" Nor does Davidson ever limit himself to human languages. He both mentions hypothetical non-human languages, "Saturnian" and "Plutonian" (2001d/1984, p. 186), and invokes an omniscient interpreter who *qua* omniscient would not be human but *qua* interpreter would have to appeal to the principle of charity to interpret a speaker's terms (2001d/1984, essay 14; 2002, essay 10). Davidson's principle of charity is meant to guide *all* these language users—in fact all language users generally—in interpretation and learning. Though Davidson's 'house' in his idiolect means house, Davidson's principle of charity is a principle for anyone with *any* idiolect at all. While I explain this in more detail in Chapter Five, let me note here that all Kantians can be logocentric, anthropocentric, ethnocentric, *or* idiocentric concerning subjective responses and subjective principles governing responses.

The sixth and final lesson elaborates on the fifth. Logocentrism, anthropocentrism, ethnocentrism, and idiocentrism concerning subjective responses and subjective principles can come apart. Davidson's two kinds of Kantianism are idiocentric concerning responses. Terms mean what they do and are mastered relative to responses of individual language users. Nonetheless Davidson's two kinds of Kantianism are logocentric concerning principles. Terms are interpreted and learned by appealing to a principle for all language users. For Davidson, the principle of charity is necessary for individuals particularly, members of communities specifically, human beings generally, and any language user at all to interpret or learn a language. As I explain in Chapter Five, Davidson's idiocentrism and logocentrism entail both that each language is its speaker's own and that all languages are mutually interpretable, respectively.

The converse, though not Davidson's view, is possible too. Terms could mean what they do and be mastered relative to a universal language. Perhaps there could be a language shared or at least shareable by all language users, possibly grounded on logic. Meaning and mastery would be logocentric. But a language user's interpreting and learning those terms could be guided by principles specific to her own individual method. Perhaps each individual could follow her own procedure or have her own particular way to make sense of this universal language. Such logocentrism and idiocentrism would now entail that each language is ultimately all speakers' but that each speaker interprets these languages in ways distinct to herself, respectively. Other combinations of logocentrism, anthropocentrism, ethnocentrism, and idiocentrism are possible also.

PART THREE

Defending Kantianism's Borders

FIVE

Defending Dualism

My aim in *Kantian Conceptual Geography* is to appeal to theses that can be drawn from Immanuel Kant's *Critique of Pure Reason* (1998/1787) to increase our understanding of myriad issues in analytic epistemology, philosophy of language, and metaphysics. In Part One I understood Kantianism to be any view that does satisfy Dualism and may satisfy Principlism. Principled Kantians are committed to Dualism and Principlism; un-Principled Kantians, only Dualism. While Dualism establishes Kantianism's external border, separating it from other conceptual territories, Principlism establishes an internal border, separating Principled and un-Principled kinds of Kantianism from themselves. In Part Two I examined various kinds of Kantianism resulting from various versions of Dualism and Principlism. I thereby explored the Kantian territory whose borders Dualism and Principlism establish.

Here in Part Three I defend Dualism and Principlism themselves. This reassures us that my understanding of Kantianism in Part One and exploration of Kantian territory in Part Two were not for naught. It also furthers my aim of increasing our understanding of those issues. Much about a view and issues related to it can be learned from its defense. In the next chapter I defend Principlism; in this one, Dualism:

> DUALISM: All empirical concepts, terms, or properties are linked essentially to subjective and objective sources.

Admittedly many are committed to neither Dualism nor Principlism. Absent commitment to Dualism in particular, they would not be Kantians in my sense. As we saw in Chapter One, there are in fact many who would not be. Platonic and Aristotelian realists maintain that all empirical concepts, terms, or properties are linked essentially only to an objective source. Berkeleian idealists maintain that all empirical concepts, terms, or properties are linked essentially only to a subjective source. And Lockean hybridists maintain that only some empirical concepts, terms, or properties are linked essentially to subjective and objective sources. Then there are those who deny that it is philosophically useful to talk of distinctly "subjective" or "objective" sources at all. These include most prominently in the Continental tradition Georg Wilhelm Friedrich Hegel, in the American Pragmatist tradition John Dewey, and in the analytic tradition, ironically enough, Donald Davidson. Because on certain readings of certain passages these thinkers all believe that all concepts, terms, and properties are inextricably tied to human practices, and because this view traces to Hegel, in Chapter One I identified anyone committed to such a view as a Hegelian pragmatist.

Given this understanding, Davidson would himself identify as a Hegelian pragmatist. He not only denies the philosophical usefulness of talk of "subjective" or "objective" sources however. He argues that the very idea of the distinction is unintelligible. In fact Davidson is Dualism's most determined detractor in the analytic tradition if not overall. But how can Davidson argue *against* Dualism if, as I maintained in Chapter Four, he is a Kantian and so committed *to* Dualism?[1] As I explain here, Davidson's arguments against Dualism fail. We are therefore entitled to take terminology that in Chapter Four apparently commits Davidson to Dualism actually to commit him to Dualism.

Nor is it that uncommon for a great philosopher to be committed to a position only to argue against it. On certain understandings Kant rejects speculative metaphysics only to engage in it.[2] In fact Kant himself might or might not be right when (perhaps ironically) in the *Critique of Practical Reason* he writes: "Consistency is the highest obligation of a philosopher" (1999/1788, 5:24). Nonetheless we would surely be wrong to expect that all great philosophers are always consistent. As I noted in Chapter One, shifting views—not to mention ambiguous language—might accompany all great philosophers. Perhaps given greats like Davidson *and* Kant we should split the difference between Kant's call for consistency and Ralph Waldo Emerson's oft-quoted quip: "A foolish consistency is the hobgoblin of little minds, adored by little statesmen and philosophers and divines" (2011/1841, p. 125).

Regardless Davidson really is Dualism's most determined detractor in the analytic tradition if not overall. My (unwitting) Dualist Davidson dared to dream a dream no Dualist dared to dream before: Dualism's demise. Defending Dualism against Davidson is therefore the best way to defend Dualism generally. That is my aim in this chapter.

The chapter proceeds as follows. In §1 I show that Davidson's arguments against what he calls the 'dualism of conceptual scheme and empirical content'

---

1. See Richard N. Manning (2011, §1) for different aspects of this tension.

2. See Peter F. Strawson (1975) and Paul Guyer (1987).

are arguments against what I have been calling 'Dualism'. In §2 I consider the first half of Davidson's argument against the "scheme" side of scheme/content dualism and then show that it fails. In §3 I consider the second half of Davidson's argument against the scheme side. In §4 I show that that second half also fails. In §5 I consider Davidson's argument against the "content" side of scheme/content dualism and then show that it fails as well. In §6 I conclude that Dualism's most determined detractor therefore fails to defeat Dualism. Finally in §7 I draw lessons for Kantian conceptual geography generally.

1. SCHEME/CONTENT DUALISM AND (MY) DUALISM

Discerning what Davidson means by the 'dualism of conceptual scheme and empirical content' (or 'scheme/content dualism') is difficult. Not only does Davidson sometimes sacrifice precision for poetic effect. Because his decided view is that the dualism is unintelligible, it is unclear whether he can mean anything by it at all. Let me therefore start with what Davidson takes others to claim scheme/content dualism to be and how that relates to my Dualism. Only after Davidson introduces his preferred characterization of a conceptual scheme in particular can we appreciate that his scheme/content dualists are committed to my Dualism concerning empirical concepts, terms, and properties, and so his dualism amounts to mine.

Davidson begins by trying to articulate what others take conceptual schemes to be:

Conceptual schemes, we are told, are ways of organizing experience; they are systems of categories that give form to the data of sensation; they are points of view from which individuals, cultures, or periods survey the passing scene (2001d/1984, p. 183).

Conversely empirical content would be the experience, data of sensation (Kant's "sensation" *simpliciter*), or passing scene that conceptual schemes somehow conceptualize or schematize. And, Davidson later adds, according to the dualist, "[c]ontent and scheme ... come as a pair" (2002, p. 46). This already suggests that Davidson's scheme/content dualism is a version of my Dualism. Though we see this in more detail below, conceptual schemes, *as* systems of categories or points of view, would depend on the subject. They would in fact be the subjective source of the subject's empirical concepts, terms, or properties, insofar as such schemes comprise the totality of her specific conceptual, linguistic, or perceptual capacities. Conversely empirical content, *as* the experience, data of sensation (or sensation), or passing scene, would be independent of the subject and so in my sense objective. It would in fact be the objective source of the subject's empirical concepts, terms, or properties.[3] Davidson even connects scheme/content dualism to subjective/objective dualism:

> Instead of saying it is the scheme–content dichotomy that has dominated and defined the problems of modern philosophy, then, one could as well say it is how the dualism of the objective and the subjective have been conceived (2002, p. 43).

What Davidson subsequently calls the 'myth of the subjective' (2002, essay 3) is that the subjective is ultimately distinct from the objective. The myth would apply to sources of empirical concepts, terms, and properties too.

Moreover Davidson's representative scheme/content dualists include two of our familiar Dualists. Though, as Davidson (2002, p. 40) is aware, Kant thinks that there is only one conceptual scheme, Davidson has Kant (1998/1787) in mind when he claims that conceptual schemes are "systems of categories that give form to the data of sensation" (Davidson 2001d/1984, p. 183). Singularize 'schemes' and 'systems' and this approximates Kant's view. Further, for Kant, categories (his *a priori* concepts) are subjective insofar as they derive from the subject's transcendental unity of apperception and so what unify her specific conceptual, linguistic, and perceptual capacities. Conversely the data of sensation are objective (in my sense) insofar as they do not derive from the subject at all. As Davidson later rightly remarks, all characterizations of scheme/content dualism have "a common origin in Kant" (1999a, p. 51). In fact Davidson implicitly (2001d/1984, essay 13) and explicitly (2002, p. 40; 2004, p. 237) treats Kant as the archetypal scheme/content dualist. We would be hard pressed to find disagreement.

Likewise, Davidson explains, Thomas Kuhn (2012/1962) talks about paradigms as "incommensurable systems of concepts," and so conceptual schemes, that "different observers" bring to their observations of the world (Davidson 2001d/1984, p. 187). Kuhn's paradigms (and later [2002] lexica) are subjective. The subject brings them, and thereby her community-inculcated conceptual,

---

3. Empirical content is not the same thing as what in previous chapters I have been calling a concept's 'content'. A concept's content is the concept's subject matter, the epistemological correlate of its corresponding term's meaning. For Donald Davidson, while the very idea of a concept's content is intelligible—it would, along with its corresponding term's meaning, be determinable by a radical interpreter—the very idea of empirical content is not. Moreover, as we saw in Chapter One, §2, *non-conceptual* content is the allegedly purely sensory, and so in my sense objective, subject matter of certain mental states. As I understand it, therefore, non-conceptual content would be empirical content as it figures in mental states.

linguistic, and perceptual capacities, to bear on observations of the world, itself independent of the subject and so objective.

Davidson also discusses his own mentor, Willard van Orman Quine. Quine is a scheme/content dualist and Dualist too. Quine writes: "Taken collectively, science has its double dependence upon language and experience; but this duality," Quine cautions, "is not significantly traceable into the statements of science taken one by one" (2006/1953, p. 42). Science, which consists of empirical concepts and terms used to conceive of and name empirical properties, depends on something subjective (for Quine, language and so our linguistic capacities) and something objective (experience).[4] Nonetheless, Quine explains, this "duality" is not traceable into individual statements. It is true of all statements. Now, because subjective principles would have only a subjective source—and, for Quine, no statement derives entirely from such a source—on his view there are no subjective principles. As I explain in Chapters Five and Nine, Quine, like Pettit, but unlike Kuhn, Davidson, and Kant himself, is an un-Principled Kantian.

Having considered these and other characterizations of scheme/content dualism, Davidson next proposes his preferred characterization of a conceptual scheme: "We may identify conceptual schemes with languages, then, or better, allowing for the possibility that more than one language may express the same conceptual scheme, sets of intertranslatable languages" (2001d/1984, p. 185). Empirical content would then be whatever these sets of languages process. Moreover Davidson's characterization is compatible with the characterizations offered by Kant, Kuhn, and Quine. Languages have been regarded as providing the subject *with* ways of organizing experience, systems of categories that give form to the data of sensation, and points of view to survey the passing scene. They have been thought to *be* or to *embody* paradigms and incommensurable systems of concepts. Languages in short have been taken to provide the subject with ways of conceptualizing or schematizing experience. Conversely empirical content—experience, the data of sensation, sensation itself, passing scenery, sensory promptings, *etc.*—has been thought to be something independent of the subject that her language conceptualizes or schematizes.

Hence conceptual schemes, as sets of intertranslatable languages, are meant to be subjective in my sense; empirical content, objective. Admittedly I have been understanding linguistic capacities rather than languages as subjective. Nonetheless for the sake of argument Davidson follows Quine (2006/1953, p. 42) in treating languages, and language itself, as subjective. In devising his

---

4. Willard van Orman Quine also expresses commitment to Dualism by calling subjective and objective sources "language" and "extra-linguistic fact" (2006/1953, p. 34), respectively.

account of radical interpretation Davidson follows Quine's own (1964, ch. 2) account of radical translation, which is behavioral. And, for the behaviorist, linguistic capacities can be understood only through overt behavior, here requiring language use. So Davidson's focus on sets of intertranslatable languages is a behavioral version of my focus on linguistic capacities. In fact languages, and certainly their use, would depend not only on linguistic but also on conceptual and perceptual capacities. They would depend on a subjective source in full.

As we can now finally see, Davidson's scheme/content dualist is committed to my Dualism concerning empirical concepts, terms, and properties in particular. Davidson's dualist is committed to my Dualism concerning empirical *terms* because she maintains that terms just are linked to language, which comes from the subject, and experience (*etc.*), which comes from something independent of the subject and so is objective. Conceptual scheme and empirical content are the subjective and objective sources of empirical terms, respectively. Moreover that link is essential. For the dualist, were empirical terms not linked to *language*, then they would not be *terms*. Were they not linked to *experience*, then they would not be *empirical*.

To appreciate why Davidson's dualist is committed to Dualism concerning empirical *concepts*, consider the following. In Chapter Four I focused on Davidson's philosophy of language because of its centrality to his other concerns. There is an aspect of this centrality that I have not yet examined. Davidson claims that everything speakable is necessarily thinkable and *vice versa* (2001d/1984, essay 11; 2002, essay 7).[5] For Davidson, everything speakable is necessarily thinkable, because speaking (rather than merely behaving as if one were speaking) requires understanding what one is saying. Speaking requires possessing the associated concepts. Conversely, for Davidson, everything thinkable is necessarily speakable, because of the publicity constraint on thoughts and therefore concepts. According to Davidson, only thought's vulnerability to public correction accounts for its normativity. We cannot share our thoughts directly, however, at least not *qua* thoughts. We can share them only indirectly *via* terms. If empirical terms are linked essentially to subjective and objective sources, therefore, then so too, for Davidson, are empirical concepts.

Finally Davidson's dualist is committed to Dualism concerning empirical *properties*. Davidson explains on her behalf: "Reality itself is relative to a conceptual scheme: what counts as real in one system may not in another" (2001d/1984, p. 183). What count as empirical properties that populate the

---

5. As in Chapter Four, I follow Davidson in usually talking about a "speaker" specifically rather than a "language user" generally.

world (Davidson's "reality itself") would then be relative to a conceptual scheme also. Moreover, because (for the dualist) the world *itself* is relative to a conceptual scheme, its properties would not be real were it not for that conceptual scheme, arising from the subject. The link is essential. Conversely those properties had better be (and so essentially are) linked to something independent of the subject—experience, the data of sensation, the passing scene—lest they not be empirical. For the scheme/content dualist, therefore, all empirical properties are linked essentially to subjective and objective sources too.

Hence Davidson's scheme/content dualism amounts to my Dualism. Nonetheless, having offered his preferred characterization of a conceptual scheme, Davidson argues that the very idea of such a scheme, and so the dualism itself, are ultimately unintelligible. The very idea of my own Dualism would then be unintelligible also.

2. FIRST HALF OF DAVIDSON'S ARGUMENT AGAINST THE SCHEME SIDE

What Davidson says against scheme/content dualism is complicated. My discussion of it must therefore also be complicated. Davidson presents two arguments against the dualism. The first (2001d/1984, essay 13) is against the scheme or subjective side of the dualism. The second (2002, essays 3, 10, 11; 2005b, essay 4) is against the content or objective side. For Davidson, because, as we saw in §1, "[c]ontent and scheme ... come as a pair" (2002, p. 46), each argument highlights different (alleged) problems with the same dualism.

Now Davidson divides the first argument, against the scheme side, in half. In this section I consider the first half; in the next two sections, the second. Nonetheless both halves contend that the very idea of a conceptual scheme is unintelligible because we could never have *evidence* of such a scheme.[6] What would such evidence be? Davidson proposes the possibility of non-intertranslatable languages. His reasoning is apparently this. Were sentences in your language non-intertranslatable into sentences in mine, then we each would have a conceptual scheme subsuming empirical content relative to it. Davidson then attempts to show that such non-intertranslatability is impossible. Since, as we saw in Chapter Three, non-intertranslatability is Kuhn's mature (2002) characterization of incommensurability, Davidson in effect attempts to show that incommensurability is impossible.

---

6. Adrian Haddock (2011, pp. 36–37), Stephen Turner (2011, p. 347), and, as I understand them, Ernest Lepore and Kirk Ludwig (2007, p. 307) also take Davidson to be concerned with evidence.

In the first half of his argument against the scheme side Davidson contends that *complete* non-intertranslatability is impossible. In the second half he contends that *partial* non-intertranslatability is impossible. He explains: "There would be complete failure" of intertranslatability, or complete non-intertranslatability, "if no significant range of sentences in one language could be translated into the other; there would be partial failure" of intertranslatability, or partial non-intertranslatability, "if some range could be translated and some range could not" (2001d/1984, p. 185).[7] Davidson argues against the possibility of complete non-intertranslatability by urging that the various ways of understanding how schemes interact with content "fall into two main groups" (p. 191). Conceptual schemes could "organize" ("categorize," "systematize," "divide up") or "fit" ("predict," "account for," "face the tribunal of") their empirical content. Davidson then contends that each group fails to allow there to be evidence of non-intertranslatable languages. So the very idea of a conceptual scheme and so scheme/content dualism (and my Dualism) are unintelligible.

Here is how Davidson's argument against the possibility of complete non-intertranslatability unfolds.[8] Davidson contends that a conceptual scheme, understood as a language or set of intertranslatable languages, can "organize" something only if the thing to be organized already contains parts. When one organizes an office, one organizes books, equipment, and furniture. It is impossible to organize something that has no internal differentiations. Such differentiations however would themselves be a kind of organization into parts. Hence, if a conceptual scheme can organize its empirical content, then that empirical content must itself already be organized into parts. Yet, according to the scheme/content dualist, the *conceptual scheme* does the organizing. Before its application, empirical content is meant to have *no* organization, and so no internal differentiations or parts, at all. But then for a conceptual scheme to organize its empirical content that empirical content must already both be and not be organized. We have a contradiction. Conceptual schemes cannot organize their empirical content. Since non-intertranslatability would result from schemes (understood as a language or set of intertranslatable languages) organizing their empirical content in disparate ways, non-intertranslatability

---

7. Davidson leaves 'significant' undefined. Though this is naturally understood quantitatively, Haddock (2011, p. 34) understands it qualitatively. Regardless Davidson's "partial" non-intertranslatability amounts to Thomas Kuhn's intranslatability with "residue or loss" (2002, p. 36). See Chapter Three, §4. Further, while my discussion in Chapter Three of non-intertranslatability was of individual terms, here I follow Davidson in talking about sentences.

8. See Nathaniel Goldberg (2004b, §§3–4; 2012a, §1) for lengthier discussion.

is itself then impossible. Understanding conceptual schemes as organizing their empirical content can provide no evidence of a conceptual scheme or scheme/content dualism.

The other way that Davidson contends that a conceptual scheme (again understood as a language or set of intertranslatable languages) might interact with its empirical content is by "fitting" it. Davidson decides that a language fits its empirical content only if it is true of it. He then maintains that our best understanding of truth is Alfred Tarski's (2008/1944) concept of truth in a language, encapsulated in Convention T. As we saw in Chapter Four and see again in Chapter Nine, Tarski maintains that by correlating each of a language's sentences with its meta-linguistic translation the totality of such resulting T-sentences captures what it is for any sentence to be true in the language. Yet understanding languages as fitting their empirical content was supposed to explain the possibility of complete *failure* of translatability. It cannot therefore be presupposed. Davidson summarizes:

> Since Convention T embodies our best intuition as to how the concept of truth is used, there does not seem to be much hope for a test that a conceptual scheme is radically different from ours if that test depends on the assumption that we can divorce the notion of truth from that of translation (2001d/1984, p. 193).

We have another contradiction. Conceptual schemes cannot fit their empirical content either. Since non-intertranslatability would result from such fitting, non-intertranslatability is again impossible. Understanding conceptual schemes as fitting their empirical content cannot provide evidence of a conceptual scheme or scheme/content dualism either.

This concludes the first half of Davidson's first argument against scheme/content dualism. Before evaluating it, let me consider one further point. Having told us that "organizing" and "fitting" are ways to understand complete non-intertranslatability specifically, Davidson acts as if they are ways to understand non-intertranslatability generally. The notion of *complete* non-intertranslatability itself plays no role. The argument is as much against complete non-intertranslatability as it is against partial non-intertranslatability. If we cannot understand how conceptual schemes and empirical content can interact, then we cannot understand how they can give rise to completely *or* partially non-intertranslatable languages. Though Davidson does not realize it, the first "half" of his first argument against scheme/content dualism could therefore function as an argument *in toto*.

Nonetheless Davidson is fortunate that his argument has a second half. Problems abound with the first. Perhaps the most obvious concern Davidson's appropriation of Tarski's work. Even if Convention T does "embody our best intuition as to how the concept of truth is used," that convention requires only that all *true* sentences in one language be *translatable* into *one other* language, its meta-language. Three problems follow for Davidson. First, Convention T does not require that *all* sentences be intertranslatable, just the true ones. Second, Convention T does not require that all sentences in one language be intertranslatable into *all* languages, just its meta-language. And third, Convention T does not allow that all true sentences in one language be *inter*translatable into its meta-language in particular on pain of semantic paradox.[9] Yet Davidson's argument against the possibility of complete non-intertranslatability requires all three.

Whether or not these problems can be overcome, Davidson's argument faces a fourth problem that cannot be. Davidson has offered an argument from elimination. He claims that all the various ways of understanding how scheme and content interact fall into two groups, neither of which allows there to be evidence of non-intertranslatable languages. But then, if there are ways to understand their interaction that do not fall into those two groups, his argument fails. In fact there are many such ways including relatively obvious ones. I need only one. Here are four:

(a) If empirical content is understood as "fluid," then, as Davidson himself initially suggests, a conceptual scheme might be understood as "giv[ing] form to" (2001d/1984, p. 183) it. Empirical content, the objective source of empirical concepts, terms, or properties, could take the form of whatever subjective conceptual scheme constrains it. Nor does a fluid's taking a form require that it already have a form (unlike the "organizing" notion, which requires that empirical content already be organized) or implicate truth and translatability (unlike the "fitting" notion, which arguably implicates both).

(b) A conceptual scheme might be understood as "interpreting" its empirical content. The subjective source of empirical concepts, terms, or properties might "make sense of" the objective source by assigning it epistemological, linguistic, or metaphysical value, respectively. This way of understanding their interaction not only avoids both the "organizing" and the "fitting" notions but, as we saw in Chapter Four, is also how Davidson himself relates the principle of charity, the subjective source, to a speaker's observable behavior and environment, the objective source, of her empirical terms.

---

9. Davidson (2001d/1984, pp. 28–29) himself counsels that we accept the intertranslatability between object and meta-language except concerning the object language's truth-predicate.

Defending Dualism

(c) A conceptual scheme might be understood as "synthesizing" its empirical content. This both avoids the "organizing" and "fitting" notions and invokes Kant's (1998/1787, A8/B12) own understanding of how concepts relate to sensation as contained in empirical intuition.

(d) Likewise Kant talks about what is independent of the subject (the "manifold") as having been "gone through, taken up, and combined in a certain way for a cognition to be made out of it" (B102/A77). A conceptual scheme's going through, taking up, and combining empirical content would be distinct from its organizing or fitting that content also. None of Davidson's objections concerning the "organizing" and "fitting" notions applies here either.

Because Davidson needs yet fails to eliminate relatively obvious ways of understanding how scheme and content interact, the first half of Davidson's argument against the scheme side of his dualism—and so the subjective side of my Dualism—fails.[10]

3. SECOND HALF OF DAVIDSON'S ARGUMENT AGAINST THE SCHEME SIDE

The second half of Davidson's argument against the scheme side of scheme/content dualism is meant to show that *partially* non-intertranslatable languages are impossible. Because it is more elliptical than the first, let me focus more on stepwise interpolation than on Davidson's explicit text.

Davidson's argument begins by recalling his point about evidence, now applied to the possibility of partial non-intertranslatability:

> STEP 1. The possibility of partially non-intertranslatable languages would be evidence of a conceptual scheme and so scheme/content dualism (and my Dualism).[11]

He then turns to the procedure of the radical interpreter:

> STEP 2. For a normal radical interpreter under normal conditions of radical interpretation to interpret a term in L, the interpreter would construct a charitable, Tarski-style truth theory for L based on the observable behavior and environment of a speaker of L.

---

10. See Richard Rorty (1979, pp. 99) and Goldberg (2004b, p. 420) for more on this objection.

11. Steps that are premises I simply state. Steps that follow from previous steps I state and then indicate parenthetically those steps from which they follow.

As we saw in Chapter Four, because the charitable, Tarski-style truth theory is *charitable*, in basic cases the interpreter would correlate a speaker's sentences with truth conditions that describe what from the interpreter's perspective would be perceptually salient features of the environment were the interpreter in the speaker's spot. Because it is a *Tarski-style truth theory*, in non-basic cases the interpreter would systematically correlate a speaker's sentences with conditions under which each is true. Further, for Davidson, these truth conditions amount to beliefs that the radical interpreter attributes to the speaker. Suppose that the radical interpreter constructs the following T-sentence:

(T) 'La rosa es roja' is true in the speaker's language if and only if the rose is red.

She would then attribute to the speaker the belief that the rose is red. And, because belief attribution follows from charitable, Tarski-truth theory construction, beliefs that the radical interpreter attributes would be charitable and systematic too. Hence this follows from STEP 2:

STEP 3. The radical interpreter would charitably and systematically attribute to the speaker beliefs. (STEP 2)[12]

Now, while in earlier writing Davidson focuses on the radical interpreter, in his argument against scheme/content dualism he applies lessons from the radical interpreter to us. Davidson wants his conclusion to hold not only for the radical interpreter but also for us. Thus he assumes this:

STEP 4. The radical interpreter's methodology is sufficiently similar to our own.

How similar are they? As we saw in Chapter Four, we (non-radicals) do not interpret speakers' sentences by explicitly constructing charitable, Tarski-style truth theories. Nonetheless we might do this implicitly. We might interpret 'la rosa es roja' in a speaker's language as meaning that the rose is red, because (i) 'la rosa es roja' is uttered under the condition in the speaker's environment that the rose is red, the *charity* constraint (required by the principle of charity), and (ii) doing so is more or less consistent with interpretations that we give to the compositional parts of 'la rosa es roja' when occurring in other sentences, the *systematicity* constraint (required by Tarski's recursive method). And, even if we did not appeal to charity and systematicity exactly as the radical interpreter would, Davidson is right that they are both part of

---

12."The interdependence of belief and meaning springs from the interdependence of two aspects of the interpretation of speech behavior: the attribution of beliefs and the interpretation of sentences" (Davidson 2001d/1984, p. 195).

our interpretive methodology. Unless we assume that a speaker believes more or less what we would in her spot, we would not know where to begin interpreting. Unless we have a baseline for her beliefs pegged to our reactions to her empirical surroundings, we would have no good way of determining what beliefs her utterances are expressing. Likewise, unless we interpret a speaker's utterances systematically, we would have no good way of interpreting utterances not directly keyed to her environment in the first place.

Consider what so far follows. If the radical interpreter would construct a charitable, Tarski-style truth theory for a speaker's language (STEP 2), which involves charitably and systematically attributing to the speaker beliefs (STEP 3), and we ordinary interpreters would implicitly appeal to sufficiently similar charity and systematicity constraints (STEP 4), then:

> STEP 5. "Given the underlying methodology of interpretation, we could not be in a position to judge that others had concepts or beliefs radically different from our own" (2001d/1984, p. 197). (STEPS 2, 3, 4)

In basic cases we, like the radical interpreter, would correlate a speaker's sentences with truth conditions that describe what from our perspective would be perceptually salient features of the environment were we in the speaker's spot. We would thereby find the speaker to believe what we would were we in her spot. In non-basic cases we would interpret a speaker's sentences based on these basic ones. Basic-case beliefs would make non-basic ones similar enough to our own that we could not be in a position to judge that *any* speaker had concepts radically different from our own.

Davidson aims however to show that partially non-intertranslatable *languages* are impossible. He therefore needs to move from concepts and beliefs to terms and sentences. As we saw in §1, Davidson maintains this:

> STEP 6. Everything speakable is necessarily thinkable and *vice versa*.

And STEPS 5 and 6 entail STEP 7:

> STEP 7. We could not be in a position to judge that any significant part of anyone's language is non-intertranslatable into our own. (STEPS 5, 6)

Admittedly one might think that STEP 7 does not in fact follow from STEPS 5 and 6. STEP 5 entails that we must judge others as having concepts and beliefs similar to our own. STEP 6 entails that all concepts and beliefs are expressible as speech. Hence we must judge others as saying things that are by and large translatable into our language. This makes it sound as if the proper conclusion is this:

> STEP 7′. We could not be in a position to judge that any significant part of anyone's language is *in*translatable into our own.

The impossibility of non-*inter*translatability might seem to strong. Nonetheless the "we" in STEP 5 can be any language user. As we (initial) interpreters could not be in a position to judge that any significant part of anyone's language is non-intertranslatable into our own, so we speakers who are being interpreted, were we ourselves interpreters, could not be in a position to judge this either. STEP 7 and with it non-intertranslatability do follow.

So far we have been talking about "judging." Though Davidson is never explicit about what that means, this much is clear. If we could not be in a position to judge that any significant part of anyone's language is non-intertranslatable into our own, then

> STEP 8. We could not be in a position to interpret terms in L to mean things radically different from our own. (STEP 7)

If we cannot ever judge them to be radically different, then we cannot treat their meaning to be radically different either.

We have already seen Davidson's appeal to radical interpretation. We come now to the connection between radical interpretation and meaning. As we saw in Chapter Four, Davidson's account of radical interpretation is a kind of Ontological Kantianism concerning terms, encapsulated in RI. That is Davidson's next step:

> STEP 9. RI: For any empirical term in L, the term means what it does if and only if a normal radical interpreter under normal conditions of radical interpretation would interpret it in L to have that meaning.

Nonetheless Davidson's actual view concerning radical interpretation is stronger. As we saw in Chapter Four, Davidson thinks that the radical interpreter can determine *all* the semantic details of a situation. "What a fully informed interpreter," and therefore a radical interpreter, "could learn about what a speaker means is all there is to learn" (2002, p. 148). Likewise "[m]eaning is entirely determined by observable behavior" (2005b, p. 56).[13] Of course, if radical interpretation ultimately concerns *all* terms, then it concerns all *empirical* terms. So RI is not false. Nonetheless, while in Chapter Four I limited RI to empirical terms out of expediency, because that is all that Dualism required, we can see here that Davidson's actual view is not so limited. Radical interpretation does concern all terms. Moreover that is precisely what this stage of Davidson's argument requires. STEP 9 should therefore be emended:

---

13. As we saw in Chapter Four, §1, Lepore and Ludwig themselves observe that, for Davidson, the position of the radical interpreter is "the fundamental standpoint from which to consider questions of thought and meaning" (2007, p. 338)—and *a fortiori* empirical thought and meaning.

STEP 9'. RI': For any term in L, the term means what it does if and only if a normal radical interpreter under normal conditions of radical interpretation would interpret it in L to have that meaning.

Because RI' entails RI, Davidson remains committed to Dualism and Kantianism. More importantly for the argument at hand, other results follow quickly. If the radical interpreter's methodology is sufficiently similar to our own (STEP 4); we could never interpret terms in L to mean things radically different from our own (STEP 8); and, for any term in L, the term means what it does if and only if a normal radical interpreter under normal conditions of radical interpretation would interpret it in L to have that meaning (STEP 9'), then:

STEP 10. No term in L could mean anything radically different from our own. (STEPS 4, 8, 9')

Since translation preserves meaning, this follows straightaway:

STEP 11. No language can be partially non-intertranslatable into our own. (STEP 10)

Finally, if no language can be partially non-intertranslatable into our own (STEP 11), yet the possibility of partially non-intertranslatable languages would be evidence of a conceptual scheme and so scheme/content dualism (and my Dualism) (STEP 1), then this apparently follows:

STEP 12. There can be no evidence of a conceptual scheme or scheme/content dualism (or my Dualism). (STEPS 1, 11)

Absent the possibility of such evidence, Davidson concludes that the very idea of a conceptual scheme is unintelligible. So the very idea of scheme/content dualism is unintelligible too. But then the very idea of my Dualism is unintelligible also. And, if the very idea of Dualism is unintelligible, then so is the very idea of Kantianism. My entire project is for naught.

There is much to evaluate here. I do so in the next section. In the remainder of this section let me instead explain three further points about Davidson's argument itself. First, though Davidson's argument against partial non-intertranslatability is the second half of his first argument against scheme/content dualism, this second "half" can itself function as an argument *in toto*. If Davidson is right, then "[g]iven the underlying methodology of interpretation, we could not be in a position to judge that others had concepts or beliefs radically different from our own" (2001d/1984, p. 197). And that would be radically different from our own in part *or* whole. If the second half of Davidson's first argument succeeds, therefore, then partially *and* completely non-intertranslatable languages are impossible. While

Davidson introduces the notion of partial non-intertranslatability to mean that *only some* range of sentences is non-intertranslatable,[14] his argument against the possibility in effect leaves the "*only*" out. For, if it is not the case that *some* range (or part) of two languages is non-intertranslatable, then it is not the case that *all* of two languages (or their whole) are non-intertranslatable. Because, as we saw in §2, the first "half" of Davidson's argument can function as an argument *in toto* too, *each* of the two "halves" of Davidson's first argument against scheme/content dualism are self-subsistent wholes.

Second, STEP 11 in particular is surprisingly strong. Consider two steps that, Davidson is right, follow from it. On the one hand, if no language can be partially non-intertranslatable into our own, then:

STEP 13. All languages are necessarily and completely intertranslatable into our own. (STEP 11)

On the other hand, if all languages are necessarily and completely intertranslatable into our own, then *via* translation into our own, which is translatable into all languages:

STEP 14. All languages are necessarily and completely intertranslatable into each other. (STEP 13)

Hence Davidson has apparently shown *sans* empirical investigation that Algonquin and Zulu, "Saturnian" and "Plutonian" (Davidson 2001d/1984, p. 186),[15] and every other language are necessarily and completely intertranslatable. All language users must then be able in principle to understand one another. This is remarkable. Perhaps though we should not be surprised. Davidson's argument relies on considerations from radical interpretation, including the principle of charity and its systematic application. And, as we saw in Chapter Four, that principle is logocentric. It is meant to guide all language users—radical interpreters, ourselves, and every other language user too. Admittedly, as we also saw, Davidson thinks that meaning is idiocentric. It is centered on the individual. For Davidson, however, whether it is idiocentric or otherwise, meaning is interpretable in a way shareable by all language users.[16] So, idiocentric or otherwise, meaning would be expressible in all languages. Davidson's idiocentrism and logocentrism entail both that each

---

14. As we saw in §2, Davidson says that partial non-intertranslatability would occur "if some range [of sentences] could be translated *and* some range could not" (p. 185, emphasis mine).

15. See Chapter Four, §5.

16. As I put it in Chapter Four, §5, Davidson is an idiocentric Kantian concerning responses and a logocentric Kantian concerning principles.

language is its speaker's own and that all languages must be mutually interpretable, respectively. I return to that in Chapter Nine.

And third, Davidson uses the unintelligibility of scheme/content dualism to reach related conclusions. Sentences and beliefs express truths *simpliciter* rather than truths about empirical content relative to a conceptual scheme. Hence conceptual relativism is false. Similarly we have "unmediated touch with the familiar objects whose antics make our sentences and opinions true or false" (2001d/1984, p. 198). A kind of direct realism follows. Finally, endorsing Quine's (2006/1953, essay 2) dismissal of the first two "dogmas of empiricism," which I discuss in Chapter Six, Davidson claims that scheme/content dualism

> is itself a dogma of empiricism, the third dogma. The third, and perhaps the last, for if we give it up it is not clear that there is anything distinctive left to call empiricism (2001d/1984, p. 189).

Empiricism itself, Davidson surmises, is beyond repair. So too is any view that relies on a philosophically significant distinction between subjective and objective sources. Dualism and with it Kantianism are beyond repair as well.[17]

4. EVALUATING THAT SECOND HALF

Unfortunately for Davidson, the second half of his first argument against scheme/content dualism, against the possibility of *partial* non-intertranslatability, is invalid. The invalid inference occurs from STEPS 1 and 11 to STEP 12:

> STEP 1. The possibility of partially non-intertranslatable languages would be evidence of a conceptual scheme and so scheme/content dualism (and my Dualism).
> STEP 11. No language can be partially non-intertranslatable into our own. (STEP 10)
> STEP 12. There can be no evidence of a conceptual scheme or scheme/content dualism (or my Dualism). (STEPS 1, 11)

The inference is invalid because STEP 1 does not disqualify anything *else* from being evidence of scheme/content dualism. STEPS 1 and 11 could therefore both be true. Since that is consistent with something else being evidence, STEP 12 could be false.

---

17. See Rorty (1979), Jonathan Lear (1982), Eva Schaper and Wilhelm Vossenkul (1989), Michael N. Foster (1998), Haddock (2011), and Joel Smith and Peter Sullivan (2011a) for the sense in which Davidson's argument is "transcendental."

The obvious remedy is to replace STEP 1 with this:

STEP 1'. *Only* the possibility of partially non-intertranslatable languages would be evidence of a conceptual scheme and so scheme/content dualism (and my Dualism).

Nonetheless Davidson makes two moves in tension with STEP 1'. First, as we saw in §1, he remarks: "We may identify conceptual schemes with languages, then, or better, allowing for the possibility that more than one language may express the same conceptual scheme, sets of intertranslatable languages" (2001d/1984, p. 185). If sets of intertranslatable languages are themselves conceptual schemes, then the existence of such sets—and not necessarily non-intertranslatable languages themselves—would be evidence of a conceptual scheme and so scheme/content dualism. That contradicts STEP 1'. Now perhaps Davidson was speaking loosely, tentatively, or not in his own voice in this identification. If so then he could simply deny that we may identify conceptual schemes with sets of intertranslatable languages. It is unclear however whether Davidson should deny it. As we saw in §2, Davidson apparently reasons that, were sentences in your language non-intertranslatable into sentences in mine, then we each would have a conceptual scheme subsuming empirical content relative to it. Yet, by parallel reasoning, Davidson should maintain that, were sentences in every language intertranslatable into every other, then we each would have a conceptual scheme subsuming empirical content relative to it too. In the former case our schemes would differ; in the latter, they would be the same.

I do not know whether this tension can be resolved.[18] So let me merely flag Davidson's remark about identifying conceptual schemes with sets of intertranslatable languages and continue. The second move that Davidson makes in tension with STEP 1' is this. STEP 1' focuses on the scheme side of the dualism. Davidson however offers a *second full argument* against scheme/content dualism, which focuses on the content side. Moreover there he argues that something besides non-intertranslatable languages would be evidence of empirical content. That something is anything non-conceptual yet justificatory. Because this evidence of empirical content would also be evidence of scheme/content dualism—for the dualist, "[c]ontent and scheme ... come as a pair" (2002, p. 46)—Davidson's offering it as evidence is in tension with STEP 1' too.

Hence (at best) Davidson needs to replace STEP 1' with this:

STEP 1''. Only the possibility of *either* partially non-intertranslatable languages *or* anything non-conceptual yet justificatory would be evidence of a conceptual scheme and so scheme/content dualism (and my Dualism).

---

18. See Goldberg (2004b, pp. 424–27; 2012a, pp. 5–6) for discussion.

Defending Dualism

For the second half of Davidson's first argument to succeed, therefore, he must show that there can be nothing non-conceptual yet justificatory either. That he does in his second (full) argument against scheme/content dualism.

Thus the second half of Davidson's first argument against scheme/content dualism is entwined with Davidson's second (full) argument against scheme/content dualism itself. Because STEP 1″ remains part of the second half of Davidson's argument against the scheme side, that second half can succeed only if Davidson can show that there can be no evidence of empirical content [in the form of anything non-conceptual yet justificatory. And he attempts to do that in his second argument against the dualism, which focuses on the content side. Davidson can therefore show that the very idea of a conceptual scheme and so scheme/content dualism are unintelligible only by showing that the very idea of empirical content is unintelligible first.

5. DAVIDSON'S ARGUMENT AGAINST THE CONTENT SIDE

Davidson's argument against empirical content, like both halves of his argument against conceptual schemes, is an argument against intelligibility. Unlike either half of his argument against conceptual schemes, however, Davidson's argument against empirical content is relatively straightforward. According to him (2002, essays 3, 10, 11; 2005b, essay 4), empirical content, as the alleged sensation that conceptual schemes conceptualize, is meant to be non-conceptual and so causal. But, Davidson adds, empirical content is also meant to justify perceptual beliefs. My belief that this patch of snow is white is on this view meant to be justified by sense-data, sensory stimulations, or some other causal source deriving from the patch of white snow itself. Davidson then asks whether anything non-conceptual can justify beliefs. He answers that each time some alleged empirical content apparently justifies a belief, *awareness* of it justifies the belief instead. But awareness, Davidson insists, is just another belief.[19] Hence the alleged empirical content never itself does the justifying. In fact, Davidson explains, sensation and other candidate kinds of empirical content are the wrong logical kind to do any such justifying at all:

> The relation between a sensation and a belief cannot be logical, since sensations are not beliefs or other propositional attitudes. What then is the relation? The answer is, I think, obvious: the relation is causal. Sensations cause some beliefs and in *this* sense are the basis or ground of those beliefs. But a causal explanation of a belief does not show how or why the belief is justified (2002, p. 143).

19. "[J]ustification seems to depend on awareness, which is just another belief" (Davidson 2002, p. 142).

Instead Davidson counters that "nothing can count as a reason for holding a belief except another belief" (p. 141) and that "all that counts as evidence or justification for a belief must come from the same totality of belief to which it belongs" (p. 155). This is just as true for perceptual beliefs, supposedly justified by empirical content, as for any other. The problem with the very idea of empirical content, Davidson concludes, is that because such content is meant to be non-conceptual, it *cannot* be justificatory; yet, because it is meant to justify perceptual beliefs, it *must* be justificatory. Once more we have a contradiction. The very idea of empirical content is therefore unintelligible. And because, as we saw in §1, they amount to the same, the very idea of an objective source of empirical concepts, terms, or properties would be unintelligible too. So go scheme/content dualism and my Dualism themselves.

What should we think of Davidson's argument against the content side of scheme/content dualism? Unfortunately for Davidson, there are four reasons that his argument fails. First, *contra* Davidson, awareness is not just another belief. Grammar already suggests a mismatch. 'Awareness' is a mass noun. Some people possess *more* awareness than others. 'Belief' is a count noun. The only *thing* that can justify *one* belief is *another* belief. More importantly, awareness need not be propositional, while, for Davidson, belief does. I can possess awareness of a patch of white snow without being interpretable as bearing a certain attitude toward an intentional object analyzable in subject/predicate form. Yet, for Davidson, my belief that there is a patch of white snow involves my being precisely so interpretable. Presumably penguins and polar bears can possess *awareness of* patches of white snow, and so can I. Nonetheless, for Davidson, only I can *believe that* there are such patches. For only I can utter sentences that are radically interpretable, and so only I could be attributed beliefs. But then Davidson is simply wrong. Awareness is not a belief. Worse still, if Davidson is nevertheless right that awareness justifies some beliefs, then he has shown that beliefs can be justified by something *other* than other beliefs. He has disposed of his own argument.

Second, awareness instead is similar to what Kant took to be empirical intuition. For Kant, empirical intuition is unmediated by concepts (1998/1787, A19–20/B33–4). Empirical intuition therefore is not propositional. Beliefs, conversely, for Davidson, are similar to Kant's empirical judgments. Empirical judgments are mediated by concepts (B143). Empirical judgments are propositional. Now, for Kant, empirical intuition contains empirical content (A20/B34). It contains the non-conceptual matter, or sensation, that the categories conceptualize into empirical judgments. But then, because awareness is similar to Kant's empirical intuition, awareness is itself a candidate conduit for empirical content. Moreover, while, for Kant, empirical intuition *contains* empirical content, Davidson (2002, p. 40) himself classifies Kant's empirical intuition as a species

Defending Dualism

of (alleged) empirical content. Hence Davidson's invoking awareness commits him—indirectly on my view, directly on his—to empirical content itself. He seems again to have disposed of his own argument.

Of course Davidson contends that awareness is conceptual while empirical content is merely causal. He would not *himself* connect awareness to empirical content. Yet, and this is the third reason that Davidson's argument fails, it is unclear that something cannot be both causal and justificatory in the first place. David Hume (2000/1739, I.i.1–2; 1999/1748, §2) maintains that concepts (his "ideas") are faded sensations ("impressions"). *Qua* conceptual, concepts would be justificatory; yet, *qua* faded remnants of something causal, they would be causal. Concepts do double-duty for Hume. Where is the problem?

Davidson in fact discusses Hume on just this issue. According to Davidson, Hume identifies basic beliefs about the world with sensations, which Davidson rejects for two reasons:

first, if the basic beliefs do not exceed in content the corresponding sensation, they cannot support any inference to an objective world; and second, there are no such beliefs (2002, p. 142).[20]

The first point is that Hume's view cannot be used to prove the existence of a world beyond our beliefs. This is an odd point for Davidson to make in the context of Hume, who does not care about supporting any such inference. More importantly, it is an odd point for Davidson to make in the context of his own argument. It is to say that we should reject a view because it has a separate consequence that Davidson does not like. The view does not let him counter the skeptic. Yet this does not show that the view is false. If anything it shows that Davidson begs the question against the skeptic.

The second point that Davidson makes about Hume is that there are no basic beliefs. Davidson's reason for this however is his reason for thinking that only beliefs can justify beliefs. Sensations (and other candidate kinds of empirical content) are the wrong logical kind. But then this second point adds nothing to Davidson's argument. Davidson has yet to provide a non-circular reason that empirical content cannot be both causal and justificatory. He has yet to show that its very idea is unintelligible.

The fourth and final reason that Davidson's argument against the content side of scheme/content dualism fails is this. Suppose that Davidson is right. Empirical content cannot be causal and justificatory. Suppose also that what

---

20. By a belief's 'content' Davidson means what I mean by a concept's 'content', its subject matter, the epistemological correlate of the corresponding sentence's meaning.

he thinks follows does follow. The only thing that can justify beliefs are other beliefs. Regardless something still *causes* those beliefs. For Davidson, there are still "causal intermediaries" (2002, pp. 144) between subjects and objects in the world. These intermediaries are simply not justificatory. So Davidson apparently replaces empirical content with causal intermediaries. The problem however is that the "replacement" is *merely* apparent. Davidson in effect replaces empirical content with itself.

To appreciate this, we have much to consider. For starters, we should note that Davidson offers two different notions of empirical content. In the two halves of his argument against the scheme side of scheme/content dualism (2001d/1984, essay 13), empirical content is meant to be the content of a conceptual scheme. It is what the scheme allegedly organizes or fits. Nowhere in the notion of being organized or being fit is there any notion of justification. Nor need there be. Something can be the content of something else without justifying it. Davidson's argument against the scheme side of the dualism does not appeal to the allegedly justificatory nature of empirical content at all. Given this initial notion, however, Davidson's causal intermediaries would themselves seem to be instances of empirical content. The causal intermediaries that Davidson thinks exist when he (2002, essays 3, 10, 11; 2005a, essay 4) argues *against* empirical content can play the role *of* empirical content when he (2001d/1984 essay 13) argues against schemes. Rather than arguing against the unintelligibility of the very idea of empirical content, Davidson makes that very idea intelligible.

Admittedly in these later articles Davidson bundles the justificatory idea into the content idea. In this, his later notion, content is meant to be causal *and* justificatory. There are however two reasons to prefer Davidson's initial notion of content. First, that notion comes closer to being canonical. Davidson's argument against the very idea of a conceptual scheme has received more attention than has his argument against the very idea of empirical content.[21] Second, and more importantly, Kant himself is committed at best only to the initial notion. And, as we saw in §1, Davidson is right that all characterizations of scheme/content dualism have "a common origin in Kant" (Davidson 1999a, p. 51). Because only by preferring Davidson's initial notion of content can we have any chance at preserving Kant's status as a scheme/content dualist, we have no choice but to prefer it.

This second reason needs explaining. Strictly speaking Kant's candidate empirical content, sensation, is meant to be non-causal and non-justificatory. It is meant to be *non-causal* because **cause and effect** is a category and so

---

21. See Goldberg (2004b, p. 432, n. 2) and surrounding text for comparative bibliographies.

conceptual (A80/B106). Nothing non-conceptual can be causal. Sensation is meant to be *non-justificatory* because it is the wrong kind of thing to justify anything. Consider my judgment that there is a white patch of snow. For Kant, this judgment would presumably be justified directly by my experiencing white snow and indirectly by experience and inferences. Yet experience is "a synthetic combination of intuitions" (A8/B13) and so combined *by* concepts, while inferences are themselves conceptual. Sensation itself would not do the justifying.[22]

Hence, for Kant, empirical content can be neither causal nor justificatory. Nonetheless Kant might count empirical content as causal in the following attenuated sense. Kant requires that things in themselves or considered in themselves somehow *affect* us. Though such "affectation" cannot be (conceptual) causation, it must be a means by which empirical content is contributed to judgments. Commitment to empirical content would itself then commit Kant to something *like* causal intermediaries between things in themselves or considered in themselves and us. Moreover Davidson himself uses 'causal' to *mean* non-conceptual. For him, causal intermediaries just are non-conceptual contributions from the world to beliefs and sentences. Let me therefore count both Kant's sensation and Davidson's intermediaries as non-conceptual and in *some* sense causal. Neither however is in *any* sense justificatory. But then Kant's own notion of empirical content can at most satisfy Davidson's initial notion of empirical content. It can at most be non-conceptual and in some sense causal. Kant's notion cannot satisfy Davidson's later notion of empirical content. It cannot in any sense be justificatory. So we must privilege Davidson's initial notion of empirical content ourselves. Otherwise Kant is not a scheme/content dualist.

We are finally in a position to appreciate the fourth and final reason that Davidson's argument against the content side fails. Because only Davidson's initial notion of empirical content can be operative in any of his arguments against scheme/content dualism lest Kant not be a scheme/content dualist, Davidson must treat empirical content as non-conceptual *simpliciter* rather than non-conceptual *and justificatory*. This makes empirical content causal in Davidson's sense. But then Davidson's initial notion of empirical content is indistinguishable from his notion of causal intermediaries. For Davidson, both empirical content and causal intermediaries are meant to be the causal, non-conceptual source of (empirical) beliefs and sentences. Neither is meant to be justificatory. Hence, not only can the causal intermediaries

---

22. As I understand Immanuel Kant (1998/1787, A20/B34), sensation, insofar as it figures in judgments, is his version of non-conceptual content. See Chapter One, §2. As we also saw there, Kant identifies empirical cognition, which is conceptual, with experience (B147).

that Davidson thinks exist when he argues against empirical content play the role of empirical content when he argues against schemes. Davidson, by "replacing" empirical content with causal intermediaries, "replaces" empirical content with itself.

I may now conclude my analysis of Davidson's argument against the content side of scheme/content dualism. Not only does Davidson's invoking awareness reveal that beliefs can be justified by things other than beliefs. Not only does that invocation commit him (indirectly or directly) to empirical content. Not only does he fail to present a non-circular reason that the very idea of empirical content is unintelligible. But Davidson replaces empirical content with itself and is thereby committed to it after all. For all these reasons Davidson's argument against the content side of scheme/content dualism—and so the objective side of Dualism—fails.

6. DUALISM DEFENDED

What does this mean for Dualism? Recall where we have been. In §1 I observed that Davidson's arguments against scheme/content dualism amount to the most serious arguments against Dualism. In §2 I showed that the first half of Davidson's first argument against scheme/content dualism, against the scheme side, fails. For the first half is an argument from elimination that fails to eliminate relatively obvious alternatives. In §§3–4 I showed that the second half of Davidson's first argument, (still) against the scheme side, relies on the impossibility of evidence for the dualism yet fails to eliminate all possible evidence. In particular it fails to eliminate the possibility of evidence of empirical content itself.

Moreover in §5 I showed that Davidson's second full argument against scheme/content dualism is itself an argument against the very idea of empirical content. Hence Davidson's second argument is meant to double duty. On the one hand, if it establishes that the very idea of empirical content is unintelligible, then it eliminates the possibility of the holdout evidence from the second half of Davidson's first argument. On the other hand, according to the scheme/content dualist, "[c]ontent and scheme ... come as a pair" (2002, p. 46). So, if Davidson's second argument shows that the very idea of empirical content is unintelligible, then it disqualifies scheme/content dualism and Dualism on its own.

Yet I then showed in §5 that there are four reasons that Davidson's second argument, against the content side, also fails. Instead, if anything, Davidson's argument commits him *to* empirical content. So there is no hope of rehabilitating the second half of Davidson's first argument either. And, recall, the first half of his first argument fails too. *All* of Davidson's arguments *in toto* against scheme/content dualism, and so by extension my Dualism, therefore fail.[23]

What should we make of Davidson's view overall? Because Davidson is committed to empirical content, and because he agrees with the dualist that "[c]ontent and scheme ... come as a pair," Davidson is himself committed to scheme/content dualism and my Dualism too. But more than that, Davidson is committed to a particular subjective scope concerning subjective principles. To appreciate this, recall that problems with the second half of Davidson's first argument concern only its first step. Steps not relying on the first nevertheless do follow. STEP 14 itself then does:

STEP 14. All languages are necessarily and completely intertranslatable into each other.

Davidson reaches STEP 14 by appealing to his logocentric subjective principle, the principle of charity, and other considerations from radical interpretation applied to us. Now it is unlikely that any non-Kantian would grant Davidson the principle of charity let alone in logocentric scope. Certainly no non-logocentrist, Kantian or otherwise, would. Regardless, if Davidson is a scheme/content dualist (or Dualist) who thinks that all languages are necessarily and completely intertranslatable, then he is a dualist who thinks that there is only one conceptual scheme, shared by all subjects *qua* language user. That makes him a logocentric Kantian concerning principles. Nor might this be surprising. As we saw in §5, we flagged Davidson's remark: "We may identify conceptual schemes with languages, then, or better, allowing for the possibility that more than one language may express the same conceptual scheme, sets of intertranslatable languages" (2001d/1984, p. 185). If sets of intertranslatable languages are themselves conceptual schemes, then the existence of a single such set would be evidence of a single such scheme. It would be a scheme shared by all subjects *qua* language user.

7. LESSONS FOR KANTIAN CONCEPTUAL GEOGRAPHY

In this chapter we have seen that Davidson is Dualism's most determined detractor in the analytic tradition if not overall. We have then seen that all his arguments against Dualism fail. In this conclusion I draw three lessons for Kantian conceptual geography generally.

---

23. See Goldberg (2004b, §4; 2004c, §2; 2009c, p. 84, n. 11; 2012a, §2) for additional reasons that Davidson's arguments fails.

First, Davidson's arguments *do* fail. Dualism has therefore been defended against its most determined detractor. In fact Davidson himself is a Dualist of a logocentric sort.

Second, I am therefore justified in Chapter Four in taking Davidson to be not a Hegelian pragmatist but a Kantian. Because Davidson's accounts of radical interpretation and language learning apparently commit him to different kinds of Kantianism, and his arguments against Dualism and so Kantian fail, I am entitled to take those accounts to be kinds of Kantianism. This is so even though, as we saw in Chapter Four, Davidson should reject his account of language learning itself.

And third, I can fulfill a promissory note issued in Chapter Four. It concerns how Davidson's accounts of radical interpretation and language learning relate to noumenalism and the possibility of incommensurability. Let me say something about each in turn.

We saw in Chapter Two that all kinds of Kantianism are committed to noumenalism, the thesis that reality possesses an intrinsic nature or aspect that remains unknowable. We can now see here that this is so for Davidson's in particular. For Davidson, all empirical terms are linked essentially to subjective and objective sources. Because such an objective source would be distinct from any subjective source, it would remain unknowable in itself, if construed ontologically, or considered in itself, if construed epistemologically, by the subject. And, because Davidson's account of radical interpretation is ontological, while his account of language learning is ontological and epistemological, Davidson is committed to noumenalism construed both ontologically and epistemologically.[24]

Incommensurability's relation to Davidson's accounts is more complicated. We saw in Chapter Three that languages would be incommensurable were they at least partially non-intertranslatable. Now, because incommensurability concerns the meaning of terms, it concerns Ontological Kantianism concerning terms. We also saw that the possibility of incommensurability follows from any kind of Ontological Kantianism concerning terms that allows there to be relevantly distinct subjects, and so relevantly distinct conceptual, linguistic, and perceptual capacities. Because ethnocentric Ontological Kantianism concerning terms allows there to be more than one community whose members have such capacities, the possibility of incommensurability follows. Likewise, because anthropocentric Ontological Kantianism concerning terms allows there to be more than one species whose members have such capacities, the possibility of incommensurability follows too.

---

24. As we saw in Chapter Two, these different construals are not so easily segregated.

Now, as we saw in Chapter Four, according to Davidson's accounts of radical interpretation and language learning, meaning is idiocentric. That would suggest that he too is committed to incommensurability. Nonetheless, as we also saw, Davidson's version of Principlism is logocentric. While terms do mean what they do relative to the individual, all subjects *qua* interpreter would be able to determine—and, especially in the radical interpretation case, constitute—their meaning regardless. For all interpreters (radical or otherwise) rely on the principle of charity, itself a logocentric principle. Hence, for Davidson, though all terms do mean what they do relative to an individual, because all subjects can determine what they mean, this relativism does not itself entail non-intertranslatability. Davidson's logocentrism instead entails that there is a universally shareable language into which idiocentric terms could be translated.[25]

Hence Davidson relies on considerations of radical interpretation generally and the principle of charity specifically to conclude that all languages are necessarily and completely intertranslatable. But then, though his accounts of radical interpretation and language learning entail noumenalism, at least his account of radical interpretation entails the *im*possibility of incommensurability. All languages, necessarily and completely intertranslatable, are necessarily and completely commensurable. Davidson however remains a Kantian, not a Hegelian pragmatist. He himself observes: "Even those thinkers who are certain there is only one conceptual scheme are in the sway of the scheme concept; even monotheists have religion" (2001d/1984, p. 184). Davidson presumably has in mind Kant, who thinks that all human beings have the same conceptual scheme. Nonetheless Davidson should have in mind himself, who thinks that all language users have the same such scheme. Even monotheists have religion. Even Kantians with logocentric principles are Kantians.

---

25. Again, as I put it in Chapter Four, §5, Davidson is an idiocentric Kantian concerning responses and a logocentric Kantian concerning principles.

SIX

Defending Principlism

While all Kantians are committed to Dualism, only some are committed to Principlism:

PRINCIPLISM: The subjective source of all empirical concepts, terms, or properties takes the form of subjective principles.

In Chapter One we saw that Immanuel Kant is a Principled Kantian. His subjective principles are synthetic *a priori* judgments. In Chapter Two we saw that Philip Pettit is an un-Principled Kantian. He has no subjective principles. In Chapter Three we saw that Thomas Kuhn is a Principled Kantian. His subjective principles are implicit within his paradigms, disciplinary matrices, and lexical taxonomies. In Chapter Four we saw that Donald Davidson is a Principled Kantian. His subjective principle is the principle of charity. Finally, it is worth mentioning, in Chapter Five we saw that Willard van Orman Quine is an un-Principled Kantian.

Though not all Kantians are Principled, those who are make Principlism central to their view. Kant announces: "The real problem of pure reason is now contained in the question: **How are synthetic judgments *a priori* possible?**" (1998/1787, B19). Kant's answer is the topic around which the second edition of the *Critique of Pure Reason* is organized, and synthetic *a priori* judgments are fundamental to the entire Critical *corpus*. Further, no term is more closely associated with Kuhn than 'paradigm', whose present-day ubiquity traces to him. Moreover the evolution of Kuhn's notion of a paradigm into his notions of a disciplinary matrix and lexical taxonomy tracks the evolution of his thought. Finally, whether or not he succeeds, Davidson relies on the principle of charity to give accounts of interpretation and language learning (as we saw in Chapter Four); arguments against scheme/content dualism, conceptual relativism, and empiricism (as we saw in Chapter Five); and arguments against skepticism about other minds and the external world (as I have shown elsewhere [2003]). Davidson's one principle is meant to perform many a philosophical feat.

Even though not all Kantians are Principled, therefore, those who are make Principlism *so* central that it is worth investigating whether Principlism is defensible. It is worth learning whether this internal border between Principled and un-Principled kinds of Kantianism can stand. My aim in this chapter is to show that it can. Moreover, as with Dualism, Principlism's defense serves two purposes. On the one hand, it shows that my definition of 'Kantianism' (and 'Principlism' in particular) has not been for naught. On the other hand, it furthers my aim of increasing our understanding of issues in epistemology, philosophy of language, and metaphysics.

There are however two differences in strategy between the last chapter and this. First, my strategy in Chapter Five was to defend Dualism by showing that its most determined detractor fails on his own terms. My strategy here is to demonstrate that there is a version of Principlism that the most important arguments against Principlism fail to impugn. Second, my strategy there was to focus on Davidson's view because Davidson is Dualism's most determined detractor. My strategy here is to consider the historical progression of versions of Principlism and their opponents from which to extract that version itself.

Now I have already defended Principlism once by defending Dualism against Davidson. Though not all of Dualism's detractors claim that there are neither a subjective nor an objective source of all empirical concepts, terms, or properties, Davidson does. Were Davidson right, then there would be no subjective principles either. Nonetheless one can reject Principlism yet retain Dualism. One can maintain that all empirical concepts, terms, or properties are linked essentially to subjective and objective sources generally but deny that the subjective source takes the form of subjective principles specifically. Un-Principled Kantianism is Pettit's and Quine's view. Quine is important in this chapter also. We saw in the last chapter that Davidson is Dualism's most determined detractor in the analytic tradition if not overall. We see here that Davidson's mentor, Quine, is himself Principlism's principal opponent *par excellence*.

The chapter proceeds as follows. In §1 I consider Kant's Principlism, according to which subjective principles are synthetic *a priori*. In §2 I consider classic arguments against synthetic apriority, culminating in those of the logical empiricists, including Rudolf Carnap. In §3 I consider the historically next key Principlism, Carnap's own, according to which subjective principles are analytic. In §4 I consider the most famous arguments against analyticity, *viz.*, Quine's. In §5 I consider Michael Friedman's contemporary version of Principlism, according to which subjective principles are relativized *a priori*. In §6 I show that Friedman's Principlism remains unimpugned by classic arguments against Kant's and Quine's arguments against Carnap's. In §7

I conclude that this defends Principlism itself. Finally in §8 I draw lessons for Kantian conceptual geography generally.

1. KANT'S PRINCIPLISM

Principlism, like Dualism, traces to Kant, who contends: "Synthetic *a priori* judgments are contained as principles in all theoretical sciences of reason" (1998/1787, A10/B14). Kant however neither intends all his principles to be synthetic *a priori* (those of pure general logic are analytic *a priori*) nor calls all his synthetic *a priori* judgments 'principles' (he does not call particular arithmetic and geometric claims that). Nonetheless I have adopted his term 'principle' generally to name any claim, distinct from any empirical one, that is the form or basic epistemological or linguistic unit that the subjective source of empirical concepts, terms, or properties takes.

While in Chapter One I showed that Dualism and Principlism can both be drawn from the *Critique of Pure Reason* generally, here I draw from the *Critique* to show that Kant's synthetic *a priori* judgments count as subjective principles in my sense specifically. As in Chapter One, I aim to achieve not so much exegetical fidelity as thematic acquaintance with Kant's view. I would again be content to provide an understanding of a view recognizably like Kant's own that is useful to consider here in understanding Principlism itself.

For Kant, judgments are something like complete thoughts. They fall under two sets of distinctions: analytic and synthetic, and *a priori* and *a posteriori*. Kant introduces the first distinction:

> In all judgments in which the relation of a subject to the predicate is thought (if I consider only affirmative judgments, since the application to negative ones is easy), this relation is possible in two different ways. Either the predicate B belongs to the subject A as something that is (covertly) contained in this concept A; or B lies entirely outside the concept A, though to be sure it stands in connection with it. In the first case I call the judgment **analytic**, in the second **synthetic**. Analytic judgments (affirmative ones) are thus those in which the connection of the predicate is thought through identity, but those in which this connection is thought without identity are to be called synthetic judgments. One could also call the former **judgments of clarification**, and the latter **judgments of amplification**, since through the predicate the former do not add anything to the concept of the subject, but only break it up by means of analysis into its component concepts, which were already thought in it (though confusedly); while the latter, on the contrary, add to the concept of the subject a predicate that was not thought in it at

all, and could not have been extracted from it through any analysis (A6–7/B10–11).

I take Kant to be offering three related characterizations of the analytic/synthetic distinction here. First, analytic judgments have grammatical subjects that *conceptually contain* their predicates, while synthetic judgments do not.[1] Second, analytic judgments are those in which the connection of the predicate to the subject is *thought through* (and so involve a kind of conceptual) *identity*, while synthetic judgments are not.[2] And third (and combining the first two), analytic judgments *clarify* their subjects by pairing them with predicates merely expressing concepts contained in, or thought through, them.[3] Conversely synthetic judgments *amplify* their subjects by pairing them with predicates not merely expressing concepts contained in, or thought through, them.[4]

In these three characterizations Kant targets analyticity, characterizing syntheticity relative to it. Nonetheless we can say something about syntheticity directly. If synthetic judgments do not concern conceptual containment, are not thought through identity, and do not clarify but instead amplify, then something must be added to their grammatical subjects to form them. Indeed, Kant explains, synthetic judgments have "in addition to the concept of the subject something else" (A8/B11). That something else, as I explain below, is intuition.

---

1. Later in the *Critique of Pure Reason* Kant distinguishes conceptual from spatial containment (1998/1787, A25/B39–40).

2. I take Kant to be developing this second characterization when he explains that "the principle of contradiction," that the contrary of an analytic judgment " ... is always correctly denied[,] ... is the universal and completely sufficient **principle of all analytic cognition**" (A151/B190–91).

3. In the *Prolegomena to Any Future Metaphysics* Kant connects this third characterization with the principle of contradiction:

> All analytic judgments depend wholly on the principle of contradiction. ... For the predicate of an affirmative analytic judgment is already thought in the concept of the subject, of which it cannot be denied without contradiction (2010/1783, 4: 267).

4. Though I am unsure whether he is right, R. Lanier Anderson (2010, §3.ii) takes the second and third characterizations to collapse into the first. Further, Anderson is right, philosophers from Kant's contemporary J. G. Maaß to our near contemporary Willard van Orman Quine fault the notion of conceptual containment. Nonetheless Anderson (§3.iii) himself defends it, and in §6 I show that Quine's arguments against analyticity themselves fail. Finally Robert Hanna (2001, ch. 3.1.1–3.1.3) further divides Kant's characterization of analyticity into two notions of conceptual containment, two notions of identity, and four notions of contradiction. Hanna himself (ch. 3.2–3.5) then defends Kant's notion of analyticity generally.

Kant introduces the *a priori/a posteriori* distinction in terms not of "judgments" but of "cognitions," of which judgments are a species (A68/B93):

> [W]e will understand by *a priori* cognitions not those that occur independently of this or that experience, but rather those that occur *absolutely* independently of all experience. Opposed to them are empirical cognitions, or those that are possible only *a posteriori*, i.e., through experience (B3).

Now just above Kant declares: "But although all our cognition commences **with** experience, yet it does not on that account arise **from** experience" (B1). Since *a priori* cognition is cognition, its *occurring* independently of all experience means not that it commences *without* experience but that it does not arise *from* experience. Moreover, as we saw throughout Part Two, there are ontological and epistemological senses of apriority. For consistency let me focus on judgments.[5] In the ontological sense *a priori* judgments derive from a subjective source. This is one way of understanding Kant's claims about how they "occur" or "arise." Kant himself explains that "cognition derived from experiential *sources*" (B2, emphasis mine) would not be *a priori*. *A priori* judgments have as their source not experience but the subject herself (ultimately her transcendental unity of apperception). In the epistemological sense *a priori* judgments are insusceptible to empirical justification or verification. That is consistent with Kant's claim about occurring and arising. One reason that *a priori* judgments would be so insusceptible is their deriving purely from a subjective source—and so independent of anything objective like sensation.[6]

Conversely Kant talks not about how *a posteriori* cognitions—and let me again focus on judgments—"occur" or "arise" but about what makes them "possible." They are possible "only *a posteriori*, i.e., through experience." They are therefore empirical. This "possibility" itself has ontological and epistemological senses. Ontologically it concerns how *a posteriori* judgments come to be in virtue of an objective source. Epistemologically it concerns how they come to be justified or verified in virtue of an objective source. Hence *a posteriori* judgments are linked essentially to an objective source (and so are empirical). But Kant also thinks that insofar as *a posteriori* judgments are rule-governed—which, for him, they must be to count as judgments at all—they necessarily depend on *a priori* judgments (A127). In fact Kant calls the understanding,

---

5. I focus on judgments also because, unlike certain other kinds of cognitions, judgments can be justified or verified. See below.

6. Hanna (2001, ch. 5.2) calls Kant's ontological sense of apriority 'semantic' because it concerns the source of the (semantic) content of cognition. As Anderson (2010, p. 78) explains, the epistemological sense is normally taken to be basic in Kant.

the source of these *a priori* judgments, "the **faculty of rules**" (A126). This necessary dependence itself entails that *a posteriori* (or empirical) judgments are linked essentially to a subjective source also. I return to this below.[7]

Now Kant claims that all philosophers before him assumed that all analytic judgments are *a priori* and all synthetic judgments *a posteriori*. Kant agrees that there are analytic *a priori* and synthetic *a posteriori* judgments. According to him, the former pair their grammatical subjects with predicates expressing concepts contained in those subjects (making them analytic) and derive purely from a subjective source, the transcendental subject's mind (making them *a priori*). Kant's example is "All bodies are extended" (A7/B11), where he thinks that **being extended** is contained in **body** and that the total claim derives exclusively from the subject's own (hence subjective) conceptual capacities. Analytic *a priori* judgments are therefore conceptual claims. Conversely synthetic *a posteriori* judgments pair their subjects with predicates not merely expressing concepts contained in those subjects (making them synthetic) and derive partly from an objective source (making them *a posteriori*). Kant's example is "All bodies are heavy" (A7/B11), where he thinks that **being heavy** is not contained in **body** and that the total claim derives from the subject's own conceptual capacities along with something objective like sensation. Synthetic *a posteriori* judgments are therefore empirical claims. This entails that, unlike analytic *a priori* judgments, synthetic *a posteriori* ones are linked essentially to subjective and objective sources: conceptual (and in fact intuitive or perceptual—more below) capacities and sensation, respectively.[8]

Kant claims to have discovered a third kind of judgment: synthetic *a priori*. They pair their grammatical subjects with predicates not merely expressing concepts contained in those subjects (making them synthetic) but nevertheless derive purely from a subjective source (making them *a priori*).[9] As we saw above, Kant explains: "The real problem of pure reason is now contained in the question: **How are synthetic judgments *a priori* possible?**" (B19). This is "[t]he real problem" because *a priori* judgments derive from a subjective source, yet synthetic judgments are not mere clarifications of concepts. And in the rationalist and empiricist traditions preceding Kant the only candidate subjective source are concepts and conceptual capacities deriving from the

---

7. I return to it in Chapter Nine also.

8. This is so, for Kant, regardless of the persuasiveness of his examples. While we might understand synthetic *a posteriori* judgments as being linked essentially to conceptual capacities and *experience*, for Kant, experience is already intuited and conceptualized. See below.

9. Kant claims that there can be no analytic *a posteriori* judgments (1998/1787, A7/B11; *cf.* 2010/1783, 4: 267).

subject's mind. Kant must therefore find a subjective source distinct from the conceptual from which synthetic *a priori* judgments derive (and are justified and verified).

Kant turns to pure intuition. Pure intuition is something like the mental canvass on which subjects perceive experience but which is structured prior to experience by the pure forms of space and time—which themselves derive from the transcendental subject's mind. Thus pure intuition amounts to the totality of human perceptual capacities, where these capacities are specifically spatial and temporal. Pure intuition and its pure forms are themselves therefore *a priori* and in my sense subjective. In turn synthetic *a priori* judgments are meant to derive from *a priori* conceptual constructions in the pure forms of space and time. Consider Kant's paradigmatic synthetic *a priori* judgments, principles of arithmetic, geometry, and pure natural science. For Kant, arithmetic principles involve conceptual constructions in time. Geometric principles—which, for Kant, are necessarily Euclidean—involve conceptual constructions in space. Finally principles of pure natural science are the most fundamental laws of nature presupposed by empirical inquiry. They include this: "In all changes of appearances substance persists, and its quantum is neither increased nor diminished in nature" (B224). This law, Kant's First Analogy, an *a priori* version of the law of conversation of matter, results from the *a priori* concept (or category) **substance** intuited over time.[10]

Now, according to Kant, synthetic *a priori* judgments are necessary for both judgments about experience and experience itself. Judgments about experience—empirical judgments—are synthetic *a posteriori*. And experience itself is described by synthetic *a posteriori* judgments. In fact, as we saw in Chapter One, Kant claims that empirical cognition, of which judgment is a species, is not distinct from experience (B147). Moreover, according to Kant, as we saw above, empirical judgments are rule-governed. Experience then is also. Both must obey Kant's synthetic *a priori* judgments—and so the principles, or rules, of arithmetic, geometry, and pure natural science. As we saw in Chapter One as well, Kant can be understood as maintaining that empirical concepts and terms are linked essentially to subjective and objective sources. Empirical judgments, comprised of empirical concepts and, if understood linguistically, empirical terms, would likewise be so linked. And, because empirical cognition is experience, experience—itself consisting of empirical properties—is itself

---

10. As I explain in Chapter Nine, §1, in the *Metaphysical Foundations of Natural Science* (2010/1786) Kant attempts to derive the mechanical theory of Isaac Newton from these fundamental laws of nature.

then so linked. Hence Kant can be understood as maintaining that empirical properties are linked essentially to subjective and objective sources too.

Further, as we also saw, this essential link can be construed ontologically or epistemologically. While in Chapter One I compared these construals to influential analytic construals of transcendental idealism, let me here explore generic ontological and epistemological construals of transcendental idealism in their own right. On such an ontological construal, empirical judgments and experience itself are both *constituted essentially out of* Kant's synthetic *a priori* judgments and sensation somehow arising from things in themselves. These subjective principles allow the subject to put sensation into conceptual and intuitive (or perceptual) form. What results is the constitution of synthetic *a posteriori*, or empirical, judgments and experience itself. Construed ontologically, therefore, synthetic *a priori* judgments are constitutive of the parts of empirical judgments, including empirical concepts and terms, as well as the parts of experience, including empirical properties. Hence Kant can be understood as committed to Ontological Principlism:

> ONTOLOGICAL PRINCIPLISM: The subjective source of all empirical concepts, terms, or properties takes the form of subjective principles constitutive of those concepts, terms, or properties.

Kant's synthetic *a priori* judgments are those constitutive principles.

Conversely, on a generic epistemological construal of transcendental idealism, judgments about experience and experience itself are both *acquired by a subject's appealing essentially to* synthetic *a priori* judgments and sensation. These subjective principles allow the subject to track sensation as it fits into conceptual and intuitive (or perceptual) form. What results is the acquisition of synthetic *a posteriori*, or empirical, judgments and experience itself. On an epistemological construal, therefore, synthetic *a priori* judgments are acquisitive of the parts of empirical judgments, including empirical concepts and terms, as well as the parts of experience, including empirical properties.[11] Hence Kant can be understood as committed to Epistemological Principlism:

> EPISTEMOLOGICAL PRINCIPLISM: The subjective source of all empirical concepts, terms, or properties takes the form of subjective principles acquisitive of those concepts, terms, or properties.

Kant's synthetic *a priori* judgments are now those acquisitive principles.

Regardless of how we understand him, Kant is therefore a Principled Kantian. Moreover, as we saw in Chapters Three and Four, Kant's Principlism

---

11. See Chapter One, §1, on its potentially sounding infelicitous to say that properties (and therefore experience) is acquired in the sense in which concepts and terms are acquired.

is anthropocentric. His subjective principles are meant to guide all human beings *qua* human in their constitutive or acquisitive activities.

2. CLASSIC ARGUMENTS AGAINST KANT'S PRINCIPLISM

Kant's Principlism, according to which subjective principles are synthetic *a priori*, was revolutionary. It was also controversial. Bracketing concerns about Kant's transcendental idealism generally, two classic arguments confront his Principlism specifically. I consider both as they played out historically.

The first argument, made in successive steps by Friedrich Ludwig Gottlob Frege and his logicist heirs, and by Hermann von Helmholtz and Henri Poincaré, is that no claim that Kant thinks is synthetic *a priori* in fact is. Frege (1964/1893 & 1903, 1980/1884) in particular argued that arithmetic is reducible to logic alone. He did so by broadening logic to encompass his predicate calculus, expressively more powerful than Kant's Aristotelian logic. Frege thereby claimed to clarify (though he really expanded) Kant's notion of analyticity by speaking not of conceptual containment but of "general logical laws and ... definitions" (1980/1884, p. 4). Moreover Frege emphasized analyticity as a property of statements and propositions.[12] Now, as Bertrand Russell observed, Frege's reduction relies on his Basic Law V: the extension of concept F is identical with the extension of concept G if and only if the same objects fall under F and G (Frege 1964/1893, §§3, 20). Nonetheless, as Russell showed, this law is inconsistent when applied to the concept of the set of all sets not containing themselves. So Frege's reduction fails. Regardless Russell joined Alfred North Whitehead to propose a replacement reduction of arithmetic. According to Russell and Whitehead (1997/1923), arithmetic reduces to logic plus "types," set-like objects that cannot contain anything at or below their own type. Now Russell and Whitehead have not persuaded everyone. Moreover, while others have tried other variations on Frege's logicism,[13] the issue remains unsettled. Regardless a general consensus remains to this day that arithmetic claims are not synthetic *a priori*. They do not rely on pure intuition. They are instead, if the logicists were themselves right, analytic *a priori*.

What Frege did for arithmetic, Helmholtz and Poincaré did for geometry, and in Poincaré's case the lesson was extended to what Kant took to be pure natural science, the most fundamental laws of nature presupposed by empirical

---

12. For Friedrich Ludwig Gottlob Frege, judgments are psychological and therefore philosophically unimportant. See J. Alberto Coffa (2008/1991, pp. 62–76) and Hanna (2001, pp. 159–64) for more on Frege on analyticity.

13. See Hanna (2001, p. 122).

inquiry. Helmholtz (1977/1921, chs. 1, 2, 4) showed that non-Euclidean geometries are conceivable and usable in science. While Helmholtz's positive view meandered between treating such geometries as conventional and empirical, his negative view persuaded many that geometry generally does not rely on pure intuition. Its claims are then not synthetic *a priori*. Poincaré (1946/1902, bk. 1, ch. 3) took geometries to be possible in virtue of linguistic convention. The role allegedly played by pure intuition was instead played by definition. Geometric claims are again not synthetic *a priori*. Reinforcing Helmholtz's and Poincaré's arguments was the apparent empirical success of Albert Einstein's theory of general relativity. Because general relativity presupposes the non-Euclidean geometry postulated by Bernhard Riemann—and, according to Kant's theory of synthetic apriority, non-Euclidean geometry is impossible—there now was apparently empirical confirmation that geometric claims are not synthetic *a priori*.[14]

Finally the synthetic apriority of what Kant took to be claims of pure natural science was likewise put into doubt. Carnap (1988/1952, suppl. A) expanded Poincaré's conventionalism to argue that the most fundamental laws of nature presupposed by empirical inquiry, like Kant's version of the law of conversation of matter, have nothing to do with pure intuition either. They are themselves conventional and so not synthetic *a priori*. As I explain in §3, Carnap treated them as analytic *a priori*—which, for him, made them analytic *simpliciter*.

Thus, if the likes of Frege, Russell and Whitehead, Helmholtz, Poincaré, and Carnap are right, then Kant's notion of synthetic apriority fails to apply to any particular claim to which he thinks that it does. Collectively this is the first classic argument against Kant's Principlism:

ARGUMENT FROM INAPPLICABILITY: Kant's notion of synthetic apriority is inapplicable to his own alleged cases.

The second classic argument against Kant's Principlism is simpler to trace. It was made by Carnap and his fellow logical empiricist, Moritz Schlick. Following Frege in talking about "statements" or "propositions," Carnap (2003/1934, 1935, 1959) maintained that synthetic *a priori* statements generally are not constructed according to universal rules of syntax. No claims then can be synthetic *a priori* at all. Amplifying Carnap's argument, Schlick (1979/1921, 1949) maintained that

---

14. See Coffa for more on Hermann von Helmholtz (Coffa 2008/1991, pp. 49–57) and Henri Poincaré (pp. 128–40). See Michael Friedman (1999, chs. 1–4) and Hanna (2001, pp. 270–79) for more on how research into the foundations of geometry shook Kant's synthetic apriority. Hans Reichenbach (1965/1920) and Ernst Cassirer (1980/1921) take the apparent empirical success of general theory to *confirm* Kant's view insofar as they take general relativity to maintain that all measurements are observer-relative.

synthetic *a priori* statements generally are meaningless. They are neither analytically true nor verifiable, where meaningful statements must be one or the other. So, for Schlick, there can be no synthetic *a priori* statements either. Hence the second classic argument against Kant's Principlism is an argument not from mere inapplicability but from necessary inapplicability:

> ARGUMENT FROM NECESSARY INAPPLICABILITY: Kant's notion of synthetic apriority is necessarily inapplicable to any case at all.

It is necessarily inapplicable because synthetic apriority is itself impossible. Without synthetic apriority, however, we are without Kant's version of Principlism.[15]

3. CARNAP'S PRINCIPLISM

Though the logical empiricists rejected Kant's Principlism, according to which subjective principles are synthetic *a priori*, they did not reject Principlism altogether. They merely reworked it. Ironically Carnap's (1988/1952, suppl. A) analytic statements are their most developed version. Because the logical empiricists contrasted analytic statements (*simpliciter*) with synthetic ones (*simpliciter*), their Principlism involves the analytic/synthetic distinction (*simpliciter*).

To appreciate this, we must first consider Carnap's fellow empiricist, Hans Reichenbach. As we saw in Chapter Three, Friedman uses Reichenbach's view to explain Thomas Kuhn's (2012/1962, 2012/1970, 2002). As I explain here, Reichenbach's view illuminates Kant's and Carnap's views as well as Principlism itself. Giving what I have been calling an 'ontological construal' of transcendental idealism, Reichenbach claimed that "Kant's concept of a priori"—and as the context makes clear he means Kant's concept of synthetic *a priori* in particular—"has two different meanings. First, it means 'necessarily true' or 'true for all times', and secondly, 'constituting the concept of object'" (1965/1920, p. 48). Regarding the first meaning, Reichenbach (p. 55) knew that Kant's synthetic *a priori* concerns only human beings. So by "necessarily true" or "true for all times" he means true *for* human beings specifically. Regarding the second, Reichenbach described "constituting the concept of object" itself as concerning "the object of knowledge" (p. 48) rather than merely its concept, and later as concerning "the object of science" (p. 49). Now, for Kant, the object of science is empirical. And Reichenbach is clear that the objects in which he was interested are those constituted when "perceptions

---

15. See Hanna (2001, pp. 236–37) and Paolo Parrini (2003, pp. 349–56) for more on this second argument.

present the material" (p. 49), or empirical content, for conceptualization. The concept of such objects itself therefore is empirical. So Reichenbach took the second meaning of Kant's concept to concern the constitution of all empirical concepts ("the concept of object") and objects ("the object of knowledge" and "the object of science"). Moreover, because all objects are the objects that they are in virtue of their properties, the second meaning would also concern the constitution of all empirical properties. Finally, as we saw in Chapter One, Kant himself talks about "predicates," which are linguistic; Carnap and the other logical empiricists generally prefer talk not of "concepts" but of their linguistic correlates, "terms"; and we have no reason to think that Reichenbach would reject talk of "terms" himself. So the two meanings of Kant's synthetic apriority would concern the constitution of empirical terms too.

Hence, construing Kant's view ontologically, Reichenbach is committed to the following. Kant's synthetic *a priori* judgments are meant to be

(a) necessarily true or true for all times (for human beings); and
(b) constitutive of all empirical concepts, terms, and properties.

Indeed on an ontological construal Kant's synthetic *a priori* judgments are meant to be (a) because they are supposed to derive from *a priori* conceptual constructions in pure intuition, which is shared by all human beings. As we saw in §1, Kant's principles are anthropocentric. On the assumption that Kant never challenges—that our nature as humans is immutable[16]—his synthetic *a priori* judgments are therefore necessarily true or true for all times for human beings. Likewise Kant's synthetic *a priori* judgments are meant to be (b) because they are supposed to be principles constitutive of judgments about experience and of experience itself. And judgments about experience are comprised of empirical concepts and, if understood linguistically, empirical terms. Similarly experience itself is comprised of empirical properties. So Kant's synthetic *a priori* judgments are meant to be constitutive of all empirical concepts, terms, and properties. Now, because Reichenbach would understand Kant as committed to his synthetic *a priori* judgments being constitutive of all these (and because these judgments are subjective in my sense of deriving exclusively from the transcendental subject's mind), Reichenbach would in my terms understand Kant as committed to Ontological Principlism:

ONTOLOGICAL PRINCIPLISM: The subjective source of all empirical concepts, terms, or properties takes the form of subjective principles constitutive of those concepts, terms, or properties.

---

16. See Reichenbach (1965/1920, p. 56).

Because Reichenbach construes Kant's Principlism as ontological, he would construe Kant's synthetic *a priori* judgments themselves as constitutive principles. On an ontological construal I agree.

Nonetheless there is something misleading about Reichenbach's (a) and (b). Though only (a) explicitly concerns necessity, they both ultimately concern necessity that is relative. *Qua* (a), synthetic *a priori* judgments are meant to be necessary insofar as their truth holds for all times for human beings. The necessity explicit in (a) is relative to human beings. Conversely, *qua* (b), synthetic *a priori* judgments are meant to be necessary *for* the constitution of all empirical concepts, terms, and properties. Their truth is necessary relative to those concepts, terms, and properties—and ultimately to judgments about experience (consisting of empirical concepts or terms) and experience itself (consisting of empirical properties). The necessity implicit in (b) is therefore ultimately relative to the empirical claims that they make possible.

Now, as we saw in Chapter Three from Reichenbach and Kuhn, one can be a Principled Kantian by countenancing claims that are (b) but not (a). Subjective principles can be constitutive of all empirical concepts, terms, and properties without also being necessarily true or true for all times for human beings. In fact, Reichenbach himself maintains, we should understand geometric principles thus. So suppose that one does countenance claims that are (b) but not (a). Because pure intuition is supposed to be anthropocentric and so necessary relative to human beings, those claims would not derive from *a priori* conceptual constructions in pure intuition. They would derive from some other subjective source. Schlick therefore persuaded Reichenbach that he "should designate [his] *a priori* principles as conventions" (Schlick 1979/1921, p. 324) in Poincaré's fashion.[17] Subjective principles would derive from linguistic convention in particular. And, for these theorists, because linguistic convention differs across different (linguistic) communities, such principles are not anthropocentric but ethnocentric. They involve the linguistic (and likely conceptual and perceptual) capacities that subjects have as members of a community.[18] It is not Reichenbach but Carnap who developed this idea fully. I consider Carnap now.

---

17. See Coffa (2008/1991, pp. 202–03), Friedman (1999, pp. 62–68), and Jonathan Y. Tsou (2003, pp. 575–76).

18. Albert Einstein apparently agreed with Reichenbach, retaining (at least) parts of (b) while rejecting (a):

> The theoretical attitude here advocated [in the general theory of relativity] is distinct from that of Kant only by the fact that we do not conceive of the "categories" as unalterable (conditioned by the nature of the understanding) but as (in the logical sense) free

Carnap's subjective principles are meant to derive from linguistic convention, and so from the subject's "language" or "linguistic framework" (1988/1952, suppl. A), as employed by her community. Because that language or framework articulates the legitimate linguistic capacities of that community, the framework is subjective in my sense. Moreover, for Carnap, because his subjective principles derive purely linguistically, they are analytic. They are not however analytic in Kant's or Frege's sense. Carnap broadens the notion of analyticity beyond theirs—even beyond what Schlick encouraged Reichenbach himself to do.[19] For Carnap, the set of analytic statements includes semantic rules (2003/1934), meaning postulates (1988/1952, suppl. B), and ultimately any claim that, as conventional, is part of a background language or framework that the subject chooses within which to articulate and empirically verify empirical claims (1988/1952, suppl. A).[20]

The effect of Carnap's making his principles analytic can be illuminated *via* Kant's distinction among analytic *a priori*, synthetic *a priori*, and synthetic *a posteriori*. As we saw in §2, Carnap rejected Kant's synthetic *a priori* judgments. For Carnap, *a priori* statements just are analytic. As I would put it, for Carnap, statements can derive from a subjective source (and so be *a priori* in an ontological sense), and be insusceptible to empirical justification or verification (and so be *a priori* in an epistemological sense), only if they are purely linguistic claims (and so are analytic). Consequently Carnap's analytic statements are meant to play two roles. First, they are meant to play the role of Kant's synthetic *a priori* judgments. Both Kant's judgments and Carnap's statements are meant to be subjective, and ultimately constitutive, principles. Second, Carnap's analytic statements are meant to play the role of Kant's analytic *a priori* judgments. Admittedly Kant's analytic *a priori* judgments are meant to express conceptual claims; Carnap's analytic statements, linguistic claims. Yet linguistic claims just are conceptual claims expressed in

---

conventions. They appear to be *a priori* only insofar as thinking without the positing of categories and of concepts in general would be as impossible as is breathing in a vacuum (1970/1949, p. 674).

19. As Thomas Uebel argues, Rudolf Carnap effects "a considerable widening [of Poincaré's notion of convention] to … entire language systems" (2012, p. 8).

20. Because Carnap (1988/1952, suppl. A) accepts the analytic/synthetic distinction, he accepts the existence of synthetic statements, which, for him, would be true in virtue of language (a subjective source) and experience (an objective source). Carnap is therefore a Dualist and Kantian too. Indeed in Chapter Nine, §2, I explain that he is a Principled Kantian. Moreover, while Kant takes experience to be conceptual and *sensation* to be non-conceptual, Carnap takes *experience* to be non-conceptual (and so an objective source). Previously (2003/1928) Carnap had contrasted concepts not with experience but with *sense data*.

language. Each conveys no more than what is contained in its grammatical subject. As Kant (1998/1787, A7/B10–11) himself might say, Carnap's analytic statements express "clarification" not "amplification" because, in virtue of their grammatical subjects "conceptually [or semantically] containing" their predicates, they can be "thought" (or meant) through "identity" (specifically the semantic identity of definition). Finally Kant's one kind of *a posteriori* judgment, the synthetic *a posteriori*, is itself replaced with Carnap's one kind of synthetic statement, which is synthetic *simpliciter*. Each plays the same role also. Kant's synthetic *a posteriori* judgments and Carnap's synthetic statements both serve as empirical claims. Hence Kant's threefold distinction among analytic *a priori*, synthetic *a priori*, and synthetic *a posteriori* collapses into Carnap's twofold distinction between analytic and synthetic.

Carnap's notion of analyticity promised to allow the logical empiricists to retain Principlism while avoiding the arguments against Kant's version of it. Nonetheless Quine soon took issue with the view of Carnap, his mentor.

4. QUINE'S ARGUMENTS AGAINST CARNAP'S PRINCIPLISM

As we saw in Chapter Five, Quine is an un-Principled Kantian. He embraces Dualism:

DUALISM: All empirical concepts, terms, or properties are linked essentially to subjective and objective sources.

but shuns Principlism:

PRINCIPLISM: The subjective source of all empirical concepts, terms, or properties takes the form of subjective principles.

For Quine, the subjective source, along with its objective dual, is holistically distributed across the whole of one's theory or language.

Quine not only shuns Principlism however. He publicly impugns it more vigorously than anyone else before or since. Further, because with the demise of Kant's notion of synthetic apriority Carnap's notion of analyticity was thought to be the best way of making sense of Principlism, Quine is not only analyticity's but also Principlism's principal opponent. In fact Quine offers six arguments against analyticity and so ultimately Carnap's Principlism. The arguments fall into three groups.[21] Here I consider each in turn.

---

21. See Friedman (1999, chs. 7, 9) for his take on the Carnap/Quine debate. See Richard Creath (2008, p. 327) for various understandings of Quine's arguments. See Scott Soames (2003b, ch. 16) for discussion more sympathetic to Quine, and Gillian Russell (2007; 2011, chs. 4–6) for recent research on analyticity including an alternative summation of Quine's arguments.

Quine's first group of arguments against analyticity has two members:

(i) Quine (2008/1936) argues that, if statements in logic and mathematics, which are supposedly analytic, can be regarded as conventional, then so can any statement. But then, unfortunately for Carnap, convention is too weak to establish any non-arbitrary distinction between analytic and synthetic, and so any clear characterization of analyticity.

(ii) Not just Kant's synthetic *a priori* but also his analytic *a priori* judgments are meant to be necessarily true or true for all times (for human beings),[22] Reichenbach's (a). Regarding the analytic *a priori*, that is because they are meant to express conceptual claims. So one property of analyticity, albeit Kant's rather than Carnap's, is such necessity. Now, as a behaviorist, Quine (2006/1953, essay 2, §6) glosses a necessary statement as one "held true come what may" (p. 43). He then argues that, because any statement *can* be held true come what may given adjustments elsewhere, the alleged class of analytic statements lacks identity conditions. Since (for Quine) there is no entity without identity, there is no such class. Though as stated this argument is not against Carnap's notion of analyticity, it can be modified into one. Quine merely needs to argue that any statement can be held true *relative to other statements* given adjustments elsewhere. Again the alleged class of analytic statements lacks identity conditions. Again there is no such class.[23]

Quine's point in these two arguments is that, because we can always rationally reconstruct how statements relate to one another, those relations are not linguistically significant. For Carnap, since the analytic/synthetic distinction is linguistic, Quine concludes that Carnap's notion of analyticity in particular is not viable. Because of the role that rational reconstruction plays in it, we might understand this first group of arguments as expressing Quine's Argument from Rational Reconstruction:

ARGUMENT FROM RATIONAL RECONSTRUCTION: Because theories can always be rationally reconstructed, the actual relations among their statements are linguistically irrelevant. *A fortiori* any perceived analyticity relation is itself linguistically irrelevant.

---

22. Kant's analytic *a priori* are meant to be necessarily true or true for all times *simpliciter*, and so *a fortiori* for human beings.

23. I follow Roger Gibson (1986, pp. 104–05), Georges Rey (1994, pp. 79–81), and Russell (2007, p. 719; 2011, pp. 135–42) in taking Quine to argue from holism against analyticity. Michael Dummett (1993/1973) and Gila Sher (1999) take Quine to argue conversely.

The second group of Quine's arguments has three members:

(iii) Quine (2008/1936) urges that because there is an infinity of logical truths, which are paradigmatically analytic, logical truths must be characterized by convention. "[L]ogic" itself, however, "is needed for inferring logic from conventions" (p. 104). This results in an infinite regress. Because convention cannot do the work that Carnap needs it to do, no statements can be true in virtue of it. But then none can be analytic.[24]

(iv) Quine (2006/1953, essay 2, §§1–5) argues that no attempt to characterize analyticity so far proposed avoids relying on other problematic intensional notions. Recognizing that Kant characterizes analyticity in terms of conceptual containment, Quine contends that Kant's "intent, evident more from the use he makes of the notion of analyticity than from his definition of it, can be restated thus: a statement is analytic when it is true by virtue of meanings and independently of fact" (p. 21). Quine then argues that characterizing analyticity in terms of meanings makes an unnecessary metaphysical commitment to meanings as objects (§1). Characterizing analyticity in terms of synonymy, definition, interchangeability *salva veritate*, or necessity is circular (§§2–4). And characterizing analyticity in terms of semantic rules is both arbitrary (and so reminiscent of argument (i)) and at best characterizes analytic-in-*L* not analytic *simpliciter* (§5). Carnap himself appeals to the intensional notions of synonymy, definition, and semantic rules when attempting to characterize analyticity in terms of linguistic convention. So Carnap's and, Quine claims, all other intensional characterizations fail.[25]

(v) Pressed by Quine in all these ways, Carnap eventually (1988/1952, suppl. B) tried characterizing analyticity behaviorally.[26] Yet Quine (1964, ch. 2) maintains that analyticity cannot be detected by a radical translator, whose data for translation are purely behavioral. Since, Quine believes, any such property is detectable by

---

24. Quine's inspiration is Lewis Carroll (1895), who argues that logical inference rules must be taken as postulates lest an infinite regress concerning their justification result.

25. See Herbert Paul Grice and Peter F. Strawson (1956), Paul A. Boghossian (1999), Eliot Sober (2000), and Russell (2007, pp. 718–19; 2011, pp. 129–35) for more on (iv).

26. See Thomas G. Ricketts (1982, pp. 123–27).

the radical translator, analyticity is illegitimate. Hence this new characterization by Carnap also fails.[27]

In each argument Quine purportedly eliminates ways to characterize analyticity and with it Carnap's principles: (iii) conventionally, (iv) intensionally, and (v) behaviorally. We might then think of this second group of arguments as expressing Quine's Argument from Elimination:

ARGUMENT FROM ELIMINATION: Analyticity cannot be characterized conventionally, intensionally, or behaviorally. Yet all attempts at characterizing it have chosen one of these. No attempt at characterizing analyticity therefore succeeds.

The last group of Quine's arguments against analyticity has one member:

(vi) Quine maintains that, even if a statement is introduced into a theory by "legislative postulation" (2008/1960, p. 75), the statement is not thereby analytic. For it can eventually enter into holistic relations with other, clearly empirical statements.

He offers as example:

When in relativity theory momentum is found to be not quite proportional to velocity, despite its original definition as mass times velocity, there is no flurry over redefinition or contradiction in terms, and I don't think there should be. The definition served its purpose in introducing a word for subsequent use, and the word was thereafter ours to use in the evolving theory, with no lingering commitments (p. 60).

"Definition," Quine concludes, making the same point as he did with postulation, "is episodic." Postulation and definition, and therefore Carnap's linguistic convention, are themselves "epistemologically insignificant" (p. 61). In fact to take a statement's origin in postulation, definition, or convention to indicate its status as true by postulation, definition, or convention—and so to be analytic—is to confuse epistemology with genealogy. Quine is thus warning against a kind of genetic fallacy regarding the status of statements. We might therefore think

---

27. Quine's radical translator inspired Donald Davidson's radical interpreter, considered in Chapters Four and Five. Nonetheless, while Davidson invokes the radical interpreter to elucidate meaning, Quine invokes the radical translator to eliminate meaning. See Davidson (2002, essay 5).

of this third group of arguments against analyticity as expressing Quine's Argument Invoking the Genetic Fallacy:

> ARGUMENT INVOKING THE GENETIC FALLACY: Though some statements are introduced into a theory by postulation, such genealogy entails nothing about their epistemology. Postulation is therefore no indicator of analyticity either.

Hence, as I understand Quine, his six arguments reduce to three.[28] Now, if Quine is right, then Carnap has no license to his notion of analyticity. But then Carnap has no license to Principlism. Pending a replacement, we therefore have none either.

5. FRIEDMAN'S PRINCIPLISM

Fortunately Friedman has recently (2000, 2001, 2002a, 2008, 2010a, 2010c) proposed his own version of Principlism. He does so by combining elements of Carnap's and Kuhn's.[29] As we saw in §§3–4, Carnap's principles are analytic statements. As we saw in Chapter Three, Kuhn's principles are implicit within his paradigms (2012/1962), disciplinary matrices (2012/1970; 1979, essay 12), and lexical taxonomies (2002, essays 1–4, 11).

Friedman calls his own subjective principles 'relativized a priori principles'. Following both Carnap and Kuhn, Friedman proposes that his principles are *relativized* because they are not necessarily true or true for all times (for human beings), Reichenbach's (a). They are instead necessary relative to the empirical claims, and derivatively their empirical terms, from which they are constituted, part of Reichenbach's (b). And Friedman follows both Carnap and Kuhn in maintaining that his Principlism is (in my terms) ethnocentric. Different communities have different principles relative to them. Moreover,

---

28. Morton White (1973/1950), whom Quine (2006/1953, p. 46, n. 22) cites, anticipates many of these. Like Quine (essay 2, §§1–4), White focuses on explaining analyticity in terms of synonymy. He then presents three arguments against being able to explain synonymy itself:

   (i) Appealing to counterfactual conditionals is inadequate, because counterfactuals themselves require explanation (1973/1950, p. 135).
   (ii) Appealing to behavior is inadequate, because strong assent to allegedly synthetic statements is behaviorally indistinguishable from strong assent to allegedly analytic ones (pp. 132–34).
   (iii) Appealing to "artificially constructed languages" with "definitional rules" is inadequate, because it not only fails to explain synonymy in ordinary language but also relies on the notion of a definitional rule, which is itself arbitrary (pp. 126–29).

29. Friedman is ubiquitously explicit about his own debt to Kant. Mauricio Suárez (2012) calls Friedman's project "developmental Kantianism."

Defending Principlism

again following both Carnap and Kuhn, Friedman proposes that, though his principles are necessary relative to empirical claims and terms, they are not themselves empirical. As I understand them, Friedman's principles are meant to be *a priori* in both ontological and epistemological senses. Ontologically they are meant to derive from a subjective source. As I explain below, that source is a kind of convention different from Carnap's. Epistemologically they are meant to be insusceptible to empirical justification or verification within the requisite community. Friedman's relativized *a priori* principles are in fact meant to be necessary relative to empirical claims of that community without themselves being vulnerable to experience.

Now, because Friedman thinks that his principles satisfy (b), he is committed to Ontological Principlism:

ONTOLOGICAL PRINCIPLISM: The subjective source of all empirical concepts, terms, or properties takes the form of subjective principles constitutive of those concepts, terms, or properties.

Friedman cares about empirical concepts and terms, and potentially also properties. As we see below, he even calls his relativized *a priori* principles "constitutively relativized a priori."[30] Moreover, from Carnap specifically, Friedman takes the idea that his relativized *a priori* principles should be explicit. Though Carnap's analytic statements are meant to derive from linguistic frameworks, those statements are themselves his principles. They are not implicit within larger, often ambiguous structures, as is the case for principles implicit in Kuhn's paradigms, disciplinary matrices, or lexical taxonomies. From both Carnap and Kuhn, Friedman takes the idea that his principles should be conventions upon which members of a community agree. Finally, from Kuhn specifically, Friedman takes the idea that the relevant conventions are ethnocentric in a historically situated way. While Carnap's analytic statements are conventional insofar as they are relative to a linguistic framework adopted by a community, Kuhn's are conventional insofar as they are relative to a "time, place, and culture" (Kuhn 2002, p. 245). Friedman intends his own relativized *a priori* principles to be the same.

It is worth pausing on this last point. For Carnap, which statements are analytic is a matter not of which statements subjects do or did treat as conventional. It is a matter instead of which statements philosophers should treat as conventional when understanding the practices of a community. And, for Carnap, philosophers should be guided by ahistorically logical rather than

---

30. See Friedman (*e.g.*, 2001, pp. 30, 31, 39, 71, 83; 2008, pp. 95–96). Though I cannot discuss it here, Friedman is also committed to Ontological Dualism. Indeed in Chapter Nine, §2, I explain that he is a Principled Kantian.

actually historical considerations. In particular Carnap approves of rational reconstruction to distill the allegedly non-rational (psychological, sociological, historical) factors from science. Conversely, for Friedman (following Kuhn), which statements are relativized *a priori* just is a matter of which statements subjects do or did treat as conventional. For him, there is no reconstructing history to make sense of some ahistorical logic. As K. Brad Wray notes:

> Kuhn thought the history of science was the data from which philosophers would develop an accurate descriptive account of science and how it works. ... Rational reconstructions were unacceptable as far as Kuhn was concerned (2012, p. 5).

As Friedman himself explains: "[M]y implementation of this idea of relativized constitutively a priori principles ... essentially depends on an historical argument" (2008, p. 96). Richard Creath is right to take Friedman's point even further: "The history is not an illustration of [Friedman's] argument ... ; it *is* the argument" (2010, p. 504).

Thus Friedman sides with Kuhn over Carnap on the relevance of historical situatedness of communities.[31] There is another difference between Carnap and Friedman, also tracing to Kuhn. Friedman urges that "one could attempt to combine basic aspects of Carnap's philosophy of formal languages or frameworks with fundamental features of Thomas Kuhn's much less formal theory of scientific revolutions." Moreover, Friedman continues, doing so would allow one to avoid

> ... the drawbacks of Carnapian formal *Wissenschaftslogik*. In particular, W. V. Quine's well-known and widely accepted attack on the Carnapian conception of analytic truth need no longer compel us to adopt a thoroughgoing epistemological holism according to which there is nothing left of the a priori at all (2001, p. xii).

Friedman's point is that "Carnapian formal *Wissenschaftslogik*," or logical regimentation of science, makes Quine's arguments against analyticity compelling. Friedman later explains:

> Carnap's theory of formal languages or linguistic frameworks was to be developed ... within what Carnap called *Wissenschaftslogik* and, as such, within mathematical logic. ... In particular, then, the fundamental

---

31. Friedman's commitment to Ontological Dualism would commit him to a related view for non-scientists, as it did for Kuhn. See Chapter Three, §2.

distinction, in the context of any given formal or linguistic framework, between logical and empirical rules, analytic and synthetic sentences, was itself supposed to be a purely formal or logical distinction. But one of the main pillars of Quine's attack on the analytic/synthetic distinction [and so on the notion of analyticity] is simply that, from a purely formal or logical point of view, all sentences derivable within a given formal system are so far completely on par—so that, more specifically, Carnap's attempt further to characterize some subset of derivable sentences as analytic ultimately amounts to nothing more than an otherwise arbitrary label (p. 40).

Friedman is describing one element of Quine's Argument from Elimination, *viz.*, that characterizing analyticity in terms of semantic rules is arbitrary (Quine 2006/1953, §5). Though Friedman himself never demonstrates that this is so, he nevertheless thinks that replacing Carnap's *Wissenschaftslogik* with "Kuhn's much less formal theory" permits his Principlism to avoid the fate of Carnap's.

There is much here to track. Fortunately Friedman illustrates his Principlism.[32] According to him, classical mechanics as actually developed by Isaac Newton divided into three components:

(1) a form of mathematics, the calculus;
(2) conceptions of force and mass embodied in his three laws of motion; and,
(3) a universal law of nature, the law of universal gravitation.

Friedman takes Newton to assume the truth of (1) and (2) to articulate and in turn empirically verify (3). For Newton, while (3) is amenable to empirical testing, (1) and (2) are not.[33] In fact, for Friedman, (1) and (2) are constitutive of (3). That makes (1) and (2) relativized *a priori* principles in Friedman's sense and subjective principles in mine.

---

32. I focus on Friedman on classical mechanics (2001, pp. 35–37, 39–40, 75–77, partly repeated in 2002a, pp. 177–79 and 2002b, pp. 374–75; and 2010, pp. 574–85). Friedman makes a similar historical argument based on special and general relativity (2001, pp. 39–40, 61–63, 77–80, 83–84, 86–99, partly repeated in 2002a, pp. 179–80 and 2002b, pp. 376–77, 380–81; and 2008 and 2010a, pp. 653–63). He also discusses quantum mechanics (2001, pp. 120–23), modern chemical theory (2001, pp. 124–26), and evolutionary biology (2001, pp. 126–29).

33. Newton assumes (or stipulates) the truth of the calculus because he takes it to describe the structure of absolute space and time. See Robert DiSalle (2002). Friedman claims that (1) and (2) correspond to Kant's principles of arithmetic and geometry, and pure natural science, respectively.

Friedman maintains that as a matter of historical fact Newton's formulation of (2) required him first to assume and so stipulate the mathematical resources encoded within (1). Why is that? Essential to Newton's second law of motion specifically was acceleration understood as velocity's instantaneous rate of change. Yet the idea of acceleration as such was unintelligible without the notion *of* an instantaneous rate of change, which was supplied by the calculus. Indeed, according to Friedman, had Newton not stipulated (1), then any statement of (2) would have had "no meaning or truth-value at all" (2001, p. 36). As I would put it, (1) was constitutive of the terms, and ultimately the meaning, of (2), thereby allowing (2) to be true or false. For the concepts to which (2) appealed were meaningful only against the background language provided by (1). Without stipulating the calculus, therefore, Friedman believes, Newton could not have articulated his second law. Further, those who came to accept classical mechanics came to agree on (1), and in that sense (1) could be seen as true by convention.

Friedman likewise maintains that as a matter of historical fact Newton's formulation of (3) required the fundamental conceptual resources encoded within (2). For what Friedman takes to be Newton's empirical law of universal gravitation could not have been hypothesized without the concept of an inertial frame of reference. Yet such a reference frame is one in which objects obey Newton's laws of motion. Without (2), (3) would likewise have had no meaning or truth-value. Here the notions to which (3) appealed were meaningful only against the background language provided by (1) and (2). Newton's notion of force in particular as used in the law of universal gravitation would have been ill-defined had his laws of motion not first been stipulated. And those who came to accept classical mechanics came to agree on accepting (1) and (2), and in that sense (1) and (2) could both be seen as true by convention.

Further, Friedman contends that as a matter of historical fact Newton had to assume or stipulate (1) and (2) not merely to articulate (3) but also to make (3) amenable to empirical verification. While (1) established the mathematical framework in which empirical claims were to be analyzed, (2) served as "coordinating principles" (2001, p. 74) or general rules coordinating the application *of* the mathematical framework to the physical phenomena described by the law of universal gravitation. Coordinating principles provide the linguistic means necessary for the description of concrete observations by abstract mathematical representations. In that sense relative to classical mechanics (2) is a fundamental law of nature presupposed by empirical inquiry. Stipulating (1) and (2) thereby permitted Newton to count empirical data as evidence for or against (3). Stipulating them therefore permitted the law of universal gravitation to be not merely empirically possible but also empirically verifiable.

For the sake of argument let me grant that Friedman got the history right. For him, the epistemological relations among claims like (1), (2), and (3), as they hold not merely historically but also generally, are themselves illuminated historically. According to Friedman, were scientists today to verify Newton's law of universal gravitation, then they would first have to assume or stipulate those claims, the calculus and laws of motion, which he takes to be constitutive of it. Only then could they coordinate empirical phenomena with the mathematical structure that the law of universal gravitation presupposed. Admittedly, were scientists today to verify some rationally reconstructed version of the law of universal gravitation, then this might not be true. But Newton's law itself, Friedman maintains, does require for its verification assumptions embodied in the calculus and laws of motion. Then *and* now (1) and (2) serve as principles constitutive of the language within which (3) could be articulated and empirically verified.

Regardless of whether Friedman is right, he has proposed an account of constitutive principles that are explicit, like Carnap's, and historically situated, like Kuhn's. Now Friedman's resulting Principlism is rich and promising.[34] It is also central to my defense of Principlism. Though Friedman himself never shows this, as I explain next, the most important arguments against other versions of Principlism fail to impugn it.

6. DEFENDING FRIEDMAN'S PRINCIPLISM

We saw in §2 that Kant's Principlism faces two classic arguments:

ARGUMENT FROM INAPPLICABILITY: Kant's notion of synthetic apriority is inapplicable to his own alleged cases.
ARGUMENT FROM NECESSARY INAPPLICABILITY: Kant's notion of synthetic apriority is necessarily inapplicable to any case at all.

Friedman's Principlism involves relativized *a priori* principles, meant to derive from historically situated linguistic convention. It does not involve Kant's synthetic *a priori* judgments, meant to derive from *a priori* conceptual constructions in pure intuition. Because both the Argument from Inapplicability and the Argument from Necessary Inapplicability are arguments against Kant's notion of synthetic apriority in particular, neither applies to Friedman's notion of relativized apriority. Nor should this be surprising. Friedman's notion of relativized apriority draws on Carnap's notion of analyticity, which Carnap developed with those classic arguments against Kant's notion of synthetic apriority in mind.

---

34. See especially Mary Domski and Michael Dickson (2010) and Suárez and Uebel (2012).

Nonetheless, because Friedman's notion *does* draw on Carnap's, Friedman's notion of relativized apriority, it might be impugned by Quine's arguments. We saw in §4 that Quine's arguments reduce to three. The first is this:

ARGUMENT FROM RATIONAL RECONSTRUCTION: Because theories can always be rationally reconstructed, the actual relations among their statements are linguistically irrelevant. *A fortiori* any perceived analyticity relation is itself linguistically irrelevant.

Carnap's Principlism is vulnerable to the argument because, as we saw in §§4–5, Carnap appeals to rational reconstruction to distil the allegedly non-rational elements from science, thereby claiming to identify statements that are analytic. Quine then appeals to rational reconstruction to show that which statements appear analytic is arbitrary. We might therefore think of Quine's argument as a *reductio ad absurdum* of Carnap's view. Friedman himself however does not appeal to rational reconstruction at all. For Friedman, it is irrelevant that the historical case of classical mechanics could be rationally reconstructed so that (3) the law of universal gravitation would be conventional and (1) the calculus would be empirical, or that (1) *or* (3) could—with enough ingenuity—be held true come what may. For him, which statements are constitutive principles is determined by appealing to the history of science. Quine's argument misses the mark.[35]

Next consider Quine's Argument from Elimination:

ARGUMENT FROM ELIMINATION: Analyticity cannot be characterized conventionally, intensionally, or behaviorally. Yet all attempts at characterizing it have chosen one of these. No attempt at characterizing analyticity therefore succeeds.

Though the argument is in terms of 'analyticity' rather than 'relativized a priority', Friedman's view is close enough to Carnap's that I should consider whether the argument *modulo* this difference impugns Friedman's version of Principlism. It does not. As we saw in Chapter Five, an argument from elimination is only as strong as it eliminates all relevant alternatives. Now it requires an inductive leap to think that merely because all attempts at characterizing analyticity *have* been conventional, intensional, or behavioral in the past (even if true), all attempts *will* be so in the future. In fact we already know that this is false. Noam Chomsky (1969, 2002) has attempted to characterize analyticity by appealing to syntactic data of natural languages. Likewise Laurence BonJour has attempted to characterize analyticity in

---

35. As I argued elsewhere (2009a, §3), Quine should himself be sympathetic to Friedman's appeal.

terms of "rational insight or rational intuition" (1998, p. 102, his emphasis suppressed). Moreover, and more importantly, Friedman's own principles are meant to derive from neither the kind of ahistorical rationally reconstructed convention that Quine targets, nor intension or behavior. They are meant to derive from historically situated convention instead. Friedman's historically situated conventionalism in particular therefore fails to make Quine's eliminative list.[36]

Quine's final argument remains:

ARGUMENT INVOKING THE GENETIC FALLACY: Though some statements are introduced into a theory by postulation, such genealogy entails nothing about their epistemology. Postulation is therefore no indicator of analyticity either.

According to Friedman, however, Newton's postulation of (1) and (2) was not irrelevant to the epistemological role that they played relative to (3). It illuminated the role. On Friedman's view understanding how classical mechanics could and still does yield successful empirical predictions requires understanding some of its claims as principles stipulated to constitute the terms in which concrete observations can yield scientific knowledge. For Friedman, history informs, and perhaps is even part of, epistemology. Genealogical properties are not necessarily "epistemologically insignificant" (Quine 2008/1991, p. 61). Not all alleged instances of the genetic fallacy are actually instances of it. In fact, if Friedman is right, then we have to rethink the scope of the genetic fallacy itself.

Further, even independent of such thinking, on internal grounds Quine should not advance the Argument Invoking the Genetic Fallacy in the first place. Quine maintains that epistemology studies how "the meager input" from sensation gives rise to the "torrential output" (1969, p. 83) of theory. Whether or not he is right, Quine believes that epistemology studies this without declaring it insignificant that the input is *from* sensation:

> Two cardinal tenets of empiricism remain unassailable however and so remain to this day. One is that whatever evidence there is for science is sensory evidence. The other ... is that all inculcation of meanings of words must rest ultimately on sensory evidence (p. 75).

But then, by parity of reasoning, Quine ought to believe that epistemology should study how a statement enters a theory by postulation without declaring it epistemologically insignificant that the input is *from* postulation either.

---

36. Creath (2010, p. 498) thinks that Quine's argument fails against Friedman even on behavioral, and so Quine's own, terms.

If genealogical facts about sensation have epistemological import, and Quine thinks that they do, then genealogical facts about postulation have epistemological import also. Quine cannot consistently maintain that postulation is epistemologically insignificant. Hence independent of Principlism—Kant's, Carnap's, or Friedman's—Quine should withdraw his Argument Invoking the Naturalistic Fallacy altogether.[37]

7. PRINCIPLISM DEFENDED

What does this mean for Principlism? Recall where we have been. In §1 I considered Kant's Principlism, according to which subjective principles are synthetic *a priori*, and in §2 classic arguments against this. In §3 I considered Carnap's Principlism, according to which subjective principles are analytic, and in §4 Quine's arguments against that. Next in §5 I considered Friedman's Principlism, according to which subjective principles are relativized *a priori*, and now in §6 concluded that classic arguments against Kant's and Quine's arguments against Carnap's versions of Principlism fail to impugn Friedman's.

Though this does not show that Principlism is true, it does respond to everyone important on record who thinks it false. For I have shown that no important argument against Principlism impugns it. I have thereby shifted the burden to Principlism's opponents to propose other arguments against it. This amounts to defending Principlism itself.

There is one more noteworthy part of my defense. Though he never actually illustrates this, we saw in §5 that Friedman thinks that the informal nature of his subjective principles spares his Principlism the same fate as Carnap's. As we saw implicitly in §6, however, Friedman's informalism is irrelevant. The historical nature of Friedman's principles protects them from Quine. I have therefore defended Friedman's own project in an informative way.

8. LESSONS FOR KANTIAN CONCEPTUAL GEOGRAPHY

In this chapter we have seen the history of Principlism, arguments against Principlism, and Principlism's defense. In this conclusion I draw three lessons for Kantian conceptual geography generally.

---

37. Quine might argue that Friedman's alleged relativized *a priori* principles seem necessary because due to their empirical centrality scientists shield them from revision. See Nathaniel Goldberg (2009a, §§2-3) for why this argument also fails.

Defending Principlism

First, Principlism *has* been defended. Though I have not proved Principlism true, I have shifted the burden against those who think it false. I have also along the way advanced Friedman's view in its own right.

Second, according to Reichenbach, Kant's synthetic *a priori* judgments are meant to be:

(a) necessarily true or true for all times (for human beings); and
(b) constitutive of all empirical concepts, terms, and properties.

We can now appreciate how that maps onto my own analysis of Kant's version of Principlism. That Kant's synthetic *a priori* judgments are meant to be (a) maps onto my claim that Kant's principles are anthropocentric. They are meant to be necessarily true or true for all times for human beings. That Kant's synthetic *a priori* judgments are meant to be (b) maps onto my claim that Kant's principles are subjective constitutive principles. Subjective principles (constitutive or acquisitive) are claims, distinct from any empirical ones, that are the form or basic epistemological or linguistic unit that the subjective source of empirical concepts, terms, or properties takes. So Reichenbach's particular insight is that Kant's subjective principles (on an ontological construal) are both anthropocentric, (a), and constitutive, (b).

And third, that insight can be generalized to all versions of Principlism. According to Kant, subjective principles are anthropocentric; according to Carnap, Kuhn, and Friedman, they are ethnocentric; according to Davidson, they are logocentric; and we can imagine a kind that is idiocentric. Likewise, according to at least Kuhn and Davidson, as well as an epistemological construal of Kant's transcendental idealism, subjective principles can be acquisitive. Hence generalizing Reichenbach's insight yields the following. Subjective principles might be meant to be

(a′) necessarily true or true for all times for human beings generally, members of communities specifically, individuals particularly, *or* language users overall; and
(b′) constitutive *or* acquisitive of all empirical concepts, terms, or properties.

(a′) specifies the principles' subjective scope, and (b′) specifies whether the principles are constitutive or acquisitive. While (a)–(b) describe Kant's Principlism specifically, (a′)–(b′) describe any Principlism generally.

PART FOUR

Looking for New Land Within Kantianism's Borders

SEVEN

From Dualism to a Kantian Account of Meaning

In Part One of *Kantian Conceptual Geography* I defined 'Kantianism' as any view that does satisfy Dualism and may satisfy Principlism. In Part Two I explored the resulting Kantian territory by considering how Dualism and Principlism play out in Philip Pettit's, Thomas Kuhn's, and Donald Davidson's views. In Part Three I defended Kantianism's borders by defending Dualism and Principlism themselves. Now in Part Four I look for new land within those borders by searching for previously uncharted parts of Kantian territory itself. In this chapter I rely on Dualism to disclose a Kantian account of meaning and in the next chapter consider problems that such an account faces. In the chapter that follows I rely on Principlism to disclose Kantian thoughts on the nature of empirical truth. Because meaning and truth are issues central to analytic philosophy, relying on Dualism and Principlism, respectively, to say substantive things about them further demonstrates the value of Kantian conceptual geography itself.

Now by a 'Kantian account of meaning' I do not mean Immanuel Kant's account of meaning, even if one could be gotten from his view. Instead I mean an account of meaning entailed by Kantianism generally and Dualism specifically. In fact, as I explain below, there are accounts of meaning in the analytic literature that count as Kantian in my sense. Nonetheless I am after a general account, one that reveals what a Kantian account of meaning *qua* Kantian would be. Moreover locating a Kantian account of meaning in the conceptual landscape situates other accounts of meaning relative to it. It thereby illuminates meaning itself. Finally, though as a Kantian conceptual geographer my aim is to survey rather than to settle on any particular view, I do show that a Kantian account of meaning faces none of the problems that I show these other accounts face. We therefore have reason to prefer a Kantian account to them.

The chapter proceeds as follows. In §1 I identify three general formulations and three specific examples of a Kantian account of meaning. In §2, after exploring that account, I explain that we can put it into better focus by considering contrasting accounts of meaning. In fact each view that in Chapter One I contrasted with Kantianism—Platonic and Aristotelian realism, Berkeleian idealism, Lockean hybridism, and Hegelian pragmatism—has a correlative account of meaning that contrasts with a Kantian account. Moreover there exist accounts of meaning in the analytic literature approximating most of these. In §3 I argue that Friedrich Ludwig Gottlob Frege's (1993/1892) account of sense and reference approximates a Platonic realist account of meaning. In §4 I argue that Hilary Putnam (1993/1975) and Saul Kripke's (2005/1980) "new theory of reference" approximates an Aristotelian realist account of meaning. In §5 I argue that Herbert Paul Grice's (1991, chs. 5, 6, 14) account of speaker meaning approximates a Berkeleian idealist account of meaning. In §6 I argue that, though there is no approximation of a Lockean hybridist account of meaning in the literature, we can nevertheless imagine one. And in §7 I argue that Davidson's accounts of radical interpretation and language learning are intended (even if they ultimately fail) to approximate a Hegelian pragmatist account of meaning.[1] In each section I also consider one problem that each contrasting account of meaning faces that a Kantian account does not. Finally in §8 I draw lessons for Kantian conceptual geography generally.

1. KANTIAN ACCOUNT OF MEANING

What is a Kantian account of meaning? Let me answer this by offering three general formulations and three specific examples of such an account. The first general formulation relies on Dualism:

DUALISM: All empirical concepts, terms, or properties are linked essentially to subjective and objective sources.

My focus is on empirical terms. As we have seen, there are two ways for such terms to be "linked essentially" to subjective and objective sources. First, those terms could be *constituted essentially out of* subjective and objective sources. Such sources go into the terms' very being. In that sense subjective and objective

---

1. As we saw in Chapter Four, §1, Donald Davidson officially introduces his account of radical interpretation in an eponymous article (2001d/1984, essay 9) and elaborates on it throughout his career (*e.g.*, 2002, essay 10; 2005a, ch. 3). He presents his account of language learning over several different articles (2002, essays 2, 3, 6, 8, 9, 13; 2004, essay 9; 2005b, essays 1, 4, 7, 8, 9).

sources go into their meaning. On this view the meaning in English of 'gold' would be constituted, or constructed, essentially out of something subjective (ultimately a subject's specific conceptual, linguistic, or perceptual capacities) and something objective (ultimately something independent of the subject). Its meaning derives from both. Second, those terms could be *acquired by a subject's appealing essentially to* subjective and objective sources. Such sources now go into a subject's very knowledge of the terms. In that sense subjective and objective sources go into a subject's learning them—without impacting their meaning. On that view 'gold' would be acquired, or learned, by a subject's appealing essentially to something subjective and something objective. Its mastery would depend on both. Hence Ontological Dualism concerning terms involves their meaning while Epistemological Dualism concerning terms involves merely their mastery:

> ONTOLOGICAL DUALISM: All empirical concepts, terms, or properties are constituted essentially out of subjective and objective sources.
>
> EPISTEMOLOGICAL DUALISM: All empirical concepts, terms, or properties are acquired by a subject's appealing essentially to subjective and objective sources.

Ontological Dualism concerning terms is itself the first general formulation of a Kantian account of meaning. It tells us that meaning is connected to subjective and objective sources. As we saw in my discussion of Kuhn and Davidson in Chapters Three and Four, respectively, all empirical terms mean what they do *in virtue of* subjective and objective sources. To appreciate this, recall Kuhn's and Davidson's kinds of Ontological Kantianism concerning terms. They are Kuhn's account of language learning, and Davidson's accounts of radical interpretation and language learning. These three accounts themselves amount to three specific examples of a Kantian account of meaning.

According to Kuhn's account of language learning, all empirical terms are constituted essentially out of ethnocentric responses to objects in the world. Taxonomic empirical terms mean what they do in a community's language if and only if normal members of that community under normal conditions of observation would respond to objects in the world by taxonomizing them in particular ways. And *via* these taxonomic ones whatever we can say about the world generally depends on how our historically situated community's practices, theories, and values teach us to respond to that world. Hence, for Kuhn, all empirical terms mean what they do in virtue of these subjective and objective sources.

Likewise, according to Davidson's accounts of both radical interpretation and language learning, all empirical terms are constituted essentially out of idiocentric responses to objects in the world. Concerning radical interpretation, empirical terms for directly triangulated objects mean what they do in a language if and only if a radical interpreter would *via* triangulating objects with a speaker of the language determine that they have that meaning. Other empirical terms get their meaning indirectly from these triangulated ones. Concerning language learning, empirical terms for directly triangulated objects mean what they do in a language if and only if a language learner learned the meaning of those terms by triangulating objects with her teacher. Again other empirical terms get their meaning indirectly from these triangulated ones. For Davidson, concerning both radical interpretation and language learning, all empirical terms mean what they do in virtue of these subjective and objective sources. This is so even though, as we saw in Chapter Four, Davidson's subjective principle, the principle of charity, is logocentric. It is also so even though, as we saw there as well, Davidson should reject his account of language learning. And it is so even though, as we saw in Chapter Five, Davidson's account of radical interpretation (and, I can add here, his account of language learning too) ultimately concern all terms, empirical or otherwise.[2]

So far we have seen the first general formulation and now three specific examples of a Kantian account of meaning. Generalizing these examples in particular reveals the second and third general formulation of such an account. To appreciate the second general formulation, consider the particular response-dependence biconditionals to which Kuhn's and Davidson's particular accounts commit them. Kuhn is committed to this:

> ETHNOCENTRIC CONCEPT-AND-TERM: Something is x for a community if and only if normal members of that community under normal conditions of observation for that community would conceive of it as falling under x and call it ⌜y⌝ to mean x in their language.

The subjective source of empirical concepts and terms are ethnocentric responses (and ultimately specific conceptual, linguistic, and perceptual capacities). The objective source are objects in the world—falling under 'normal conditions of observation for that community'. Ethnocentric Concept-and-Term counts as a response-dependence biconditional because it satisfies the first three requirements that I agreed with Crispin Wright were required of all such biconditionals.[3] First, it holds *a priori*. Second, it is non-reductive and non-eliminative. And third, it is to be specified non-trivially. Moreover Ethnocentric Concept-and-Term is a version of Dualism because it concerns

---

2. I say more about Davidson's logocentrism in Chapter Nine. Because in the context of a Kantian account of meaning it remains instructive to consider Davidson's account of language learning, I do so without worry here. Likewise, because concerning all terms entails concerning empirical terms, I limit myself to the empirical ones without worry here too.

3. See Crispin Wright (1988, pp. 19–22; 1989, p. 247; 1999/1992, pp. 114–17; 1993, pp. 77–82) regarding the first and Wright (1989, p. 247–48; 1999/1992, pp. 112, 120–23; 1993, p. 78) regarding the third. The second requirement is implicit in these and proximal passages.

all empirical terms. And it is a version of Ontological Dualism because something's being x for a community either (following Wright) constitutively depends on or (following Mark Johnston) is constitutively interdependent with subjective responses to objects in the world.[4]

Likewise Davidson is committed to these:

RI TERM: Something is x for a speaker if and only if a normal radical interpreter under normal conditions of radical interpretation would interpret the speaker's term ⌜y⌝ for it to mean x in the speaker's language.

LL TERM: Something is x for a speaker if and only if as a normal language learner under normal conditions of language learning she learned to call it ⌜y⌝ to mean x in her language.

In RI Term the subjective source are the radical interpreter's responses (and ultimately her specific conceptual, linguistic, and perceptual capacities) as she and the speaker triangulate objects in the world. The objective source are the speaker's observable behavior (including her utterances) and the objects that she and the speaker triangulate—falling under 'normal conditions of radical interpretation'. In LL Term the subjective source are the language learner's responses (ultimately the same specific capacities) as she and her teacher triangulate objects in the world. The objective source are those objects and her teacher's behavior given them—falling under 'normal conditions of language learning'. Both RI Term and LL Term count as response-dependence biconditionals because they too satisfy the first three of Wright's requirements. They hold *a priori*, are non-reductive and non-eliminative, and are to be specified non-trivially. They also amount to versions of Dualism because they concern all empirical terms. Moreover RI Term expresses either (following Wright) constitutive dependence or (following Johnston) constitutive interdependence and so would be a version of Ontological Dualism, while LL Term expresses both (following Wright or Johnston) a constitutive relation (of either kind) and (following Philip Pettit) an acquisitive relation and so would be a version of both Ontological and Epistemological Dualism, respectively. For present purposes only Ontological Dualism is relevant.

Now Kuhn's Ethnocentric Concept-and-Term and Davidson's RI Term and LL Term generalize:

GENERALIZED TERM: Something is x for a suitable subject under suitable conditions if and only if a suitable subject under suitable conditions would call it ⌜y⌝ to mean x in the second speaker's language.

---

4. See Wright (1999/1992, ch. 3 append.; 1993, pp. 77–82; 2001, pp. 191–99) and Mark Johnston (1993).

Generalized Term is the second general formulation of a Kantian account of meaning. Like Ethnocentric Concept-and-Term, RI Term, and LL Term, Generalized Term concerns subjective and objective sources. The subjective source is the second subject's responses to objects in the world, while the objective source is the first subject's behavior and the objects in the world to which it is directed.[5] Like Ethnocentric Concept-and-Term, RI Term, and LL Term, Generalized Term is meant to satisfy Wright's three requirements to count as response-dependent. Like these others, Generalized Term is meant to concern all empirical terms. Generalized Term is therefore a version of Dualism. Finally, like Ethnocentric Concept-and-Term, RI Term, and LL Term, Generalized Term understands something's being x for a subject as either constitutively depending on or constitutively interdependent with subjective responses to objects in the world. Generalized Term is therefore a version of Ontological Dualism. According to it, all empirical terms mean what they do in virtue of the subjective and objective sources associated with General Term itself. That makes it the second general formulation of a Kantian account of meaning.[6]

The third and final general formulation of a Kantian account of meaning is within reach. Because RI Term and LL Term are not especially intuitive versions of Davidson's two response-dependence theories of meaning, I replaced each with biconditionals that emphasize the connection between empirical terms and meaning:

> RI: For any empirical term in L, the term means what it does if and only if a normal radical interpreter under normal conditions of radical interpretation would interpret it in L to have that meaning.
>
> LL: For any empirical term in L, the term means what it does if and only if a normal language learner of L under normal conditions of language learning learned that the term has that meaning.

I can use RI and LL to formulate the third general formulation of a Kantian account of meaning. Because it is the most intuitive, let me call it 'Kantian Meaning' (*simpliciter*):

> KANTIAN MEANING: For any empirical term in L, the term means what it does if and only if a suitable subject under suitable conditions would take it to have that meaning.

---

5. Generalized Term is phrased to allow the "two" subjects to be numerically identical.

6. Generalized Term does not generalize RI Term's ahistoricism and LL Term's historicism. As we saw in Chapter Four, §4, these entail inconsistent results. Instead Generalized Term sides with ahistoricism. There are two reasons for this. First, Thomas Kuhn's Ethnocentric Concept-and-Term is itself ahistoricist. So Generalized Term generalizes two of the three specific response-dependence biconditionals. Second, as I argued in Chapter Four, §4, ahistoricism better respects the nature and purpose of meaning.

Kantian Meaning involves the same subjective and objective sources as does General Term. The subject's responses to objects in the world are subjective. Those objects—falling under 'suitable conditions'—are objective. Moreover Kantian Meaning, like Generalized Term, concerns all empirical terms and is a constitutive claim. According to Kantian Meaning, all empirical terms mean what they do in virtue of a suitable subject under suitable conditions taking them to have that meaning. It is then a version of Ontological Dualism also.

2. KANTIAN ACCOUNT EXPLORED

Hence I have found three general formulations of a Kantian account of meaning: Ontological Dualism concerning terms, Generalized Term, and Kantian Meaning. I have also found three specific examples of a Kantian account of meaning: Kuhn's account of language learning, and Davidson's accounts of radical interpretation and language learning. Nonetheless one might still ask how exactly a Kantian account of meaning imparts meaning to empirical terms. I explore this now.

Consider the first general formulation:

ONTOLOGICAL DUALISM: All empirical concepts, terms, or properties are constituted essentially out of subjective and objective sources.

Focusing on terms, Ontological Dualism says that the meaning of empirical terms has two sources. In reverse order, their *objective source* would be things like the world, objects in the world, or other persons and their behavior in the world. These all count from the subject's perspective as objective because they are independent of her specific conceptual, linguistic, or perceptual capacities. Conversely their *subjective source* would be the specific conceptual, linguistic, or perceptual capacities of the subject herself. Concerning Ontological Dualism in particular those capacities would interact with the objective source to constitute terms with meaning. Moreover, as we saw in Chapters Two, Three, and Four, the relevant subject might be counted in four different ways: *qua* individual, *qua* community member, *qua* human being, or *qua* language user. The resulting Dualism (and therefore Kantianism) would be idiocentric, ethnocentric, anthropocentric, or logocentric, respectively.

To appreciate how this imparts meaning to empirical terms, consider these subjective scopes in the order in which we encountered them. To simplify my examples, let me phrase things in terms of English as used by speakers *qua* human being, *qua* community member, *qua* individual, and *qua* language user (in that order). Though Pettit is an anthropocentric Epistemological Dualist, Kant is himself construable as an anthropocentric Ontological Dualist. So we can imagine a kind of Ontological Dualism concerning terms that is *anthropocentric*. On that account 'gold' in English as used by human beings generally would mean gold for them in virtue of normal human beings under normal conditions taking it to mean gold. Though not all human beings speak English, 'gold' in English would mean gold for any human being who did. Nonetheless members of other species might mean something else by it. Further, Kuhn presents a kind of Ontological Dualism concerning terms that is *ethnocentric*. 'Gold' in English as used by a specific community would mean gold for that community in virtue of normal members of that community under normal conditions taking it to mean gold. Though not all (or even any) members of that community might speak English, 'gold' in English as used by that community would mean gold for any member of that community who did. Nonetheless members of other communities might mean something else by it. Moreover Davidson presents two kinds of Ontological Dualism concerning terms that are *idiocentric*. 'Gold' in English as used by a particular individual would mean gold for that individual in virtue of the individual under normal conditions taking it to mean gold. Though not all individuals speak English, 'gold' in English as used by that individual would mean gold for that individual if she did. Nonetheless other individuals might mean something else by it. Finally, because Davidson's principle of charity is itself logocentric, his work suggests that there could be a kind of Ontological Dualism concerning terms that is itself *logocentric*. 'Gold' in English as used by any language user at all would mean gold for that language user in virtue of any normal language user under normal conditions taking it to mean gold. Though not all language users speak English, 'gold' in English as used by any language user would mean gold for any language user who did. This time no language user would mean anything else by it.

I can put a Kantian account of meaning into better focus by considering accounts of meaning contrasting with it. Because Ontological Dualism, the first general formulation, itself maintains that all empirical concepts, terms, or properties are constituted essentially out of subjective and objective sources, four accounts that contrast with a Kantian account of meaning come to mind. First, all empirical terms are constituted essentially out of only an objective source. Second, all empirical terms are constituted essentially out of only a subjective source. Third, only some empirical terms are constituted essentially out of subjective and objective sources. And fourth, no empirical terms are constituted essentially out of subjective or objective sources.

These contrasting accounts of meaning correlate with the views that in Chapter One I contrasted with Kantianism generally: realism, Platonic and Aristotelian; Berkeleian idealism; Lockean hybridism; and Hegelian pragmatism, respectively. In the next several sections I consider these contrasts. I also identify which if any account of meaning in the analytic literature approximates each, thereby revealing a new taxonomy for influential analytic views. Finally, for each contrasting account, I present a problem that it faces. I then show that, though a Kantian account of meaning faces its own problems—considered in Chapter Eight—it does not face these. Hence I reveal something about the conceptual contours of Kantianism itself by showing that a Kantian account of meaning does not share the same weaknesses as these other accounts. Moreover this provides reason to prefer it to them.

3. PLATONIC REALIST ACCOUNT OF MEANING

By a 'realist account of meaning' I mean any account of meaning that maintains that all empirical terms are constituted essentially out of only an objective source. Empirical terms would therefore mean what they do purely in virtue of that source. As we saw in Chapter One, Plato proclaims, and Aristotle agrees, that reality or the world itself comes constituted into species. "[S]pecies [have] ... natural joints" (*Phaedrus* 265e). Thus

> [s]uppose, for example, that we undertake to cut something. If we make the cut in whatever way *we* choose and with whatever tool *we* choose, we will not succeed in cutting. ... If we try to cut contrary to nature, ... we'll be in error (*Cratylus* 387a).[7]

The *Platonic* realist understands these "natural joints," or species-markers, as existing "*ante res*," or prior to the objects in the world whose speciation they make possible. By a 'Platonic realist account of meaning' I therefore mean any realist account that appeals to such *ante-res* objects. The *Aristotelian* realist understands these natural joints as existing only "*in rebus*," or in the objects in the world whose speciation they make possible. By an 'Aristotelian account of meaning' I therefore mean any realist account that appeals only to such *in-rebus* objects.

There are two influential accounts of meaning in the analytic literature approximating Platonic and Aristotelian realist accounts of meaning, respectively. Here I consider the former; in the next section, the latter. Frege's (1993/1892) account of sense and reference approximates a Platonic realist account of meaning. According to Frege, an empirical term's meaning concerns both its sense and reference. The reference of an empirical term—or the "referent," or object in the world, to which it refers—is the object that it is in

---

7. The *Phaedrus* translation is Alexander Nehamas and Paul Woodruff's; the *Cratylus*, C. D. C. Reeve's—both in John M. Cooper (1997). See also *Statesman* 262b.

virtue of the senses that pick it out. Senses themselves are *ante-res* objects. They exist in a supermundane realm of pure thought accessible to all rational beings independent of their specific conceptual, linguistic, or perceptual capacities. Senses are therefore akin to Platonic forms. Because senses, which are independent of such capacities, are sufficient to pick out referents that exist in the mundane realm, referents are independent of specific conceptual, linguistic, or perceptual capacities also. For Frege, while ideas are psychological and therefore "wholly subjective" (p. 145), senses and referents are neither. Senses and referents of empirical terms are instead constituted essentially out of only an objective source, reality (supermundane and mundane, respectively) independent of all subjects.

Frege's account, like all those contrasting with the Kantian one, is more nuanced than I can discuss here.[8] Nonetheless, because it does approximate a Platonic realist account of meaning, it faces a problem a version of which all forms of Platonic realism face. For Frege, senses exist independently of subjects in a separate realm and referents exist independently of subjects in this realm. Yet the mechanism by which subjects can epistemologically bridge this double ontological divide, between and within realms, is obscure. Moreover to say, as Frege does, that subjects are simply capable of "grasping" (p. 145) senses—and then stipulate that they can *via* such grasping simply pick out referents—fails to appease the Platonic realist's opponents. Nor can Frege appeal to specific subjective conceptual, linguistic, or perceptual capacities to explain how subjects can grasp senses and so refer to objects. For Frege, appealing to subjective capacities "psychologizes" meaning. It therefore fails to recognize its true, objective nature. Instead, for Frege, subjects grasp senses and so pick out referents by using something like pure reason, independent of any specifically subjective capacities. But "pure reason" is as obscure as the "grasping" that it is meant to do.

While a Kantian account of meaning faces other problems, it does not face the problem of epistemologically bridging a double ontological divide. The Kantian maintains that all empirical terms are constituted essentially out of subjective and objective sources. For her, there would be no supermundane divide to bridge to reach the realm of senses. Meaning is constituted by a subjective source, residing in the subject, and an objective source, residing in the mundane realm. And the subject can bridge the mundane divide to this objective source by appealing to her own specific capacities. There is no obscure "grasping" or more obscure "pure reason" required. Though the subject cannot know the objective source in itself, her empirical terms are nevertheless

---

8. Nuances include that not all senses have referents, that the referent of propositional-attitude phrases are senses, and that some referents (*e.g.*, of 'subjective') are themselves subjective.

meaningful in virtue of these subjective and objective sources themselves. This provides reason to prefer a Kantian account of meaning to a Platonic realist one.

4. ARISTOTELIAN REALIST ACCOUNT OF MEANING

Like the Platonic realist, the Aristotelian realist maintains that all empirical terms are constituted essentially out of only an objective source. Again reality or the world itself has "natural joints," and again a subject can use her terms to track them. Unlike the Platonic realist, however, the Aristotelian realist does not understand these joints (or species markers) as existing prior to the objects in the world whose speciation they make possible. The Aristotelian understands them as existing only in the objects themselves.

The "new theory of reference," associated with Putnam (1993/1975) and Kripke (2005/1980), approximates an Aristotelian realist account of meaning. Putnam and Kripke's (roughly shared)[9] idea is that (at least certain—more below) empirical terms are constituted essentially out of only an objective source, their reference. Empirical terms therefore mean what they do purely in virtue of their reference. And Putnam and Kripke understand the reference of empirical terms roughly as Frege would *sans* sense: as something independent of the subject's specific conceptual, linguistic, or perceptual capacities.

Putnam and Kripke themselves focus on (empirical) natural-kind terms and proper names. As they describe it, the subject uses such terms to "baptize" objects in the world containing essences, or objective properties that make the objects the species of object that they are. And these essences are constituted essentially out of only an objective source. They are natural joints embedded in objects. Essences are themselves *in rebus*. Moreover these terms, referring to those essences, can then be passed on to others in one's community across space and time. Anyone in the resulting chain of persons using these terms is thereby causally connected to those essences. Finally, because terms mean what they do in virtue of their referents, and these referents are the referents that they are in virtue of their essences, meaning is itself constituted essentially out of only an objective source, objects (and specifically their essences) in the world. The subject's terms track those essences themselves.

Now, because Putnam and Kripke limit themselves to natural-kind terms and proper names, unless these are exhaustive of all empirical terms, Putnam and Kripke do not themselves count as full-blooded Aristotelian realists concerning meaning. Nor are natural-kind terms and proper names so exhaustive.

---

9. See Robert Hanna (2006, p. 144, n. 7) and Ian Hacking (2007) for differences between Hilary Putnam's and Saul Kripke's views.

Nonetheless others have extended their account,[10] and we can for the sake of argument suppose that such an extension can cover (directly or indirectly) all empirical terms. A full-blooded Aristotelian account of meaning would result.

Such an account faces its own problem. Before considering it, however, it is noteworthy that an Aristotelian account also faces part of the problem faced by a Platonic realist account. As we saw in §3, in Frege's version of it, the Platonic realist must explain how subjects can epistemologically bridge the ontological divide between themselves and, on the one hand, senses that exist independently of them in a separate realm, and, on the other hand, referents that exist independently of them in this realm. While the Aristotelian realist does not have to provide a bridge to a separate realm, she does have to provide a bridge to objects existing independently of subjects in this realm. Moreover she must do so without appealing essentially to the subject's specific conceptual, linguistic, or perceptual capacities. And to say, as Putnam and Kripke do, that subjects can simply "refer" to essences fails to appease the Aristotelian's opponents. Some subject's ability to pick out *the* referent for her term is what is in question. Ironically Putnam later (1981) can be seen as making this point when distancing himself from his earlier (1993/1975) realist view by proposing an explicitly Kantian view called 'internal realism'. Now, according to Putnam (1981), subjective and objective sources are both essential to constitute an empirical term's meaning. Otherwise it is unclear which of the infinite ways in which subjects and objects relate is *the* reference relation.[11] Simply stipulating that, or leaving unanalyzed how, subjects can refer to particular objects is inadequate.

As we saw in §3, a Kantian account of meaning does not face this problem. The Kantian does not try to account for meaning independently of the subject's conceptual, linguistic, or perceptual capacities. So the Aristotelian realist inherits part of the problem that the Platonic realist faces which the Kantian does not face. Nonetheless let me for the remainder of this section focus on a different problem that an Aristotelian account of meaning specifically faces. It is the problem of empty names.

By 'empty name' I mean any natural-kind term or proper name with no referent. Consider 'phlogiston', which, though once thought to refer to a substance, in fact does not, and 'Sherlock Holmes', which, though in fiction

---

10. See especially Scott Soames (2003a).

11. Thus, Putnam (1981, essay 2) maintains, according to the realist (and he has in mind the metaphysical realist, who would be Platonic or Aristotelian), the reference of 'cat' in English could as easily be a cat or a cherry. See Nathaniel Goldberg (2008a, pp. 472, 484, 486, ns. 8–9; 2011, pp. 740, 747, n. 6) for more on Putnam, and Yemima Ben-Menahem (2005, p. 120, n. 18) for the evolution of Putnam's internal realism into his pragmatic realism.

referring to a person, in fact does not. Because these terms refer to nothing, for Putnam, Kripke, and any full-blooded Aristotelian, they mean the same thing, *viz.*, nothing. Yet 'phlogiston' and 'Sherlock Holmes' do not seem synonymous. While a Platonic realist account of meaning does not face this problem—there can be Platonic forms without objects instantiating them just as there can be Fregean senses without referents—an Aristotelian account has nothing to which to turn besides objects or referents themselves.

Regardless of what Putnam or Kripke would themselves do, a full-blooded Aristotelian realist might offer two replies to the problem of empty names. Reply one is that 'phlogiston', 'Sherlock Holmes', and other empty names are non-empirical terms. The Aristotelian realist is therefore absolved from having to account for them. Reply two is that not all empirical terms are constituted essentially out of only an objective source. Empty names that are empirical terms—"empty empirical terms"—themselves therefore need not be. So the Aristotelian realist could have more than merely referents to which to turn.[12]

The Aristotelian realist should not choose reply one because it is doubtful that all empty names are non-empirical. 'Phlogiston' in particular seems empirical. It was part of an empirical theory, a theory tested against objects in the world independent of its theorizers. Moreover, if 'phlogiston' is non-empirical because it is part of a falsified empirical theory—and if pessimistic induction about the truth of our own current empirical theories holds—then perhaps most current allegedly empirical terms are non-empirical also. Not just 'phlogiston' but also 'oxygen' and myriad others might be non-empirical. But then science itself, insofar as it relies on such terms, teeters on being non-empirical. Most of its subject matter would be non-empirical. Reply one, that empty names are non-empirical and so the Aristotelian realist is absolved from saying more, is therefore unsatisfying.[13]

Consider instead reply two, that not all empirical terms are constituted essentially out of only an objective source. Hence empty empirical terms need not be. The Aristotelian now has a choice. She can argue that empty empirical terms are constituted essentially out of either *both* subjective and objective sources or *only* a subjective source. Regardless both choices are problematic

---

12. The Aristotelian realist also might offer reply three, that 'phlogiston', 'Sherlock Holmes', and other empty names *are* synonymous. This however would be reason to prefer a Kantian account to an Aristotelian realist account straightaway.

13. Kripke himself later (2013, lecture III) offers reply one for fictional names like 'Sherlock Holmes'. He contends that they refer to "abstract" fictional objects, which would presumably be non-empirical. Nonetheless this fails to allay worries about terms like 'phlogiston' from falsified empirical theories. While 'Sherlock Holmes' might refer to a fictional character, 'phlogiston' does not refer to a fictional substance. It refers to nothing at all, though it was once thought to refer to a factual substance.

for the same reason. Were the "Aristotelian realist" to argue that *any* empirical term (empty or otherwise) is not constituted essentially out of only an objective source, then she would not be an Aristotelian realist. Were she to argue that (only) some empirical terms are constituted essentially out of subjective and objective sources, then she would be a Lockean hybridist, whom I consider in §6. Were she to argue that (only) some are constituted essentially out of only a subjective source, then she would be some other kind of theorist outside my taxonomy.

Hence the Aristotelian realist is caught in a dilemma. On the one hand, she can choose reply one, argue that empty names are non-empirical, and attempt to absolve herself from solving the problem. Yet it is unclear that she should do so. On the other hand, she can choose reply two and argue that not all empirical terms are constituted essentially out of only an objective source. Yet she is then not an Aristotelian realist.

Though it faces other problems, a Kantian account of meaning does not face this. I am unsure whether the Kantian should maintain that fictional names, like 'Sherlock Holmes', are empirical or non-empirical terms. Nonetheless I am persuaded by pessimistic-induction worries that she should maintain that terms from falsified empirical theories, like 'phlogiston', are empirical. According to the Kantian, the latter would, like all (other) empirical terms, be constituted essentially out of subjective and objective sources. And, unlike with the Aristotelian realist, this does not turn the Kantian into some other kind of theorist.

Admittedly this might raise a different worry. If both non-empty empirical terms, (presumably) like 'oxygen', and empty empirical terms, like 'phlogiston', are constituted essentially out of subjective and objective sources, then how can the Kantian distinguish them? This worry however is easily allayed. While the non-empty ones refer, the empty ones do not. That distinguishes them. And which terms do and do not refer is itself empirically determinable. Moreover the Kantian can explain the difference in referring as follows. Non-empty empirical terms would be constituted essentially out of subjective and objective sources in an evenhanded way. Terms would result equally from the subject's specific capacities and objects in the world. As one might put it, the subjective would not "overshoot" the objective. Conversely empty empirical terms would be constituted essentially out of subjective and objective sources in an unevenhanded way. Terms would result more from the subject's specific capacities than from objects in the world. Here the subjective would "overshoot" the objective. In that latter case the subject might begin by applying her capacities to those objects but then extrapolate beyond them in ways not supported by the objects themselves. The meaning of 'oxygen' and 'phlogiston' would both result from subjective responses to objects in the world.

Concerning 'oxygen' the responses would not go beyond the objects to which subjects are responding. Concerning 'phlogiston' they would.

5. BERKELEIAN IDEALIST ACCOUNT OF MEANING

A Berkeleian idealist account of meaning maintains that all empirical terms are constituted essentially out of only a subjective source. All empirical terms would then mean what they do purely in virtue of that source.

Grice's (1991, chs. 5, 6, 14) account of meaning approximates a Berkeleian idealist account. Grice understands meaning in terms of speaker meaning, and speaker meaning itself in terms of reflexive intentions between speaker and audience. Roughly a speaker means something by a term if and only if she speaks it with the intention of inducing a belief in her audience by having the audience recognize her intention to induce that belief by her speaking that term.[14] Grice therefore reduces meaning to intention and ultimately to the psychology of speakers and audiences. Meaning is explicated mentally and so in my sense subjectively. In fact, though Grice does not make this point, his account does not require that there be subjects *besides* the speaker. A speaker can speak a term with the intention of inducing a belief in her audience without inducing such a belief and without there being such an audience. Thus, for Grice, all terms—and *a fortiori* all empirical ones—are constituted essentially out of only a subjective source. Maximally they are constituted essentially out of the speaker's and audience's psychological states (and so conceptual if not also linguistic and perceptual capacities) together. Minimally they are constituted essentially out of the speaker's psychological states (and so conceptual if not also linguistic and perceptual capacities) alone. Regardless there would be no objective source at all.

Grice's account faces the same problem facing any form of Berkeleian idealism. Intuitions are strongly against any view that grants no role to objects in the world. As Davidson himself puts it: "idealism ... reduce[s] reality to so much less than we believe there is" (2002, p. 178). Most believe that there is a world in some sense independent of subjects. Likewise at least many believe that an account of meaning should take that into account. As long as there are accounts that do so, a Berkeleian idealist account would be the last account of meaning that one might prefer.

A Kantian account of meaning itself grants a role to both subjects and objects. By linking all empirical terms essentially to subjective and

---

14. See especially Herbert Paul Grice (1991, p. 219). Grice himself calls speaker meaning 'non-natural meaning' and 'utterer's meaning'.

objective sources, a Kantian account of meaning avoids idealism. As we saw in §1, Kuhn's Ontological Dualism concerning terms involves interactions between teachers and students as the former ostends to objects in the presence of the latter. Likewise Davidson's two different kinds of Ontological Dualism concerning terms involve interactions between speakers and radical interpreters, and teachers and students, as they triangulate objects in the world.

One might object that Grice either never intended to exclude objects in the world from his account of meaning or could easily include them even if he did. Insofar as this is right, however, Grice's account itself is or collapses into a Kantian one. To say that meaning involves subjects and objects is to be a kind of Ontological Dualist concerning terms and so a Kantian about meaning. Grice would therefore be a proponent of a Kantian account himself. Hence, because a Berkeleian idealist account of meaning either excludes objects from the world or at least regarding Grice's collapses into a Kantian account, we again have reason to prefer the Kantian.

6. LOCKEAN HYBRIDIST ACCOUNT OF MEANING

So far I have considered accounts of meaning concerning *all* empirical terms. All are constituted essentially out of subjective and objective sources (Kantian), all are constituted essentially out of only an objective source (Platonic and Aristotelian realist), and all are constituted essentially out of only a subjective source (Berkeleian idealist). A Lockean hybridist account of meaning concerns *only some* empirical terms. It maintains that only some such terms are constituted essentially out of subjective and objective sources.

Hence a Lockean hybridist account leaves open how *other* empirical terms are constituted. Now, as we saw in §4, the most natural way to divide empirical terms that are, and those that are not, constituted essentially out of subjective and objective sources is to have that division mirror the division between empty and non-empty names—where, for the division to work here, all such names must themselves be empirical terms. So let me divide terms as such. But then empirical terms constituted essentially out of subjective and objective sources are themselves *either* the empty *or* the non-empty ones. Moreover, if *empty* empirical terms are constituted essentially out of subjective and objective sources, then non-empty empirical terms are constituted essentially out of either only a subjective or only an objective source. Likewise, if *non-empty* empirical terms are constituted essentially out of subjective and objective sources, then empty empirical terms are constituted essentially out of either only a subjective or only an objective source. Which combination should the Lockean hybridist countenance?

Let me propose the following. If the Lockean hybridist maintains that *empty* empirical terms are constituted essentially out of subjective and objective sources, then she should maintain that non-empty empirical terms are constituted essentially out of only an objective source. It makes little sense for non-empty empirical terms, which do refer, to be *less* objective than empty ones, which do not refer. Conversely, if the Lockean hybridist maintains that *non-empty* empirical terms are constituted essentially out of subjective and objective sources, then she should maintain that empty empirical terms are constituted essentially out of only a subjective source. It likewise makes little sense for empty terms, which do not refer, to be *more* objective than non-empty ones, which do refer.

These then are the two most plausible versions of a Lockean hybridist account of meaning. First, empty empirical terms are constituted essentially out of both sources; non-empty empirical terms, only an objective source. Second, non-empty empirical terms are constituted essentially out of both sources; empty empirical terms, only a subjective source. Now I know no account in the analytic literature approximating either version of a Lockean hybridist account of meaning. Let me nevertheless evaluate each of the two most plausible versions in turn.

The first plausible way that one could be a Lockean hybridist is to maintain that empty empirical terms are constituted essentially out of subjective and objective sources, while non-empty empirical terms are constituted essentially out of only an objective source. I considered this possibility in §4 in the context of an Aristotelian account of meaning. Now there are two reasons that the Lockean hybridist should not choose this way. On the one hand, by a similar pessimistic-induction argument to the one considered in §4, the Lockean hybridist account would collapse into a Kantian one. For perhaps most empirical terms currently thought non-empty in fact are empty. Not just 'phlogiston' but also 'oxygen' and myriad others might be empty. They would be constituted essentially out of subjective and objective sources, as the Kantian contends. So the Lockean hybridist would for all practical purposes be a Kantian. On the other hand, even if many (or perhaps most) of our empirical terms are instead non-empty, the Lockean hybridist faces the problem faced by the Aristotelian and Platonic realist, considered in §§3–4. Non-empty empirical terms would be constituted essentially out of only an objective source. But then, like the Platonic and Aristotelian realist, the Lockean hybridist must herself explain how subjects can epistemologically bridge the ontological divide between themselves and objects that exist independently of them—again without appealing to the subject's specific conceptual, linguistic, or perceptual capacities. And once more, if she did appeal to them, then she would be a Kantian rather than a Lockean hybridist.

The second plausible way that one could be a Lockean hybridist is to maintain that non-empty empirical terms are constituted essentially out of subjective and objective sources, while empty empirical terms are constituted essentially out of only a subjective source. The Lockean hybridist should not choose this way either. By similar pessimistic induction, the Lockean hybridist account would now collapse into a Berkeleian idealist one. Again perhaps most empirical terms currently thought non-empty in fact are empty. They would then be constituted essentially out of only a subjective source, as the Berkeleian idealist contends. This time the Lockean hybridist would for all practical purposes be a Berkeleian idealist.

A Kantian account of meaning faces none of these problems. By maintaining that all empirical terms, empty or otherwise, are constituted essentially out of subjective and objective sources, pessimistic induction would not cause the Kantian account to collapse into any other. Nor need the Kantian provide an epistemological bridge between a subject's terms and objects in the world that does not itself appeal to the subject's specific conceptual, linguistic, or perceptual capacities. She again builds those capacities into her account. Admittedly the Kantian might be asked why, if all empirical terms are constituted essentially out of subjective and objective sources, some are empty while others are not. But we know what she might say. As we saw in §4, the Kantian could explain that, though empty and non-empty empirical terms are constituted essentially out of subjective and objective sources, in the case of the former the subjective overshoots the objective, while in the case of the latter it does not. Hence we have reason to prefer a Kantian account of meaning to a Lockean hybridist account as well.

7. HEGELIAN PRAGMATIST ACCOUNT OF MEANING

A final account of meaning maintains that no empirical term is constituted essentially out of subjective or objective sources. Such an account would deny the philosophical usefulness of talk of distinctly "subjective" or "objective" sources of empirical terms altogether. Examples approximating such an account might be so-called "use," "social-practice," or "inferentialist" accounts of meaning—where uses and inferences are themselves kinds of practices. The American Pragmatists, the later Ludwig Wittgenstein (2009/1958), Wilfrid Sellars (1991/1963, 1968), Robert Brandom (1998), and perhaps Georg Wilhelm Friedrich Hegel (1977/1807) say things at times along these lines. Were John McDowell (1996) to offer an account of meaning, presumably it would approximate a Hegelian account insofar as it denied any useful distinction between "subjective" and "objective" sources too. Moreover, as I understand them, Davidson's accounts of meaning, both radical interpretation and language learning, are meant to be social-practice accounts. They explicate meaning in terms of the social practices of radical interpretation and language learning, respectively. And, as we saw in Chapter Five concerning radical interpretation in particular, they are part of Davidson's reason for denying the subjective/objective divide and with it Dualism itself. In fact, relying on considerations from radical interpretation, Davidson concludes that "we have erased the boundary between knowing a language," a subjective source of meaning, "and knowing our way around in the world," an objective source (2002, p. 107). Because Davidson's and all these other accounts are or descend from Hegel's, and most make practices central, let me call each an instance of a 'Hegelian pragmatist account of meaning'.[15]

Such a Hegelian pragmatist account faces its own problem. If meaning just is what is used between subjects, or is constituted merely out of inferences and social practices, then it is unclear how objects enter the picture.[16] Hence it is unclear whether a Hegelian pragmatist account of meaning does not collapse into a Berkeleian idealist account. Admittedly Davidson himself provides a model of how objects can enter the picture, *viz.*, through language users triangulating them. But Davidson's accounts of meaning turn out not to be examples of a Hegelian pragmatist account. As we saw in Chapter Four, Davidson's account of radical interpretation is a form of Ontological Dualism concerning terms. It is therefore an example of a Kantian account of meaning. Conversely his account of language learning is a form of Ontological and Epistemological Kantianism concerning terms. It is therefore in the former form an example of a Kantian account of meaning also. Moreover, as we saw in Chapter Five, the best arguments against the distinction between subjective and objective sources of terms, Davidson's own arguments against the dualism of conceptual scheme and empirical content, fail.

Hence not only is a Hegelian pragmatist account robbed of prominent exemplars. Because Davidson's are the best arguments against Dualism and so

---

15. In fact Davidson's pairing of interpreter and speaker, and teacher and language learner, are philosophical descendants of Georg Wilhelm Friedrich Hegel's pairing of master and slave. Each member of each pair is engaged in a social practice constitutive of each one's status in the pair. Because these statuses are co-constituted and arise from a common source, the practice itself, the statuses are themselves not ultimately distinct.

16. This is John McDowell's (1996, lecture I; afterward, part I) objection to Davidson (especially 2002, essay 10), and McDowell (2005) objects similarly to Robert Brandom (1998). Regarding Davidson, as I would put it, McDowell is objecting that Davidson fails to leave room for objects, when McDowell does just that. And this is so even though, for McDowell, objects are not distinct in kind from subjects. They are both ultimately linguistic. That is McDowell's own attempt at being a Hegelian pragmatist.

the subjective/objective divide, and they fail, the burden is shifted against those denying a philosophically useful distinction between subjective and objective sources in the first place. So the burden is shifted against those arguing for a Hegelian pragmatist account of meaning itself.

A Kantian account of meaning faces none of this. For the Kantian, it is clear how objects enter the picture. For Kuhn, language learning happens *via* a teacher's ostending to objects in the presence of her student. For Davidson, radical interpreter and speaker, and language learner and teacher, each triangulate objects for her mate. More generally a Kantian account of meaning maintains that meaning is constituted essentially out of subjective and objective sources themselves. Objects are built into the account. Further, while a Hegelian pragmatist account of meaning is robbed of prominent exemplars, a Kantian account has three: one from Kuhn and two from Davidson. Hence we have reason to prefer a Kantian account of meaning to a Hegelian account too.

8. LESSONS FOR KANTIAN CONCEPTUAL GEOGRAPHY

In this chapter we have seen what a Kantian account of meaning is, how Dualism is connected to such an account, and three general formulations and three specific examples of the account itself. We have also considered contrasting accounts of meaning, which revealed a new taxonomy of influential views in the analytic literature. And we have seen that a Kantian account of meaning does not face problems faced by these others. In this conclusion I draw four lessons for Kantian conceptual geography generally.

First, Kantianism lends itself to an account of meaning. Ontological Dualism concerning terms in particular, and its other general formulations, is such an account. So Kantian conceptual geography is useful for philosophy of language especially.

Second, accounts of meaning that contrast with a Kantian account are the linguistic correlates of those views that contrast with Kantianism generally. As I understand them, Platonic realism, Aristotelian realism, Berkeleian idealism, Lockean hybridism, and Hegelian pragmatism all have correspondingly contrasting accounts of meaning.

Third, there exist accounts of meaning in the analytic literature that approximate nearly all these other accounts of meaning just considered. Frege's account of sense and reference, Putnam and Kripke's new theory of reference, and Grice's account of speaker meaning approximate Platonic realist, Aristotelian realist, and Berkeleian idealist accounts of meaning, respectively. Various use, social-practice, or inferentialist accounts of meaning approximate a Hegelian pragmatist account. And Kuhn's account of language learning and

Davidson's accounts of radical interpretation and language learning are each examples of a Kantian account of meaning.

And fourth, a Kantian account of meaning faces none of the problems considered here that any of these other accounts do. Though I remain a Kantian conceptual geographer rather than a settler, I have shown that we therefore have reason to prefer a Kantian account of meaning to these others.

EIGHT

Problems That a Kantian Account of Meaning Faces

In Chapter Seven I relied on Dualism to disclose a Kantian account of meaning. To put that account into better focus, I then considered accounts of meaning that contrast with it and problems that each contrasting account faces that a Kantian account of meaning does not. This not only illuminated the Kantian account but also provided reason to prefer it to these others. Here I consider eight putative problems that a Kantian account does face. As I explain, only three are genuine problems—and all three have replies. Hence we have even more reason to prefer a Kantian account of meaning to these others.

The chapter proceeds as follows. In §1 I consider three putative problems that a Kantian account of meaning faces: meaning indeterminacy, meaning relativism, and meaning incommensurability. In §2 I consider a fourth and fifth putative problem: infinite regression and truth-value relativism. In §3 I consider a sixth putative problem: empirical-property (and in fact empirical-world) relativism. In §4 I consider a seventh putative problem: a possible plurality of empirical worlds. In §5 I consider an eighth putative problem: the possible movability between such worlds. Having either disqualified or replied to each of these, in §6 I show that anyone committed to a Kantian account of *meaning* (concerning terms) is committed to Kantian accounts of *content* (concerning concepts) and *nature* (concerning properties), and *vice versa*. Finally in §7 I draw lessons for Kantian conceptual geography generally.

1. FIRST THREE PUTATIVE PROBLEMS: INDETERMINACY, RELATIVISM, AND INCOMMENSURABILITY

A first putative problem that a Kantian account of meaning faces concerns meaning indeterminacy. As we saw in Chapter Seven, Donald Davidson's account of radical interpretation is a specific example of a Kantian account of meaning. As we saw in Chapter Four, according to Davidson, any radical interpreter could interpret a term to mean $x_1, x_2, x_3,\ldots$, or x_n, with compensatory adjustments elsewhere, without there being a fact of the matter about which is right. Any term would then *mean* any of these without there being a fact of the matter about which is right. If Davidson is himself right, then a Kantian account of meaning allows there to be no fact of the matter *about* meaning. That would apparently undermine its being an account *of* meaning.

It is unclear whether indeterminacy would infect a Kantian account of meaning beyond Davidson's specific example of one. Regardless, even if it did, such indeterminacy would be innocuous. Suppose that there were no fact of the matter about what *the* meaning of a term is. There would still be facts of the matter about what its meaning*s* are. It would (presumably) be a fact that 'gold' means gold in English given one interpretation, even if given enough changes in the interpretation of other terms it would mean something else. Moreover indeterminacy would obtain—there would be no fact of the matter about whether *the* meaning of the term is $x_1, x_2, x_3,\ldots$, or x_n—only if speakers could develop and carry out their projects regardless of whether the meaning of the term is $x_1, x_2, x_3,\ldots$, or x_n. Davidson himself (2001d/1984, pp. 224–25; 2002, pp. 65, 79, 81, 132, 214–15, 218) analogizes the indeterminacy of meaning (or interpretation) to the indeterminacy of temperature. As long as two interpretations track the same behavior, there is no more fact of the matter about whether a term means x_1 or x_2 than there is about whether under standard conditions water freezes at 0° Celsius or 32° Fahrenheit. Davidson explains: "Indeterminacy of meaning... does not represent a failure to capture significant distinctions; it marks the fact that certain apparent distinctions are not significant" (2001d/1984, p. 154). Hence the first putative problem that a Kantian account of meaning faces is not a genuine problem.

A second putative problem that a Kantian account of meaning faces concerns meaning relativism. According to a Kantian account, because empirical terms are constituted essentially out of subjective and objective sources, their meaning would be relative to a particular subject—*qua* individual, *qua* community member, *qua* human being, or *qua* language user. Empirical terms could then mean different things *for* different subjects. And this difference would be in addition to any indeterminacy. It would parallel, not the same temperature's being a certain number of degrees Celsius or Fahrenheit, but different temperatures altogether.

Indeed meaning relativism does follow from a Kantian account of meaning. We can see this by considering the four subjective scopes that such an account can take. If the account is *idiocentric*, then an empirical term in a language means what it does for an individual in virtue of that individual under normal conditions taking it to have that meaning in that language. And different individuals can take empirical terms to have different meanings. If the account is *ethnocentric*, then an empirical term in a language means what it does for a community in virtue of a normal member of that community under normal conditions taking it to have that meaning in that language. And different communities can take empirical terms to have different meanings. If the account is *anthropocentric*, then an empirical term in a language means what it does for all human beings in virtue of a normal human being under normal conditions taking it to have that meaning in that language. Though we have no uncontroversial evidence of non-human language users, different linguistic species (were there any) could take different empirical terms to have different meanings. Finally, if the account is *logocentric*, then an empirical term in a language means what it does for all language users in virtue of a normal language user under normal conditions taking it to have that meaning in that language. Though not all language users would use the same language, they would all agree (*pace* indeterminacy) on what a particular term in a particular language means. In the logocentric case as in all the others meaning remains relative. For the logocentrist, a term would have no meaning in anything *not* a language.

Meaning relativism is not a genuine problem either. It is not even controversial. Everyone agrees that 'red' in English means red and in Spanish network, while 'hell' in English means hell and in German bright. A Kantian account of meaning merely adds that subjective scope of such relativism is relevant. In these examples one can ask whether the terms mean what they do relative to those languages in virtue of what subjects *qua* individual, *qua* community member, *qua* human being, or *qua* language user would mean.

A third putative problem that a Kantian account of meaning faces concerns meaning incommensurability. As I understood it in Chapter Three, incommensurability occurs when terms in one language are non-intertranslatable into another language. The possibility of incommensurability follows from the possibility of relevantly distinct subjects, *i.e.*, subjects having relevantly distinct subjective capacities. Who would these relevantly distinct subjects be? For an *idiocentric* account, each subject *qua* individual would be relevantly distinct. For an *ethnocentric* account, each subject *qua* member of a different community would be relevantly distinct. For an *anthropocentric* account, each subject *qua* member of a different (linguistic) species would be relevantly distinct. And, for a *logocentric* account, no subject *qua* language user would be relevantly distinct from any other, though each would be relevantly distinct from any non-language user.

Given idiocentrism, meaning would be relative to the individual and so terms from one subject *qua* individual might be non-intertranslatable into another individual's language. Given ethnocentrism, meaning would be relative to the community and so terms from one subject *qua* community member might be non-intertranslatable into another community's language. Given anthropocentrism, meaning would be relative to human beings and so terms from one subject *qua* human being might be non-intertranslatable into another species' language. And, because logocentrism denies the possibility of relevantly distinct (linguistic) *subjects*, a logocentric Kantian account of meaning does not entail incommensurability at all. In fact, as we saw in Chapter Five, Davidson uses his logocentric subjective principle, the principle of charity, to establish that all languages are necessarily and completely intertranslatable. This is so even though Davidson's account of meaning is itself otherwise idiocentric.

Regardless incommensurability is at least possible given a Kantian account of meaning. And that possibility is a third putative problem that a Kantian account faces. For some might find the possibility worrisome. Let me offer three replies. Reply one is that given certain subjective scopes worries concerning the possibility of incommensurability would (at least for now) be nil. Concerning anthropocentrism, so far our linguistic dealings have been exclusively with other humans, and we have no uncontroversial evidence of any other language users. So far the possibility of incommensurability on the anthropocentric view is *merely* a possibility. Concerning logocentrism, there would be no incommensurability at all. All subjects would have the same specific conceptual, linguistic, and perceptual capacities. None would be relevantly distinct from any other. The *im*possibility of incommensurability would follow.

Suppose however that incommensurability could or would arise, given anthropocentrism, ethnocentrism, or idiocentrism. Reply two is that such incommensurability might not be dramatic. Thomas Kuhn himself claims that communities before and after scientific revolutions have languages with incommensurability that is merely "local" (1999, p. 34; 2002, p. 36). Ethnocentric Kantianism can permit large overlap between otherwise ethnocentrically different languages. Anthropocentric and idiocentric Kantianism can permit the same.

And reply three is that there are ways for incommensurability to be partially overcome. Kuhn helps here too. He (1999, pp. 34–35; 2002, pp. 38–40, 61) claims that members of different communities might be able to learn one another's language, and thereby acquire the specific conceptual, linguistic, and perceptual capacities relevant to a different community. Ethnocentric differences therefore can be ameliorated. Given idiocentrism and anthropocentrism, individuals might be able to do the same.

Because meaning incommensurability would not actually arise in one case or even possibly arise in another, might not be dramatic, and might be partially overcome, this third putative problem that a Kantian account of meaning faces is not a genuine problem either. None of these first three is.

2. FOURTH AND FIFTH PUTATIVE PROBLEM: INFINITE REGRESSION AND TRUTH-VALUE RELATIVISM

To appreciate a fourth putative problem that a Kantian account of meaning faces, consider how such an account connects with concepts. Recall Ontological Dualism:

> ONTOLOGICAL DUALISM: All empirical concepts, terms, or properties are constituted essentially out of subjective and objective sources.

While Ontological Dualism concerning terms is the first general formulation of a Kantian account of meaning, our concern now is with concepts *and* terms. Empirical concepts and terms would both be constituted essentially out of subjective and objective sources. Ontological Dualism concerning concepts and terms maintains that subjective and objective sources go into those concepts' and terms' very being. In that sense they go into the content of the concepts and the meaning of the terms. If Ontological Dualism concerning terms is a formulation of a Kantian account of *meaning*, therefore, then Ontological Dualism concerning concepts is a formulation of a Kantian account of *content*. Concerning the former, all empirical terms mean what they do in virtue of subjective and objective sources. Concerning the latter, all empirical concepts have the content that they do in virtue of the same.

Now anyone committed to a Kantian account of meaning would be committed to a Kantian account of content. As we saw in Chapter Five, according to Davidson (2001d/1984, essay 11; 2002, essay 7), speaking (rather than merely behaving as if one were speaking) requires understanding what one is saying. Because that requires being able to think the concepts expressed by one's terms, everything speakable is necessarily thinkable. I believe that Davidson is right about this. Nor am I alone. Everyone whom I have considered who is committed to Ontological Dualism concerning terms (Immanuel Kant on an ontological understanding, Kuhn, and Davidson twice) is committed to Ontological Dualism concerning concepts. Conversely everyone whom I have considered who is committed to Epistemological Kantianism concerning terms (Kant on an epistemological understanding and Philip Pettit) is committed to Epistemological Kantianism concerning concepts. These Kantian kinds coincide.

For convenience let me phrase things in terms of the third general formulation of a Kantian account of meaning, Kantian Meaning:

> KANTIAN MEANING: For any empirical term in *L*, the term means what it does if and only if a suitable subject under suitable conditions would take it to have that meaning.

Kantian Meaning, like Ontological Dualism concerning terms, should be understood as a constitutive claim. All empirical terms mean what they do *in virtue of* a suitable subject under suitable conditions taking them to have that meaning. Anyone committed to Ontological Dualism concerning concepts would be committed to Kantian Content:

> KANTIAN CONTENT: For any empirical concept, the concept has the content that it does if and only if a suitable subject under suitable conditions would take it to have that content.

Kantian Content should itself be understood as a constitutive claim. All empirical concepts have the content that they do *in virtue of* a suitable subject under suitable conditions taking them to have that content. Moreover, because anyone committed to Ontological Dualism concerning terms is committed to Ontological Dualism concerning concepts, anyone committed to Kantian Meaning is likewise committed to Kantian Content.

We can now appreciate the fourth putative problem that a Kantian account of meaning faces. Anyone committed to a Kantian account of meaning is committed to a Kantian account of content, which apparently involves an infinite regress. That a concept has the content that it does if and only if someone would *take* it to have that content apparently requires that that someone *have a certain mental state* relative to the content. Yet mental states themselves are or involve concepts. Hence the content of *that* mental state or concept apparently requires its *own* constitution. But then that a concept has the content that it does if and only if someone would take it to have the content apparently requires that someone *else* take the first someone's "taking" to have the content that it does—*ad infinitum.*

This fourth putative problem is not a genuine problem either. There is no need for an infinity of mental states. Conceptual content can be shared. The content of more than one person's concepts can depend on the content of the same suitable subject under suitable conditions. Neither is it the case that a suitable subject under suitable conditions *does* have to take one's concept to have the content that it does for it to have that content. Such a subject merely *would* have to take it to have that content. Content could bottom out counterfactually rather than infinitely regressively.

To appreciate a fifth putative problem that a Kantian account of meaning faces, now consider how such an account connects with truth values. All empirical statements mean what they do in virtue of the meaning of their terms, including how those terms relate and so would be arranged relative to other terms. Moreover all empirical statements have the truth value that they do in virtue of what those statements mean. Conjoining the connection between the meaning of empirical statements and their component terms, and the truth values of empirical statements and their meaning, Kantian Meaning entails this:

> KANTIAN TRUTH VALUE: For any empirical statement in L, the statement has the truth value that it does if and only if a suitable subject under suitable conditions would take it to have that truth value.

Like Kantian Meaning and Kantian Concept, Kantian Truth Value should be understood as a constitutive claim. All empirical statements have the truth value that they do *in virtue of* a suitable subject under suitable conditions taking them to have that truth value.

The fifth putative problem that a Kantian account of meaning faces follows. Anyone committed to such an account of meaning would be committed to Kantian Truth Value. Kantian Truth Value however makes truth values relative to subjects. 'Gold exists in the earth's crust' would have the truth value that it does in English in virtue of a suitable subject under suitable conditions taking it to have that truth value. The same would be so for the truth value of every other empirical statement. Yet that empirical statements are true or false depending on whether a *subject* would take them to be so might seem worrisome insofar as it makes truth value relative *to* subjects.

Should it be worrisome? Such relativism of truth value is no more problematic than the relativism of meaning, the second putative problem that a Kantian account of meaning faces, considered in §1. In fact truth-value relativism follows from it. Because all empirical statements have the truth value that they do in virtue of their meaning, if meaning is relative to the subject then truth value is also. Hence my reply to meaning relativism applies here too. Moreover, because meaning would already be relative, the relativism of truth value need not entail that statements with the *same meaning* have *different truth values*. Since relevantly different subjects could mean different things by their statements, they need not be entertaining the *same statements*. No *single* statement would necessarily have the truth value that it does relative to some subjects and not others. The fifth putative problem that a Kantian account of meaning faces is itself not a genuine problem either. None of the first five is.

3. SIXTH PUTATIVE PROBLEM: EMPIRICAL-PROPERTY RELATIVISM

A sixth, seventh, and eighth putative problem that a Kantian account of meaning faces also concern its connection with truth values. The sixth follows directly from the fifth. If the truth values of empirical statements are relative to a subject (the fifth), then empirical properties are themselves relative to a subject (the sixth). Consider this substitution instance of Kantian Truth Value:

(a) 'Gold exists in the earth's crust' has the truth value that it does in English if and only if a suitable subject under suitable conditions would take it to have that truth value.

Now the statement 'gold exists in the earth's crust' has one particular truth value, true, if and only if such a subject would take it to be true. So (a) entails:

(b) 'Gold exists in the earth's crust' is true in English if and only if a suitable subject under suitable conditions would take it to be true.

We were to understand Kantian Truth Value as a constitutive claim. Hence (b) should itself be understood as this:

(c) 'Gold exists in the earth's crust' is true in English in virtue of a suitable subject under suitable conditions taking it to be true.

To say that some statement is true in virtue of a subject's taking "it" to be true is to say that the statement is true in virtue of the subject's taking *the statement* to be true. So (c) expands:

(d) 'Gold exists in the earth's crust' is true in English in virtue of a suitable subject under suitable conditions taking 'gold exists in the earth's crust' to be true in English.

My conclusion is within reach. We just need to recognize this disquotational truth:

(e) 'Gold exists in the earth's crust' is true in English if and only if gold exists in the earth's crust.

And (d) and (e) entail this:

(f) Gold exists in the earth's crust in virtue of a suitable subject under suitable conditions taking 'gold exists in the earth's crust' to be true in English.

Gold has the property of existing in the earth's crust—and every other empirical property that it has—in virtue of a suitable subject under suitable conditions taking the corresponding statement to be true. This is startling. We have seen through empirical truth values to the empirical properties that they concern.

Consider what follows. Empirical properties are relative to subjective responses *to* objects in the world. Gold has the property of existing in the earth's crust in virtue of suitable subjects *under suitable conditions* taking the corresponding statement to be true. And those conditions include the presence of *objects in the world* to which those subjects respond. Hence the constitution of the property is linked essentially to subjective *and* objective sources. Empirical properties are relative to subjects because those properties are themselves constituted essentially out of subjective and objective sources. The relativism of empirical properties therefore amounts to Ontological Kantianism concerning properties. Anyone committed to Ontological Kantianism concerning terms would therefore be committed to Ontological Kantianism not only concerning concepts, as we saw in §2, but also concerning properties, as I explained here. All empirical concepts, terms, and properties would be constituted essentially out of subjective and objective sources. This time these three Kantian kinds coincide. And that is startling too.

Further, while Ontological Kantianism concerning terms involves their *meaning*, and Ontological Kantianism concerning concepts concerns their *content*, Ontological Kantianism concerning properties concerns their *nature*. Hence, if Ontological Dualism concerning terms is a Kantian account of meaning, and Ontological Dualism concerning concepts is a Kantian account of content, then Ontological Dualism concerning properties is a Kantian account of nature. It is an account of the nature of empirical properties themselves. So anyone committed to a Kantian account of meaning would be committed to a Kantian account of nature in this sense. We can also see this by focusing on particular formulations. We have already seen in §2 that commitment to Kantian Meaning entails commitment to Kantian Content and Kantian Truth Value. By parity of reasoning, we can see here that commitment to Kantian Truth Value entails commitment to Kantian Nature:

> KANTIAN NATURE: For any empirical property, the property has the nature that it does if and only if a suitable subject under suitable conditions would take it to have that nature.

Moreover Kantian Nature, like these others, should be understood as a constitutive claim. All empirical properties have the nature that they do *in virtue of* a suitable subject under suitable conditions taking them to have that nature.

Consequences of this are profound. The empirical world *in toto* is nothing beyond the totality of empirical properties and objects instantiating them. But then the empirical world *in toto* has the nature that it does if and only if a suitable subject under suitable conditions would take it to have that nature. Empirical terms, no less than the empirical world, would be constituted essentially out of subjective and objective sources. My modest exploration in Chapter Seven of a Kantian account of meaning has led to my immodest finding here that anyone committed to such an account would be committed to a Kantian account of the empirical world. Not just the meaning of empirical terms (and, as we saw in §2, the content of empirical concepts) but also the nature of empirical properties and with it the empirical world itself would be relative to subjects—*qua* individual, *qua* community member, *qua* human being, or *qua* language user.

Consider what else follows. As we saw in Chapter One, empirical properties constituted essentially out of subjective and objective sources would be ones that subjects could in principle learn. Robert Hanna calls a world comprised of such properties "user-friendly" (2006, p. 50). Its properties are "in-principle knowable by means of our cognitive faculties," what I have been calling 'subjective capacities'. Hanna's focus is on Kant's (1998/1787) anthropocentric view. That view entails an *anthropocentric* user-friendly world, what Hanna describes as a world of "human experience" (2001, ch. 1). Expanding Hanna's idea, I can say that the relativism of empirical properties entails a world of *individual* experience, if the subjective scope is idiocentric. It entails a world of *community* experience, if the subjective scope is ethnocentric. It entails (as Hanna himself observes) a world of *human* experience, if the subjective scope is anthropocentric. And it entails a world of (overall) *language-user* experience, if the subjective scope is logocentric. Thus, expanding Hanna's idea, we see that a Kantian account of meaning entails that subjects live in *subject*-friendly worlds. Those are worlds in which all empirical properties are in-principle knowable *by* subjects *qua* specific sort.

I can expand Hanna's idea further. A Kantian account of meaning entails that subjects use empirical concepts and terms that are themselves constituted essentially out of the same subjective and objective sources as are those empirical properties. Hence a Kantian account of meaning entails that all such concepts and terms have what Kant calls "objective validity" (A97, A89–90/B122, A93/B126, A111). They are all in-principle applicable to empirical properties and the empirical world.[1] A Kantian account of meaning therefore entails that subjects live in subject-friendly worlds *in which* their empirical concepts and terms are in-principle applicable to those worlds' empirical properties. In this sense those worlds *themselves* would then be idiocentric, ethnocentric, anthropocentric, or logocentric depending on the subject scope of the Kantian account of meaning.

All this follows from the relativism of empirical properties and the empirical world. Of course not everyone would endorse that relativism. Many would

---

1. Immanuel Kant's own concern is with the objective validity of *a priori* concepts. My understanding of objective validity is roughly Robert Hanna's (2001, pp. 28, 84), which he distinguishes from objective reality. Henry Allison (2004, p. 88) understands objective validity to be the capacity to be true or false. Because the capacity of empirical, or synthetic *a posteriori*, judgments to be true or false concerns their being in-principle applicable to the empirical world, in the case of empirical judgments Allison's understanding collapses into mine.

find it and its consequences rankling to say the least. For some, the thought that empirical properties and the empirical world are not in principle independent of subjects might be reason enough to reject a Kantian account of meaning altogether. Hence in this, the sixth putative problem that a Kantian account of meaning faces, I have finally found a genuine problem.

What should we think of this first genuine problem, that a Kantian account of meaning entails the relativism of empirical properties (and world and all that follows)? Let me offer three replies. Reply one here mirrors reply one to the incommensurability worry from §1. Given certain subjective scopes, worries about the relativism of empirical properties would (at least for now) be nil. If a Kantian account of meaning is anthropocentric, then empirical properties are relative to subjects *qua* human. All human beings therefore could in principle take all objects to have the same properties. Since we have no uncontroversial evidence of other beings with the requisite conceptual, linguistic, and perceptual capacities, as yet no such relativism would be relevant. Conversely, if a Kantian account of meaning is logocentric, then empirical properties are relative to subjects *qua* language user. All linguistic beings therefore could in principle take all objects to have the same properties. So no such relativism would be relevant at all.

Reply two is that, while many might find the relativism of empirical properties rankling, each of Kantianism's competitors has consequences that should be at least as rankling. *Platonic realism* maintains that empirical properties are constituted essentially out of only an objective source existing in a supermundane realm. Whatever the virtues of Platonic realism, the idea of such a realm, as well as the need for an epistemological bridge to that realm, should rankle as much as the relativism of empirical properties would. *Aristotelian realism* maintains that empirical properties are constituted essentially out of only an objective source existing in a mundane realm. A proponent of such a view must then explain how subjects can come to know these properties without appealing to those subjects' specific conceptual, linguistic, or perceptual capacities. And it should be less rankling to say, with Kantianism and against Aristotelian realism, that appealing to just those capacities is essential to coming to know those properties. *Berkeleian idealism* maintains that empirical properties are constituted essentially out of only a subjective source. As we saw in Chapter Seven, Davidson rightly explains: "idealism ... reduce[s] reality to so much less than we believe there is" (2002, p. 178). Berkeleian idealism perhaps should rankle most of all. Moreover, because *Lockean hybridism* agrees with Kantianism that *some* empirical properties are relative to subjects, it makes no progress on that front. Nonetheless it disagrees with Kantianism that *all* empirical properties are so relative. And such hybridization is itself rankling— let alone, as George Berkeley (2000/1713) himself argued, potentially unstable.

Finally *Hegelian pragmatism* maintains that all talk of "subjective" or "objective" sources of empirical properties is philosophically useless. That should be at least as rankling as saying that such talk is useful, as Kantianism does.

Finally reply three is that, even if the relativism of empirical properties does rankle, a Kantian account of meaning remains preferable to these other accounts. For, as we saw in Chapter Seven, a Kantian account faces none of the problems that we saw they themselves face. Hence, though some worries about the relativism of empirical properties might remain, we still have reason to prefer a Kantian account to these other accounts.

4. SEVENTH PUTATIVE PROBLEM: A PLURALITY OF EMPIRICAL WORLDS

A seventh putative problem follows from the sixth. If a Kantian account of meaning makes empirical properties and the empirical world relative to subjects (the sixth putative problem), then depending on how many relevantly distinct subjects it countenances such an account entails a plurality of empirical worlds (the seventh).

In fact a Kantian account of meaning entails that there are as many empirical worlds as there are relevantly distinct subjects. Given *idiocentrism*, there are as many relevantly distinct subjects as there are individuals who have relevantly distinct conceptual, linguistic, and perceptual capacities. For the idiocentric Kantian, subjects *qua* individual would live in their own empirical world. These empirical worlds often would be very similar and overlap but would nevertheless differ. Given *ethnocentrism*, there are as many relevantly distinct subjects as there are communities whose members have relevantly distinct conceptual, linguistic, and perceptual capacities. For the ethnocentric Kantian, subjects *qua* member of a community would live in the same empirical world, while subjects *qua* member of different communities would live in different ones. As I explain below, examples of these empirical worlds could be those in which, according to Kuhn (2012/1962), scientists live before and after scientific revolutions. Given *anthropocentrism*, there are as many relevantly distinct subjects as there are species whose members have relevantly distinct conceptual, linguistic, and perceptual capacities. For the anthropocentric Kantian, subjects *qua* human being would live in the same empirical world, while subjects *qua* member of different species with such capacities would live in different ones. As Kant (1998/1787) himself maintains, our empirical world is the human world.[2] And we as yet have no uncontroversial evidence

---

2. "We can accordingly speak of space, extended beings, and so on only from the human standpoint" (1998/1787, A26/B42).

of any other such species. Finally, given *logocentrism*, no subject *qua* language user is relevantly distinct from any other. For the logocentric Kantian, subjects *qua* language user would live in the same empirical world. As we saw in Chapter Five by considering Davidson's arguments (allegedly) against the dualism of conceptual scheme and empirical content, such subjects would all have the same scheme. Though John McDowell (1996, pp. 115–21), following Hans-Georg Gadamer (1992, pp. 438–56), is making a different point, the logocentric Kantian might follow both in saying that by contrast *non*-language users live not in a "world" but in a mere "environment."[3]

Hence a Kantian account of meaning that is idiocentric or ethnocentric entails a plurality of empirical worlds. A Kantian account of meaning that is anthropocentric might entail a plurality of empirical worlds. And a Kantian account of meaning that is logocentric entails a singularity of empirical worlds. So a Kantian account of meaning *possibly* entails a plurality of empirical worlds. Regardless such a possibility would presumably be even more rankling than the relativism of the empirical world *per se*. This seventh putative problem that a Kantian account of meaning faces is a genuine problem also. For some, the thought that a Kantian account of meaning could entail this might itself be reason enough to reject the account altogether.

What should we think of this problem? Let me again offer three replies. Reply one is that a Kantian account of meaning entails a plurality of empirical worlds only given certain subjective scopes. And there might be reasons to reject those scopes. In fact one such reason might be the subjective scope's entailing a plurality of empirical worlds.

Reply two is that we have reason to accept a Kantian account of meaning's plurality of empirical worlds even if its subjective scope does entail it. For we have reason to accept an ontology of worlds that contains this plurality. Because reply two is complicated, let me take it slowly.

A "plurality of worlds" recalls David Lewis's eponymous work (2001/1986) in which he argues for modal realism, the thesis that possible worlds exist just as the actual world does. According to Lewis, possible-worlds talk

---

3. Though John McDowell argues for the Hegelian pragmatist view that there is no philosophically useful distinction between subjective and objective sources, he nevertheless wants to distinguish humans from lower animals. He does so by adopting Hans-Georg Gadamer's idea that language reveals the world in itself to humans, who are linguistic, because the world in itself is linguistic. As I would put it, the subjective is already operative in the objective. (See Chapter One, §3.) Since lower animals do not have language, they cannot appreciate the world for what it (objectively) is. (See Jeff Malpas 2011a, essays 9–14, for comparisons between Gadamer and Davidson himself.)

has clarified questions in many parts of the philosophy of logic, of mind, of language, and of science—not to mention metaphysics itself. Even those who officially scoff often cannot resist the temptation to help themselves abashedly to this useful way of speaking (2003/1986, p. 3).

Given its utility, Lewis argues, we should treat possible-worlds talk as referring to possible worlds. We should then treat possible worlds as on ontological par with the actual world. In fact, for Lewis, the only difference between (merely) possible worlds and the actual world is that there is only one actual world, which we (as opposed to our counterparts) inhabit.

Many might disagree that the utility of a kind of talk provides reason to take that talk to refer to existing things.[4] Nonetheless, even if inconclusive, such utility provides *some* reason. Now consider how Lewis's ontology of worlds compares to the Kantian's ontology of worlds. Since reply one makes the point that the Kantian's commitment to that ontology depends on which subjective scope she accepts, in reply two let me suppose that the Kantian accepts a subjective scope that does commit her to a plurality of worlds.

Lewis's possible worlds are merely logically possible. Any maximally consistent state of affairs amounts to a possible, and so, for Lewis, real, world. Conversely the Kantian's empirical worlds are empirical worlds relative to relevantly distinct subjects—*qua* individual, *qua* community member, and perhaps *qua* human being, as we are assuming. They are worlds all of whose empirical properties are constituted essentially out subjective and objective sources. And, because a Kantian account of meaning, besides entailing a Kantian account of nature, also entails a Kantian account of content, these worlds would be ones in which subjects' empirical concepts and terms are themselves constituted essentially out of subjective and objective sources. As we saw in §3, they would be worlds of subjective experience (or properties) and the objective validity of subjective empirical concepts and terms to that experience (or those properties). While Lewis's worlds are *logically possible*, therefore, we might understand the Kantian's worlds as *subjectively empirical*. A subjectively empirical world is a world in which subjects *qua* individual, *qua* community member, *qua* human being, or *qua* language user can learn every empirical property and whose empirical concepts and terms can in principle be applied to them.

---

4. Willard van Orman Quine (2006/1953, essay 1), who rejects *possibilia*, would nevertheless agree with David Lewis on this point.

Hence Lewis is committed to a plurality of logically possible worlds that exist, while a Kantian account of meaning is (given certain subjective scopes) committed to a plurality of subjectively empirical worlds that exist. Now all empirical properties, concepts, and terms are logically possible properties, concepts, and terms, respectively. But then all subjectively empirical worlds are themselves logically possible worlds. All worlds that a Kantian account of meaning entails are worlds that Lewis accepts. The Kantian's ontology is contained in Lewis's.

I can now conclude reply two to the seventh putative problem that a Kantian account of meaning faces, its (possibly) entailing a plurality of worlds. As we saw above, one has some reason to accept Lewis's ontology. As Lewis himself explains, doing so is useful. Moreover, as I myself explained here, if one has some reason to accept Lewis's ontology of worlds, then one has some reason to accept the Kantian's. For Lewis's contains it. Hence one has some reason to accept the Kantian's.

Finally reply three to the worry about a plurality of empirical worlds mirrors reply three to the worry about the relativism of the empirical world, which I considered in §3. Even if such a plurality does arise from a Kantian account of meaning, that account continues to face none of the problems that we saw in Chapter Seven its competitors face. Hence we still have reason to prefer a Kantian account of meaning to them.

5. EIGHTH PUTATIVE PROBLEM: MOVABILITY BETWEEN EMPIRICAL WORLDS

An eighth, and for my purposes final, putative problem that a Kantian account of meaning faces is related to the seventh. As Kuhn himself contends, subjects sometimes change worlds. They in effect move between them. As we saw in Chapter Three, Kuhn initially (2012/1962) talks about "worlds," though he eventually retracts such talk. As I explain in §6, Kuhn should not have retracted it. Regardless Kuhn's talk generalizes beyond just ethnocentric Kantianism. Given an *idiocentric* Kantian account of meaning, individuals would change empirical worlds, however so slightly, should their specific idiocentric conceptual, linguistic, or perceptual capacities change. Given an *ethnocentric* account, members of communities would change empirical worlds should they change communities. That would involve changing their specific ethnocentric conceptual, linguistic, or perceptual capacities. Given an *anthropocentric* account, human beings would change empirical worlds should they change species and with it their species-specific capacities. While, as we saw in Chapter Six, Kant assumes that our human nature is fixed, we need not assume this ourselves. Nonetheless, because of human plasticity, any change to our species-specific capacities would likely have to be significant for us to change empirical worlds. Finally, given a *logocentric* account, language users would not change empirical worlds but instead surrender their empirical world, *the* empirical world, should they cease being language users. As I suggested in §4, by going from linguistic to non-linguistic they would move from a world to a mere environment.

Hence an eighth putative problem that a Kantian account of meaning faces is that it allows (under certain subjective scopes) movability between empirical worlds. This is a genuine problem also but why? There might be different reasons. To avoid redundancy, let me bracket problems with the relativism of empirical properties and the empirical world (considered in §3) and the possible plurality of such worlds (considered in §4). Instead let me suggest that movability between empirical worlds presupposes some fixed point relative to which such movability is intelligible. And it is unclear what such a point could be.

Ironically Davidson himself suggests something that it might be. Leading up to his (2001d/1984, essay 13) first argument against the dualism of conceptual scheme and empirical content, Davidson maintains that there must be a "common co-ordinate system" (p. 184), and so a common origin point, for different perspectives to be intelligible. Now Davidson also contends that the necessity of such a point belies any difference between conceptual schemes and that without any difference there could be no evidence of such schemes in the first place. Regardless Davidson elsewhere (2002, p. 41) considers treating empirical content as itself a fixed point relative to which different perspectives are intelligible. Movability between perspectives would presumably be intelligible too. Admittedly Davidson dismisses this consideration because he argues against the very idea of a conceptual scheme and empirical content. Nonetheless, as we saw in Chapter Five, Davidson's arguments fail. Moreover I can myself treat empirical content as the fixed point relative to which movability between empirical worlds is intelligible. I can myself make good on Davidson's (as it turns out) wrongly rejected consideration.

This is what I have in mind. For Davidson, empirical content is meant to be the objective source here specifically of empirical properties and ultimately worlds. The objective source of these together with its subjective dual would be constitutive essentially of such properties and worlds. Now *ex hypothesi* such empirical content, this objective source, is logically independent of the subjective source. Further, as we saw in Chapter Two, the objective source just is the intrinsic nature (if construed ontologically) or aspect (if construed epistemologically) of reality. Since a Kantian account of meaning is a kind of Ontological Kantianism, the objective source is itself then this intrinsic nature.

Of course, for the Kantian, any such intrinsic nature remains unknowable. That is the thesis of noumenalism construed ontologically. But then noumenalism itself provides a way to make intelligible a point logically independent of any *particular* reality, now understood as any *particular* empirical world. While the subjective source of empirical worlds can vary, this objective source—this empirical content, entailing the truth of noumenalism—remains fixed. It is intrinsic to all empirical worlds while being independent of any variable subjective capacities partly constitutive of those worlds. In that sense the objective source is intrinsic to reality (or Reality) itself. Various empirical worlds would be constituted, or constructed, essentially out of subjects applying their specific conceptual, linguistic, and perceptual capacities to it. Because of its connection to noumenalism, let me call this purely objective source the 'noumenal world'. We might then call these various empirical worlds 'phenomenal worlds'. Hence the noumenal world itself is a non-variable, or fixed, point relative to which movability between empirical, or phenomenal worlds, is intelligible. So this eighth putative problem, while also genuine, nevertheless also has a reply.

In fact, as we saw in Chapter Three, Kuhn himself says something similar to all this:

> Underlying all these processes of differentiation and change, there must, of course, be something permanent, fixed, and stable. But, like Kant's *Ding an sich*, it is ineffable, undescribable, undiscussible. Located outside of space and time, this Kantian source of stability is the whole from which have been fabricated both creatures and their niches, both the "internal" and the "external" worlds (2002, p. 104).

As Kuhn describes it, the permanent, fixed, and stable something would in fact be Kant's *Ding an sich*, or thing in itself. It would therefore be my noumenal world.[5] Underlying everything ethnocentric is this world, this purely objective source of all subjects' empirical concepts, terms, or properties. Now we might or might not follow Kuhn (and Kant) in saying that this noumenal world is outside of space and time. Regardless we should follow Kuhn (and Kant) in regarding the noumenal world as a source of stability, the fixed point. For the noumenal world remains unchanged by various subjects' specific (and potentially changing) conceptual, linguistic, and perceptual capacities. Instead a subject's empirical (or phenomenal) world changes relative to it.

---

5. See Allison (2004, ch. 3.I–3.III) and Hanna (2001, ch. 2.4) for competing discussions of Kant's uses of "thing in itself," "noumenon," and "transcendental object."

Now Kuhn's discussion is applicable to other subjective scopes besides the ethnocentric. Nonetheless his thought that the noumenal world is "ineffable, undescribable, undiscussible" is not right. For Kant sees while Kuhn does not that we can distinguish between positive and negative senses of Kant's 'noumenon' and so my 'noumenal world':

> If by a noumenon we understand a thing **insofar as it is not an object of our sensible intuition**, because we abstract away from the manner of our intuition to it, then this is a noumenon in the **negative** sense (1998/1787, B307).[6]

When we talk about a noumenon in the negative sense, we say what it is *not*. It is *not* an object of our sensible (or empirical) intuition. There are two ways to read this. First, we can recognize that something that is not an object of *our* sensible intuition nevertheless can be the object of *another* sensible intuition. Indeed Kant (B72) himself recognizes the possibility of other kinds of sensible intuition. Second, recognizing that when we abstract away from the manner of *our* intuition we neither leave nor add a *different* manner of intuition, we can take something that is not an object of our sensible intuition to be something that is not an object of *any* sensible intuition. On this reading, when Kant talks about a thing insofar as it is not an object of "our" sensible intuition, he means that it is not an object of our *kind* of intuition, which is necessarily sensible. Moreover, consistent with this second reading, Kant goes on to talk about "the doctrine of the noumenon in the negative sense, i.e., of things that the understanding must think without this relation to our *kind* of intuition" (B308, emphasis mine) and to say that "one cannot assert of sensibility that it is the only possible *kind* of intuition" (B310, emphasis mine). Kant also explains: "The concept of a noumenon is therefore merely a **boundary concept**, in order to limit the pretension of sensibility, and therefore only of negative use" (B310–11). The negative concept of a noumenon limits the pretension not just of our sensibility but also of sensibility *simpliciter*. For all these reasons I read Kant's claim in the second way. By a 'noumenon in the negative

---

6. In the *Prolegomena to Any Future Metaphysics* Kant anticipates Thomas Kuhn's "underlying" metaphor:

> In fact, if we view the objects of the senses as mere appearances, as is fitting, then we thereby admit at the very same time that a thing in itself *underlies* them. ... Therefore the understanding, just by the fact that it accepts appearances, also admits to the existence of things in themselves, and to that extent we can say that the representation of such beings as *underlie* the appearances, hence of mere intelligible beings, is not merely permitted but also unavoidable (2010/1783, 4: 314–15, emphases mine).

sense' I take him to mean something that is not an object of sensible intuition *tout court*.[7]

Continuing the quotation, Kant explains that, rather than understanding a noumenon in this negative sense, we might instead understand it in a positive sense:

> But if we understand by that an **object of a non-sensible intuition**, then we assume a special kind of intuition, namely intellectual intuition, which, however, is not our own, and the possibility of which we cannot understand, and this would be the noumenon in a **positive** sense (B307).

When we talk about a noumenon in the positive sense, we say what it *is*. It is an object of *non*-sensible intuition. For Kant, because our intuition is necessarily sensible, an object of non-sensible intuition would be something that could be intuited only by a being with a kind of intuition different from ours. That kind of intuition would be not sensible but intellectual. That would make it a kind of intuition whose possibility we cannot understand.[8]

Kant concludes that we should say nothing about a noumenon in the positive sense. We should not say what a noumenon is. As Kuhn himself might remark, that is because a noumenon in the positive sense is "ineffable, undescribable, undiscussible." Nonetheless Kuhn fails to realize that we can say something about a noumenon in the negative sense. We can say what it is not. In particular, by saying that it is not an object of sensible intuition, we can follow Kant in treating its concept as a boundary concept to limit the pretension of sensibility. For Kant, sensibility is responsible for sensibly intuiting objects (A19/B33) in space and time (B147). The concept of a noumenon, as a boundary concept, would limit the pretension of sensibility, because a noumenon is *ex hypothesi* not itself in space or time. But then a noumenon in the negative sense cannot be an object of sensible intuition or ultimately empirical knowledge. A noumenon in the negative sense, and indeed my own notion of a noumenal world, therefore marks the boundary of what we can sensibly intuit

---

7. Allison (2004, p. 63) supports my reading. Moreover, as we saw in Chapter One, §1, my initial definition of 'objective source' was a source that is not subjective. This is tantamount to treating it as a noumenon in the negative sense.

8. According to Kant, intellectual intuition would be had by "an understanding that itself intuited (as, say, a divine understanding, which would not represent given objects, but through whose representation the objects would themselves at the same time be given, or produced)" (1998/1787, B145). For such an intellect, the subjective/objective distinction apparently collapses. See Sally Sedgwick (2012, chs. 1–2) for Georg Wilhelm Friedrich Hegel's attitude toward Kant's notion of intellectual intuition.

and so empirically know. Moving from Kant's view back to Kantianism, for the Kantian, if empirical worlds are constituted essentially out of subjective and objective sources, then the noumenal world, as the objective source itself, would itself lie beyond the boundary of the empirical.

Moreover invoking the notion of a noumenon, or noumenal world, in the negative sense explains how subjects can move between phenomenal worlds. All subjects live in their various phenomenal worlds. Beyond their boundary is the noumenal world. It is the intrinsic nature of all these various phenomenal worlds, left after abstracting away our manner of intuition, and so our perceptual (and, I might add, conceptual and linguistic) capacities, to it. As we saw above, a subject changes phenomenal worlds when her capacities change. She moves from one world to another. Nonetheless her noumenal world, indeed *the* noumenal world, stays the same.[9]

An analogy might help. Suppose that we think of the noumenal world analogously with a purely physical world—a world containing only natural kinds. In that world there are natural kinds like gold and humans. We might understand a particular empirical world, constituted essentially out of this noumenal world and subjective responses to it, as a social world—a world containing social kinds and "socialized" natural kinds, *i.e.*, natural kinds granted social use and import. In this world there are social kinds like coins and citizens. The noumenal world would still be a boundary of what kinds of things can have social use and import. Gold is the raw material for coins while plutonium is not. Humans are potential citizens of political states while viruses are not. Now, continuing the analogy, suppose that we are ethnocentric Ontological Kantians like Kuhn. Members of other communities might not treat gold as the raw material for coins or agree that all humans can be citizens instead of some necessarily being slaves and others sovereigns. Members of different communities might then have different uses for and ideas about what is important regarding each. Regardless beyond all their social uses would be their intrinsic nature, the noumenal world itself: gold and humans. Their differing social uses entail that moving between worlds involves learning new social uses for these objects. It does not entail that there are no objects, or intrinsic nature, of these worlds between which subjects move.[10]

---

9. Employing Kant's metaphors from the *Prolegomena* (2010/1783, 4: 314–15) we might say that the noumenal world "underlies" all phenomenal worlds.

10. This analogy is similar to John Searle's (1995) description of how "institutional facts," which are social, derive from "brute facts," which are physical. Nonetheless Searle's description is not meant analogically. Searle takes the physical world (and its brute facts) as given rather than constituted; he is some sort of realist rather than an Ontological Kantian concerning properties. Relatedly Searle thinks that there is only one empirical world.

Admittedly this is only an analogy. For the Kantian, there is no subject-independent natural-kind gold to recur. Likewise, for her, talk of "humans" as much as "citizens," "slaves," and "sovereigns," presupposes that such talk is itself meaningful in virtue of subjective and objective sources. Nonetheless the analogy helps make intelligible a noumenon, albeit analogically, as a boundary concept. It is analogous not to a socialized natural kind but to a natural kind that lies beyond the socialized boundary. A noumenon is the purely objective, analogically purely physical, material out of which phenomena, or empirical objects, are *via* specific subjective capacities constituted. It is like gold, or even humans, that different communities conceive of and name differently. A noumenon is their objective ground. Discharging the analogy I can say that the noumenal world is whatever lies beyond the boundary of every subject's empirical—or phenomenal—world.

So what should we think of this eighth putative problem that a Kantian account of meaning faces, its possibly allowing the movability between empirical worlds? Not only can empirical content, as Davidson suggests (only wrongly to reject), make intelligible such movability. Not only would such empirical content, as Kuhn suggests, amount to a noumenal world that is "permanent, fixed, and stable." Such a world would, as Kant himself suggests, be discussible as what is beyond the boundary of the empirical, analogous to how a natural kind is beyond the boundary of its socialized uses. And that makes the possibility of movability between worlds intelligible. Thus this eighth putative problem that a Kantian account of meaning faces, though a genuine problem, has a reply. Moreover that reply should on internal grounds be particularly persuasive. It uses noumenalism, a consequence of Kantianism, to good effect. Given all that—plus the conclusion from Chapter Seven that a Kantian account faces none of the problems that we there saw its competitors themselves face—we have even more reason to prefer a Kantian account of meaning to these others.

6. THE UNITY OF REASON

There is one more thing to say about a Kantian account of meaning before concluding. As we saw in §2, anyone committed to a Kantian account of meaning is also committed to a Kantian account of content. As we saw in §3, anyone committed to a Kantian account of meaning is also committed to a Kantian account of nature. As I explain here, anyone committed to any of these Kantian accounts is committed to each of the others. Anyone who is an Ontological Dualist concerning terms, concepts, *or* properties, is ultimately an Ontological Dualist concerning terms, concepts, *and* properties. Anyone in for one is in for all.

By having shown that anyone committed to a Kantian account of meaning is also committed to a Kantian account of content and nature, I have shown that anyone committed to Ontological Dualism concerning terms is also committed to Ontological Dualism concerning concepts and properties. Now anyone committed to Ontological Dualism concerning properties is committed to Ontological Dualism concerning concepts and terms as well. If empirical properties are constituted essentially out of subjective and objective sources, then the concepts and terms for these properties must themselves be so constituted. Otherwise they would not be the concepts under which these properties fall or terms by which these properties are named.

Hence, if I can show that commitment to Ontological Dualism concerning concepts itself entails commitment to Ontological Dualism concerning properties, then I can show that commitment to any one kind of Ontological Dualism entails and is entailed by commitment to them all. And indeed I can. For I can formulate (a)–(f), from §3, in terms of statements and terms as easily as I can in terms of thoughts and concepts. The claim that the *statement* 'gold exists in the earth's crust' has the truth value that it does in English would itself be true if and only if the *thought* **gold exists in the earth's crust** has the truth value that it does. Moreover, paralleling empirical statements, empirical thoughts have the content that they do in virtue of the content of their concepts (as well as their arrangement). And empirical thoughts have the truth value that they do in virtue of the content of those thoughts. Hence empirical thoughts have the truth value that they do if and only if a suitable subject under suitable conditions would take them to have that truth value. (a) can then be replaced with (a'):

(a') **Gold exists in the earth's crust** has the truth value that it does if and only if a suitable subject under suitable conditions would take it to have that truth value.

Thus (b)–(e) can themselves be replaced with (b')–(e') modeled on this. The conclusion, (f'), follows:

(f') Gold exists in the earth's crust in virtue of a suitable subject under suitable conditions taking **gold exists in the earth's crust** to be true.

Gold has the properties that it does in virtue of subjective responses to objects in the world. Kantian accounts of meaning (as we saw in §3) and content (as I explained here) both entail that. Kantian accounts of meaning and content therefore both entail a Kantian account of nature. Hence commitment to

Ontological Dualism concerning concepts and terms entails commitment to Ontological Dualism concerning properties.

Now, as promised, because commitment to Ontological Dualism concerning concepts and terms entails commitment to Ontological Dualism concerning properties (as I explained here), and commitment to Ontological Dualism concerning properties entails commitment to Ontological Dualism concerning concepts and terms (as we saw above), commitment to Ontological Dualism concerning empirical concepts, terms, or properties entails commitment to Ontological Dualism concerning empirical concepts, terms, and properties. One can be an Ontological Dualist—and therefore Kantian—concerning all or none. Ontological Kantian kinds concerning concepts, terms, and properties stand or fall together.

Ontological Dualism itself can therefore be strengthened:

> STRENGTHENED ONTOLOGICAL DUALISM: All empirical concepts, terms, *and* properties are constituted essentially out of subjective and objective sources.

As we saw in Chapter One, though Kant himself (if understood as an Ontological Kantian) believes that all empirical concepts, terms, and properties are so constituted, I phrased Ontological Dualism disjunctively (albeit inclusively) to cover Kantians who might not. As I explained here, anyone believing this of such concepts, terms, or properties must, like Kant, believe it of all of them. The disjunction of Ontological Dualism becomes the conjunction of Strengthened Ontological Dualism. Ontological Kantianism can itself then be strengthened:

> STRENGTHENED ONTOLOGICAL KANTIANISM: All empirical concepts, terms, *and* properties are constituted essentially out of subjective and objective sources. The subjective source may take the form of subjective constitutive principles.

Moreover, by parity of reasoning, commitment to either Kantian Content, Kantian Meaning, or Kantian Nature itself entails commitment to all three:

> KANTIAN CONTENT: For any empirical concept, the concept has the content that it does if and only if a suitable subject under suitable conditions would take it to have that content.
> KANTIAN MEANING: For any empirical term in L, the term means what it does if and only if a suitable subject under suitable conditions would take it to have that meaning.
> KANTIAN NATURE: For any empirical property, the property has the nature that it does if and only if a suitable subject under suitable conditions would take it to have that nature.

Hence I can combine all three into a single Inclusive Kantian Account:

INCLUSIVE KANTIAN ACCOUNT: For any empirical concept, term in *L*, and property, respectively, the concept, term, and property has the content, meaning, and nature that it does if and only if a suitable subject under suitable conditions would take it to have that content, meaning, and nature.

In fact, because Kantian accounts of content, meaning, and nature all do individually entail commitment to one another, my Kantian conceptual geography might be said in Kant's own spirit to be exploring the "unity of reason." By the 'unity of reason' I do not mean Kant's notion of such a unity expressed in the Transcendental Dialectic: "If the understanding may be a faculty of unity of appearances by means of rules, then reason is the faculty of the unity of the rules of understanding under principles" (1998/1787, A302/B359). Though, Kant continues, this "bring[s] the highest possible *unity of reason* into our cognition" (A309/B366, emphasis mine), reason is thereby relegated to regulating the understanding's work. As Kant later explains, reason therefore has "only a **project** united" (A647/B675).[11] Instead by the 'unity of reason' I mean what on my reading Kant means when he writes in the Canon of Pure Reason:

> All interest of my *reason* (the speculative as well as the practical) is *united* in the following three questions:
> 1. **What can I know?**
> 2. **What should I do?**
> 3. **What may I hope?** (A804–05/B832–33, italicized emphases mine)

This unity of reason concerns reason's uniting the domains of what we might recognize as epistemology, ethics, and philosophy of religion, respectively. A single capacity (Kant's "faculty") plays a central role in each. Epistemology, ethics, and philosophy of religion are themselves elements of a larger endeavor.[12]

Now, as I have shown, a subject's "reason"—not in Kant's sense but in my sense of her specific conceptual, linguistic, and perceptual capacities—is partly constitutive of empirical concepts and so their content, terms and so their meaning, and properties and so their nature. We might therefore say

---

11. See Nathaniel Goldberg (2004a) for how Kant nevertheless both needs yet cannot allow reason to be more than merely regulative.

12. Susan Neiman (1997) explores this notion of the "unity of reason," correlating Kant's questions with science, ethics and politics, and faith, respectively.

in Kant's spirit that Kantian conceptual geography unites all interest of my reason in *these* three questions:

1. **What can I empirically think?**
2. **What can I empirically say?**
3. **What empirically exists?**

This unity of reason concerns "reason's"—or the subject's subjective capacities'—uniting the domains of epistemology, philosophy of language, and metaphysics, respectively. A single set of capacities plays a central role in each. Epistemology, philosophy of language, and metaphysics are themselves elements of a larger endeavor.

Nor can this unity be broken. This is so even though we have encountered someone who tries to break it. As we saw in Chapter Three, while early on (2012/1962) Kuhn writes that members of different communities "are responding to a different world" (p. 111), that those before a scientific revolution "lived in a different world" (pp. 116–17), and that "though the world does not change with a change of paradigm, the scientist afterwards works in a different world" (p. 121), later (2002) he retracts such claims. As I argued there, Kuhn could present his later view as a kind of Ontological Kantian concerning concepts and terms, and not properties. That would explain his retraction. Nonetheless that explanation can be no justification. As I have shown here, commitment to Ontological Kantianism concerning concepts and terms entails commitment to Ontological Kantianism concerning properties. Talk of "the world," and in fact "worlds," is non-retractable without also retracting talk of "terms" and "concepts," and so Kuhn's view *in toto*.[13]

7. LESSONS FOR KANTIAN CONCEPTUAL GEOGRAPHY

In this chapter we have seen eight putative problems that a Kantian account of meaning faces, only three of which are genuine problems, all three of which

---

13. As we saw in Chapters Two and Three, according to Kuhn, the Ptolemaic and Copernican conceive of and name the same object in the world, the sun, differently. I concluded that, for Kuhn, such objects would be tantamount to Pettit's "pre-existing things" (2002, p. 75). Nonetheless on that view Kuhn is not an Ontological Kantian concerning properties. Because, as I have now shown, Kuhn is such a Kantian, he remains committed to there being an objective source of the Ptolemaic's and Copernican's concept and term—something like the noumenal world discussed in §5. Such a world would not however contain the sun as an object. Regardless, if the Ptolemaic's and Copernican's conceptual, linguistic, and perceptual capacities are sufficiently similar, then they might take themselves to be conceiving of and naming the same object, the sun, differently. The sun would be constituted, or constructed, similarly enough by each that each could regard it as pre-existing when in fact it is not.

have replies. In this conclusion I draw four lessons for Kantian conceptual geography generally.

First, I can strengthen a lesson from Chapter Seven. There we learned that a Kantian account of meaning faces none of the problems that we saw its competitors face. So we had reason to prefer that account to them. Because we learned here that the putative problems that a Kantian account does face are either not genuine problems or have replies, we have even more reason to prefer a Kantian account of meaning. Though I am a conceptual geographer rather than a settler, evaluating a Kantian account of meaning has helped us appreciate its conceptual contours—including the relative durability of those contours against criticism especially when compared to a Platonic realist, Aristotelian realist, Berkeleian idealist, Lockean hybridist, or Hegelian pragmatist account of meaning.

Second, I can elaborate on that lesson from Chapter Seven as well. There we also saw that there are accounts of meaning in the analytic literature approximating nearly all these competitor accounts. Friedrich Ludwig Gottlob Frege's (1993/1892) account of sense and reference, Hilary Putnam (1993/1975) and Saul Kripke's (2005/1980) new theory of reference, and Herbert Paul Grice's (1991, chs. 5, 6, 14) account of speaker meaning approximate Platonic realist, Aristotelian realist, and Berkeleian idealist accounts of meaning, respectively. Various use, social-practice, or inferentialist accounts of meaning associated with the American Pragmatists, the later Ludwig Wittgenstein (2009/1958), Wilfrid Sellars (1991/1963, 1968), Robert Brandom (1998), and perhaps Georg Wilhelm Friedrich Hegel (1977/1807)—and that would be associated with McDowell (1996) were he to offer an account of meaning—approximate a Hegelian pragmatist account. Taken with the previous lesson, I conclude that we have reason to prefer a Kantian account to all these specific accounts in the literature too.

Third, and concerning a Kantian account of meaning in its own right, such an account entails the existence of one subjectively empirical world if the subjective scope is logocentric. It entails the existence of at least one subjectively empirical world if that scope is anthropocentric. And it entails the existence of more than one subjective empirical world if that scope is ethnocentric or idiocentric. Moreover these are "subject-friendly" worlds—worlds all of whose properties subjects can in principle conceive of, name, and perceive.

And fourth, anyone committed to a Kantian account of meaning is committed to Kantian accounts of content and nature, and *vice versa*. Anyone committed to Ontological concerning concepts, terms, or properties is committed to Ontological Kantianism concerning all three. There is a "unity of reason" concerning Kantianism itself. Kantianism treats epistemology, philosophy of language, and metaphysics each as elements of a larger endeavor.

NINE

From Principlism to Kantian Thoughts on Truth

In Chapters Seven and Eight I examined the connection between Dualism and a Kantian account of meaning, thereby disclosing new land within Kantianism's borders, and then putative problems that the Kantian account faces. Here in Chapter Nine I examine the connection between Principlism and not a Kantian account of but instead Kantian thoughts on truth, disclosing more new land. Moreover, as surveying a Kantian account of meaning illuminated the nature of meaning, surveying Kantian thoughts on truth illuminates the nature of truth. This further demonstrates the value of Kantian conceptual geography itself.

Now by 'Kantian thoughts on truth' I do not mean Immanuel Kant's thoughts on truth, though I do consider some of them. Nor do I mean what in Chapter Eight I called a 'Kantian account of truth value'. The topic here is not what it is for some claim to be true or false. It is instead the nature of truth (and empirical truth in particular) itself. Nor finally do I mean what, following my theme from Chapter Seven, one might call a 'Kantian account of truth'. I have nothing as explicit as such an account, with general formulations and specific examples, in mind. Instead by 'Kantian thoughts on truth' I mean ideas about the nature of truth, and empirical truth in particular, suggested by Kantianism generally and Principlism specifically.

There are four other ways in which my discussion of Kantian thoughts on truth differs from my discussion of a Kantian account of meaning. First, I do not appeal to non-Kantian thoughts on truth for contrast. I focus on the Kantian alone. Second, I do not consider problems that Kantian thoughts on truth face. Not only is my discussion looser here than was my discussion concerning meaning, so that it is not as easy to identify such problems. It is likely that those problems that a Kantian account of meaning faces have correlates that Kantian thoughts on truth face, so that I might have already (albeit implicitly) considered them. Third, and combining the first two, I do not determine whether we have reason to prefer Kantian thoughts on truth to any other. I merely consider these thoughts in their own right. And fourth, like my defense of Principlism in Chapter Six, my discussion of its connection to Kantian thoughts on truth here is guided by the history of Principlism itself—from Kant's synthetic *a priori* judgments to Donald Davidson's principle of charity.

The chapter proceeds as follows. In §1 I consider anthropocentric Kantian thoughts on truth suggested by Kant's version of Principlism. In §2 I consider ethnocentric Kantian thoughts on truth suggested by Thomas Kuhn's, Rudolf Carnap's, and Michael Friedman's versions of Principlism. In §3 I consider un-Principled Kantian thoughts on truth suggested by Philip Pettit's and Willard van Orman Quine's version of un-Principled Kantianism.[1] In §4 I consider logocentric Kantian thoughts on truth suggested by Davidson's version of Principlism. In §5 I consider the full historical story, from Kant to Davidson, that emerges. Finally in §6 I draw lessons for Kantian conceptual geography generally.[2]

1. ANTHROPOCENTRIC KANTIAN THOUGHTS FROM KANT

Principlism is the following view:

> PRINCIPLISM: The subjective source of all empirical concepts, terms, or properties takes the form of subjective principles.

It comes in ontological and epistemological kinds:

> ONTOLOGICAL PRINCIPLISM: The subjective source of all empirical concepts, terms, or properties takes the form of subjective principles constitutive of those concepts, terms, or properties.
> EPISTEMOLOGICAL PRINCIPLISM: The subjective source of all empirical concepts, terms, or properties takes the form of subjective principles acquisitive of those concepts, terms, or properties.

To prime my consideration of anthropocentric Kantian thoughts on empirical truth from Kant, consider Kant's own remarks on truth in the *Critique of Pure Reason*:

> The old and famous question with which logicians were to be driven into a corner and brought to such a pass that they must either fall into a miserable

---

[1]. As I explain in §3, while Philip Pettit is an anthropocentric Kantian, it is unclear which subjective scope Willard van Orman Quine endorses.

[2]. I do not consider idiocentric thoughts suggested by Principlism, because I know no extant version of Principlism that is idiocentric.

circle or else confess their ignorance, hence the vanity of their entire art, is this: **What is truth?** The nominal definition of truth, namely that it is the agreement of cognition with its object, is here granted and presupposed; but one demands to know what is the universal and certain criterion of the truth of any cognition (1998/1787, A57–58/B82).

I take Kant to be doing four things here. First, he is criticizing logicians for being unhelpful in answering what seems to be a basic question.[3] Second, he is granting and presupposing that truth is the agreement of cognition with its object.[4] Third, by calling this definition "nominal" he is implying that it is not real (since real contrasts with nominal, and so is perhaps what he means by "certain").[5] And fourth, Kant is noting that one demands more than merely the nominal definition. One demands a definition (his "criterion") of 'truth' that is not only real (or "certain") but also universal (or, as I explain below, "general"). Specifically one demands to know what the nature of truth itself is. What Kant eventually says is therefore surprising: "it is clear that a sufficient and yet at the same time general sign of truth cannot possibly be provided" (A59/B83). Nothing beyond the nominal definition can be had.

Regardless I can say more on Kant's behalf about the truth of empirical claims, Kant's synthetic *a posteriori* judgments, in particular. Given Kant's Principlism in its ontological or its epistemological construal, all synthetic *a posteriori* judgments depend on, and are therefore necessarily consistent with, Kant's synthetic *a priori* judgments, which would be subjective principles in my sense.[6] As we saw in Chapter One, Kant's Kantianism concerns empirical concepts, terms, and properties, though let me for convenience focus on concepts. Given Ontological Principlism, Kant's subjective principles are constitutive of empirical concepts. Subjects would use those principles to constitute empirical concepts from sensation, where such constitution would include how those concepts relate to other concepts and intuitions and

---

3. The question is Pontius Pilate's (*John* 18:38), who happens to be a major character in Mikhail Bulgakov's (1995) *Master and Margarita*, which I mentioned in my Preface & Acknowledgments and to which I return in Chapter Ten.

4. Immanuel Kant is explicit that truth is a property of judgments (1998/1787, A293/B350).

5. I equate a "*certain* criterion of truth" with a real definition of it and emphasize the role of *certainty*. Robert Hanna (2006, ch. 5.2) equates a "*criterion* of truth" with a real definition of it and emphasizes the role of *criteriality*. Nonetheless Hanna and I agree that Kant contrasts a nominal definition with a real one. See Hanna (pp. 260–61) for further textual support.

6. As we saw in Chapter Six, §1, Kant neither intends all his principles to be synthetic *a priori* nor calls all his synthetic *a priori* judgments 'principles'.

so form empirical judgments. Likewise, given Epistemological Principlism, Kant's principles are acquisitive of his empirical concepts. Subjects would use those principles to acquire empirical concepts from sensation, where such acquisition would likewise include how those concepts relate to other concepts and intuitions and so form empirical judgments. Hence, whether Kant's Principlism is construed ontologically (and constitutively) or epistemologically (and acquisitively), the resulting empirical judgments depend on, and are therefore necessarily consistent with, his subjective principles.

Kant says nearly as much himself. Speaking of synthetic *a priori* judgments, he explains:

> these rules of the understanding are not only true *a priori* but are rather even the source of all truth, i.e., of all agreement of our cognition with objects, in virtue of containing the ground of the possibility of experience, the sum total of all cognition in which objects maybe be given to us (A237/B296).

These "rules of the understanding," or subjective principles, are not only true *a priori*. As I would put it, they are not only true in virtue of a subjective source, the categories of the understanding and forms of intuition, deriving from the transcendental subject's mind. They are the "source" of all truth insofar as such truth concerns the agreement of a subject's cognition with objects. That would include empirical truth, the truth of synthetic *a posteriori* judgments, or empirical claims. For these subjective principles contain "the ground of the possibility of experience." They make experience and so empirical claims possible. Again Kant's synthetic *a posteriori* judgments would depend on, and therefore be necessarily consistent with, his synthetic *a priori*.[7]

Now let me suggest the following elaboration on Kant's view. As we saw in Chapters Five and Six, Kant's paradigmatic synthetic *a priori* judgments are principles of arithmetic, geometry, and pure natural science. Consider arithmetic ones. Suppose that a subject sees, and so forms the empirical (or synthetic *a posteriori*) judgment, that she is in an empty room. Suppose that she then sees, and so forms the empirical judgment, that five other persons enter. Finally suppose that she sees, and so forms the empirical judgment, that seven other persons enter and none leaves. If the subject saw, and so formed

---

7. Kant later writes: "For when we consider nature, experience provides us with the rule and is the source of truth" (A318/B375), where by 'nature' Kant means the empirical world, the world *of* experience. Nonetheless the subjective source, in the form of Kant's subjective principles, still makes experience possible. Judgments about nature, which are empirical or synthetic *a posteriori*, would still depend on, and therefore be necessarily consistent with, judgments that are synthetic *a priori*.

the empirical judgment, that there were twelve persons besides herself in the room, then that empirical judgment would be true. It would be an empirical judgment, so its truth value would depend on how she used her synthetic *a priori* judgments to constitute or acquire the empirical judgment that twelve persons besides her were in the room. Hence the truth of the judgment that twelve persons besides the subject were in the room would depend on, and therefore be necessarily consistent with, the synthetic *a priori* judgment that five plus seven equal twelve. For Kant, were the empirical judgment inconsistent with the subjective principle, then the subject's empirical judgment would be false. She would be seeing an incorrect number of persons. That five plus seven equal twelve is constitutive or acquisitive of her synthetic *a posteriori* judgment. Subjective principles therefore partly determine empirical truth.

Consider an example from pure natural science. According to Kant, if a subject sees, and so forms the empirical judgment, that an apple's position changes from hanging on a tree to resting on the ground, then she must form the empirical judgment that the change is the effect of some cause. Any empirical judgment denying that would be false. It would conflict with Kant's Second Analogy: "All alterations occur in accordance with the law of the connection of cause and effect" (1998/1787, B232). In fact, because in the *Metaphysical Foundations of Natural Science* (2010/1786) Kant attempts to derive the mechanical theory of Isaac Newton from *a priori* considerations like the Analogy, the claim that the apple when changing positions did not accelerate at 9.8 m/s^2 were there no outside forces acting on it would itself be false. Even specific experimental beliefs, to be true, would depend on, and therefore be necessarily consistent with, Kant's principles. Subjective principles partly determine empirical truth here too.

I can now make general points about the nature of empirical truth suggested by all this. As we saw in Chapters Two and Six, for Kant, subjective principles are anthropocentric. They are meant to guide all human beings in the constitution (if construed ontologically) or acquisition (if construed epistemologically) of all empirical concepts, terms, and properties. Moreover, for Kant, because empirical claims are comprised of empirical concepts, the epistemological correlate of empirical terms, and describe empirical properties, subjective principles would guide all human beings in the constitution or acquisition of empirical claims themselves. Hence, for Kant, all human beings would be right to agree that there were twelve persons besides the subject in the room, that change in the apple's position is the effect of some cause, and that (*ceteris paribus*) the apple accelerates at 9.8 m/s^2. For all human beings would apply the same principle to sensation. But then empirical claims, all of which depend on, and are therefore necessarily consistent with, arithmetic, geometry, and pure natural science, have the truth value that they do for all human beings in virtue of these anthropocentric principles as used by subjects to process sensation.

Though Kant maintains that there can be no "universal and certain criterion for truth" (1998/1787, A58/B82)—by which I take him to mean no general and real definition of 'truth'—Kant's anthropocentric Principlism entails that the nature of empirical truth is itself anthropocentric. Truth concerns human beings. It relates to specifically human capacities as those capacities interact with sensation somehow arising things in themselves or considered in themselves. Though his project differs from mine, Robert Hanna makes a similar point when writing that, for Kant, "the concept of truth," and so empirical truth in particular, "is an essentially anthropocentric concept: *it's truth with a human face*" (2006, p. 270). For Kant, there is no legitimate sense of empirical truth not centered on humanity.[8]

2. ETHNOCENTRIC KANTIAN THOUGHTS FROM KUHN, CARNAP, AND FRIEDMAN

As we saw in Chapter Six, Kuhn, Carnap, and Friedman are all ethnocentric Principled Kantians. They all think that all empirical concepts, terms, or properties are linked to essentially subjective and objective sources—where the subjective source takes the form of subjective, ethnocentric principles. Kuhn's subjective principles are meant to be implicit within paradigms (2012/1962), disciplinary matrices (2012/1970; 1979, essay 12), and lexical taxonomies (2002, essays 1–4, 11). They are also meant to depend on informal historically situated convention. Carnap's (1988/1952, suppl. A) subjective principles, his analytic statements, are meant to be explicit and to derive from linguistic frameworks. They are themselves meant to depend on formal ahistorical (indeed rationally reconstructed) convention. Finally Friedman's (2000, 2001, 2002a, 2008, 2010a, 2010c) subjective principles, his relativized *a priori* principles, are meant, like Kuhn's, to depend on informal historically situated convention, yet, like Carnap's, to be explicit.

Regardless of these differences, Kuhn's, Carnap's, and Friedman's versions of Principlism are similar enough to allow Friedman's analysis of Newton's account of mechanics to illustrate their general view. As we saw in Chapter Six, according to Friedman, Newton's account contains three components:

(1) a form of mathematics, the calculus;
(2) conceptions of force and mass embodied in his three laws of motion; and,
(3) a universal law of nature, the law of universal gravitation.

---

8. Hanna (2006, ch. 5) both endorses Kant's concept of truth and tries to explain it *vis-à-vis* all of Kant's kinds of judgments. I do neither.

For Friedman, Newton took (1) and (2) to be principles constitutive of the empirical claim, (3). In particular he took Newton to construct (3) by appealing to the mathematical resources encoded within (1) and the fundamental conceptual resources encoded within (2). Hence, for Friedman, (3) depends on, and is therefore necessarily consistent with, (1) and (2). As Friedman puts it, (1) and (2) make possible the articulating and verifying of (3) against experience. Subjective principles here too partly determine empirical truth.

I am unsure whether Kuhn and Carnap would agree with Friedman on the details. I am however sure that they too would divide theories into subjective principles and empirical claims. Moreover all three would have the same general view about empirical truth. Empirical truth would itself depend on, and therefore be necessarily consistent with, subjective principles. According to all three, empirical terms, and so claims, would be constituted essentially out of subjective and objective sources—where the subjective source takes the form of these principles. All empirical claims would then have the truth value that they do in virtue of the subject's using ethnocentric principles to process experience. For each, therefore, the nature of empirical truth is itself ethnocentric. Truth concerns members of communities. It relates to specifically community capacities as those capacities interact with experience. Adapting Hanna's point from §1, one might say that, for Kuhn, Carnap, and Friedman, the concept of empirical truth is an essentially ethnocentric concept: *it's truth with a community member's face*. For Kuhn, Carnap, and Friedman, there is no legitimate sense of empirical truth not centered on community.

Consider the claim that an otherwise undisturbed object dropped near the earth's surface accelerates at 9.8 m/s^2. That claim would be true relative to the subjective principles that are implicit within Kuhn's lexicon, that are themselves Carnap's explicit analytic statements, and that are themselves Friedman's explicit relativized *a priori* principles, of Newtonian (or classical) mechanics. Its negation would be false. Nonetheless that negation need not be false relative to the subjective principles of special or general relativity as they themselves make possible the articulation and verification of that claim against experience. Other factors, including velocity's effect on mass and weight (itself a kind of force), would have to be considered. Hence, for Kuhn, Carnap, and Friedman, empirical truth is relative to ethnocentric principles and so specific communities. According to one community, that an otherwise undisturbed object dropped near the earth's surface accelerates at 9.8 m/s^2 is true, while, according to a different community, it might be false. Subjective principles still partly determine empirical truth.

Compare this with Kant's view. For Kant, empirical truth is anthropocentric because his subjective principles are themselves anthropocentric. For Kuhn, Carnap, and Friedman, empirical truth is ethnocentric because their subjective principles are instead ethnocentric. There is a related difference also. As we saw in Chapter Six, for Kant, our human nature is immutable. As we also saw there, for Kuhn, Carnap, and Friedman, our community membership is mutable. Hence Kant says nothing about the status of subjective principles not our own. Immutable in our humanity, we are immutable in our principles. Conversely Kuhn, Carnap, and Friedman each say something about a subject's choosing subjective principles from a community other than her own—and thereby changing communities.

Kuhn initially (2012/1962) maintains that a subject, or member, of one community chooses a different community's principles not because those other principles are true. Truth is lexicon- (or, at this point in his career, paradigm-) relative. Instead a subject chooses them because of "non-rational" factors. These include whether those principles and in fact the new paradigm *in toto* is "'neater', 'more suitable', or 'simpler' than the old" (p. 155). Kuhn later (2012/1970, pp. 185, 199, 206; 1979, pp. 321–22; 2002, pp. 36, 113, 119, 251) maintains that community changes can be rational if mediated by values like accuracy, consistency, efficiency, fruitfulness, and simplicity. Now, as Friedman himself notes (2001, pp. 53–57, 93–95; 2002a, pp. 83–85), the sort of rationality that these values engender would be merely instrumental. While research under a paradigm would be fully intelligible to anyone accepting the paradigm, paradigms from other communities—even those under consideration—could at best be more or less accurate, consistent, efficient, fruitful, or simple for subjects to use to process experience. For Kuhn, changing communities would itself then be a merely instrumentally rather than robustly rational affair.

Apparently independent of Kuhn, Carnap (1988/1952, suppl. A) himself says something similar.[9] Carnap phrases his discussion in terms of two kinds of questions. He claims that "Are there numbers?," if asked internally to a set of analytic statements, would be an internal question. It would have a cognitive answer. Each possible answer would be either true or false relative to these analytic statements and ultimately the linguistic framework from which they derive. Conversely the same question, if asked externally to any such set or framework, would be an external question. It would have a non-cognitive answer. That statement would have no truth value at all. Moreover Carnap recognizes that external questions might play two roles. The first role, which Carnap rejects, is metaphysical. It is to ask about ultimate reality. Anyone asking "Are there numbers?" externally is asking whether numbers *really* exist, not

---

9. Nonetheless, as I noted in Chapter Three, §2, Thomas Kuhn was influenced by neo-Kantians like Alexandre Koyré. As Michael Friedman (1999) notes, Rudolf Carnap was influenced by neo-Kantianism also.

relative to a framework but *simpliciter*. It is to ask a question about what in Chapter Eight I called the 'noumenal world', the intrinsic nature of the empirical world itself. Carnap thinks that such a question is not only non-cognitive but also futile. The second role, which Carnap accepts, is pragmatic. It is to ask about the pragmatic value of rejecting one framework in exchange for another. Anyone asking "Are there numbers?" externally in this sense is now asking whether it would be useful to choose a framework relative to which numbers exist. According to Carnap, therefore, whether one should choose a framework cannot depend on cognitive values like truth and falsity. It must instead depend on pragmatic values like efficiency, fruitfulness, and simplicity.

Not only do Carnap's pragmatic values overlap with Kuhn's instrumental ones however. Kuhn's and Carnap's accounts overlap generally. Research under a paradigm (Kuhn) involves asking and answering internal questions (Carnap). Considering whether to choose another paradigm (Kuhn) involves asking external questions (Carnap). If a new paradigm (Kuhn) or framework (Carnap) is chosen, then it is not because its principles are true. For Kuhn and Carnap, truth remains relative to a set of principles. It is instead because doing so has instrumental (Kuhn) or pragmatic (Carnap) value. Conversely choosing empirical claims relative to an already accepted set of principles would be based on whether those empirical claims—relative to those principles against experience—were true or false.[10]

So Kuhn's and Carnap's versions of ethnocentric Principled Kantianism have much in common with each other. They also both have much in common with Friedman's. As we saw in Chapter Six, Friedman's is informed by theirs. In fact, Friedman, like Kuhn and Carnap, maintains that activity internal to a set of principles can be robustly rational. Nonetheless, unlike Kuhn or Carnap, he tries to block the consequence that activity external to a set of principles could be merely instrumentally or pragmatically rational. Friedman (2001, pp. 66–68, 105–15; 2002a, pp. 89–90) does so by introducing his notion of a *meta*-paradigm. According to him, a meta-paradigm is a shared philosophical debate concerning foundational issues in science. Such debates are meant to establish what counts as intelligible and so what speculative, extra-scientific moves scientists are justified in entertaining when adjudicating between paradigms (or relativized *a priori* principles).[11] According to Friedman, engaging in such a debate might allow scientists to see a certain philosophical position as intelligible. They might regard a

---

10. Also like Kuhn, Carnap recognizes intranslatability between statements (1949/1936, p. 126) and the possibility of scientific revolutions (1997/1963, p. 921). See Chapter Three, §4 and §2, respectively.

11. When discussing meta-paradigms Friedman himself talks of "paradigms" rather than "relativized a priori principles."

paradigm that presupposes some position on that debate as itself intelligible. They might then have robustly rational reasons to choose it. Friedman argues that Albert Einstein appealed to the debate concerning absolute *versus* relative motion to allow his light principle, according to which the velocity of light in a vacuum is constant, and principle of equivalence, according to which bodies in a uniform gravitational field and uniformly accelerated frame of reference behave identically, to be taken seriously as foundations for a new paradigm in science. Einstein thereby provided the Newtonian with philosophical or "meta-paradigmatic" reasons to find his scientific paradigm intelligible. The Newtonian could then join those who already had chosen Einstein's relativistic paradigm to see whether it was explanatory of the physical world. According to Friedman, mediation by a meta-paradigm can allow members of one community to choose principles of another based on robustly rational grounds generally.

Nonetheless Friedman's attempt to go beyond Carnap's and Kuhn's shared view is unsuccessful. Suppose that Friedman is right that community changes can be mediated by a meta-paradigm. Friedman is then caught in a dilemma. On the one hand, the meta-paradigm is *ex hypothesi* something for which a subject searches to make sense of another community's paradigm. If choosing a new paradigm without a mediating meta-paradigm cannot be robustly rational, however, then choosing a meta-paradigm without a mediating *meta*-meta-paradigm cannot be robustly rational either. An infinite regress results. On the other hand, Friedman can block the regress by accepting that meta-paradigm choice is itself not robustly but instead merely instrumentally rational. Scientists from different communities would appeal to a shared meta-paradigm because of its accuracy, consistency, efficiency, fruitfulness, and simplicity in facilitating the choice of a particular paradigm. In fact that might better describe Einstein's actions than Friedman himself does. Einstein's appealing to the debate concerning absolute *versus* relative motion was efficient and fruitful in facilitating others to choose his paradigm in particular. Regardless, no matter how intelligible a philosophical debate might make another community's subjective principles seem, the debate cannot itself be chosen on robustly rational grounds. On pain of infinite regress, at some level some debate would have to be chosen on merely instrumental grounds. But then anything chosen based on that debate would have ultimately been chosen based on the instrumental value of the debate itself. This is no genuine improvement on Kuhn's or Carnap's view.[12]

Because infinite regression is less desirable than instrumental rationality, Friedman should opt for the second horn. He should follow Kuhn and Carnap

---

12. See Nathaniel Goldberg (2009c, §§4–6), where I discuss Friedman's proposal further.

in maintaining that choosing another community's subjective principles is itself ultimately (even if in his case indirectly) an instrumentally or pragmatically rational affair. Hence Kuhn, Carnap, and Friedman have a combined view. For each, empirical truth is internal to a set of subjective principles. An empirical claim is true or false relative to them. Subjective principles themselves however are neither true nor false in any absolute or external sense. Rather they are (ultimately) more or less instrumental or pragmatic.[13]

3. UN-PRINCIPLED KANTIAN THOUGHTS FROM PETTIT AND QUINE

Kantian thoughts on truth suggested by Kant are that empirical truth depends on, and is therefore necessarily consistent with, anthropocentric principles. Kantian thoughts on truth suggested by Kuhn, Carnap, and Friedman are that empirical truth depends on, and is therefore necessarily consistent with, ethnocentric principles; and that extra-ethnocentric principles are neither true nor false but more or less instrumental or pragmatic. Kantian thoughts on truth suggested by Pettit and Quine are more difficult to discern. For their Kantianism is un-Principled. While Pettit and Quine are both committed to Dualism, neither is committed to Principlism.

Because Pettit himself is sufficiently removed from discussions of empirical truth, little can be gleaned from his view. So let me focus on Quine. Following the historical story again helps. Quine responds directly to Carnap's distinction between internal and external questions, and so cognitive and pragmatic value:

> Carnap, [C. I.] Lewis, and others take a pragmatic stand on the question of choosing between language forms, scientific frameworks; but their pragmatism leaves off at the imagined boundary between the analytic and the synthetic. In repudiating such a boundary I espouse a more thorough pragmatism. Each man is given a scientific heritage plus a continuing barrage

---

13. Of course subjective principles are true or false relative to other subjective principles. Statements that are analytic (to recur to Carnap's version) in one framework are true relative to it; false, otherwise. This is one sense in which Kuhn (2012/1962, p. 94) maintains that arguments in support of a paradigm are circular. Moreover what I am calling Kuhn's, Carnap's, and Friedman's 'combined views' themselves trace to Kant. For Kant, though we cannot go outside our anthropocentric perspective to gain theoretical knowledge, we can go outside it to investigate ethics, a practical discipline, and to order our knowledge, a practical task. Conversely Kuhn, Carnap, and Friedman think that we can go outside our ethnocentric perspective to choose a different such perspective. And, for them, as for Kant, going outside our perspective is a practical (their "instrumental" or "pragmatic") endeavor.

of sensory stimulation; and the considerations which guide him in warping his scientific heritage to fit his continuing sensory promptings are, where rational, pragmatic (2006/1953, p. 46).

As we saw in Chapters Five and Six, Quine rejects the distinction between analytic and synthetic statements. In my terms he rejects the distinction between subjective principles and empirical claims. Quine maintains that subjective and objective sources of empirical concepts and terms are always mixed. The truth of statements always depends on both. Moreover, as I explain here, Quine takes his rejection of the analytic/synthetic distinction to entail a rejection of Carnap's pragmatic/cognitive distinction. For Carnap, while internal questions have cognitive value and so are true or false, external questions have (at best) pragmatic value and so are about the practical value of choosing languages, frameworks, or sets of analytic sentences themselves. "In repudiating such a boundary" between subjective principles and empirical claims, therefore, Quine explains, "I espouse a more thorough pragmatism."

Now there are two ways to understand Quine's espousal. One way is that Quine *rejects* the notion of cognitive value. Statements are not really true or false but instead merely more or less pragmatic. Euclid's parallel postulate is not, as it would be for Carnap, true relative to Newton's framework of classical mechanics and false relative to Einstein's framework of general relativity. The parallel postulate overall is simply less pragmatic than is its negation. For its negation leads to views, like general relativity, that more accurately predict physical phenomena. The other way to understand Quine's espousal is that he *collapses* cognitive into pragmatic value. Saying that a statement is true is not ultimately distinct from saying that it is pragmatic. The parallel postulate is again not true relative to the framework of classical mechanics and false relative to the framework of general relativity. It is false overall because its negation leads to views more accurately predicting physical phenomena.

Quine intends to be understood the second way. He does close:

Each man is given a scientific heritage plus a continuing barrage of sensory stimulation; and the considerations which guide him in warping his scientific heritage to fit his continuing sensory promptings are, *where rational*, pragmatic (2006/1953, p. 46, emphasis mine).

Quine collapses cognitive into pragmatic value itself. But what does this mean for empirical truth? For Quine, there are no claims, distinct from any empirical ones, that are the form or basic epistemological or linguistic unit that the subjective source of empirical concepts, terms, or properties takes. Rather empirical truth depends on, and is therefore necessarily consistent with, no subjective principles at all. Instead it depends on, and is necessarily consistent with, all empirical claims. Moreover, absent subjective principles in particular, the nature of empirical truth is itself, "where rational, pragmatic."

Hence Quine, unlike Kuhn, Carnap, or Friedman, does not have a combined view. For him, it is not the case that statements relative to a set of principles are true or false, while principles are themselves more or less instrumental or pragmatic. All statements are true or false relative to subjective and objective sources generally *because* subjects can use them more or less efficiently, fruitfully, or simplistically to process the "flux of experience" (2006/1953, p. 44).[14] For Quine, therefore, the nature of empirical truth is itself pragmatic. Adapting Hanna's point from §1, one might say that, for Quine, the concept of empirical truth is an essentially pragmatic concept: *it's truth with a pragmatic face*. For Quine, there is no legitimate sense of empirical truth that is not pragmatic.[15]

Such truth-*cum*-pragmatism however says nothing about the scope of the subjective. Though for my purposes the importance of Quine's and Pettit's views is that they are un-Principled, it remains worth asking whether Quine, as well as Pettit himself, is an idiocentric, ethnocentric, anthropocentric, or logocentric un-Principled Kantian.

Pettit's case is clear. He is anthropocentric. As we saw in Chapter Two, Pettit takes subjective capacities to be shared by all human beings.

Quine's case is unclear. Sometimes Quine's sympathies lie with anthropocentrism: "If people's innate spacing of qualities"—and so their perceptual, if not also conceptual and linguistic, capacities—"is a gene-linked trait, then the spacing that has made for the most successful inductions will have tended to predominate through natural selection" (1969, p. 126). "People" here are human beings, and natural selection is generally thought to operate on species, here again human beings. Similarly Quine explains: "Natural selection had heightened man's responsiveness and that of other animals to the sight and

---

14. For the Principled Kantians Kant, Kuhn, Carnap, and Friedman, empirical truth would be consistent with all empirical claims also. For all empirical claims would themselves depend on, and therefore themselves be necessarily consistent with, subjective principles. Nonetheless, for Principled Kantians, consistency among empirical claims would follow from a logically prior dependence on principles, while, for un-Principled Kantians, the dependence would be direct.

15. Quine also talks about how theories are undetermined by their empirical content, so that there are multiple empirical theories having equal predictive value. For Quine, such theories are "empirically equivalent." Though initially (1975; 1981; 1986, pp. 156–57) wavering on whether to count confirmed empirically equivalent theories as all true, Quine ultimately (2004/1992, §42) counts as true only the simplest among each equivalent set. (See Donald Davidson 2005a, pp. 43–44.) For him, truth again collapses into pragmatic value, here simplicity.

smell of bodies" (1998, p. 35), and so "man's" subjective responses to "bodies," or objects, in the world. Besides appealing again to natural selection, Quine contrasts "other animals" with "man," by which he means humankind.[16]

Other times Quine's sympathies lie elsewhere. Though this apparently begins sympathetically with anthropocentrism, its conclusion supports anthropocentrism or ethnocentrism: "This public harmony of private standards of perceptual similarity"—a subjective source of all empirical concepts, terms, or properties—"is accounted for by natural selection." Appealing to natural selection, that seems anthropocentric. But Quine continues: " ... [T]hanks to shared ancestry and shared environment, [these private standards] will tend to harmonize across the tribe" (1998, p. 21). While by 'tribe' Quine perhaps means species rather than community, a tribe, as a genetically related community, would itself have a shared ancestry and environment more specific than humanity's at large.

In fact Quine's sympathies occasionally lie clearly with ethnocentrism: "[O]bservation sentences," meant to be empirical checkpoints on theories,

> are the sentences on which all members of the community will agree under uniform stimulation. And what is the criterion of membership in the same community? Simply general fluency of dialogue. This criterion admits of degrees, and indeed we may usefully take the community more narrowly for some studies than for others. What count as observation sentences for a community of specialists would not always so count for a larger community (1969, p. 87).

Observation sentences, which Quine explains are community specific, are comprised of empirical terms, express empirical concepts, and concern empirical properties. But then, if "stimulation"—the *objective* source of such concepts, terms, or properties—is "uniform," agreement *or* disagreement on observation sentences must be due to their *subjective* source. Since, Quine explains, members of the same community will agree on observation sentences, such members must themselves contribute the same subjective source.

Other times still Quine apparently straddles ethnocentrism and idiocentrism:

> Different persons growing up in the same language are like different bushes trimmed and trained to take the shape of identical elephants. The anatomical details of twigs and branches will fulfill the elephantine form differently from bush to bush, but the outward results are alike (1964, p. 8).

---

16. See Quine (1998, pp. 28, 50).

For Quine, "growing up in a language" is presumably an ethnocentric activity. Different linguistic communities have their own subjective source of empirical concepts, terms, or properties. They inculcate in their members shared linguistic (if not also conceptual and perceptual) capacities. But then Quine is here apparently saying that language learning, which operates on subjects *qua* community member, masks differences among subjects *qua* individual. Nonetheless this ethnocentrism does not cause those divergent idiocentric capacities to be lost. It merely pushes them below observable behavior. Yet at some level the idiocentric subjective source remains.

4. LOGOCENTRIC KANTIAN THOUGHTS FROM DAVIDSON

The last Kantian to consider is Davidson. Unlike Pettit's and Quine's, Davidson's Kantianism is Principled. Unlike Kant's, Kuhn's, Carnap's, and Friedman's, Davidson's Principlism is logocentric. For Davidson, the principle of charity is shared by all subjects *qua* language user. All language users would use the principle of charity to interpret any speaker's utterances. This is so even though Davidson remains an idiocentric Kantian concerning responses. For him, the meaning of a speaker's utterances, though in principle interpretable by any language user, nevertheless remains relative to each speaker's own idiolect.

Now Davidson, like Kant, writes directly about truth. As we saw in Chapters Four and Five, Davidson appeals to Alfred Tarski's (2008/1944) semantic conception of it. So let me consider what Tarski says. As we saw there, Tarski maintains that specifying all the conditions under which any sentence in a language is true defines the concept of truth in that language. But then, like Kant (as we saw in §1), Tarski thinks that no *universal* definition of the concept of truth can be had. Nonetheless, unlike Kant, he thinks that we can define truth in a particular language.

As we also saw, Davidson modifies Tarski's conception in three ways. First, he applies Tarski's conception to natural languages. Second, he applies it officially to utterances of sentences—even though unofficially Davidson continues to talk of "sentences." And third, while Tarski contends that one can define truth in a language by presupposing a notion of translation (and so meaning), Davidson wishes to determine sentences' interpretation (and so meaning) by presupposing the concept of truth. Nonetheless, I can now add to this third difference, Davidson does agree with Tarski that one can define truth in a particular language.

Let me focus on this third point. It concerns what Davidson takes the nature of truth itself (in a universal sense) to be. Though Davidson does think that one can define truth in a language in Tarski's manner, Davidson presupposes the concept of truth itself. According to him, "[t]ruth is beautifully transparent…, and I take it as a primitive concept" (2002, p. 139). Davidson continues:

> Any further attempts to explain, define, or explicate the concept will be empty or wrong. … [A]ll such theories either add nothing to our understanding of truth or have obvious counterexamples. Why on earth should we expect to be able to reduce truth to something clearer or more fundamental? (pp. 155–56).

And, "[i]f we want to speak the truth about truth, we should say no more than need be" (p. 191), which, for Davidson, means leaving it undefined. Finally Davidson explains:

> It is a mistake to look for an explicit definition or outright reduction of the concept of truth. Truth is one of the clearest and most basic concepts we have, so it is fruitless to dream of eliminating it in favor of something simpler or more fundamental (2005a, p. 55).

Hence Davidson agrees with Kant and Tarski that there can be no universal definition of the concept of truth. He also agrees with Tarski that there can be a definition of truth in a particular language.[17] Nonetheless Davidson disagrees with Kant and Tarski by taking the concept of truth itself as primitive. This suggests that Davidson would take the nature of truth (empirical or otherwise) as unanalyzable. If the concept has no further analysis, then neither does truth itself.[18]

Nonetheless Davidson (2005a, essay 3) does say that he can describe some of the content of the concept of truth itself. According to him, because presupposing the concept of truth is required for interpretation, truth is linked to interpretation and meaning. Because, as we saw in Chapters Four and Five, the radical interpreter, when constructing a charitable, Tarski-style

---

17. See Davidson (2005a, ch. 1) on agreement between Alfred Tarski and himself, and Hanna (2006, ch. 5) on agreement among Kant, Tarski, and Davidson.

18. Though Davidson initially (2001d/1984, essay 3) takes himself to be offering a weak correspondence theory of truth, and then (2002, essay 10) a coherence theory of truth consistent with a correspondence theory, he ultimately (2002, essay 10, "Afterthoughts"; 2005a, ch. 2) recants all these. See Hans-Johann Glock (2003, pp. 107–08). Hence Davidson would agree with Hilary Putnam that "[t]ruth and falsity are the most fundamental terms of rational criticism" but disagree that " … any adequate philosophy must give some account of these, or, failing that, show that they can be dispensed with" (1976, pp. 606). Davidson instead regards truth as primitive (defining 'falsity' in terms of it)—even if, as I explain below, Davidson says more about it.

theory of meaning for a speaker's languages, simultaneously attributes to the speaker beliefs, truth is also linked to belief. Though I merely alluded to this in Chapter Four, because Davidson thinks that his account of radical interpretation is part of a unified theory of meaning, thought, and action—where the radical interpreter needs to discern which statements a speaker prefers to be true and so her desires—truth is linked to desire too. And, for Davidson, by interpreting a speaker's utterances and thereby attributing to her beliefs and desires, the radical interpreter can discern her behavior as actions. She therefore reveals that the speaker is rational, thereby linking truth to rationality itself. Moreover, as we saw in Chapter Five, Davidson maintains that our own methodology of interpretation is sufficiently similar to the radical interpreter's. The methodology of any language user would be. Hence all interpretation, radical or otherwise, links truth to meaning, belief, desire, and rationality.

Hence Davidson's stated view on truth is threefold. First, Tarski's semantic conception of truth can define truth in a particular language. Second, the concept of truth itself must be presupposed and cannot be defined. And third, the concept of truth itself is nevertheless linked to interpretation, meaning, belief, desire, and rationality, giving the concept its "content."

Now, as I did with Kant, I can say more about the nature of empirical truth—and in Davidson's case empirical truth about interpretation in particular—on Davidson's behalf. As we saw in Chapter Four, Davidson maintains:

> A theory of meaning (in my mildly perverse sense) is an empirical theory, and its ambition is to account for the workings of a natural language. Like any theory, it may be tested by comparing some of its consequences with the facts (2001d/1984, p. 24).

Interpretive claims are themselves empirical, deriving from the principle of charity (a subjective source) as applied by the interpreter to the speaker's observable behavior and environment (from the interpreter's perspective, an objective source). As *per* that principle, in basic cases the interpreter correlates a speaker's sentences with truth conditions that describe what from the interpreter's perspective would be perceptually salient features of the environment were the interpreter in the speaker's spot. As *per* the systematic nature of theory construction, in non-basic cases the interpreter matches the speaker's sentences with their truth conditions recursively in a way modeled on Tarski's. Thus the interpreter might construct the empirical claim that 'snow is white' in the speaker's idiolect of English means that snow is white. She might construct other empirical claims besides. Regardless, for Davidson, all such constructions depend on, and are therefore necessarily consistent with, the principle of charity. That subjective principle partly determines the empirical truth of claims like those concerning the meaning of 'snow is white'.

Davidson therefore provides a view of empirical truth of interpretive claims themselves. Moreover, for him, all language users would be right to agree that 'snow is white' in many idiolects of English means that snow is white. That interpretation follows from applying the logocentric principle of charity (and the rest of Davidson's "methodology of interpretation" [2001d/1984, p. 197]) to the speaker's observable behavior and environment. Nonetheless, for Davidson, this would be so even though all language users would also be right to agree that 'snow is white' can mean something else, *modulo* alternate interpretations of other utterances—so long as those interpretations follow from the same. As we saw in Chapters Four and Eight, Davidson maintains that there is no fact of the matter about which interpretation is *the* right one. More than one interpretation of any utterance is possible. Meaning is indeterminate.[19] For Davidson, therefore, all interpretations are universally determin*able* while none is determin*ate*.

Regardless, for him, all language users would be able to agree that some claim about what an utterance means is true or false. For they would all be able to determine whether the claim follows from applying the principle of charity (and the rest of his methodology) to a speaker's observable behavior and environment. Now, because the principle of charity is logocentric, Davidson has nothing like Kuhn's, Carnap's, or Friedman's combined view of truth and instrumental or pragmatic value. For Davidson, all interpretation is an "internal" activity. Interpreting is like answering one of Carnap's internal questions. It is always relative to the principle of charity. There is no other "methodology of interpretation," and so no other subjective principle, besides his own.

Nor does Davidson have anything like Quine's view that truth collapses into pragmatic value. A claim about what an utterance means is true or false, not because it is more or less instrumental or pragmatic, but because the claim does or does not follow from a charitable, Tarski-style truth theory. Admittedly some interpretations might be more instrumental or pragmatic than others. Regardless the truth of an interpretation would be distinct from its being merely instrumental or pragmatic.

The picture that emerges on Davidson's view then in this. What a speaker means, believes, and desires is idiocentric. The meaning of her terms and content of her concepts are relative to her interpreter's subjective capacities. But the truth *that* she means, believes, and desires what she does is logocentric. Truths about those terms or concepts *having* that meaning or content are relative to

---

19. As we saw in Chapter Eight, §1, such indeterminacy is innocuous.

the principle of charity. Any language user, insofar as she can interpret the speaker, would do so by appealing to the principle of charity—and could (in principle) come up with the same empirical result. And this is so even though interpretation remains indeterminate. Regardless the empirical truth of the interpreter's interpretations depends on, and is therefore necessarily consistent with, the principle of charity. All such empirical claims would have the truth value that they do in virtue of an interpreter's applying the principle of charity to a speaker's utterances. For Davidson, therefore, the nature of empirical truth concerning interpretation is itself logocentric. It concerns language users generally. It relates to general language-user capacities as they interact with a speaker's observable behavior and environment. I can therefore adapt Hanna's point from §1 as follows. For Davidson, the concept of empirical truth in interpretation is an essentially logocentric concept: *it's truth with any language user's face at all*. For Davidson, there is no legitimate sense of empirical truth in interpretation not centered on language use generally.

5. THE HISTORICAL STORY IN FULL

Having reached the end of the historical story, from Kant to Davidson, I can now recapitulate its highlights in full. Though Kant is pessimistic about saying more about truth than that it involves the agreement of a cognition with its object, his anthropocentric Principlism suggests that the nature of empirical truth in particular is anthropocentric. Empirical truth depends on, and is therefore necessarily consistent with, anthropocentric principles.

Conversely Kuhn, Carnap, and Friedman each are committed to the view that the nature of empirical truth is ethnocentric. Empirical truth depends on, and is therefore necessarily consistent with, ethnocentric principles. Moreover, while such principles are true or false internal to the paradigm or framework from which they derive, they are merely more or less instrumental or pragmatic external to it. Kuhn, Carnap, and Friedman have combined views.

Then there is Quine (and perhaps Pettit). Because Quine is un-Principled, he collapses truth into instrumental or pragmatic value. For him, empirical claims are true or false relative to subjective and objective sources generally because they can all be used more or less efficiently, fruitfully, and simplistically to process the "flux of experience" (2006/1953, p. 44). And this is so regardless of the subjective scope to which Quine is committed.

Finally Davidson accepts Tarski's concept of truth in a language while taking truth itself to be primitive. Nonetheless he also says that truth is linked to interpretation, meaning, belief, desire, and rationality. And the truth of empirical claims about interpretation in particular depends on, and is therefore necessarily consistent with, the principle of charity. So, for Davidson, though meaning remains idiocentric, the interpretation of meaning would be guided by the principle of charity, which is logocentric. Hence, on the one hand, Davidson's is not a combined view, as are Kuhn's, Carnap's, and Friedman's. For Davidson, there can be no work done under, or question asked relative to, one set of principles rather than another. All empirical claims about interpretation are true or false relative to the principle of charity. Nor, on the other hand, does empirical truth collapse into pragmatic value, as it does for Quine. There is a subjective principle relative, and in that sense internal, to which interpretations are true or false. Again this is so even though interpretation remains indeterminate.

6. LESSONS FOR KANTIAN CONCEPTUAL GEOGRAPHY

In this chapter we have reviewed the history of Principlism to glean Kantian thoughts on truth suggested by Principlism (and, regarding Pettit and Quine, its absence). In this conclusion I draw four lessons for Kantian conceptual geography generally.

First, according to Principled Kantianism, because empirical claims depend on, and are therefore necessarily consistent with, subjective principles, the nature of empirical truth is itself so dependent and consistent. In that sense subjective principles partly determine empirical truth. Likewise the subjective scope of those principles determines the subjective scope of empirical truth. If the subjective principles are idiocentric, ethnocentric, anthropocentric, or logocentric, then empirical truth is also.

Second, for the non-logocentric Principled Kantians whom we have considered, those principles which the particular subject in question does not endorse are neither true nor false but more or less instrumental or pragmatic. Those Principled Kantians therefore have combined views. While truth is a property internal to a set of principles, instrumental or pragmatic value is a property external to a set of principles—and therefore the basis on which those principles can be chosen.

Third, according to un-Principled Kantianism, there are no principles relative to which empirical claims can be true or false. Such claims must therefore be true or false relative to subjective and objective sources generally. For Quine, that means that, though empirical claims can still be true, their being so is not ultimately distinct from their having pragmatic value.

And fourth, in the case of logocentric Principlism, empirical claims are true because they depend on, and are therefore necessarily consistent with, the only possible principles that there are. Hence a logocentric Principled Kantian has no combined view. There is no such thing as work done under, or questions asked relative to, one set of principles rather than another. All empirical statements are true or false relative to the same principles. Nonetheless a logocentric Principled Kantian is not an un-Principled Kantian. Because there is a subjective principle, the logocentric Principled Kantian distinguishes truth from instrumental or pragmatic value.

PART FIVE

Lessons for Us

TEN

"Some Idea Had Seized the Sovereignty of His Mind"

In one of the more poetic passages of the *Critique of Pure Reason* Immanuel Kant proffers:

> We have now not only traveled through the land of pure understanding, and carefully inspected each part of it, but we have also surveyed it and determined the place for each thing in it. But this land is an island, and enclosed in unalterable boundaries by nature itself. It is the land of truth (a charming name), surrounded by a broad and stormy ocean (1998/1787, A235/B294–95).

At the point in the *Critique* that Kant is writing he has completed the positive part of his own conceptual geography. By traveling through the land of pure understanding, Kant has surveyed his *a priori* concepts, forms, and principles. He thereby claims to have determined the place—in conceptual space—for all the positive notions of the Critical philosophy itself. Kant's conceptual geography has also revealed that this land, or territory, of pure understanding is surrounded by a broad and stormy ocean.

Similarly at the point in *Kantian Conceptual Geography* that I am writing I have completed the entirety of my own conceptual geography. By traveling through Kantian territory, I have surveyed the nature of the subjective, objective, and empirical; potential scopes of the subjective; what can (and cannot) be said about a subject-independent reality; empirical concepts and their content, empirical terms and their meaning, and empirical properties and their nature; analyticity, syntheticity, apriority, and aposteriority; constitutive principles, acquisitive principles, and empirical claims; meaning, meaning indeterminacy, meaning relativism, meaning incommensurability, and truth-value relativism; logically possible *versus* subjectively empirical worlds;

and the nature of empirical truth. I thereby have determined the place—in conceptual space—for all their corresponding concepts. My Kantian conceptual geography has also revealed that this land, or Kantian territory, has as its borders two broad and diversely specifiable theses, Dualism and Principlism.

Having reached the final part of *Kantian Conceptual Geography*, I now look back at the full expanse of Kantian territory not only in isolation but also in relation to the broader conceptual world. While at the end of each of the preceding chapters after the first we saw what lessons my survey holds for Kantian conceptual geography, here at the end of this book we see what lessons it holds not only *for* Kantian conceptual geography but also *from* Kantian conceptual geography for us philosophers—Kantian or otherwise.

The chapter proceeds as follows. In §1 I consider what we have learned about subjectivity, objectivity, principles, and the empirical. In §2 I consider what we have learned about response-dependence, noumenalism, and incommensurability. In §3 I consider what we have learned about the various scopes that subjectivity can take and the timing with which it might take them. In §4 I consider what we have learned about the dualism of conceptual scheme and empirical content, as well as analyticity, apriority, subjective principles, their history, and their viability. In §5 I consider what we have learned about meaning, possible worlds, and truth. Finally in §6 I explain the title of this chapter and thereby recall from the Preface & Acknowledgments the sense in which, like Fyodor Dostoevsky, Kant is immortal.

1. SUBJECTIVITY, OBJECTIVITY, PRINCIPLES, AND THE EMPIRICAL

The first series of lessons from Kantian conceptual geography for us are those we learned in Part One, "Establishing Kantianism's Borders." In Chapter One, "Dualism, Principlism, Kantianism," we encountered theses in epistemology, philosophy of language, and metaphysics worth our attention. Those theses can be drawn from Kant's *Critique of Pure Reason*; exist in various forms in the works of analytic philosophers like Philip Pettit, Thomas Kuhn, and Donald Davidson; and come in many kinds besides. The theses are of course Dualism, Principlism, and Kantianism:

> DUALISM: All empirical concepts, terms, or properties are linked essentially to subjective and objective sources.
> PRINCIPLISM: The subjective source of all empirical concepts, terms, or properties takes the form of subjective principles.
> KANTIANISM: All empirical concepts, terms, or properties are linked essentially to subjective and objective sources. The subjective source may take the form of subjective principles.

Because we have spent much time discussing Dualism, Principlism, and Kantianism, let us see what lessons there are to learn from each.

Though I dropped its full name after introducing it, 'Dualism' is short for 'Empirical Dualism'. It is a thesis about the empirical. According to Dualism, the nature of the empirical is twofold. In particular all concepts, terms, or properties that are empirical are linked essentially to two separate sources. There is the *subjective* source, deriving ultimately from the specific conceptual, linguistic, or perceptual capacities in an individual subject's mind, shared across a group of subjects' minds, or encoded in a subject's or subjects' language or (other) conventions. Then there is the *objective* source, deriving from something independent of the subject. As I put it in Chapter One when introducing the term, Dualism concerns how certain epistemological, linguistic, and metaphysical items are ineluctably bound to both minded subjects and mind-independent objects.

Likewise, though I dropped its full name after introducing it, 'Principlism' is short for 'Subjective Principlism'. It is a thesis about subjective principles insofar as they relate to the empirical. According to Principlism, the nature of the subjective source, of which Dualism speaks, itself might take the form of subjective principles—claims distinct from any empirical ones whose constitution or acquisition these principles make possible. If Dualism concerns how certain items are ineluctably bound to both minded subjects and mind-independent objects, then Principlism concerns the form that such subjective binding might take.

Finally Dualism and Principlism figure together in Kantianism. All kinds of Kantianism satisfy Dualism; only some, Principlism. Those that do satisfy Principlism I called kinds of 'Principled Kantianism'; those that do not, 'un-Principled Kantianism'. Kantianism therefore recognizes the possibility rather than the necessity of the subjective source of all empirical concepts, terms, or properties taking the form of principles. There is always binary binding; the subjective binding may or may not be principled.

Exploring these theses revealed two ways of understanding how subjectivity, objectivity, and subjective principles, and empirical concepts, terms, and properties might relate generally. The "essential link" specified by Dualism and "form taken" specified by Principlism can come in *ontological* or *epistemological* kinds. As kinds of Kantianism *in toto*, they are these:

ONTOLOGICAL KANTIANISM: All empirical concepts, terms, or properties are constituted essentially out of subjective and objective sources. The subjective source may take the form of subjective constitutive principles.

EPISTEMOLOGICAL KANTIANISM: All empirical concepts, terms, or properties are acquired by a subject's appealing essentially to subjective and objective sources. The subjective source may take the form of subjective acquisitive principles.

Moreover from these kinds of Kantianism we learned the difference between *constituting* and *acquiring* empirical concepts, terms, and properties. The former involves constructing those concepts' content, terms' meaning, and properties' nature, while the latter involves learning those concepts, terms, and properties themselves. We also learned the difference between constitutive and acquisitive principles. Both are subjective principles, distinct from any empirical claim, that are the form or basic epistemological or linguistic unit that the subjective source of empirical concepts, terms, or properties takes. Subjects use constitutive principle to constitute, or construct, empirical concepts, terms, or properties from their correlative objective source. Subjects use acquisitive principles to acquire, or learn, those concepts, terms, or properties from the same.

So from Dualism, Principlism, and Kantianism we learned how subjectivity, objectivity, principles, and the empirical might relate—and how that relation might itself be ontological, and involve constitution, or epistemological, and involve acquisition. But more than that, because Dualism and Principlism establish the borders of Kantian territory, exploring them taught us not only what Kantianism is but also what it is not. Kantianism is neither *Platonic* nor *Aristotelian realism*, which maintain that all empirical concepts, terms, or properties are linked essentially only to an objective source. For Platonic realism, the objective exists *ante res*, or prior to objects in the world whose speciation they make possible, while, for Aristotelian realism, it exists only *in rebus*, or in such objects. Nor is Kantianism *Berkeleian idealism*, which maintains that all empirical concepts, terms, or properties are linked essentially only to a subjective source. Neither is Kantianism *Lockean hybridism*, which maintains that only some empirical concepts, terms, or properties are linked essentially to subjective and objective sources. Finally Kantianism is not *Hegelian pragmatism*, which maintains that there is no philosophically useful subjective/objective distinction at all.

My engaging in Kantian conceptual geography therefore offers multiple ways—Kantian and otherwise—of understanding the nature of the empirical itself. Regardless of whether one is a Kantian, this exploration can nevertheless inform her foray into epistemology, philosophy of language, and metaphysics generally.

2. RESPONSE-DEPENDENCE, NOUMENALISM, AND INCOMMENSURABILITY

In Part Two, "Exploring Kantian Territory," I turned to Kantian territory proper. I began my exploration in Chapter Two, "Philip Pettit." While local response-dependence theorists, like Mark Johnston and Crispin

Wright, connect only some empirical concepts, terms, or properties in an *a priori* manner to paradigmatic responses to objects in the world, *global response-dependence* theorists, and Pettit is the only explicit example, connect them all. From Pettit moreover we learned that global response-dependence entails Dualism and with it Kantianism. In fact, while Johnston and Wright take their inspiration from John Locke's distinction between primary and secondary qualities, Pettit takes his from Kant's transcendental idealism.

We also learned from Pettit that all kinds of Kantianism entail *noumenalism*, the thesis that reality possesses an intrinsic nature (if construed ontologically) or aspect (if construed epistemologically) that remains unknowable. Though Pettit engages in a debate with Michael Smith and Daniel Stoljar concerning noumenalism, which I complicated, the cause for Kantianism's commitment to noumenalism is clear. For Kantianism, since all empirical concepts, terms, or properties are linked essentially to subjective and objective sources, it is impossible to know the purely objective source *per se*. For both concepts and terms are integral to knowledge, and properties themselves would concern what is to be known.

We then turned to Chapter Three, "Thomas Kuhn." Though Kuhn is not explicitly a global response-dependence theorist, we saw that he nevertheless fits the description. That revealed things about *incommensurability*. Following Kuhn and construing incommensurability as non-intertranslatability, we saw that all kinds of Ontological Kantianism concerning terms, if they allow relevantly distinct subjects—subjects with relevantly distinct subjective capacities—entail its possibility. I return to this in §3.

Finally I turned to Chapter Four, "Donald Davidson." Though Davidson is not explicitly a global response-dependence theorist either, we saw that he nevertheless fits the description too. This revealed that different kinds of Kantianism—even when proposed by the same person—are not always consistent. Davidson's first kind of Kantianism is connected to his notion of radical interpretation; his second and third, like Pettit's and Kuhn's own, language learning. We also learned about the connection between language learning and Kantianism more generally.

Though global response-dependence, noumenalism, incommensurability, and Kantian inconsistencies are all of interest from the perspective of Kantianism, they are of interest from other perspectives too. Response-dependence is popular in many areas of philosophy. Pettit's explicit, and Kuhn's and Davidson's implicit, globalizations of it should therefore be of interest to many. Moreover, even for those opposed to Kantianism, there is much to gain by seeing how global response-dependence can itself be a version of Kantianism. Insofar as Pettit, Kuhn, and Davidson can all be understood as global response-dependence theorists, Kantians and non-Kantians alike can appreciate affinities between their views and Kant's. Likewise, while noumenalism might itself be a mere curiosity to those outside Kantian territory, the idea that knowledge has limits is not. Kantianism provides a model, both ontological and epistemological, of such limits, and explores some of their consequences. Kantianism also helps us understand how ontological and epistemological versions of theses themselves differ. Further, incommensurability has itself been of central concern to philosophers of science, while in its non-intertranslatability form it is important to philosophers of language. It has epistemological and metaphysical implications (some of which we saw) too. By engaging in Kantian conceptual geography we learned why incommensurability might arise, what forms it might take, and some of the consequences that it might have. By illuminating what is at stake concerning all these issues, engaging in Kantian conceptual geography has been a boon to Kantianism's friends as well as foes.

3. SUBJECTIVE SCOPE AND RELEVANT TIMING

Pettit's, Kuhn's, and Davidson's views taught us other lessons too, including that kinds of Kantianism can come in a spectrum of subjective scopes. The subjective source to which all empirical concepts, terms, or properties are essentially linked can be *anthropocentric*, or paradigmatically human-centered, as Kant and Pettit maintain. It can be *ethnocentric*, or paradigmatically community-centered, as Kuhn claims. It can be *idiocentric*, or paradigmatically individual-centered, to which Davidson is committed. Or it can be *logocentric*, or paradigmatically language-centered, to which Davidson is also committed.

Moreover Dualism and Principlism can themselves diverge on subjective scope. The subjective source specified in Dualism can be (in order) idiocentric, ethnocentric, anthropocentric, or logocentric. It can involve the specific conceptual, linguistic, or perceptual capacities of subjects *qua* individual, *qua* community member, *qua* human being, or *qua* language user. Conversely subjective principles can guide the application of that source for any subject *qua* individual, *qua* community member, *qua* human being, or *qua* language user too.

Philosophers generally have much to learn here. Though all self-identifying response-dependence theorists, as well as Locke and Kant, are explicitly anthropocentrist, it likely never occurred to them that a suitable subject under suitable conditions could be anything other than a normal human being under normal conditions of observation. Moreover, while others have realized that the subjective has more potential scopes—Kuhn, Rudolf Carnap, and Michael Friedman favor ethnocentrism, while Davidson favors idiocentrism and logocentrism albeit in different ways—none has ever realized that *all* these exist in conceptual space. Hence anyone, Kantian or otherwise, who finds subjectivity significant should take note of all these potential scopes. Those who find it insignificant should take note too, if only to become acquainted with views that they reject. Idiocentrism, ethnocentrism, anthropocentrism, and logocentrism are all worth all philosophers' attention.

The idea of subjective scope also adds to my discussion of incommensurability. Suppose that a theorist is an Ontological Kantian concerning terms. Any subjective scope that such a theorist endorses that allows there to be relevantly distinct subjects, or subjects with relevantly distinct subjective capacities, entails the possibility of incommensurability. For there can then be more than one subject with relevantly different conceptual, linguistic, or perceptual capacities, relative to which her terms (and with it their meaning) are constituted. Idiocentric, ethnocentric, and anthropocentric Ontological Kantianism concerning terms therefore entails the possibility of incommensurability. Concerning the idiocentric, ethnocentric, and anthropocentric, it is possible that there be subjects with different subjective capacities. Logocentric Ontological Kantianism concerning terms, however, because it does not permit relevantly distinct subjects, does not entail the possibility of incommensurability. Concerning logocentrism, it is not possible that there be subjects with relevantly different subjective capacities. All subjects would be subjects *qua* language user overall.

Finally, though not concerning subjective scope, we learned from Davidson too that the relevant timing of the subjective is itself variable. All the other theorists considered have a dispositional view. When empirical concepts, terms, or properties are linked essentially to a subjective source, their idea is that the link is to some capacity and so disposition of the subject to respond in some way. This dispositionalism traces to Locke, is inherited by Kant, and is without question taken on by many analytic philosophers. Davidson however makes us realize that a dispositional view is not the only view. Empirical concepts, terms, or properties might be linked essentially to a subjective source in the form, not of their (mere) capacities or dispositions, but of the activation of those capacities or dispositions. While Davidson maintains that a term means what it does in a language if and only if a radical interpreter *would* interpret it to have that meaning in that language, he also maintains that a term means what it does in a language if and only if a learner of that language *did* learn that the term has that meaning in that language. The former, concerning mere capacities or dispositions, is *ahistoricist*. It does not require a history of subjective responses. The latter, concerning the activation of capacities or dispositions, is *historicist*. It does require a history of subjective responses.

Because timing is orthogonal to scope, ahistoricism and historicism are each compatible with idiocentrism, ethnocentrism, anthropocentrism, and logocentrism alike. That is a lesson for Kantians and non-Kantians, and so something that we all should learn, also. And it is something that we did learn by engaging in Kantian conceptual geography.

4. DUALISM AND PRINCIPLISM DEFENDED

We learned much as well, for both Kantian conceptual geography and ourselves, from my defenses—in Part Three, "Defending Kantianism's Borders"—of Dualism and Principlism. From Chapter Five, "Defending Dualism," we learned how Davidson himself is ironically Dualism's most determined detractor in the analytic tradition if not overall. We also learned how his arguments against the very idea of a conceptual scheme and empirical content (or scheme/content dualism) amount to arguments against Dualism. And we learned about the nature and structure of Davidson's arguments themselves.

Thus we saw how Davidson's first argument against scheme/content dualism is an argument specifically against the very idea of a conceptual scheme. Then we saw how the two halves of that argument rely on Davidson's creative use of metaphors, misuse of Alfred Tarski's semantic conception of truth, and reuse of his own account of radical interpretation. Next we saw how that first half of Davidson's first argument is unsuccessful, while the second half, to succeed, depends on his second argument—specifically against the very idea of empirical content. This revealed Davidson's different ways of construing empirical content. Finally we saw how Davidson's argument against the very idea of empirical content, and both halves of his argument against the very idea of a conceptual scheme, all fail.

We saw the synergy in Davidson's failure also. From the second half of his first argument Davidson is committed to all languages being necessarily and completely intertranslatable. From the failure of his second argument Davidson is committed to empirical content and so scheme/content dualism. For Davidson, therefore, the set of necessarily and completely intertranslatable languages itself amounts to a single conceptual scheme that interacts with its empirical content. Nor should this be surprising. Davidson is a Kantian with a logocentric subjective principle.

This is relevant beyond Kantianism too. Davidson's views on all these issues remain important and importantly misunderstood. Moreover, regardless of his arguments' failure, by considering them I considered other ways of understanding scheme/content dualism and its component duals, thereby further elaborating on Dualism and with it Kantianism. Finally Davidson's own confusion concerning the nature of empirical content is itself instructive.

Of course, for us, the most important lesson is that Davidson's arguments do not defeat Dualism. Kantianism's external border is secure. Kantian territory can itself then be settled. And that should be interesting to those who want to settle it as well as those who do not.

Likewise from Chapter Six, "Defending Principlism," we learned about the history of Principlism, versions of Principlism, arguments against Principlism, and Principlism's vindication. We saw the nature of Kant's synthetic *a priori* judgments, his subjective principles. We were reminded of Kuhn's paradigms, disciplinary matrices, and lexicons, within which his subjective principles are embedded. And we recalled Davidson's principle of charity, his subjective principle. We also learned about two other Principled Kantians, Carnap and Friedman, with their analytic statements and relativized *a priori* principles, respectively. Finally I considered classic arguments against Kant's Principlism, Willard van Orman Quine's arguments against Carnap's Principlism, and both arguments against Friedman's Principlism—itself meant to incorporate the best from Kuhn's and Carnap's.

We then saw that Friedman's Principlism remains unimpugned. At least one version of Principlism so far remains viable. Kantianism's internal border can therefore hold. But there are more general lessons too. Regardless of one's view toward synthetic apriority, understanding its strengths and weaknesses can only help epistemologists and philosophers of language (if not more besides). Regardless of one's taste or distaste for Carnap's logical empiricism, the history of analytic philosophy does inform contemporary analytic philosophy; and, especially if Friedman is right, Carnap's view is not as moribund as often thought. Further, Friedman's program in the history and philosophy of science is itself important to epistemology, philosophy of language, and metaphysics. Nor should this last point be surprising. Friedman's program is important to Kantianism.

Finally many think that Quine has had the last word on analyticity if not also apriority. If so then he would have had the last word on Principlism too. By showing not only that Quine lacks the last word but also that the word that he did have is unpersuasive, I have reestablished the respectability of Principlism and perhaps even Quine's other targets. Besides analyticity and apriority, these include meanings, synonymy, and necessity. Quine has cast a long shadow over the conceptual landscape. If I am right, then there are broad swaths of unnoticed sun.

Of course, again for us, the most important lesson is that neither classic nor Quine's arguments against Principlism are successful against Friedman's version. Though this does not show that Principlism is true, it does shift the burden to those who think it false. We therefore have reason to think that Kantianism's internal border is secure. Those who want to settle on Principled land may therefore proceed. Those who do not should nevertheless know that the land is so far defended.

5. MEANING, SUBJECTIVELY EMPIRICAL WORLDS, AND EMPIRICAL TRUTH

Having established Kantianism's borders, explored Kantian territory, and defended those borders themselves, in Part Four, "Looking for New Land within Kantianism's Borders," I looked for new land to chart. In Chapter Seven, "A Kantian Account of Meaning," I turned to Dualism to disclose a Kantian account of meaning. Here the lessons for Kantian conceptual geography and philosophy generally were many. First, we learned what a Kantian account of meaning is. While I considered three general formulations and three specific examples, such an account ultimately says that all empirical terms mean what they do in virtue of subjective and objective sources. Second, we learned that every view that in Chapter One I contrasted with Kantianism generally has a correlative account of meaning contrasting with a Kantian account of meaning specifically. And third, we learned that many influential views on meaning approximate Kantianism and its contrasts.

Platonic and *Aristotelian realist accounts of meaning* maintain that all empirical terms mean what they do in virtue of only an objective source. While, for the Platonic realist, the objective source exists *ante res*, or prior to objects in the world, and so such a realist distinguishes between a supermundane and mundane notion of meaning, for the Aristotelian realist, the objective source exists only *in rebus*, or in the objects in the world, so there is only the mundane. Moreover Friedrich Ludwig Gottlob Frege's account of meaning, which divides senses from referents, approximates a Platonic realist account. Hilary Putnam and Saul Kripke's (roughly shared) new theory of reference, which eschews senses and endorses only referents, approximates an Aristotelian realist account.

A *Berkeleian idealist account of meaning* maintains that all empirical terms mean what they do in virtue of only a subjective source. Herbert Paul Grice's account of meaning, which focuses on speakers, audiences, and their intentions approximates such an account. A *Lockean hybridist account of meaning* maintains that only some empirical terms mean what they do in virtue of subjective and objective sources. Though we found no philosophers whose accounts approximate a Lockean hybridist one, we did consider different versions of such an account. Finally a *Hegelian pragmatist account of meaning* denies the philosophical usefulness of talk of "subjective" and "objective" themselves. Accounts of meaning that approximate a Hegelian pragmatist account include various use, social-practice, or inferentialist accounts of meaning, among which are meant to be (even if they are ultimately not) Davidson's accounts of radical interpretation and language learning.

Beyond all that, we also learned that each non-Kantian account of meaning faces a problem that a Kantian account itself does not. A Platonic realist account has difficulty explaining how subjects can epistemologically bridge ontological divides. An Aristotelian realist account has difficulty handling empty names. A Berkeleian idealist account has the unintuitive consequence of leaving no room for objects. For all practical purposes a Lockean hybridist account collapses into, or in virtue of being a hybridist account inherits problems from, other accounts. Finally a Hegelian pragmatist account both seems to exclude objects and is denied Davidson's accounts of radical interpretation and language learning as exemplars. Hence my engaging in Kantian conceptual geography both provided a new taxonomy for accounts of meaning in the analytic literature and showed that a Kantian account does not face problems that they do. But more than that, my engaging in Kantian conceptual geography provided us reason to prefer a Kantian account to a Platonic or Aristotelian realist, Berkeleian idealist, Lockean hybridist, or Hegelian pragmatist account of meaning and so accounts of meaning in the literature approximating any of them.

In Chapter Eight, "Problems That a Kantian Account of Meaning Faces," I considered eight putative problems that a Kantian account of meaning does face. A Kantian account of meaning allows meaning to be indeterminate; it entails that meaning is relative to the subject; and it entails that such meaning can be incommensurable with terms from other languages. These first three putative problems, we learned, are not genuine. A Kantian account of meaning also apparently involves an infinite regress and recognizes truth values as relative to subjects. These fourth and fifth putative problems, we learned, are not genuine either. Finally a Kantian account of meaning recognizes empirical properties and the empirical world as relative to subjects; possibly entails a plurality of empirical worlds; and possibly permits movability between such worlds. These sixth, seventh, and eighth putative problems, we learned, are in fact genuine. Nonetheless I offered multiple replies to each. Hence, while in Chapter Seven we saw that a Kantian account of meaning does not face problems that its competitors do, in Chapter Eight we saw that only three of the eight putative problems that a Kantian account does face are genuine problems—and that they all have replies. We therefore have even more reason to prefer a Kantian account of meaning to these others.

We learned more things from those putative problems besides. We learned that a subjectively empirical world is a world in which subjects (*qua* individual, *qua* community member, *qua* human being, or *qua* language user) can in principle conceive of, name, and perceive all its empirical properties. We also learned that subjectively empirical worlds are a subset of David Lewis's logically possible worlds, where Lewis's worlds are merely maximally consistent state of affairs. Though we did not discuss this there, the notion of a subjectively empirical world itself has the potential to illuminate areas *well* beyond Kantian territory by making specific what kinds of worlds are of interest to what kinds of subjects. Such worlds should therefore be of interest to all kinds of philosophers.

Finally we learned that anyone committed to Ontological Kantianism concerning concepts, terms, or properties is committed to Ontological Kantianism concerning all three. Kantianism itself therefore reveals a kind of "unity of reason." Its lessons for empirical concepts' content, terms' meaning, and properties' nature are themselves united. What I can empirically think, what I can empirically say, and what empirically exists can all be asked and answered together. Kantianism therefore treats epistemology, philosophy of language, and metaphysics themselves as elements of a larger endeavor. Kantianism's friends and foes might both be surprised. They should all take note.

Having considered meaning in Chapters Seven and Eight, I turned to Chapter Nine, "Kantian Thoughts on Truth." There I explored what thoughts on empirical truth in particular can be gotten from relying on Principlism (or its absence). I did so by reviewing the historical record of Principlism from Kant to Davidson.

We learned that, for Kant, the truth of empirical judgments depends on, and is therefore necessarily consistent with, the truth of synthetic *a priori* judgments, his subjective principles. Hence, for Kant, the nature of empirical truth is anthropocentric. Conversely, for Kuhn, Carnap, and Friedman, the truth of empirical claims depend on, and is therefore necessarily consistent with, the subjective principles implicit within Kuhn's paradigms, disciplinary matrices, or lexical taxonomies; the subjective principles that are themselves Carnap's analytic statements; and the subjective principles that are themselves Friedman's relativized *a priori* principles, respectively. So, for them, unlike for Kant, the nature of empirical truth is ethnocentric. Moreover, while, for Kant, who is an anthropocentrist, human nature is immutable, for these others, who are ethnocentrists, community membership is mutable. Thus, for Kuhn, Carnap, and Friedman, claims relative to a set of subjective principles are true or false, while subjective principles are themselves chosen because doing so is more or less instrumental or pragmatic. Kuhn, Carnap, and Friedman combine an ethnocentric view of the nature of empirical truth, relative (or internal) to a set of subjective principles, with a view of instrumental or pragmatic value, independent of (or external to) any particular set of principles itself.

Further, by considering the view of Quine (and perhaps Pettit), we saw how un-Principled Kantianism affects thoughts on truth. For Quine, because there are no subjective principles, empirical truth depends on, and is therefore necessarily consistent with, the totality of empirical claims. And this is so regardless of the subjective scope to which Quine is committed. Moreover, because he has no subjective principles, Quine has no distinction between the truth of empirical claims relative to a set of principles and the instrumental or pragmatic value of those principles themselves. Unlike Kuhn, Carnap, and Friedman, therefore, Quine collapses empirical truth into instrumental or pragmatic value.

Finally we saw how logocentric Principlism—and here the model is Davidson's—has elements of other versions of Principled Kantianism as well as Quine's un-Principled Kantianism. Like all versions of Principled Kantianism, Davidson's makes empirical truth (at least concerning interpretation) depend on, and be necessarily consistent with, subjective principles. For Davidson, that is the logocentric principle, the principle of charity. The nature of empirical truth is therefore logocentric. Nonetheless, like Quine, and unlike Kuhn, Carnap, and Friedman, Davidson does not have a combined view. There is no other set of subjective principles, and so no sense in which one can get outside the principle of charity to ask whether the principle is itself instrumental or pragmatic. Regardless, unlike Quine, Davidson does not collapse empirical truth into instrumental or pragmatic value. Though some empirical claims are true, others perhaps are instrumental or pragmatic, and many might be both, empirical truth and instrumental or pragmatic value remain distinct.

Though this revealed lessons for Kantian conceptual geography specifically, it also revealed lessons for philosophy generally. The idea that empirical truth depends on non-empirical factors is important to all philosophers, regardless of whether it is right. So are the ideas that truth is an internal property while something distinct from it like instrumental or pragmatic value is an external property, and that truth (empirical or otherwise) does—or does not—collapse into instrumental or pragmatic value. As we saw in Chapter Nine, Kant himself worries about lack of progress on understanding the nature of truth:

> The old and famous question with which logicians were to be driven into a corner and brought to such a pass that they must either fall into a miserable circle or else confess their ignorance, hence the vanity of their entire art, is this: **What is truth?** (1998/1787, A57–58/B82).

Logicians and philosophers have in fact made progress since Kant's day. Kantian conceptual geography in particular makes a little more.

Finally and more generally no issues might be more central to analytic philosophy if not philosophy overall than meaning and truth. My discussion of them therefore cannot help but illuminate Kantian territory and much beyond.

Because Kantian conceptual geography guided that discussion, Kantian conceptual geography has further earned its keep. Engaging in it has illuminated issues of the utmost importance to analytic epistemology, philosophy of language, and metaphysics overall. In fact, as I suggested in Chapter One, one might think of Kantian conceptual geography as a *prolegomenon* to any future epistemology, philosophy of language, or metaphysics—Kantian or otherwise.

6. DOSTOEVSKY IS (STILL) IMMORTAL!

In the Preface & Acknowledgments to *Kantian Conceptual Geography* we encountered Mikhail Bulgakov's story of Satan and his minions' visit to Soviet Moscow. As we saw, one day in particular Satan's minions tried entering a restaurant affiliated with the Moscow Association of Writers. Because they lacked a membership card, they were turned away. When they asked whether Dostoevsky himself would face the same resistance, the receptionist explained: "Dostoevsky is dead" (1995/1967, p. 300). One of Satan's minion indignantly replied: "Dostoevsky is immortal!"

Indeed, as I explained there, Dostoevsky is immortal in the sense that his work continues to inspire others, implicitly or explicitly, in their own discussions of humanity, humility, and the divine. Similarly, and more relevant for us, we can now appreciate more fully that Kant is immortal in the sense that his work continues to inspire others, implicitly or explicitly, in their own discussions of knowledge, meaning, and reality.

Now in *Kantian Conceptual Geography* we have been concerned mostly with Kantianism, a little with Kant, and not at all with Dostoevsky. In closing it is worth turning briefly to Dostoevsky's own work. The title of the present chapter is from *The Brothers Karamazov*, Dostoevsky's *magnum opus*. It comes from a passage describing an experience had by Alexei Fyodorovich Karamazov—affectionately "Alyosha," our hero. Here is the passage *in toto*:

> Alyosha stood, gazed, and suddenly threw himself down on the earth. He did not know why he embraced it. He could not have told why he longed so irresistibly to kiss it, to kiss it all. But he kissed it weeping, sobbing, and watering it with his tears, and vowed passionately to love it, to love it forever. "Water the earth with the tears of your joy and love those tears," echoed in his soul.
> What was he weeping over?
> Oh! in his rapture he was weeping even over those stars, which were shining to him from the abyss of space, and "he was not ashamed of that ecstasy." There seemed to be threads from all those innumerable worlds of God, linking his soul to them, and it was trembling all over "in contact with

other worlds." He longed to forgive everyone for everything, and to beg forgiveness. Oh, not for himself, but for all men, for all everything. "And others are praying for me too," echoed again in his soul. But with every instant he felt clearly and, as it were, tangibly, that something firm and unshakable as that vault of heaven had entered into his soul. It was as though *some idea had seized the sovereignty of his mind*—and it was for all his life and forever and ever. ...

Within three days he left the monastery in accordance with the words of his elder, who had bidden him to "sojourn in the world" (1976/1880, pp. 340–41, emphasis mine).

The idea that seized the sovereignty of Alyosha's mind is the idea of universal love. It is Dostoevsky's idea. It is not Kant's idea and even less so ours. Perhaps it is a good idea. Definitely it is a debated idea. Certainly it is not a universally shared idea—as comparisons among Alyosha and his brothers Karamazov make clear. Nonetheless it is *Alyosha's* idea. It moves him to tears. It gives his life guidance. And it helps him map out his plans to "sojourn in the world."

The idea of universal love, though a philosophical idea, is not an idea in epistemology, philosophy of language, or metaphysics. It is not the sort of idea with which we in *Kantian Conceptual Geography* have been concerned. Nonetheless, though less romantic than Dostoevsky's, the idea with which we have been concerned is as philosophical. It is the idea of Kantianism, that all empirical concepts, terms, or properties are linked essentially to subjective and objective sources—and that the subjective source may take the form of subjective principles. That idea has seized, if not the sovereignty of our mind, then at least the span of this book. What should we say about that?

Like the idea of universal love, perhaps the idea of Kantianism is a good idea. Definitely it is a debated idea. Certainly it is not a universally shared idea—as comparisons among Kantians and their non-Kantian sisters and brothers make clear. Nonetheless Kantianism has for the span of this book been *our* idea. It has moved us to map out issues of the utmost importance to analytic philosophers in ways that were informative and often unexpected. It has given this book guidance. And it might even help a reader map out her plans as she herself sojourns in the conceptual world.

WORKS CITED

Allison, Henry. 2004. *Kant's transcendental idealism: an interpretation and defense*, revised and expanded. New Haven, CT: Yale University Press.
Anderson, R. Lanier. 2010. The introduction to the *Critique*: framing the question. In Guyer 2010, essay 3 (75–92).
Anishchuk, Alexei. 2013, September 16. Unreasonable critique of Kant leads to man being shot in Russian shop. *Guardian*. http://www.theguardian.com/world/2013/sep/16/kant-philospohy-argument-turns-violent [sic] (accessed February 19, 2014).
Aquila, Richard E. 1983. *Representational mind: a study of Kant's theory of knowledge*. Bloomington, IN: Indiana University Press.
Ben-Menahem, Yemima. 2005. Putnam on skepticism. In *Hilary Putnam*, ed. Ben-Menahem. New York: Cambridge University Press, essay 5 (125–55).
Bennett, Jonathan. 1971. *Locke, Berkeley, Hume: central themes*. New York: Oxford University Press.
Berkeley, George. 2000/1713. *A treatise concerning the principles of human knowledge*. In Readings in Modern Philosophy, vol. 2: Locke, Berkeley, Hume and Associated Texts, ed. Roger Ariew and Eric Watkins. Indianapolis: Hackett Publishing Co., selection 4 (130–74).
Bird, Alexander. 2002. *Thomas Kuhn*. Princeton, NJ: Princeton University Press.
Bird, Graham. 1962. *Kant's theory of knowledge: an outline of one central argument in the* Critique of Pure Reason. New York: Routledge & Kegan Paul.
BonJour, Lawrence. 1998. *In defense of pure reason*. New York: Cambridge University Press.
Braithwaite, John and Philip Pettit. 1992. *Not just deserts: a republican theory of criminal justice*. New York: Oxford University Press.
Brandom, Robert B. 1998. *Making it explicit*. Cambridge, MA: Harvard University Press.
Brennan, Geoffrey and Philip Pettit. 2006. *The economy of esteem: an essay on civil and political society*. New York: Oxford University Press.
Bridges, Jason. 2006. Davidson's transcendental externalism. *Philosophy and Phenomenological Research* 73: 290–315.
Brink, Ingar. 2004. Joint attention, triangulation and radical interpretation: a problem and its solution. *Dialectica* 58: 179–205.

Bulgakov, Mikhail. 1995/1967. *The master and margarita*, tr. Diana Burgin and Katherine Tiernan O'Connor. Dana Point, CA: Ardis Publishers.

Byrne, Alex. 1998. Interpretivism. *European Review of Philosophy* 3: 199–223.

Carnap, Rudolf. 1935. *Philosophy and logical syntax*. London: Kegan Paul.

———. 1949/1936. Truth and confirmation. In *Readings in philosophical analysis*, ed. Herbert Feigl and Wilfrid Sellars. New York: Appleton-Century-Crofts, 119–27.

———. 1959. The elimination of metaphysics through logical analysis of language. In *Logical positivism*, ed. Alfred Jules Ayer. New York: Free Press, essay 3 (60–81).

———. 1988/1952. *Meaning and necessity: a study in semantics and modal logic*, 2d ed. Chicago: University of Chicago Press.

———. 1997/1963. Replies and systematic expositions. In *The Philosophy of Rudolf Carnap*, ed. Paul Arthur Schilpp. Library of Living Philosophers, vol. 11.La Salle, IL: Open Court, part 3 (859–1015).

———. 2003/1928. *The logical structure of the world*. In *The logical structure of the world and Pseudoproblems in philosophy*, tr. Rolf A. George. Chicago: Open Court, 3–303.

———. 2003/1934. *The logical syntax of language*, tr. Amethe Smeaton. London: Kegan Paul.

Carroll, Lewis. 1895. What the tortoise said to Achilles. *Mind* 4: 278–80.

Cassirer, Ernst. 1980/1921. *Substance and function & Einstein's theory of relativity*. Mineola, NY: Dover Publications.

Child, William. 2001. Triangulation: Davidson, realism, and natural kinds. *Dialectica* 55: 29–49.

Chomsky, Noam. 1969. *Aspects of the theory of syntax*. Cambridge, MA: MIT Press.

———. 2000. *New horizons in the study of language and mind*. New York: Cambridge University Press.

Coffa, J. Alberto. 2008/1991. *The semantic tradition from Kant to Carnap: to the Vienna Station*. New York: Cambridge University Press.

Conant, James and John Haugeland. 2002. Editors' introduction. In Kuhn 2002, 1–9.

Cooper, John M. 1997. *Plato: complete works*. Indianapolis: Hackett Publishing Co.

Creath, Richard. 2008. Quine's challenge to Carnap. In *Cambridge companion to Carnap*. New York: Cambridge University Press, ch. 14 (316–35).

———. 2010. The construction of reason: Kant, Carnap, Kuhn, and beyond. In Domski and Dickson 2010, essay 22 (493–510).

Davidson, Donald. 1993. Reply to Andreas Kemmerling. In *Reflecting Davidson*, ed. Ralf Stoecker. Bielefeld, Germany: Centre for Interdisciplinary Research, 117–20.

———. 1994. Radical interpretation interpreted. In Tomberlin 1994, 121–28.

———. 1999a. Intellectual autobiography of Donald Davidson. In Hahn 1999, part 1 (3–70).

———. 1999b. Reply to Dagfinn Føllesdal. In Hahn 1999, reply to essay 31 (729–32).

———. 2001a. Comments on Karlovy Vary papers. In Kotatko, Pagin, and Segal 2001, essay 15 (285–307).

———. 2001b/1980. *Essays on actions and events*. New York: Oxford University Press.

———. 2001c. Externalisms. In Kotatko, Pagin, and Segal 2001, essay 1 (1–16).

———. 2001d/1984. *Inquiries into truth and interpretation*. New York: Oxford University Press.

———. 2002. *Subjective, intersubjective, objective*. New York: Oxford University Press.
———. 2004. *Problems of rationality*. New York: Oxford University Press.
———. 2005a. *Truth and predication*. Cambridge, MA: Harvard University Press.
———. 2005b. *Truth, language, and history*. New York: Oxford University Press.
DiSalle, Robert. 2002. Newton's philosophical analysis of space and time. In *Cambridge companion to Newton*, ed. I. Bernard Cohen and George E. Smith. New York: Cambridge University Press, essay 2 (57–84).
Domski, Mary and Michael Dickson, eds. 2010. *Discourse on a new method: reinvigorating the marriage of history and philosophy of science*. Chicago: Open Court.
Dostoevsky, Fyodor. 1976/1880. *The brothers Karamazov*, ed. Ralph E. Matlaw, tr. Constance Garnett. New York: W. W. Norton & Co.
Dretske, Fred. 1969. *Seeing and knowing*. Chicago: University of Chicago Press.
———. 1999/1981. *Knowledge and the flow of information*. Cambridge, MA: MIT Press.
Dummett, Michael. 1993/1973. *Frege: philosophy of language*. London: Duckworth.
Einstein, Albert. 1970/1949. Remarks to the essays appearing in this collected volume. In *Albert Einstein: philosopher-scientist*, 3rd ed., ed. Paul Arthur Schilpp. Library of Living Philosophers, vol. 7. New York: Open Court, part 3 (663–88).
Emerson, Ralph Waldo. 2011/1841. Self-reliance. In *Emerson's prose and poetry*, ed. Joel Porte and Saundra Morris. Norton Critical Edition. New York: W. W. Norton & Company, Inc., 120–37.
Evans, Gareth. 1982. *Varieties of reference*, ed. John McDowell. New York: Oxford University Press.
Evnine, Simon. 1991. *Donald Davidson*. Stanford, CA: Stanford University Press.
Fennell, John. 2000. Davidson on meaning normativity: public or social. *European Journal of Philosophy* 8: 139–54.
Fodor, Jerry A. 1994. Is radical interpretation possible? In Tomberlin 1994, 101–20.
———. 1995. Encounters with trees. (Review of John McDowell's *Mind and World*.) *London Review of Books* 17 (8): 10–11.
———. 2005/1975. *The language of thought*. Cambridge, MA: Harvard University Press.
——— and Ernest Lepore. 1992. *Holism: a shopper's guide*. Cambridge, MA: Blackwell.
Frege, Friedrich Ludwig Gottlob. 1964/1893 (vol. 1) & 1903 (vol. 2). *Basic laws of arithmetic*, tr. Montgomery Furth. Berkeley, CA: University of California Press.
———. 1980/1884. *The foundations of arithmetic*, tr. John Langshaw Austin. Evanston, IL: Northwestern University Press.
———. 1993/1892. On sense and reference. In Harnish 1993, essay 7 (221–74).
Friedman, Michael. 1999. *Reconsidering logical positivism*. New York: Cambridge University Press.
———. 2001. *Dynamics of reason*. Stanford, CA: Center for the Study of Language and Information.
———. 2002a. Kant, Kuhn, and the rationality of science. *Philosophy of Science* 69: 171–90.
———. 2002b. Transcendental philosophy and a priori knowledge: a neo-Kantian perspective. In *New essays on the a priori*, ed. Paul Boghossian and Christopher Peacocke. New York: Oxford University Press, essay 15 (367–83).
———. 2008. Einstein, Kant, and the a priori. In *Kant and philosophy of science today*, ed. Michela Massimi. Royal Institute of Philosophy Suppl. 63. New York: Cambridge University Press, 95–112.

———. 2010a. Ernst Cassirer and Thomas Kuhn: the neo-Kantian tradition in history and philosophy of science. In *Neo-Kantianism and contemporary philosophy*, ed. Rudolf A. Makkreel and Sebastian Luft. Bloomington, IN: Indiana University Press, ch. 8 (177–91).

———. 2010b. Remarks on the history of science and the history of philosophy. In Horwich 2010/1993, 37–54.

———. 2010c. Synthetic history reconsidered. In Domski and Dickson 2010, essay 26 (571–814).

Gadamer, Hans-Georg. 1992. *Truth and method*, tr. Joel Weinsheimer and Donald Marshall. New York: Crossroad.

Galileo Galilei. 1957/1623. The assayer. In *Discoveries and opinions of Galileo*, tr. Stillman Drake. New York: Random House, 229–80.

Gibson, Roger. 1986. *The philosophy of W. V. Quine: an expository essay*. Gainesville, FL: University Press of Florida.

———, ed. 2008. *Quintessence: basic readings from the philosophy of W. V. Quine*. Cambridge, MA: Harvard University Press.

Glock, Hans-Johann. 2003. *Quine and Davidson on language, thought and reality*. New York: Cambridge University Press.

Glüer, Kathrin. 2006. The status of charity I: conceptual truth or a posteriori necessity? *International Journal of Philosophical Studies* 14: 337–59.

Gödel, Kurt. 1995/1946. Some observations about the relationship between theory of relativity and Kantian philosophy (version C1). *In Kurt Gödel: collected works*, vol. 3, ed. Solomon Feferman, John W. Dawson, Jr., and Stephen C. Kleene. New York: Oxford University Press.

Goldberg, Nathaniel. 2003. Actually *v.* possibly the case: on Davidson's omniscient interpreter. *Acta Analytica* 18: 143–60.

———. 2004a. Do principles of reason have "objective but indeterminate validity"? *Kant-Studien* 95: 405–25.

———. 2004b. *E pluribus unum*: arguments against conceptual schemes and empirical content. *The Southern Journal of Philosophy* 42: 411–38.

———. 2004c. The principle of charity. *Dialogue* 43: 671–83.

———. 2008a. Response-dependence, noumenalism, and ontological mystery. *European Journal of Philosophy* 17: 469–88.

———. 2008b. Tension within triangulation. *The Southern Journal of Philosophy* 46: 367–83.

———. 2009a. Historicism, entrenchment, and conventionalism. *Journal for General Philosophy of Science* 40: 259–76.

———. 2009b. Triangulation, untranslatability, and reconciliation. *Philosophia* 37: 261–80.

———. 2009c. Universal and relative rationality. *Principia* 13: 67–84.

———. 2011. Interpreting Thomas Kuhn as a response-dependence theorist. *International Journal of Philosophical Studies* 19: 729–52.

———. 2012a. Davidson, dualism, and truth. *Journal for the History of Analytic Philosophy* 1 (7): 0–16.

———. 2012b. Swampman, response-dependence, and meaning. In *Donald Davidson on truth, meaning, and the mental*, ed. Gerhard Preyer. New York: Oxford University Press, essay 6 (148–63).

——— and Mark LeBar. 2012. Psychological eudaimonism and interpretation in Greek ethics. In *Virtue and happiness: essays in honour of Julia Annas*, ed. Rachana Kamtekar. Oxford Studies in Ancient Philosophy, ed. Brad Inwood, suppl. vol. New York: Oxford University Press, 287–320.

——— and Matthew Rellihan. 2008. Incommensurability, relativism, scepticism: reflections on acquiring a concept. *Ratio* 21: 147–67.

Grice, Herbert Paul. 1991. *Studies in the way of words*. Cambridge, MA: Harvard University Press.

——— and Peter F. Strawson. 1956. In defense of a dogma. *Philosophical Review* 65: 141–58.

Guyer, Paul. 1987. *Kant and the claims of knowledge*. New York: Cambridge University Press.

———, ed. 2010. *Cambridge companion to Kant's* Critique of Pure Reason. New York: Cambridge University Press.

Hacker, Peter M. S. 1991. *Appearance and reality: a philosophical investigation into perception and perceptual qualities*. Cambridge, MA: Blackwell.

———. 1998. Davidson on intentionality and externalism. *Philosophy* 73: 539–52.

Hacking, Ian. 1983. *Representing and intervening: introductory topics in the philosophy of natural science*. New York: Cambridge University Press.

———. 1986. The parody of conversation. In *Truth and interpretation: perspectives on the philosophy of Donald Davidson*, ed. Ernest Lepore. New York: Blackwell, 447–58.

———. 2007. Putnam's theory of natural kinds and their names is not the same as Kripke's. *Principia* 11: 1–24.

———. 2010/1993. Working in a new world: the taxonomic solution. In Horwich 2010/1993, 275–310.

Haddock, Adrian. 2011. Davidson and idealism. In Smith and Sullivan 2011b, essay 2 (24–41).

Hahn, Lewis Edwin, ed. 1999. *The philosophy of Donald Davidson*. Library of Living Philosophers, vol. 27. La Salle, IL: Open Court.

Haldane, John, and Crispin Wright, eds. 1993. *Reality, representation, and project*. New York: Oxford University Press.

Hanna, Robert. 2001. *Kant and the foundations of analytic philosophy*. New York: Oxford University Press.

———. 2006. *Kant, science, and human nature*. New York: Oxford University Press.

———. 2011. Review of Leslie Stevenson's *Inspirations from Kant: essays*. *Notre Dame Philosophical Review*, December 24.

Harnish, Robert M, ed. 1993. *Basic topics in the philosophy of language*. Englewood Cliffs, NJ: Prentice Hall.

Hegel, Georg Wilhelm Friedrich. 1977/1807. *Phenomenology of spirit*, tr. A. V. Miller. New York: Oxford University Press.

Helmholtz, Hermann von. 1977/1921. *Epistemological writings: the Paul Hertz/Moritz Schlick centenary edition of 1921*, tr. Malcom Lowe, ed. Robert S. Cohen and Yehuda Elkana. Boston, MA: D. Reidel Publishing Company.

Horwich, Paul. 2010/1993. *World changes: Thomas Kuhn and the nature of science*. Cambridge, MA: MIT Press.

Howell, Robert. 2013. Kant and Kantian themes in recent analytic philosophy. *Metaphilosophy* 44: 42–47.

Hoyningen-Huene, Paul. 1993. *Reconstructing scientific revolutions: Thomas S. Kuhn's philosophy of science*, tr. Alexander T. Levine, foreword by Thomas S. Kuhn. Chicago: University of Chicago Press.

Hume, David. 1999/1748. *An enquiry concerning human understanding*, ed. Tom L. Beauchamp. New York: Oxford University Press.

———. 2000/1739. *A treatise of human nature*, ed. David Fate Norton and Mary J. Norton. New York: Oxford University Press.

Hurley, Susan. 2002/1998. *Consciousness in action*. Cambridge, MA: Harvard University Press.

Jackson, Frank and Philip Pettit. 2002. Response-dependence without tears. *Noûs* suppl. vol. 36: 97–117.

———, ———, and Michael Smith. 2004. *Mind, morality, and explanation: selected collaborations*. New York: Oxford University Press.

Johnston, Mark. 1989. Dispositional theories of value. *Proceedings of the Aristotelian Society*, suppl. vol. 63: 139–74.

———. 1991. Explanation, response-dependence, and judgment-dependence. In *Response-dependent concepts*, ed. Peter Menzies. Working Papers in Philosophy No. 1. Philosophy Program, Research School of Social Sciences. Canberra: Australian National University, 122–83.

———. 1993. Objectivity refigured: pragmatism without verificationism. In Haldane and Wright 1993, 85–103.

Kant, Immanuel. 1998/1787. *Critique of pure reason*, 2d ed., tr. Paul Guyer and Allen W. Wood. New York: Cambridge University Press.

———. 1999/1788. *Critique of practical reason*, tr. Mary J. Gregor. In *Practical philosophy*. New York: Cambridge University Press, 133–272.

———. 2010/1783. *Prolegomena to any future metaphysics*, tr. Gary Hatfield. In *Theoretical philosophy after 1781*. New York: Cambridge University Press, 29–170.

———. 2010/1786. *Metaphysical foundations of natural science*, tr. Michael Friedman. In *Theoretical philosophy after 1781*. New York: Cambridge University Press, 171–270.

Kotatko, Petr, Peter Pagin, and Gabriel Segal. 2001. *Interpreting Davidson*. Stanford, CA: Center for the Study of Language and Information.

Kripke, Saul. 2005/1980. *Naming and necessity*. Cambridge, MA: Harvard University Press.

———. 2013. *Reference and existence*. New York: Oxford University Press.

Kuehn, Manfred. 2002. *Kant: a biography*. New York: Cambridge University Press.

Kuhn, Thomas S. 1979. *The essential tension: selected studies in scientific tradition and change*. Chicago: University of Chicago Press.

———. 1990. Dubbing and redubbing: the vulnerability of rigid designation. In *Scientific theories*, ed. C. Wade Savage. Minnesota Studies in the Philosophy of Science, ed. C. Kenneth Waters, vol. 9. Minneapolis: University of Minnesota Press, 300–18.

———. 1999. Remarks on incommensurability and translation. In *Incommensurability and translation: Kuhnian perspectives on scientific communication and theory change*, ed. Rema Rossini Favretti, Giorgio Sandri, and Roberto Scazzieri. Northampton, MA: Edward Elgar Publishing, Inc., 33–38.

———. 2002. *The road since* Structure, ed. James Conant and John Haugeland. Chicago: University of Chicago Press.

———. 2012/1970. Postscript to *The structure of scientific revolutions*. Chicago: University of Chicago Press, postscript (174–210).

———. 2012/1962. *The structure of scientific revolutions*. Chicago: University of Chicago Press, 4th ed., 1st ed. without postscript.

Langton, Rae. 2004/1998. *Kantian humility*. New York: Oxford University Press.

Lasonen, Maria and Tomáš Marvan. 2004. Davidson's triangulation: content-endowing causes and circularity. *International Journal of Philosophical Studies* 12: 177–95.

Lear, Jonathan. 1982. Leaving the world alone. *Journal of Philosophy* 79: 382–403.

Lepore, Ernest and Barry Loewer. 2011. *Meaning, mind, and matter: philosophical essays*. New York: Oxford University Press.

——— and Kirk Ludwig. 2007. *Donald Davidson: meaning, truth, language, and reality*. New York: Oxford University Press.

——— and ———. 2009. *Donald Davidson's truth-theoretic semantics*. New York: Oxford University Press.

Lewis, Clarence Irving. 2004/1929. *Mind and the world order*. White Fish, MT: Kessinger Publishing.

Lewis, David. 2001/1986. *On the plurality of worlds*. Hoboken, NJ: Wiley-Blackwell.

Lipton, Peter. 2003. Kant on wheels. *Social Epistemology* 17: 215–19.

List, Christian and Philip Pettit. 2011. *Group agency*. New York: Oxford University Press.

Locke, John. 1979/1689. *An essay concerning human understanding*, ed. Peter H. Nidditch. New York: Oxford University Press.

Makkreel, Rudolf A. and Sebastian Luft. 2010. *Neo-Kantianism in contemporary philosophy*. Bloomington, IN: Indiana University Press.

Malpas, Jeff. 2011a. *Dialogues with Davidson*. Cambridge, MA: MIT Press.

———. 2011b. Triangulation and philosophy: a Davidsonian landscape. In *Triangulation: from an epistemological point of view*, ed. Marcia Cristina Amoretti and Gerhard Preyer. Philosophische Analyse (Philosophical Analysis), ed. Herbert Hochberg, Rafael Hüntelmann, Christian Kanzian, Richard Schantz, and Erwin Tegtmeier, vol. 40. New Brunswick, NJ: Ontos Verlag/Transaction Books, essay 11 (257–79).

Manning, Richard. 2006. Rationalism in the philosophy of Donald Davidson. In *A companion to Rationalism*, ed. Alan Nelson. Malden, MA: Wiley-Blackwell, ch. 25 (468–87).

———. 2011. Interpretive semantics and ontological commitment. In Malpas 2011a, essay 5 (61–86).

Marcum, James A. 2012. From paradigm to disciplinary matrix and exemplar. In *Kuhn's* The structure of scientific revolutions *revisited*, ed. Vasso Kindi and Theodore Arabatzis. New York: Routledge, essay 3 (41–63).

Martí, José Luis and Philip Pettit. 2012. *A political philosophy in public life: civic republicanism in Zapatero's Spain*. Princeton, NJ: Princeton University Press.

Masterman, Margaret. 1970. The nature of a paradigm. In *Criticism and the growth of knowledge*, ed. Imre Lakatos and Alan Musgrave. New York: Cambridge University Press: 59–89.

McDonough, Jeffrey K. 2003. A *rosa multiflora* by any other name: taxonomic incommensurability and scientific kinds. *Synthese* 136: 337–58.

McDowell, John. 1996. *Mind and world*. Cambridge, MA: Harvard University Press.

———. 2001/1998. Values and secondary qualities. In *Mind, value and reality*. Cambridge: Harvard University Press, essay 7 (131–50).

———. 2005. Motivating inferentialism: comments on *Making it explicit* (ch. 2). *Pragmatics and Cognition* 13: 121–40.

McGinn, Colin. 1983. *The subjective view: secondary qualities and indexical thoughts*. New York: Oxford University Press.

Menand, Louis. 2002. *The metaphysical club: a story of ideas in America*. New York: Farrar, Straus and Giroux.

Miščević, Nenad. 2011. No more tears in Heaven: two views of response-dependence. *Acta Analytica* 26: 75–93.

Montminy, Martin. 2003. Triangulation, objectivity and the ambiguity problem. *Critica* 35: 25–48.

Mou, Bo, ed. 2006. *Davidson's philosophy and Chinese philosophy*. Philosophy of History and Culture, ed. Michael Krausz, vol. 23. Boston: Brill.

Neiman, Susan. 1997. *The unity of reason: rereading Kant*. New York: Oxford University Press.

Pagin, Peter. 2001. Semantic triangulation. In Kotatko 2010, ch. 10 (199–212).

Parrini, Paolo. 2003. Reason and perception in defense of a non-linguistic version of empiricism. In *Logical empiricism: historical & contemporary perspectives*, ed. Parrini, Merrillee H. Salmon, and Wesley C. Salmon. Pittsburgh: University of Pittsburgh Press, 349–74.

Parsons, Charles. 1992. The transcendental aesthetic. In *Cambridge companion to Kant*, ed. Paul Guyer. New York: Cambridge University Press, essay 2 (62–100).

Peacocke, Christopher. 1995. *A study of concepts*. Cambridge, MA: MIT Press.

Pettit, Philip. 1996. *The common mind: an essay on psychology, society, and politics*. New York: Oxford University Press.

———. 1997. *Republicanism: a theory of freedom and government*. New York: Oxford University Press.

———. 1998. Terms, things and response-dependence. *European Review of Philosophy* 3: 55–66.

———. 2001. *A theory of freedom: from the psychology to the politics of agency*. Boston: Polity Press.

———. 2002. *Rules, reasons, and norms: selected essays*. New York: Oxford University Press.

———. 2005. Précis of *Rules, reasons, and norms*. *Philosophical Studies* 124: 181–83.

———. 2010. *Made with words: Hobbes on language, mind and politics*. Princeton, NJ: Princeton University Press.

Platts, Mark de Bretton. 1997. *Ways of meaning: an introduction to a philosophy of language*, 2d ed. Cambridge, MA: MIT Press.

Poincaré, Henri. 1946/1902. *Science and hypothesis*. In *The foundations of science*, ed. George Bruce Halsted. Lancaster, PA: Science Press, 9–200.

Pollok, Konstantin. 2010. The "transcendental method": on the reception of the *Critique of Pure Reason* in neo-Kantianism. In Guyer 2010, essay 16 (346–79).

Proffer, Ellendea. 1995. Commentary on *The master and margarita*. In *The master and margarita*, by Mikhail Bulgakov (originally published 1967), tr. Diana Burgin and Katherine Tiernan O'Connor. Dana Point, CA: Ardis Publishers, 337–55.

Putnam, Hilary. 1976. Philosophy of language and philosophy of science. In *Proceedings of the 1974 biennial meeting of the Philosophy of Science Association*, ed. Robert S. Cohen and Marx W. Wartofsky. Boston Studies in the Philosophy of Science, vol. 32. Boston, MA: D. Reidel Publishing Company, 603–10.

———. 1978. *Meaning and the moral sciences*. Boston: Routledge & Kegan Paul.

———. 1981. *Reason, truth and history*. New York: Cambridge University Press.

———. 1993/1975. The meaning of 'meaning'. In Harnish 1993, essay 11 (221–74).

Quine, Willard van Orman. 1964. *Word and object*. Cambridge, MA: MIT Press.

———. 1969. *Ontological relativity and other essays*. New York: Columbia University Press.

———. 1975. On empirically equivalent systems of the world. *Erkenntnis* 9: 313–28.

———. 1981. *Theories and things*. Cambridge, MA: Harvard University Press.

———. 1986. Reply to Roger F. Gibson Jr. In *Philosophy of W. V. Quine*, ed. Edwin Hahn and Paul Arthur Schilpp. LaSalle, IL: Open Court, reply to essay 5 (155–58).

———. 1998. *From stimulus to science*. Cambridge, MA: Harvard University Press.

———. 2004/1992. *Pursuit of truth*, revised ed. Cambridge, MA: Harvard University Press.

———. 2006/1953. *From a logical point of view: nine logico-philosophical essays*, 2d ed., revised. Cambridge, MA: Harvard University Press.

———. 2008/1960. Carnap and logical truth. In Gibson 2008, essay 4 (64–90).

———. 2008/1936. Truth by convention. In Gibson 2008, essay 1 (3–30).

———. 2008/1991. Two dogmas in retrospect. In Gibson 2008, essay 3 (54–63).

Ramberg, Bjørn T. 1991. *Donald Davidson's philosophy of language: an introduction*. Malden, MA: Wiley-Blackwell.

Reichenbach, Hans. 1920. *Relativitätstheorie und erkenntnis apriori*. Berlin: Springer.

———. 1965/1920. *The theory of relativity and a priori knowledge*. Los Angeles: University of California Press.

Rey, Georges. 1994. The unavailability of what we mean: a reply to Quine, Fodor and LePore. In *Holism: a consumer update*, ed. Jerry Fodor and Ernest Lepore. *Grazer Philosophische Studien* 46, ed. Rudolf Haller. Atlanta, GA: Rodopi, 61–102.

Ricketts, Thomas G. 1982. Rationality, translation, and epistemology naturalized. *Journal of Philosophy* 79: 117–36.

Rorty, Richard. 1979. Transcendental arguments, self-reference, and pragmatism. In *Transcendental arguments and science: essays in epistemology*, ed. Peter Bieri, Rolf-Peter Horstmann, and Lorenz Krüger. Synthese Library: Studies in Epistemology, Logic, Methodology, and Philosophy of Science, vol. 133, ed. Jaakko Hintikka. Boston, MA: D. Reidel Publishing Company, 77–103.

———. 1981. *Philosophy and the mirror of nature*. Princeton, NJ: Princeton University Press.

———. 1990a. Introduction: pragmatism as anti-representationalism. In *Pragmatism from Peirce to Davidson*, ed. John P. and Anna R. Murphy. Boulder, CO: Westview Press.

———. 1990b. Pragmatism, Davidson and truth. In *Objectivity, relativism, and truth*. Philosophical Papers, vol. 1. New York: Cambridge University Press, 126–50.

———. 1997. Introduction. In *Empiricism and the philosophy of mind* by Wilfrid Sellars. Cambridge, MA: Harvard University Press, 1–12. (*Empiricism and the philosophy of mind* originally published 1956, reprinted in Sellars 1991/1963, essay 5 [127–96].)

———. 2011. Davidson versus Descartes. In Malpas 2011a, essay 1 (3–6).

Russell, Bertrand and Alfred North Whitehead. 1997/1927. *Principia mathematica*, 2d ed. New York: Cambridge University Press.

Russell, Gillian. 2007. The analytic/synthetic distinction. *Philosophy Compass* 2: 712–29.

———. 2011. *Truth in virtue of meaning: a defense of the analytic/synthetic distinction*. New York: Oxford University Press.

Ryle, Gilbert. 2000/1949. *The concept of mind*. Chicago: University of Chicago Press.

Sankey, Howard. 1993. Kuhn's changing concept of incommensurability. *British Journal for the Philosophy of Science* 44: 759–74.

———. 1994. *The incommensurability thesis*. Brookfield, VT: Ashgate Publishing Company.

———. 1998. Taxonomic incommensurability. *International Studies in the Philosophy of Science* 12: 7–16.

——— and Paul Hoyningen-Huene, eds. 2001. *Incommensurability and related matters*. Boston Studies in the Philosophy of Science, ed. Robert S. Cohen, Jürgen Renn, and Kostas Gavroglu, vol. 216. Norwell, MA: Kluwer Academic Publishers.

Schaper, Eva and Wilhelm Vossenkul, eds. 1989. *Reading Kant: new perspectives on transcendental arguments and Critical philosophy*. Hoboken, NJ: Wiley-Blackwell.

Schlick, Moritz. 1949. Is there a factual *a priori*? In *Readings in philosophical analysis*, ed. Herbert Feigl and Wilfrid Sellars. New York: Appleton-Century Crofts, 277–85.

———. 1979/1921. Critical or empiricist interpretation of modern physics? In *Philosophical Papers*, vol. 1, 1909–1922, ed. H. L. Mulder and B. F. B. Van DeVelde-Schlick, tr. Peter Heath. Vienna Circle Collection. Boston, MA: D. Reidel Publishing Company, 322–34.

Searle, John. 1995. *The construction of social reality*. New York: Free Press.

Sedgwick, Sally. 1997. McDowell's Hegelianism. *European Journal of Philosophy* 5: 21–38.

———. 2012. *Hegel's critique of Kant: from dichotomy to identity*. New York: Oxford University Press.

Sellars, Wilfrid. 1968. *Science and metaphysics: variations on Kantian themes*. New York: The Humanities Press.

———. 1991/1963. *Science, perception, and reality*. Atascadero, CA: Ridgeview Publishing Company.

Sher, Gila. 1999. Is there a place for philosophy in Quine's theory? *Journal of Philosophy* 96: 491–524.

Smith, Joel and Peter Sullivan. 2011a. Introduction: transcendental philosophy and naturalism. In Smith and Sullivan 2011b, essay 1 (1–26).
——. 2011b. *Transcendental philosophy and naturalism*. New York: Oxford University Press.
Smith, Michael. 1989. Dispositional theories of value. *Proceedings of the Aristotelian Society*, suppl. vol. 63: 89–111.
—— and Daniel Stoljar. 1998. Global response-dependence and noumenal realism. *Monist* 81: 85–111.
Soames, Scott. 2003a. *Beyond rigidity*. New York: Oxford University Press.
——. 2003b. *The dawn of analysis*. Philosophical Analysis in the Twentieth Century, vol. 1. Princeton, NJ: Princeton University Press.
Sober, Eliot. 2000. Quine. *Proceedings of the Aristotelian Society*, suppl. vol. 74: 237–80.
Stevenson, Leslie. 2011. *Inspirations from Kant: essays*. New York: Oxford University Press.
Strawson, Peter F. 1975. *The bounds of sense: an essay on Kant's* Critique of Pure Reason. New York: Routledge.
Stroud, Barry. 2009/1996. The charm of naturalism. In *Naturalism in question*, ed. Mario De Caro and David Macarthur. Cambridge, MA: Harvard University Press, essay 1 (21–35).
Suárez, Mauricio. 2012. Science, philosophy, and the a priori. *Studies in History and Philosophy of Science* 43: 1–6.
—— and Thomas Uebel, eds. 2012. *Reconsidering the dynamics of reason: a symposium in honour of Michael Friedman*. Reprinted as a special issue of *Studies in History and Philosophy of Science*, vol. 43 (1).
Talmage, Catherine J. L. 1997. Meaning and triangulation. *Linguistics and Philosophy* 20: 139–45.
Tarski, Alfred. 2008/1944. The semantic conception of truth and the foundations of semantics. In *The philosophy of language*, ed. A. P. Martinich. New York: Routledge, 85–107.
Tomberlin, James E., ed. 1994. *Logic and language*. Philosophical Perspectives, vol. 8. Atascadero, CA: Ridgeview Publishing Co.
Tsou, Jonathan Y. 2003. A role for reason in science. *Dialogue* 42: 573–98.
Turner, Stephen. 2011. Davidson's normativity. In Malpas 2011a, essay 18 (343–70).
TV-Novosti. 2013, September 17. Impure reason: Russian man shot in heated Kant philosophy debate. *RT*. http://rt.com/news/russia-kant-debate-shooting-944/ (accessed February 19, 2014).
Tye, Michael. 1997. *Ten problems of consciousness*. Cambridge, MA: MIT Press.
Uebel, Thomas. 2012. De-synthesizing the relative a priori. *Studies in History and Philosophy of Science* 43: 7–17.
Van Cleve, James. 1995. Putnam, Kant, and secondary qualities. *Philosophical Papers* 24: 83–109.
——. 2003/1999. *Problems from Kant*. New York: Oxford University Press.
Verheggen, Claudine. 1997. Davidson's second person. *The Philosophical Quarterly* 47: 361–69.
——. 2007. Triangulating with Davidson. *The Philosophical Quarterly* 57: 96–103.

Westphal, Kenneth R. 2010. Kant's *Critique of Pure Reason* and analytic philosophy. In Guyer 2010, essay 17 (401–30).

White, Morton. 1973/1950. The analytic and the synthetic: an untenable dualism. In *Pragmatism and the American mind: essays and reviews in philosophy and intellectual history*. New York: Oxford University Press, 121–37.

Wiggins, David. 1998/1987. *Needs, values, truth: essays in the philosophy of value*, 3rd ed. New York: Oxford University Press.

Wilson, Neil I. 1959. Substances without substrata. *Review of Metaphysics* 12: 521–39.

Wittgenstein, Ludwig. 2009/1958. *Philosophical investigations*, tr. Peter M. S. Hacker and Joachim Schulte. Hoboken, NJ: Wiley-Blackwell.

Wray, K. Brad. 2012. Assessing the influence of Kuhn's *Structure of scientific revolutions*. *Metascience* 21: 1–10.

Wright, Crispin. 1988. Moral values, projection, and secondary qualities. *Proceedings of the Aristotelian Society*, suppl. vol. 62: 1–26.

———. 1989. Wittgenstein's rule-following considerations and the central project of theoretical linguistics. In *Reflections on Chomsky*, ed. Alexander George. Cambridge, MA: Blackwell, ch. 12 (233–64).

———. 1993. Realism: the contemporary debate—w(h)ither now? In Haldane and Wright 1993, 63–84.

———. 1999/1992. *Truth and objectivity*. Cambridge, MA: Harvard University Press.

Yalowitz, Steven. 1999. Davidson's social externalism. *Philosophia* 27: 99–136.

Yates, David. 2008. Response-dependence. *Philosophical Books* 49: 344–54.

INDEX

account of content, Kantian, 188, 192–93, 196, 201, 208–13
account of meaning, 6, 27–28, 78, 82, 89–90, 97, 167–203, 208–09, 211–14, 246–47
  Aristotelian realist, 168, 175, 177–81, 186, 213, 246–47
  Berkeleian idealist, 168, 181–82, 184–86, 213, 246–47
  Hegelian pragmatist, 168, 184–86, 213, 246–47 (*see also under* Davidson, Donald)
  Kantian, 6, 27, 28, 78, 167–214, 246–47 (*see also under* Davidson, Donald; Kuhn, Thomas)
  Lockean hybridist, 168, 180, 182–84, 213, 246–47
  Platonic realist, 168, 175–79, 183, 186, 213, 246–47
account of nature, Kantian, 188, 196–99, 208–13
acquisitive principle. *See under* subjective principle
action theory, 80, 103
ahistoricism, 27, 101–05, 172n6, 243–44
Allison, Henry, 16n18, 43n14, 45n15, 48–49, 56n20, 197n1, 204n5, 206n7
American Pragmatism, 21–22, 24n32, 26, 80n1, 110, 184, 213
analytic, 5–6, 103, 109–10, 133, 137, 146, 149–55, 159–62, 219–21, 224n13, 237–38, 245, 247–51

a posteriori, 5, 141n9, 237
a priori, 5, 69, 138, 141, 145, 149–150, 151n22, 237
  as a philosophical tradition, xii, 3, 4n1, 5–6, 15, 20, 22n28, 23, 27, 30n35, 33, 80, 143, 167–68, 174–75, 183, 186, 213, 243–44
analytic/synthetic distinction, 138–39, 146, 149n20, 151, 157, 225
anthropocentrism, 34, 37–38, 49, 58, 66, 74, 77–79, 105–06, 163, 173–74, 190–91, 197–202, 213, 224, 226–27, 232–33, 242–44
  Kant's, 26, 58, 69, 81, 147–48, 163, 197, 215, 218–20, 242, 248
  Pettit's, 33, 41, 44, 49, 58, 62, 81, 93, 242
  Quine's, 226–27
a posteriori, 5, 138, 140–43, 237–38
  See also under analytic; synthetic
a priori, 5, 8, 13–14, 35–36, 38, 40–44, 49n17, 55, 64, 68–69, 77, 96, 112, 140, 146, 159, 170–71, 197n1, 217n7, 237–38, 241, 245
  epistemological *vs.* ontological sense, 36, 42, 64, 71, 87, 90, 96, 98–99, 140, 149, 155
  See also relativized *a priori*
  See also under analytic; synthetic
Aristotelian realism, 18–20, 27, 39–40, 109, 168, 174, 186, 198, 240
  See also under account of meaning
Aristotle, 18, 23, 67, 175

Berkeleian idealism, 20n25, 22–23, 27, 109, 168, 174, 186, 198, 240
  See also under account of meaning
Berkeley, George, 20, 23, 198
Brandom, Robert, 21–23, 184, 185n16, 213
Brothers Karamazov, The, 250
Bulgakov, Mikhail, xi, 216n3, 250

calculus, 157–60, 219–20
Carnap, Rudolf, 6, 137, 145–65, 215, 219–26, 228, 231–33, 242, 245, 248–49
Cassirer, Ernst, 22n28, 145n14
categories, Kant's, 13–14, 25n33, 69n15, 70n16, 90, 105, 111–13, 130, 142, 148–49, 217
charity, principle of. *See* principle of charity
Chinese philosophy, 26, 80
Chomsky, Noam, 160
Coffa, J. Alberto, 4n1, 69n15, 144n12, 145n14, 148n17
cognitive value, 221–25
conceptual geography, 4–6, 18, 22–23, 28–30, 237, 251
  See also under Kantian
conceptual scheme, 103, 110–20, 123, 125–27, 130, 132–33, 135, 185, 200, 203, 238, 244
concepts of the understanding. *See* categories, Kant's
constitutive principle. *See under* subjective principle
Convention T, 82, 117–18
Copernican, 50–55, 62–67, 70–72, 75–77, 212n13
Cratylus, 18, 175
Critique of Practical Reason, 110
Critique of Pure Reason, 3, 6–7, 9, 12–14, 27, 29, 43n14, 109, 136, 138, 215, 237–38

Davidson, Donald, 6, 21–24, 26–27, 40n10, 57n12, 75n10, 181, 198, 215, 226n15, 238, 241–45, 247–49
  and a Hegelian pragmatist account of meaning, 184
  and a Kantian account of meaning, 163, 167–74, 185–86
  and global response-dependence, 26–27, 81, 84–89, 93–97, 101, 104, 170–73
  and incommensurability, 91, 99, 112, 115, 134–35
  and language learning, 81–82, 88, 91–106, 134–36, 169–70, 187
  and noumenalism, 91, 99, 134
  and radical interpretation, 81–90, 94–96, 98–106, 133–35, 153n27, 168–73, 184–92, 230, 241, 243–44, 247
Descartes, René, 70n16
Dewey, John, 21–22, 110
disciplinary matrix, 50n18, 68, 136
Dostoevsky, Fyodor, xi–xii, 238, 250–51
dualism of conceptual scheme and empirical content. *See* scheme/content dualism
Dualism, 7–9, 12, 18, 21n26, 25, 27, 44, 56, 66, 81, 87n16, 89, 91, 96n27, 97, 99, 109–38, 150, 155n30, 167–68, 170–72, 185–86, 188, 214, 224, 238–42, 244–46
  Epistemological, 12–13, 15, 44–45, 67, 71, 98, 169, 171, 173
  Ontological, 10, 13–15, 70–71, 89, 98, 155n30, 156n31, 169, 171–74, 182, 185, 192–93, 196, 208–10

Einstein, Albert, 69n15, 76, 145, 148n18, 223, 225
Emerson, Ralph Waldo, 110
empirical, 3, 5, 7n6, 237, 239–40
  claim, 5, 15, 28, 45, 69, 71, 99, 141, 148–50, 154–55, 158, 216–18, 220, 222, 224–26, 230, 232–33, 237, 240, 248–49
  content, 23n31, 110–11, 112n3, 113–19, 125–33, 147, 185, 200, 203–04, 208, 226n15, 238, 244
  truth (*see under* truth)

INDEX

Empirical Dualism. *See* Dualism
epistemic humility, 16, 17n19, 48–49, 53–54, 56n20
ethnocentrism, 26, 72, 79, 104–06, 134, 163, 169–74, 190–92, 197, 199–202, 207, 213, 232–33, 242–44, 248
   Carnap's, 148–49, 154–55, 219–24, 232, 242, 248
   Friedman's, 154–55, 219–24, 232, 242, 248
   Kuhn's, 49–51, 57–60, 62–64, 66–69, 74–75, 77–78, 81, 85, 93, 154–55, 219–24, 232, 242, 248
   Quine's, 227
ethocentrism, 60–61
exemplification. *See* instantiation *vs.* exemplification
external question, 221–22, 224–25

Fodor, Jerry, 29, 84n10, 91n19
forms of intuition. *See* intuition, Kant's forms of
Frege, Friedrich Ludwig Gottlob, 144–45, 149, 168, 175–78, 186, 213, 246
Friedman, Michael, 6–7, 27, 68–69, 137, 145–46, 148, 150n21, 154–163, 215, 219–24, 226, 228, 231–33, 242, 245, 248–49

Gadamer, Hans-Georg, 80, 200
Galileo (Galilei), 34n2, 62–63
genetic fallacy, 153–54, 161
Given, Myth of the, 22, 24–25
global response-dependence. *See under* Davidson, Donald; Kantianism; Kuhn, Thomas; Pettit, Philip; response-dependence
God, xin1, 20n25, 250
Grice, Herbert Paul, 152n25, 168, 181–82, 186, 213, 246
Guyer, Paul, 16–17, 47, 49, 56n20, 110n2

Hacking, Ian, 73, 76n22, 95n24, 177n9
Hanna, Robert, 4n1, 6n5, 13, 17–18, 23n31, 36n5, 43n14, 56–57n20, 139n4, 140n6, 144n13, 145n14, 146n15, 177n9, 197, 204n5, 216n5, 219–20, 226, 229, 232
Hegel, Georg Wilhelm Friedrich, 21–23, 25n33, 110, 184–85, 206, 213
Hegelian pragmatism, 21–25, 27, 110, 134–35, 168, 174, 185–86, 199, 200n3, 240
   See also under account of meaning
Helmholtz, Hermann von, 144–45
historicism, 27, 66, 101–05, 172n6, 243–44
Hume, David, 70n16, 129

idiocentrism, 27, 57n21, 81, 105–06, 163, 173–74, 189–91, 197–202, 215n2, 242–44
   Davidson's, 93, 100, 102, 124, 135n25, 169, 231, 233, 242, 249
   Quine's, 227–28
incommensurability, 5, 26, 58, 76–77, 188, 190–91, 237–38, 247
   See also under Davidson, Donald; Kantianism; Kuhn, Thomas
indeterminacy of interpretation. *See* indeterminacy of meaning
indeterminacy of meaning, 5, 84n11, 101, 188–90, 231–33, 237, 247
instantiation *vs.* exemplification, 54, 59–60
instrumental value. *See* pragmatic value
internal question, 221–22, 224–25, 231
internal realism, 19n23, 178
intuition, 13–14, 131, 139, 207, 216–17
   empirical, 13–14, 119, 128, 205–06
   intellectual, 206
   Kant's forms of, 4n1, 8n10, 13–14, 17, 57n20, 105, 142, 144–45, 147–48, 159, 217
   non-sensible (*see* intuition, intellectual)
   pure (*see* intuition, Kant's forms of)
   sensible (*see* intuition, empirical)

Jackson, Frank, 33, 40–42, 47, 59
James, William, 21–22

Johnston, Mark, 20–21, 26, 34–40, 42–43, 46n16, 49, 55–56, 64–66, 72, 79, 81, 88, 97, 101, 171, 240–41

Kant, Immanuel, xi–xii, 3–9, 12–15, 17, 18n21, 21, 23n29, 25n33, 36n5, 43, 45, 49, 57, 69–70, 79, 81, 90, 105, 110, 112–13, 119, 128, 130–31, 136–50, 152, 154, 163, 173, 192, 197, 199, 202, 204–06, 208, 210–11, 215–21, 224n13, 226n14, 228–30, 232, 237–38, 242–43, 248–50
Kantian
  account of content (*see* account of content, Kantian)
  account of meaning (*see* account of meaning, Kantian)
  account of nature (*see* account of nature, Kantian)
  conceptual geography, 4–6, 22–29, 55–57, 59, 79, 104–06, 109, 133–35, 162–63, 167, 186–87, 212–13, 233–34, 237–51
  thoughts on truth (*see* truth, Kantian thoughts on)
Kantianism, 6–12
  and global response-dependence, 26, 55–59, 79
  and incommensurability, 26, 59, 77–79, 191, 241–42
  and noumenalism, 33, 45–57, 75–79, 134, 204–08, 240–41
  and the *Critique of Pure Reason*, 13–18
  Epistemological, 11–13, 15–16, 18–20, 33, 45, 55–57, 71, 77, 79, 93, 98–100, 104, 185, 192, 239
  neo- (*see* neo-Kantianism)
  Ontological, 10, 15–17, 20, 28, 55–59, 68, 70–75, 77–79, 90, 91, 93, 99–100, 102–05, 122, 134, 169, 173, 185–86, 196, 203, 207, 210, 212–13, 239, 241, 243, 248
  Principled, 8, 12, 25, 28, 68, 72, 79, 90, 98–99, 109, 136–37, 143, 148–49, 155, 219, 222, 226, 228, 233–34, 239, 245, 249
  Un-Principled, 8, 12, 25, 28, 33, 45, 109, 113, 136–37, 150, 215, 224, 226, 232–34, 239, 248–49
Koyré, Alexandre, 70n16, 221n9
Kripke, Saul, 168, 177–79, 186, 213, 246
Kuhn, Thomas, 6, 26, 40, 49–50, 52, 81, 85, 101, 104–05, 148, 154–56, 163, 219–24, 226, 232, 238, 241–42, 248–49
  and a Kantian account of meaning, 169–70, 174, 186, 199
  and global response-dependence, 26, 43–46, 60, 63–66, 72, 79, 170
  and incommensurability, 58, 63n10, 75–79, 112–13, 191–92
  and language learning, 59–66, 70, 169, 186
  and noumenalism, 74, 202, 204–08, 212n13

Langton, Rae, 16, 43
language learning, 79, 104–106, 228
  See also under Davidson, Donald; Kuhn, Thomas; Pettit, Philip
law of universal gravitation, 157–60, 219–20
laws of motion, 157–59, 219–20
Lewis, Clarence Irving (C. I.), 17n20, 23n29, 152, 224
Lewis, David, 200–02, 248
lexical taxonomy, 50, 52, 62, 64, 67–71, 75–77, 136, 154–55, 219–21, 245, 248
lexicon. *See* lexical taxonomy
Locke, John, 20–21, 23, 26, 33–38, 43, 79, 241–43
Lockean hybridism, 21–23, 27, 34, 43, 109, 168, 174, 186, 198, 240
  See also under account of meaning
logocentrism, 27, 81, 105–06, 173–74, 190–91, 197–203, 213, 242–44
  Davidson's, 105–06, 124, 133–35, 163, 170, 215, 228, 231–34, 242

Master and Margarita, The, xi, 216n3
McDowell, John, 21–25, 29, 40, 184–85, 200, 213
meaning
  account of (*see* account of meaning)
  indeterminacy (*see* indeterminacy of meaning)
  relativism (*see* relativism, meaning)
Metaphysical Foundations of Natural Science, 142n10, 218
metaphysical realism, 19n23
Myth of the Given. *See* Given, Myth of the

naturalism, 6, 29–30
necessity, 148, 151–52, 203, 245
neo-Kantianism, 3, 22n28, 70n16, 221n9
Newton, Isaac, 76, 142n10, 157–59, 161, 218–20, 225
new theory of reference, 168, 177, 186, 213, 246
non-conceptual content, 23–25, 112n3, 126–28, 131n22, 149
normal science, 67–68
noumenal realism. *See* noumenalism
noumenalism, 26, 45–49, 205–06, 241–42
  See also under Davidson, Donald; Kantianism; Kuhn, Thomas; Pettit, Philip
noumenon, 204–08, 232, 238

objective source, 7–12, 22n28, 27, 39, 55–57, 74, 109–15, 125, 134, 137, 140–43, 168–86, 189–92, 195–96, 203–04, 206n7, 208–09, 232–34, 238–39, 251
  for Aristotle (and the Aristotelian realist), 18–20, 198, 240
  for Carnap, 149n20, 219
  for Davidson, 86, 89–90, 96–98, 169–70, 230
  for Friedman, 219
  for Johnston, 34–36
  for Kant, 8–18, 20, 141–44
  for Kuhn, 66–68, 70–72, 155, 169, 212n13, 219
  for Locke (and the Lockean hybridist), 20–21, 34, 240
  for Pettit, 43–45
  for Plato (and the Platonic realist), 18–20, 198, 240
  for Quine, 131, 150, 161, 225–28
  for Wright, 37–38
ontological mystery, 48, 50, 53–54

paradigm, 50, 67–68, 72, 75–77, 93, 105, 112–13, 136, 142, 154–55, 212, 219, 221–24, 232, 245, 248
Peirce, Charles Sanders, 21–22
Pettit, Philip, 6, 19, 26, 33, 40–57, 65–66, 72–75, 77–79, 81, 86, 88, 93–94, 97, 101, 104–05, 113, 136–37, 167, 171, 173, 192, 212, 215, 224–26, 228, 232–33, 238, 240–42, 248
  and global response-dependence, 26, 40–43, 47–49
  and language learning, 40, 51, 59–62
  and noumenalism, 33, 45–49, 51–57
Phaedrus, 18, 175
Plato, 18, 23, 175
Platonic realism, 18–20, 27, 39–40, 109, 168, 174, 186, 198, 240
  See also under account of meaning
Plurality of worlds. *See* worlds, plurality of
Poincaré, Henri, 144–45, 148–49
pragmatic realism, 178n11
pragmatic value, 28, 222–26, 231–34, 248–49
principle. *See* subjective principle
principle of charity, 83–84, 89–91, 98–99, 105–06, 118, 120–21, 124, 133, 135–36, 170, 174, 191, 215, 228, 230–33, 245, 249
Principled. *See under* Kantianism
Principlism, 7–9, 18, 25, 27–28, 44, 72, 109, 136–63, 167, 214–17, 219, 224, 228, 232–33, 238–40, 242, 244–45, 248–49
  Epistemological, 12, 15, 45, 71, 79, 99, 143, 215, 217
  Ontological, 10, 15, 71, 79, 89, 99, 143, 147–48, 155, 215–16

Prolegomena to Any Future Metaphysics, 21, 43, 139n3, 205n6, 207n9
property
 realizer-, 42n11, 47–55, 59n3, 62n6
 role-, 46–48, 52
Ptolemaic, 50–55, 62n6, 67, 72, 75–77, 212n13
Putnam, Hilary, 19, 43, 168, 177–79, 186, 213, 229, 246

quality
 primary, 20–21, 34, 241
 secondary, 20–21, 34, 37, 43, 241
Quine, Willard van Orman, 4n1, 6, 27, 45, 83n8, 113–14, 125, 139n4, 150–54, 156–57, 160–62, 201n4, 215, 224–28, 231–33, 245, 248–49

radical interpretation. *See under* Davidson, Donald
radical translation, 114, 152–53
rational reconstruction, 151, 156, 159–61, 219
Reichenbach, Hans, 68–69, 145–49, 151, 154, 163
relativism
 conceptual, 103, 125, 136
 empirical-property, 188, 196–99, 203
 empirical-world, 28, 188, 198, 200, 202–03
 meaning, 5, 135, 188–90, 194, 237
 truth-value, 5, 188, 194, 237
relativized *a priori*, 137, 154–60, 162, 219–22, 245, 248
response-dependence, 20–21, 34–40, 55–56, 73n17, 238, 240–42
 global, 19n23, 241 (*see also under* Davidson, Donald; Kantianism; Kuhn, Thomas; Pettit, Philip)
 local, 43, 55, 240–242
response-independence, 20–21, 42n11, 47–48
revolutionary science. *See* scientific revolution

Rorty, Richard, 4n1, 21–25, 81, 119n10, 125n17
Russell, Bertrand, 144–45
Ryle, Gilbert, 4

Satan, xi, 250
scheme/content dualism, 109–37, 200, 203, 208, 244
Schlick, Moritz, 145–46, 148–149
scientific revolution, 52, 67, 72–73, 156, 191, 199, 212, 222n10
Sellars, Wilfrid, 3–4, 21–25, 184, 213
sensation. *See* empirical content
sense/reference distinction, 168, 175–77
Smith, Michael, 33, 40, 45–49, 52–57, 74, 78, 241
Spinoza, Benedict (Baruch), 70n16
Statesman, 18, 175
Stoljar, Daniel, 33, 45–49, 52–57, 74, 78, 241
Strawson, Peter F., 16–17, 23, 47, 56n20, 110n2, 152n24
subjective principle, 7, 9–12, 28, 44–45, 68, 71, 89, 99, 105–06, 113, 133, 136–62, 170, 191, 214–34, 238–40, 242, 244–45, 248–49
 acquisitive principle, 5, 12, 15, 45, 71–72, 99, 143, 237, 239–40
 constitutive principle, 5, 10, 15, 70n16, 71–73, 90–91, 99, 143, 148–49, 154, 159–60, 163, 210, 237–40
Subjective Principlism. *See* Principlism
subjective scope, 5, 26–27, 57n21, 60, 62, 74–75, 100, 133, 161, 163, 173, 189–191, 197–98, 200–03, 205, 213, 215n1, 226, 232–33, 237–38, 242–44, 249
subjective source, 7–12, 22n28, 26–27, 79, 89–90, 109–15, 125, 134, 136–38, 140–43, 168–86, 189–92, 195–96, 199–203, 208–09, 211, 215, 232–34, 238–39, 242–43, 251
 for Berkeley (and the Berkeleian idealist), 20, 198, 240
 for Carnap, 148–49, 155–57, 219–220

for Davidson, 87, 89–90, 94, 97–99, 131–32, 169, 170, 230, 242–43
for Friedman, 154–57, 219–220, 242
for Johnston, 34–36
for Kant, 8–18, 20, 33, 141–44, 199, 202–03, 217, 219
for Kuhn, 64, 66–68, 70–72, 169, 199, 202, 212n13, 219–220, 242
for Locke (and the Lockean hybridist), 20–21, 34, 198, 240
for Pettit, 33, 43–45
for Quine, 131, 150, 161, 225–28
for Wright, 37–38
Swampman, 94, 101–04
synthetic, 5, 131, 138–41, 146, 150–51, 154n28, 157, 224–25, 237–38
a posteriori, 15, 69, 141–43, 149–50, 197n1, 216–18
a priori, 7n7, 9, 15, 36, 45, 68–70, 90, 105, 131, 136–49, 150–51, 159, 162–63, 215–18, 245, 248

Tarski, Alfred, 17, 82–84, 100, 103, 117–21, 228–32, 244
thing considered in itself. *See* noumenon
thing in itself. *See* noumenon
transcendental idealism, 7n6, 12–18, 23, 25–26, 33, 45n15, 47–49, 56, 68, 143–44, 146, 163, 241

triangulation, 84, 86–87, 92–95, 97–99, 169–71, 182, 185–86
truth
Davidson's thoughts on, 228–233, 249
empirical, 5, 28, 167, 195, 214–15, 217–20, 224–26, 230–33, 237–38, 248–49
Kant's thoughts on, 215–17, 249
Kantian thoughts on, 6, 28, 167, 214–34, 248
Tarski's thoughts on, 82–83, 117, 228

Un-Principled. *See under* Kantianism
unity of reason, 28, 208, 211–13, 248

Whitehead, Alfred North, 144–45
Wittgenstein, Ludwig, 184, 213
worlds
logically possible, 5, 201–02, 237, 248
noumenal, 204–08, 212n13, 222
phenomenal, 204, 207–08
plurality of, 5, 28, 188, 199–203, 247–48
subject-friendly, 197, 213
subjectively empirical, 5, 10n12, 201–02, 213, 237, 247–48
user-friendly, 197
Wright, Crispin, 20–21, 26, 33, 37–40, 42–43, 49, 56, 64–66, 72, 79, 87–88, 97, 101, 170–71, 241

Printed in the USA/Agawam, MA
March 11, 2015

610324.001